The Pagan Religions
of the
Ancient British Isles

B

Callanish Stone Circle Reproduced by kind permission of Fay Godwin

The Pagan Religions
of the
Ancient British Isles

Their Nature and Legacy

RONALD HUTTON

BLACKWELL
Oxford UK & Cambridge USA

Copyright © R. B. Hutton 1991

First published 1991

Basil Blackwell Ltd
108 Cowley Road, Oxford, OX4 1JF, UK

Basil Blackwell, Inc.
3 Cambridge Center
Cambridge, Massachusetts 02142, USA

British Library Cataloguing in Publication Data

A CIP catalogue record for this book is available from the British Library.

Library of Congress Cataloging in Publication Data
Hutton, Ronald.
The pagan religions of the ancient British Isles: their nature and legacy / Ronald Hutton.
p. cm.
ISBN 0–631–17288–2
1. Great Britain—Religion—To 449. I. Title.
BL980.G7H87 1991
291'.09361—dc20   90–27166
CIP

Typeset in 11 on 13pt Caslon
by Hope Services (Abingdon) Ltd., Oxon
Printed in Great Britain by T. J. Press Ltd., Padstow, Cornwall

Contents

Preface

The purpose of this book is to set out what is at present known about the religious beliefs and practices of the inhabitants of the British Isles before their conversion to Christianity. The term 'pagan' is used as a convenient shorthand for those beliefs and practices, and is employed in the title merely to absolve the book from any need to discuss early Christianity itself. Throughout, I have used the same word, and others such as 'faith', 'cult' and 'religion' itself, in a manner which may seem unsatisfactory to theologians and philosophers who prefer stricter definition and more precise application of these terms. I hope nevertheless that my looser usage will be deemed sufficient for a work of history (and prehistory) such as this. My principal intention is to bring to a wider public the very large amount of new evidence and ideas relating to the subject that has been published in the past two decades, much of which seems to be known only to experts within narrow areas of study. Although some more general surveys (often of superb quality) have appeared covering particular periods and places – for example, celebrated prehistoric monuments, the Roman province, the 'Celts' and the Anglo-Saxons – there exists no more general treatment. Furthermore, some of these existing surveys are already out of date or seem to me to be overconfident in certain of their judgements.

My own acknowledged expertise has hitherto lain only at the latter end of the stretch of time encompassed here. But much of the rest was already familiar territory to me before I started this book. During my adolescence I took part in a number of archaeological excavations, including some sites of relevance to the present subject, such as Ascott-under-Wychwood long barrow, the Pilsdon Pen Iron Age temple and the Harlow Romano-British temple. At university I specialized in history, but kept up with developments in archaeology by attending Glyn Daniel's seminars and by constant reading of reports, a habit I have since maintained. The substructure for another part of the work was formed by my long-standing interest in early Irish and Welsh literature, which had already stood me in good stead in providing material for my lectures on Irish history at Bristol and in enabling me to fulfil an unexpected position as patron of the university's Welsh society. My mother, Elsa Hutton, was an old-fashioned antiquarian of the best kind: her intention to publish a guide to the prehistoric chambered tombs of England and Wales was thwarted by her tragically early death, but the data which she had collected rendered me thoroughly familiar with this class of monument. In addition, each chapter of the book has been read by a specialist in the period concerned.

A work of this nature has obvious actual or potential defects. In covering such an enormous time-span, it is almost inevitable that I shall have neglected or under-emphasized items which some specialists feel to be important. I may well have failed to notice some relevant publications, and such is the pace of modern scholarship (especially in archaeology) that some of my information will probably be rendered redundant by announcements in the interval between my last revisions and publication. After the first couple of chapters I have paid little attention to comparable work in other European countries, and I draw relatively few ethnographic parallels. This is certainly a fault, but given the size of the task which I already had in hand, the addition of these other spheres of interest would have made the book unwieldy. I regret that when I was sketching objects and patterns in the field and in museum collections, I did not note down scales to be printed with them: an omission common to most authors who have included such material, but still an error. Some of my illustrations might have been better replaced by good photographs, but here financial constraints and complications of reproduction came into play. I have been concerned both to keep source-references to a minimum, and yet to ensure that no assertion should be left without one. As a result, I have sometimes provided a reference to a large modern work which contains within it precise details of ancient texts of which I make mention in my own pages, rather than citing the latter myself. Though some scholars may find this unsatisfactory, it was the best compromise I could make given the conflicting constraints of space and thoroughness. The same problem occurred on a larger scale when it became necessary to cut the text to keep the book within original unit costs. Only a few sections, such as that dealing with the claims of Glastonbury to be a pre-Saxon holy place, were excised completely: but many pieces of evidence which had been supplied to buttress assertions were struck out. The result may be a more streamlined work, and I hope that the remaining compilations of data are still sufficient to prove their points.

My greatest anxiety is that there exists no colleague whose expertise covers the whole subject of the book, so that it must be evaluated by those who find what falls within their fields all too familiar and what falls outside them all too alien. But that, of course, is the principal reason for my feeling that somebody ought to write it.

R.H.
May 1990

Acknowledgements

Each part of this book was scrutinized and criticized by specialists in the periods concerned, some acting directly for myself and some for my publisher. Of these, I would first like to thank my colleagues at Bristol, Richard Harrison, Thomas Wiedemann and Ian Wei, for dealing with the chapters concerning prehistory, the Romans and the Middle Ages respectively. Richard gave his careful attention to what became half the total number of pages, and deserves especial gratitude. The same care and honesty of approach was afforded to the 'Celtic' chapter by Miranda Green. All of them dealt mercilessly with errors of fact while taking care not to impose their opinions, which adds additional force to the conventional claim, that any mistakes which remain must be my own. Patrick Cook, of the National Monuments Service of the Irish Republic, ensured that I became as well acquainted with the prehistoric remains of his own country as with those of my own. He also introduced me to Máirín Ní Dhonnchadha, who kept me informed of the latest developments in early medieval Irish studies, to the extent of sending me photocopies of pieces which were not readily available in the United Kingdom. Their criticisms have greatly improved the book, while without their compliments I might not have had the courage to persist with it: in that sense, it is their achievement as well. My own lady, Lisa Radulovic Hutton, afforded me the additional stimulation of an intelligent and interested non-specialist, prepared to be impressed by good writing but not by dross.

The dedication is to the people of the Oak Dragon Project, an organization formed in 1986 by modern pagans, 'earth mystics' and 'alternative archaeologists' with the intention of holding debates with each other and with more orthodox scholars. I was invited into their discussions (without any previous knowledge of them) precisely because I was a professional historian who did not share any of their views. How far I have been persuaded since may be judged from this present book, but more important is the fact that the exchanges introduced me to some of the finest individuals and to some of the most exciting intellectual (and emotional) challenges of my life. A score of people among them deserve particular thanks, but I shall single out one because she has made a direct contribution to this book. This is Prudence Jones, a notable writer upon contemporary paganism. She supplied me with my reading-list for the subject, and read the section upon it which I included in my own work. While not faulting me in point of fact or interpretation, she took pains to point out that an alternative definition of contemporary paganism was both possible and desirable. To her it was not an invention of the forward-thinking imagination but an attempt to re-establish concepts and values which had existed in the ancient world and had survived vestigially in a form which is appropriate for the present day. Central to it are a recognition of the female principle of divinity and a sense of the religious importance of the natural world and the passage of seasons. She felt that the continuity of experience, albeit through Christianized practices or folk customs, was as important as the conscious re-creation of ancient and overseas (for example, native American) models. With this view I have no quarrel: my difference of perception derives solely from the fact that in this book I have had a different task in hand. Its natural opponents are those who have made statements about the old religions of these islands which are not supported by, or have ceased to be supported by, the evidence. In a sense, by establishing that we really do know very little about the subject, it provides a greater freedom to those who wish to make their own interpretations of it without any claim that these are objective or binding. I hope that it will give sceptics peace of mind, and yet leave others free to dream.

To the Clan of the Oak Dragon

Guide to Pronunciation of Celtic Words in the Text

The phonetic equivalents given below are very rough: it is impossible, for example, to provide English-speaking readers with an exact rendering of the Welsh consonant ll, as in Llyn. But some indication may be helpful, especially as those quite unfamiliar with Welsh or Irish may otherwise find themselves wildly astray! My thanks to Padraig Mac Cuaig and Geraint Evans for checking those here.

Aneirin   *anayrin*

Badhbh   *barv*
Banbha   *banva*
Barddas   *bahrtharss* (with a hard th)
Beltine   *beyaltinah*
Boudicca   *bowdeekah*
Brighid   *bree-ed*
Bron Trogain   *bron trogen*
Bryn Celli Ddu   *brun kehli thee* (th as in then)

Cáir Adomnain   *kire adomnarn*
Calan Mai   *carlarn meye*
Chrom Dubh   *krom duv*
Chrom Cruach   *krom crooahh* (hh as in Scottish 'loch')
Cimbaeth   *kimbay*
Cóir Anman   *koir ahnman*
Conall Cernach   *konall kurnahh*
Creidhne   *kreenah*
Cruachain   *krooahin*

Cú Chulainn   *koo hulin*
Cui Roi   *kwee ree*

Dafydd ap Gwilym   *davuth ap gwilum* (hard th)
Daghda   *dargda*
Diarmait Mac Cerbaill   *dermot mak kervel*
deisiol   *deshill*
Dinnshenchas   *dainshanahus*
Dún Ailinne   *doon aulin*
Dyfed   *duv-ed*

Emain Macha   *owain maha*
Eriu   *eroo*

feis   *fesh*
Fergus Mac Roich   *fergus mak rihh* (hh as in Scottish 'loch')
Fódla   *fowla*

Geisa   *gesha*
Gofannon   *govahnon*
Goibhniu   *govnoo*
Gorsedd   *gorseth* (hard th)
Gryffydd ap Adda ap Dafydd   *grifith ap ava ap davith*
Gwerthefyr   *gwertheveer* (hard th)

Imbolc   *immolk*
Iolo Morgannwg   *yolo morganoog*

Leabhar Gabhála Éireann   *lower gahwala eren* (ow as in 'ouch')
Lleu Llaw Gyffes   *hleeow hlow gufess* (ow as in 'ouch')
Llud and Llevelys   *hleeth and hlevelis*
Llyn Cerrig Bach   *hlin kerrig bahh* (hh as in Scottish 'loch')
Llyn Cwm Llwch   *hlin coom hloohh* (hh again as in 'loch')
Llyn Fawr   *hlin vawr*
Llywarch Hen   *hlowarhh hayn* (ow as in 'ouch')
Luchta   *loohtar*
Lugh   *looh*
Lughnasadh   *loonasah*

Mabon   *mahbon*

Máire MacNeill   *moyer mak neel*
Maigh Slecht   *moy sleht*
Manannán Mac Lir   *mananarn mak leer*
Manawydan fab Llyr   *manawudarn vab hleer*
Miosgan Méadhbha   *meeshgan mayva*
Mongfind   *mungfind* (find as in 'wind')
Muirchú   *moorhyoo*

Nemhain   *navan*
Nuadha Airgedlamh   *nuwa ahrgedlorth*
Nudd Llaw Ereint   *neeth hlow ereynt* (ow as in 'ouch')

Oenghus   *engus*
Ogmha   *ogvah*

Pwyll   *poyihl*

Rhiannon   *rreearnon*

Samhain   *sarwen*
Sanas Chormaic   *shanas cormac*

Tailtu   *tarltoo*
Tain Bo Cuailnge   *toin bo coolingah*
Taliesin   *tallyesin*
Tobar an Duin   *tobber an dooin*
Togail Bruidne Da Derga   *togawl breen da derga*
Torchmarc Etain   *torhhmarh eten*
Tuan Mac Cairill   *tooan mak cahril*
Tuatha de Danaan   *tooha day dahnarn*

Ui Niall   *oo nial*

I

The Mysteries Begin (c.30,000–c.5000 BC)

The human record in the British Isles goes back a very long way beyond the beginning of the islands themselves. For some half a million years human beings have wandered in the north-western limits of Europe, from which the archipelago finally severed itself only about 9000 years ago. Thus, for the whole of the Palaeolithic, or Old Stone Age, human activities in these islands represented only a corner of those scattered across the European land mass. In cultural terms there is nothing to distinguish them, and indeed the only distinction of the Palaeolithic record in Britain is that it is so intermittent. The succession of Ice Ages which coincided with early human development rendered the British area, and indeed the whole North European Plain, uninhabitable by people for long periods. It is particularly sad that one of those periods spanned the years 23,000–12,000 BC, in which the artistic achievements of people dwelling in what is now France and Spain reached their apogee. Arguably, the advance of that last ice sheet prevented British sites from becoming as rich in paintings and carvings as those of the Continent. Nevertheless, before and after that final glaciation there were human beings active in what became Britain. It seems only just to consider them, and their beliefs, from the European evidence, especially as some of that evidence has a bearing upon what is to come later.

Two aspects of the Palaeolithic record may relate to the religious beliefs of the people: burials and art. The tendency of human beings to dispose ceremonially of their dead is one of the distinguishing marks of the species, separating them from other animals. It appeared in Europe about 80,000 years ago. It is not in itself a guarantee of the existence of religion, in the strict sense of a belief in divine beings. But it does indicate either a belief in a journey to an afterlife or in the power of ancestral spirits to haunt the living. Distinguishing between these beliefs from a burial record is difficult. Gravegoods are not a guarantee of faith in a world after death. The Nankanse of Ghana placed objects in tombs to protect the living, not for the use of the dead. The Lugbara of Uganda buried goods with their dead as a sign of the status which the latter had held during life. Other tribes put the dead person's favourite possessions with the body because they had a painful emotional significance for the survivors. Nor can the position of a body furnish any conclusive evidence for a prehistorian. Much has been made of the fact that, at all periods of European prehistory, some bodies were interred upon their sides in a crouching posture. The resemblance to a foetus in a womb has encouraged speculation that these individuals were being returned to the earth to be reborn. This may be true, but as many primitive peoples sleep with knees drawn up, it may be a final rest which is indicated instead. Support for the notion of rebirth may be drawn from the fact that a sixth of known Palaeolithic burials (scattered from Wales to Russia) were sprinkled with red ochre, perhaps to represent the blood covering a baby emerging from its mother. But perhaps the mourners were trying to restore the colour which had drained from the body; or else, even more likely, the colour red had a significance in the Old Stone Age which we cannot now comprehend: this would explain why certain artefacts and ornaments deposited in caves were coated in the same ochre. The evidence is inscrutable, and associated with the additional problem that Palaeolithic burials are both rare (being found on just thirty-nine sites in Europe, spanning 70,000 years) and varied in form. We are left wondering why some people were interred crouching and most not, some with goods or ochre and most with neither, while the vast majority of the population does not seem to have been buried at all. Most of the known graves are of adult men, but women and children have also been found.[1] The British evidence is a microcosm of the European, being drawn from just three sites. One is the Goat's Cave in the Gower Peninsula, where a young man was put into a shallow grave with rods and bracelets of ivory and covered with red ochre; a mammoth's skull was placed nearby. The deposit is undatable, but the ornaments indicate that it was made shortly before the last great period of glaciation. This would put it at about 25,000 BC, making it the oldest human burial recorded in these islands. When humans resettled the British region as the ice finally retreated, a few were interred in the caves of the Mendip Hills. At Aveline's Hole in Burrington Combe four individuals were put into the floor, two apparently accompanied by fossils, perforated teeth for necklaces and flints. At Gough's Cave in Cheddar Gorge a possible burial was found without goods, and with some loose human bones nearby. In 1986–7 more bones were discovered at the same spot: these aroused great interest because the flesh had apparently been cut from them by humans before they were deposited. The British Museum (Natural History) issued a cautious press release, stating that it was possible that this feature was evidence of prehistoric cannibalism. The result was a set of lurid newspaper articles which represented good journalism but dubious prehistory. For one thing, the Museum's pathologist has not yet published her detailed report upon the bones. For another, even if she finds that the marks were indeed made by human tools, they may be traces of a burial rite in which the flesh was removed in order to free the spirit more easily from the body. So, whatever scenes of ferocity or affection have left these relics, we cannot now reconstruct them with any certainty. Nor can any of the Mendip burials yet be securely dated, estimates falling between 12,000 and 8000 BC. If closer to the latter, then they may no longer strictly be described as Old Stone Age.[2]

At first sight art promises to be a better source than burials for the study of beliefs: after all, it was presumably designed to deliver a message to the observer. It is also abundant. Carvings upon portable objects appeared around 30,000 BC and figurines and paintings on cave walls around 25,000 BC. After 17,000 BC, southern France and northern Spain became the finest hunting and fishing grounds in Europe, and the caves of this region were the setting for a very large number of wall-paintings. After 13,000 BC, as the climate began to improve, the cave art continued and the portable art reappeared in great quantity and spread out over Europe. Both forms began to decline after 11,000 BC, and by 8000 they had vanished.[3] To a student of prehistoric religion, the earliest significant works are a group of about thirty-five female figurines found on twelve sites scattered from the Pyrenees to Siberia. In view of this vast geographical range, their similarity is striking. All are relatively small, about the length of a human hand, and all are footless and faceless with swollen breasts, buttocks and/or abdomens. Within this style there are some variations. They are fashioned in clay, ivory or stone. Some are fat, some apparently pregnant, and some have the breasts and buttocks alone emphasized. Those from western and central Europe tend to be found singly and without any context, while the Russian examples are found more often in groups and on settlement sites. At Kostienki on the river Don, three were found in a niche in a hut wall. The situation could suggest that they were deities in a family shrine, but as they had been thrown there after being broken it looks more likely that they were being discarded or hidden. At Yeliseevici, on the river Desna, one was found among three mammoths' skulls arranged in a circle. At Laussel in the Dordogne, France, three reliefs of women holding objects were found carved upon boulders in a rock shelter. All are similar in style to the figurines and the best preserved holds what experts upon the fauna of the Palaeolithic have always identified as an upward-curving bison horn, marked with thirteen lines. The woman's left hand rests upon her abdomen, and she had been painted red, which, as suggested above, seems to have been the colour most often connected with sacred or arcane matters in the Palaeolithic.

No collection of male images is associated with all these females, the only masculine forms being a torso with a spear carved at Laussel and a crude and mutilated statuette from Czechoslovakia. There is also a scene engraved in the sequence at Laussel which may show an act of human copulation, though it is not plain enough to afford any certainty. The only other evidence relating to these figurines is their dating, and here another striking similarity is revealed: all those from contexts which could be dated may be attributed to the centuries between about 25,000 and about 23,000 BC. All were therefore apparently produced in a relatively short period of the Palaeolithic, that in which the ice sheets were starting to advance southward for the last time. This fact would account for their complete absence from Britain, which the ice was rendering uninhabitable.[4]

So what did they mean? Their earliest discoverers pre-empted the question by calling them 'Venuses', a name which has stuck and which indicated that they were representations of a goddess. For the first seventy years of this century it seemed to be a scholarly orthodoxy that they were representations of a universal prehistoric Earth Mother. This interpretation (which will be discussed further in the next chapter) was not the product of accumulating evidence but a theoretical construction. The figurines were slotted into a pre-existing system of thought much as earlier generations had considered Palaeolithic flints to be the discarded weapons of elves. Unlike 'elf-shot', the notion of this Mother Goddess is not susceptible of proof or disproof, but there have always been prehistorians who have noted that the Old Stone Age statuettes have no features to mark them off as divine or majestic.[5] On the other hand, the degree of effort invested in them suggests that they were far more than Palaeolithic pin-ups. Any explanation of them needs to take into account the fact that they were apparently a feature of a relatively short span of the Old Stone Age, marked by the cooling of the climate. If the Earth Mother theory is

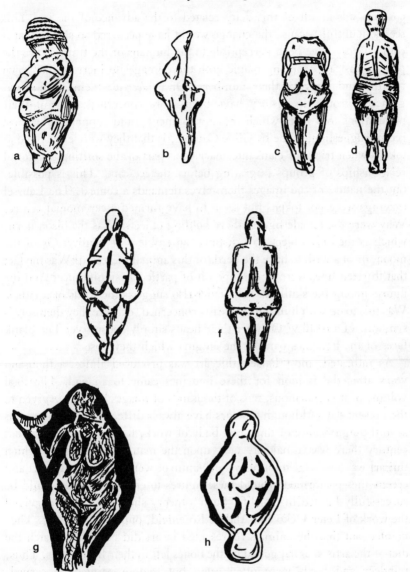

FIGURE 1.1   Old Stone Age images: figurines and reliefs from *c*.25,000 to
c.20,000 BC
a From Austria, limestone figurine ('Venus of Willendorf'); *b* from Italy, stone
figurine; *c*, *d* from Kostienski, USSR, ivory figurines; *e* from France, ivory
figurine ('Venus of Lespugue'); *f* from Czechoslovakia, baked clay figurine;
g from France, bas-relief ('Venus of Laussel'); *h* also from Laussel, France, bas-
relief of enigmatic double figure, sometimes thought to represent human
copulation.

correct, was a cult of this deity related to the advance of the ice? This seems doubtful because the change would have occurred so slowly that it could hardly have been perceptible to the humans of the time. Were the people, instead, working magic with these images to increase their own fertility and improve their numbers? Or to *decrease* them, as hunter–gatherer groups in history have been more concerned to limit their populations to a level which the environment could support? The most recent suggestion, made by Clive Gamble, is that they were exchanged as tokens when tribes or clans intermarried as part of the shifting territorial relationships of groups migrating before the ice-cap.[6] This is possible, but the nature of the images themselves demands a context. The Laussel carvings were not tokens but seem to have formed a ceremonial centre. Why were the female figures there holding objects? Was the bison horn, which is the only object now distinct, an emblem of virility? Or of the moon, or of a wish to have the herds of this animal increased? Was the fact that thirteen lines were drawn upon it of particular significance? And the figure among the skulls at Yeliseevici also suggests the focus of a ritual. Was this to do with hunting the beasts concerned, or were they themselves symbolic of a quality? Or were their heads simply decorative? The blank faces of the figurines parallel the enigma which they pose.

As indicated, most Palaeolithic art was produced almost a thousand years after the fashion for these figurines came to an end. The total volume of it is enormous, tens of thousands of images having survived to the present day. Although scholars have always differed in their opinions as to the significance of this great body of work, for much of the present century there was a majority view upon the matter, according to which this art was an aid to 'hunting magic': animals were represented in art and ceremonies performed around these figures to ensure that they could be successfully hunted in real life. Such a theory should not have survived the work of Peter Ucko and Andrée Rosenfeld, published in 1967. They pointed out that the animals represented in art did not really match the diet of the artists, as suggested by the bones left in their living sites. Thus, reindeer and birds were often eaten but seldom painted or carved. Mammoths were rare at the time and place of the artists but often feature in their work. The beasts most commonly represented are horses and bison, which were certainly hunted but not in a quantity to justify such a predominance. Some animals were indeed portrayed in traps or wounded by spears or arrows, which would support the notion of rituals to improve the hunters' catch, but most were not. An alternative proposal, that the images were intended to increase the numbers of game, and thus the food supply, does not stand up any better. No scenes of copulation appear, sexual organs are rarely indicated and female beasts are seldom shown with young. Perhaps, then, the animals selected were totems, the spiritual guardians of the clan or tribe which portrayed them? Again, the evidence does not all match the theory. Most decorated sites show a number of different species, not one dominating all. Furthermore, tribal totems are commonly predators, powerful hunting beasts which humans might admire and envy. Cave bears, lions, wolves and hyenas all abounded in the world of these Stone Age artists; but the first three appear only occasionally in the art, and the hyena never.

One way out of the problem appeared to be to study the motivation of hunter–gatherer peoples in the modern world who produce paintings and carvings, notably the Eskimo, the native Australians and the San (the so-called Bushmen) of southern Africa. The work has now been done, and has not produced the desired results. As Peter Ucko and Andrée Rosenfeld summarized the collection of research, they found that the three races had very different traditions of religion, metaphysics, art and artefacts. Clans within each of them used different symbols and they produced images for many reasons. Some were for the joy of creation, some to tell stories, some to record events, some for working sympathetic magic and some for use in initiation ceremonies. None of them put some of their finest work deep in caves in the manner of the Palaeolithic people.

So, the images from the Old Stone Age still pose us a series of riddles. Certain species of animals were selected for portrayal, and placed in a variety of locations, including the walls of caves and overhanging rocks, boulders and pieces of bone and ivory. Some of the cave art was in large chambers where a crowd could admire it; some in tiny passages accessible only to one person at a time, after a painful crawl. Footprints preserved in the mud floors of some French caverns indicate that people of all ages entered them to view the paintings. At the Tuc d'Audoubert in the French Pyrenees, the prints are in six rows, starting close together deep in the cave and fanning out near the entrance, indicating an orderly procession or dance. At El Juyo on the north coast of Spain, excavated in 1979, the cave floor had been prepared as what can only have been a ceremonial centre. Five layers of deer bones, burnt vegetation and red ochre were interspersed with cylinders of clay arranged in rosettes and capped with earth of different colours. The whole pile was studded with bone spearpoints and covered with a huge stalagmite slab set on flat stones. A few feet away, a rock had been carved into a human face upon one side and that of a snarling feline on the other. In many caves, figures were superimposed upon each other in a way that seems deliberate, and were very often paired: horses with bison, ibex with oxen or oxen with mammoths. They were commonly portrayed with parts missing or distorted, and some of the beasts which appear are fantastic, such as bears with wolves' heads and bison's tails. No landscapes are represented, nor (despite its importance to hunter-gatherers) any vegetation. On the other hand, animals are the subjects of only just over half of the total body of art. Virtually all the rest consists of geometric patterns, which may be divided into sixty basic motifs. Scholars have devoted far less time to these than to the animals, partly because they are more common in Spain than in the famous caves of France, and partly because they are even more difficult to interpret. In the art of the native Australians and of the San, such abstractions are often portions of 'spirit maps' charting supernatural journeys, and so they may have been in the Old Stone Age. But we cannot prove this.[7]

Some of the most interesting recent work upon Palaeolithic art has been that of Steven Mithen, who has regarded it as a store of information about animals which were difficult to find or to stalk. Thus, reindeer and most birds were portrayed relatively seldom because they were abundant and easy to kill. Some of the abstract designs, he suggests, are actually hoofprints, sometimes drawn in association with a picture of the animal to which they would belong. Twenty examples, all from the Pyrenees, are known of spearthrowers carved with an ibex excreting an oversized turd (upon which birds are sitting). This, according to Dr Mithen, would be a way of teaching young hunters to recognize ibex spoor. He points out that carnivores are often drawn in association with the herds upon which they preyed, indicating that they could be both a danger to human competitors and, by leading them to game, a help. Likewise, the reason why animals are only partially portrayed could be because a stalker would only partially see them: this would explain why horns and antlers in particular are often shown by themselves or oversize.[8] Now, much of this argument is splendidly perceptive. But it explains only some of the features of the art. It does not account for why a lot of it should be hidden deep in caves, nor why so much is geometric, nor why particular animals should be paired or superimposed, nor why structures such as that at El Juyo should have been made. The assumption that herds of bison and horses were scarcer than those of reindeer, and less easy to kill *en masse*, is not sufficiently confirmed by the evidence: at an earlier period, hunters had stampeded a total of 10,000 horses over a cliff at Solutré, in France. At this stage of research, it seems wisest to suggest that the people of the Palaeolithic

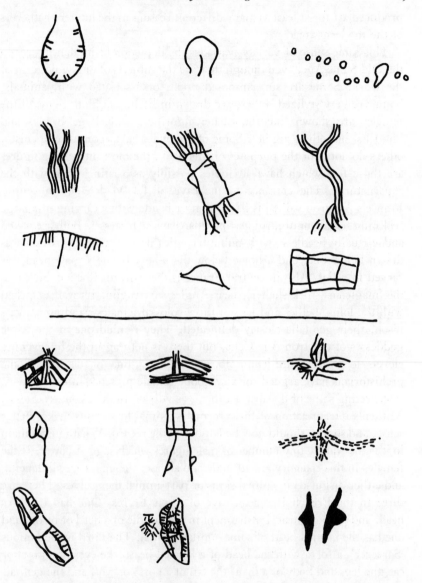

FIGURE 1.2   Old Stone Age Images: abstract forms
Those in the top half of the figure date from *c*.30,000–*c*.18,000 BC, those in the lower half from *c*.16,000–*c*.9000 BC. The three in the top row have been identified convincingly by Steven Mithen as animal footprints, but the rest remain open to anyone's guess.

produced art for at least as many different reasons as the hunter–gatherers of the modern world.

This same sense of variety pervades the depiction of human figures in the Old Stone Age, even though they are the subjects of only 3 per cent of the work. Some are superimposed upon, or associated with, animals. Some are very stylized, others are drawn in lifelike fashion. Some of the females are shown like the earlier figurines, with large breasts and buttocks, but others are not. Some of the males have accentuated penises, others do not. For the purposes of this book, the most interesting figures are those few which have attributes possibly associating them with the supernatural. The entrance to the cave of La Madeleine, in central France's Aveyron valley, is flanked on each side with a carving of a large reclining female figure, suggesting guardians or hostesses. Both are naked and virtually headless, with pubic triangles deeply etched. A bison was drawn below one, and a horse below the other. Inside a male head was carved in relief. Also in central France is the Abri du Roc aux Sorciers, the 'magicians' rock shelter', near Angles-sur-Anglin. Its wall is etched with the loins, bellies and legs of three colossal females standing above a bison, their genitalia clearly delineated. They remind one of the triple goddesses of the Iron Age Celts, but there is nothing in the intervening eleven to thirteen millennia to provide any line of descent. Some prehistorians have argued for a symbolic female presence in many caves, interpreting some of the abstract forms as vulvas. In their context, Steven Mithen's interpretation of these forms as animal hoofprints makes better sense, and so they should now be left out of the record. What must remain in it is the equally tiny number of male figures which suggest power. If the females in this category are all nude and at ease, the males are all dancing and either disguised in animal skins or part animal themselves. There are three in the French Pyrenean cave of Trois Frères. One has a bison's head, and plays a musical instrument in the middle of a herd of bison, and one has the horned head of some similar animal. The third is the famous 'Sorcerer', a form with the head of a horned beast, the eyes of an owl or cat, the legs and body of a man, the tail of a horse or wolf and the genitals of a male feline. At the cave of Le Gabillou in the Dordogne, a figure with a male human body and the head of a bison or bull, very similar to the two at Trois Frères, is carved upon a wall. Scholars have variously interpreted all these as gods or spirits, as priests or witch doctors, or as hunters disguised as animals to deceive their quarry.[9] As with all the Palaeolithic images, we lack the means to translate the artists' message.

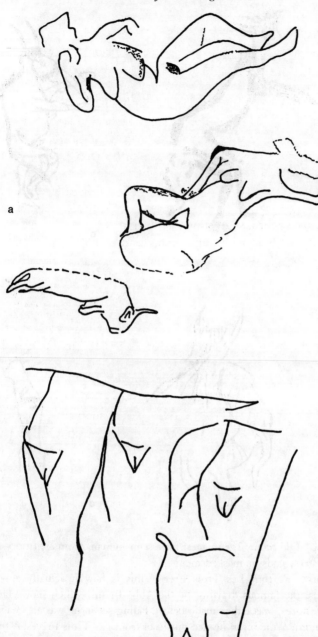

FIGURE 1.3 Old Stone Age images: female forms from *c.*13,000–*c.*11,000 BC
a The reclining women from the cave of La Madeleine; *b* the three giantesses
and bison from L'Abris du Roc aux Sorciers.

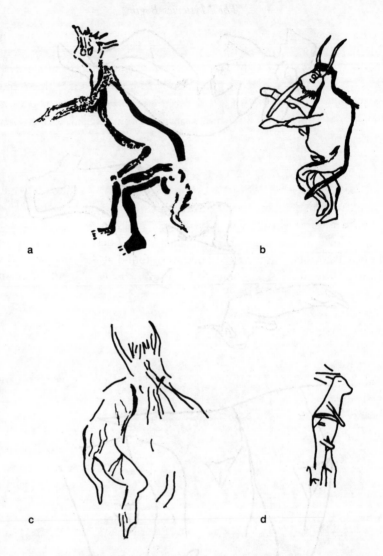

FIGURE 1.4   Old Stone Age images: male semi-humans from *c*.13,000–*c*.9000
BC – monsters, gods or masked men?
a The 'Sorcerer' from Les Trois Frères (this is how it actually appears in
photographs; the famous drawing by the Abbé Breuil, which shows far more
extensive features, was either made before fading set in or was an imaginative
reconstruction); *b* the bison-headed musician from Les Trois Frères; *c* from Le
Gabillou, engraving on wall; *d* from Pin Hole Cave, Derbyshire, engraving on
bone. The only known Palaeolithic human figure from the British Isles, it is
often described as masked and carrying a bow; the latter seems likely, but the
figure is too crude for a mask to be obvious.

British examples of Old Stone Age art are pitifully few because of the glaciation. But there are some from the period after the ice withdrew, found in the picturesquely named caves of Creswell Crags in Derbyshire. From Mother Grundy's Parlour comes a bone engraved with a reindeer. A deer's rib from Robin Hood's Cave was incised with a horse's head. From the Pin Hole Cave comes another bone etched with a chevron pattern and, most interesting, another bearing a male humanoid. This has often been described as masked and dancing like those of France, but the shapeless head may just be badly carved and half of the legs are missing. Its most obvious feature is the large penis. Finally, an etched rib bone was found with the human remains in Gough's Cave, Cheddar. Its markings consist of short strokes along the edges, often in groups of nine. The significance of this number in this context was debated for many years, but in 1989 five fragments of bone were found at the same site, all with similar grouping of incisions. The number in each group upon these varies from eight to fourteen, so it may be that the sets of nine strokes upon the first find were of no particular significance. Unless the carver was (or carvers were) simply doodling, the incisions look like tallies. But whether of kills, or days, or moons, or something else, we cannot know.[10]

With this final puzzle we may conclude our survey of the evidence for Palaeolithic beliefs. We know that the achievements of the human race had already been dramatic. It had produced stone tools of marvellous beauty as well as utility, invented the spear and the bow, and built artificial shelters and winter dwellings. It had produced art of an enduring quality. It could sew together leather and fur clothing and harvest wild plants with sickle-shaped flints. In Europe it had developed systems of exchange which could carry flint up to 250 miles and shells up to 400 miles. It had acquired the ability to slaughter whole herds of animals (as at Solutré), and to use fire not merely for warmth and protection but to clear sections of forest for habitation.[11] In brief, it had acquired a power to destroy and to create, not like that of any other species but like that of a force of nature or a deity. Yet how it conceived of its place in the natural or divine order, we cannot know.

From 12,000 BC the last Ice Age was waning, and by 8000 the European environment was changing beyond recognition. A dense forest grew over the prairies, ousting the great herds of animals. As the sea level rose, first Ireland and then Britain broke away from the continental land mass. The concentration of human beings in France and northern Spain dissolved, and the production of art there was reduced to the painting of pebbles. For the hunting bands, game was both scarcer and harder to see in the new dense woodlands, and had to be supplemented more often with plants, fish and shellfish. The change of lifestyle made necessary by these changes in the world marks the transition into the Mesolithic or Middle Stone Age. Once again, humans responded to the alteration of their environment not merely by adapting to it but by challenging it. They domesticated the dog and used fire to remove woodland on a larger scale than before. Where the natural ecosystem was fragile, the trees never grew back as the people moved on, and heaths or bogs came into being. In the clearings they created, humans seem to have penned, if not bred, cattle and deer. The only pictorial evidence for Mesolithic life is provided by the rock paintings in the gorges of eastern Spain. Unlike those of the Palaeolithic, they give great prominence to human figures, showing men hunting and women gathering plants. They also show groups of men fighting with spears. Old Stone Age artists had portrayed human bodies stuck full of these weapons, indicating that either war or executions were already a feature of society. The Middle Stone Age art leaves no doubt that warfare was now a part of the human record.[12]

But even the Spanish paintings provide no apparent indication of religious beliefs, and the British Mesolithic record is virtually as bare. There are no burials attributable to the period, unless those in the Mendip caves fall into it. At Star Carr, in Yorkshire, the site of an encampment made in about 7500 BC, excavation turned up several deer antlers fashioned to fit into human caps. These may have been the costume of priests or shamans; but they may equally as well have been disguises for hunters of the animals. Several New Stone Age sacred sites were placed upon ground which had been cleared and occupied in the Mesolithic: in the Cotswold Hills alone this is true of the Rollright stone circle, the long barrows of Ascott-under-Wychwood and Hazleton North, and the causewayed enclosure of Rendcomb.[13] This may have been because these places were already revered by the Mesolithic people; but it may also have been simply because the latter had left clearings in the forest which their Neolithic successors found easy to occupy. The most spectacular example of such possible continuity is also the most puzzling. In 1966 Lance and Faith Vatcher excavated the site of the present car park for Stonehenge, and found three large holes in an irregular line. They displayed clear signs of having held wooden posts two feet thick, including black circular organic staining, side-packing, notches in the sides for holding wedging timbers and a chalk infill at the bottom. One held a tiny piece of burnt bone, while another had a thin layer of charcoal flecks at its foot. They might, upon first sight, have derived very easily from the late Neolithic or early Bronze Ages, but the dating of two separate samples from them subsequently placed them far back in the Mesolithic. The fact that the wood which provided the samples was charred pine would also be more appropriate to the ecology of this earlier age. At this point experts upon Stonehenge lost interest in them, but experts upon the Mesolithic ignored them as well. In both local and continental terms, these holes lack a Middle Stone Age context. There is no other evidence from anywhere in Europe for the erection of such huge wooden structures in this period. Moreover, there is no sign of Mesolithic activity (such as the characteristic flint scatter) anywhere near Stonehenge, while the pollen record for that age suggests unbroken forest on the site.[14] As it stands, there is clearly something wrong with the evidence, for its import just does not make sense. There is a chance that burnt wood from a Mesolithic camp fire was dug down into early Bronze Age postholes as the latter were made, in which case these features may have formed part of the Stonehenge complex after all.

By now it must be obvious that the title of this chapter was a *double entendre*. The religious rites of the Old and Middle Stone Ages may have been mysteries in the sacred sense, but they are also mystifying to us. We do not lack data for them, but we do not know how to read those data. We do not lack for theories of explanation, but none of them is equal to the complexity of the material under study. It remains to be seen whether the yet more spectacular relics of the New Stone Age are more accessible to those interested in human belief.

2

The Time of the Tombs
(c. 5000–c. 3200 BC)

During the fifth millennium BC, the British Isles passed into the Neolithic, or New Stone Age. This transition, like that into the Mesolithic, consisted of a change in lifestyle, but unlike that earlier transformation it was the result not of natural but of human developments. Spreading from the Near East across Europe came the knowledge of sowing and reaping crops, of domesticating and breeding livestock and of making pottery. For a student of archaic religions, it would be interesting to know whether this new farming life was brought westward by new people, who overwhelmed or absorbed the existing hunter–gatherers. Until the 1970s it was often assumed that this was so, and indeed that all or most of the major changes in British prehistory were the result of immigration or invasion. After all, the story of the British Isles from the dawn of history until the High Middle Ages had followed just this pattern. The archaic Irish traditions, the oldest surviving mythology of these islands, had represented Ireland's story in terms of a succession of invasions. One of the major developments in British archaeology during the past twenty years has been a loss of confidence by its practitioners in their ability to recognize the movements of peoples. The problem is that an existing population can adopt foreign artefacts and fashions so completely as to appear to have been replaced by foreigners. Thus, according to traditional archaeological practice, had modern Britain been an illiterate society then it would have been natural to have spoken of the invasion of the 'Washing Machine People' in the 1950s and large-scale Japanese immigration in the 1970s. A glance at tribal migrations during recorded history provides further reason for caution: for example, the Athabascans moved south along the coast of North America, retaining their language and their group identity but taking on the culture of the tribes with whom they collided. They would have been utterly invisible in the archaeological record.[1]

Because of this, contemporary prehistorians have divided views upon the origins of the British and Irish Neolithic, and many withhold an opinion or favour a compromise position. The evidence does seem to support the latter. On the one hand, in northern Ireland it appears that the first Neolithic communities were established in areas away from the densest Mesolithic settlement, and some places, such as the Orkneys, were completely uninhabited before the first farmers arrived there. The earliest trace of the Neolithic found in the British Isles to date is not in Kent or Yorkshire but in County Tyrone. If this is not overtaken by further discoveries, it suggests a landfall made by a group of immigrants making a pioneering voyage into the Atlantic. Early Neolithic huts tended to be rectangular, late Mesolithic huts to be circular. All this might argue for the presence of new people. On the other hand, the major styles of Neolithic pottery tend to reproduce the geographical divisions of the major styles of Mesolithic flintwork. Most styles of Neolithic flint were derived from native Mesolithic, not European, prototypes. And in much of southern England Neolithic sites were superimposed upon those of the Mesolithic.[2] So it does seem sensible to visualize a mixture of immigration and transformation of an existing population, with more emphasis on the second factor. By whatever means, the New Stone Age reached all regions of the British Isles between 4500 and 3800 BC.

Recent research has done much to increase our sense of the sophistication which that age eventually achieved, before its end around 2000 BC. Its agriculture showed diversity and dynamism. Farming developed rapidly, adapting its methods to a range of environments and soil types. In the Northern Isles the people were building houses of stone by 3200, while in southern England they lived in timber homes, or sometimes huts of turves and skins. By 4000 their miners had learned how to pursue a seam of flint along a hillside and to excavate horizontal or vertical shafts. The flints thus produced were traded over hundreds of miles, as were stone axes and pottery. Throughout the period goods and ideas were clearly exchanged between the British Isles and with Europe. Its people were only marginally shorter than those of the present day and, all told, probably lived in as great a degree of physical comfort as those of the Middle Ages. Even if this were so, however, they still retained quite a potential for physical misery. Their skeletons reveal traces of almost every complaint which can leave a mark upon bone, including polio, sinusitis, tetanus, tuberculosis, arthritis, spina bifida and tooth abscesses. Clearly they were accomplished in neither the prevention nor the treatment of disease, and all over the British Isles most died before the age of thirty. Moreover, in some ways they were too enterprising for their own good or that of the environment. They extended the Mesolithic practice of clearing forest on a very large scale so that whole regions, such as the Wessex hills and the area around modern Sligo, were virtually stripped of their trees. In some places, such as parts of Wiltshire and Cumbria, clearance was followed by destructive farming methods leading to soil erosion. Sections of the Lake District were left uncultivable for ever, reduced from woodland to bog.

Furthermore, some Neolithic communities were at least as warlike as those of Mesolithic Spain. In the middle of this century there was a strong disposition among prehistorians to believe that the New Stone Age was one of peace. It has had a powerful influence upon 'alternative' archaeologists and 'earth mysteries' researchers. Some doubt was aroused by the bones found in the Neolithic tombs. From Wor and Crichell Down long barrows in Wiltshire came two male skeletons, each with an arrowhead in its side. In the West Kennet long barrow in the same county, an old man had an arrowhead at his throat and a slash across an arm bone. At Ascott-under-Wychwood long barrow, Oxfordshire, and the cairn of Tulloch of Assery A, in Caithness, there were arrowheads stuck in spinal columns. From Windmill Tump and Belas Knap long barrows in Gloucestershire, from the Giant's Grave long barrow in Wiltshire, and again from West Kennet, there came skulls which had been cleft or gashed before death. But all these could be explained in terms of accidents or private murders. More decisive evidence only began to accumulate at the end of the 1970s. Some came from Crickley Hill in Gloucestershire, which had been strongly fortified around the year 3200 BC. The work had been in vain, for soon after this the timber gateway and the adjoining palisade had been stuck full of arrowheads and then burned down, along with the settlement inside. In Dorset, Roger Mercer investigated Hambledon Hill, and found that this also had been fortified near the end of the mid-Neolithic. In the ditch before one rampart was found the body of a young man with an arrowhead in his throat. He had been shot from below and fallen dying, apparently still clutching a child in his arms whose bones were found with his. Then the palisade above them had been burned and toppled over them. Dr Mercer went on to excavate Carn Brea in Cornwall, long presumed to be an Iron Age hill fort. He proved that it dated from early in the Neolithic, around 3800 BC, when a massive stone wall had been raised to defend a settlement there. Only one animal is dangerous enough for such a powerful barrier to be needed against it: the human. Around 3500 BC this wall, too, was stuck with arrowheads, which littered the ground inside. The village had been destroyed by fire. Roger Mercer suggested that several other prehistoric fortresses in western England, Wales and Ireland probably also dated from the New Stone Age.

The people of that age, then, were clearly much more than brutish savages and much less than inhabitants of a time of peace, piety, natural healing and respect for the environment. What we cannot determine about them are their political systems and the balance of power between the sexes. Old-fashioned prehistorians assumed that men must have dominated, partly because of the prejudices of their own society and partly because this is true of all the agrarian societies known to history and anthropology. Some modern feminists have, with justice, challenged this picture as unprovable and preferred to believe that the New Stone Age was guided by matriarchies. Margaret Ehrenberg has made the most recent and intelligent study of the question. Drawing attention to the facts that women are or were the subservient gender in all societies which practise large-scale animal husbandry, and that such an economy spread across Europe during the mid-Neolithic, she has argued that if women had enjoyed a more equal status earlier they would probably have lost it then. The truth is probably irretrievable, though it must be said that the evidence for ruthless warfare by the mid-Neolithic increases the probability that British society had become male-dominated by then. Bellicose societies exalt aggressive masculinity.[3]

It is, however, with an enduring glory of the early western European Neolithic that this chapter is principally concerned: that its people were the first upon earth to build monumentally. Centuries before the first temple platform was raised in Mesopotamia, and one and a half millennia before the first pharaoh reigned in Egypt, imposing structures lined the western seaboard of Europe from Spain to Sweden. They were tombs, built of massive undressed stones ('megaliths') or of timbers, and covered or partially covered with tons of piled earth and stones. The mounds thus created could be conspicuous over long distances, often dominating their landscape. More than 40,000 of the stone tombs still survive in Europe, along with many hundreds of the mounds which once covered wooden structures of the same age. By the 1950s, prehistorians had achieved agreement upon the question of their origins. They were described as being the result of an idea brought up from more advanced Mediterranean civilizations, together with the cult of a Great Goddess or Earth Mother.

Both parts of this concept were shattered at the end of the 1960s, the notion of the Goddess in circumstances which will be described later, and the belief in a Mediterranean origin by the discovery of faults in the Carbon 14 dating process. When corrected, the process revealed that the western tombs were much older than the eastern civilizations which were supposed to have inspired them. The problem of how they were first conceived, and diffused over such a vast distance, remains a mystery. This is partly because the dating process, though now accurate, has provided more puzzles than it has solved. The first groups of dates for tombs in France and Spain come from around 4500 BC, in England from around 4300 BC, in Ireland from around 4200 BC, in Scotland from around 4100 BC, in Portugal and Denmark from around 3900 BC, and in the Netherlands from around 3400 BC. From these, it might be suggested that the habit of megalithic tomb construction began either in Spain or in France, and spread swiftly if unevenly northwards along the European coast. But the picture is bedevilled by earlier dates for individual tombs: 4700 BC for Kercado in Brittany and 4600 for Carrowmore 4 in Ireland.[4] They might be explained in the same fashion as the 'Mesolithic' post holes at Stonehenge, by tomb foundations being dug through a Mesolithic campfire and mixing up its remains with the Neolithic deposits. But they may be genuine. The plain truth is that at the present time we have too small a sample of dates from any country to determine whether these monuments were part of the culture of the first farmers or whether Middle Stone Age people were developing them before agriculture arrived.

If we do not know precisely *when* they appeared, can we decide *why* they did? During the 1970s the most fashionable ideas were that they were a response either to population pressure or to soil exhaustion in the westernmost margins of Europe, from which there was no escape by further migration. The first explanation suggested that these great landmarks containing ancestral bones were established to declare title to land and to deter competitors from settling nearby. The second regarded them as shrines to the pioneers who had first farmed the land, raised in supplication by descendants whose harvests were declining as the soil deteriorated with use. Neither interpretation survived for long. For one thing, tombs are often found to have been built by the earliest farmers to occupy a particular locality, in clearings in what was still thick forest. For another, the peoples of central Europe and the Balkans settled even more densely and farmed just as intensively without feeling the impulse to build tombs: they built impressive dwellings instead. To raise great landmarks such as megaliths could be as much a celebration of economic success as a reaction to economic crisis. The crucial question is why the dead, or some of them, were so important at this period. There is no doubt that these great tombs, far more impressive than would be required of mere repositories for bones, were the centres of ritual activity in the early Neolithic: they were shrines as well as mausoleums. For some reason, the success of farming and the veneration of ancestral and more recent bones had become bound up together in the minds of the people.

During the 1980s, attention was directed more towards determining the source of the tomb-builders' notions of architecture. The most prominent theory has identified two separate migrations of ideas. One was along the Atlantic coast, from Spain, and consisted of a fashion for stone tombs under circular or oval mounds. One proponent of this notion, H. N. Savory, has suggested that the original custom of collective burial was brought from the Near East, where older group burials in caves or in niches cut into rock have been discovered. The other tradition consisted of burial in pits or timber chambers under long, often trapezoidal, mounds, known in England as long barrows. This practice, suggests the current theory, originated in the long timber houses of identical shape built by farmers in the Danube basin from *c*.4800 BC. Both houses and long barrows tended to face south-east and to be entered from that end. Both had timber façades, and flanking ditches. Thus it is possible that this style of architecture migrated westward to Brittany during the next few centuries and got adapted there for tomb-building. It could then have travelled to Britain and been taken up there, before combining with the Atlantic coastal tradition to produce stone tombs under long mounds (known as chambered long barrows or long cairns). All this is plausible, though it is a very long way from the Near East to Spain with no markers between, even supposing that the megalithic tradition did start in Spain. It is a shorter distance from the Danube to Brittany, and long houses have been found in north-eastern France, in between. But even if the migration of style did occur, we still have no answer to the essential question of why the house of the living should become the house of the dead. In Spain, Britain, Ireland and most of France, there was no tradition of collective burial, let alone the building of tombs, before these great structures suddenly appear. Only in Brittany, of all the areas which have produced the earliest dates for tombs, did the late Mesolithic people have the custom of interring people in groups under cairns, in stone-lined pits. It may be that it was the 'Bretons' who first conceived a cult, for one can find no other term as appropriate, which was to spread along the whole

Atlantic seaboard of the continent.[5] Further excavation, supplying more
dates, will certainly bring us closer to a solution of this problem.

The main characteristics of that cult are remarkably consistent
throughout the vast area of its range: burial chambers under dispropor-
tionately large mounds, collective deposition of individuals who represent
both genders and all ages but only a section of the total population, and
removal of the flesh from the bones before their placement in the tomb.
Generally, also, access to the chambers was restricted by making passages
to them only large enough to be crawled along, or by installing blocking
stones or porthole entrances. In most cases gravegoods were few and
unimportant, and the front of the monument faced south or east. On the
other hand, every one of these characteristics was a rule to which there
were a great number of local exceptions. Indeed, of over 2000 such tombs
surviving in the British Isles, not one is constructed in exactly the same
way as any other. This would argue against the idea of 'megalithic
missionaries' travelling around instructing local people in a new religion.
It suggests instead the adoption by myriads of west European communities
of an idea diffused along trade routes and by fishing expeditions and
settlers. This can be illustrated by looking at the types of tomb
architecture that evolved in the British Isles during the early and mid-
Neolithic.

In Ireland three main styles appear to have existed more or less from
the beginning of the tradition: court cairns, portal dolmens and simple
passage graves. Court cairns have a long mound, with a forecourt at the
broader end leading into a stone chamber (see figure 2.1). At present 329
are known, almost all in the northern third of the island. Portal dolmens
(see figure 2.2) are stone chambers with taller uprights at one end so that
the capstone slopes backward. Some had long mounds, but many seem to
have stood more or less exposed, with only a ramp of earth or stones
behind to stabilize the uprights and to enable the capstone to be hauled
into place. They are found in the same region as court cairns, but also in
County Clare and in south-eastern Ireland, and 161 have been identified.
The simple passage grave had a circular or oval mound, containing a
round or polygonal stone chamber approached by a passage. Well over a
hundred are known, most in the northern half of the country. Portal
dolmens are also found in Britain and France, and simple passage graves
are quite widespread along the European coast, while court cairns are a
uniquely Irish feature.[6]

The distribution of such monuments in Britain is divided roughly by a
line drawn between Inverness and Bridport, Dorset. To the west of that

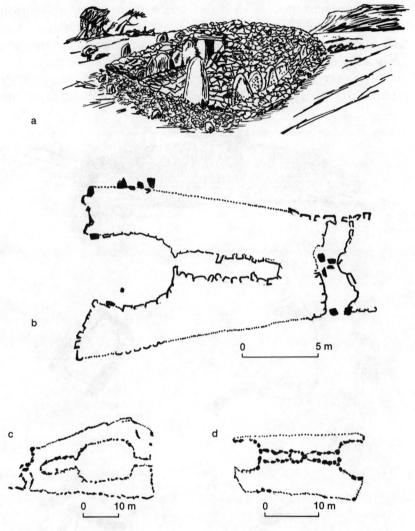

FIGURE 2.1 Irish court cairns
a Conjectural reconstruction of a court cairn; *b* plan of Annaghmare (Co. Armagh); *c* plan of Creevykeel (Co. Sligo); *d* plan of Cohaw (Co. Cavan).
Source: redrawn after Waterman, Kilbride-Jones and Hencken

are mostly stone tombs, and to the east of it the so-called earthen long barrows, with wooden chambers or pits. Included in the megalithic structures are forty-five portal dolmens, found in Wales, the Cotswolds and Cornwall, and about fifty simple passage graves scattered down the west coast of the island from the Orkneys to Cornwall. As in Ireland, it is hard at present to tell which is the older style, and they are joined in Britain by a third very early type, the box dolmen or rotunda grave. These are small stone boxes in round mounds, which were either used only once or had to be reopened by sliding off the capstone. They occurred over quite a wide area, but it is difficult to calculate as (like the simple passage graves) many were rebuilt more elaborately in later

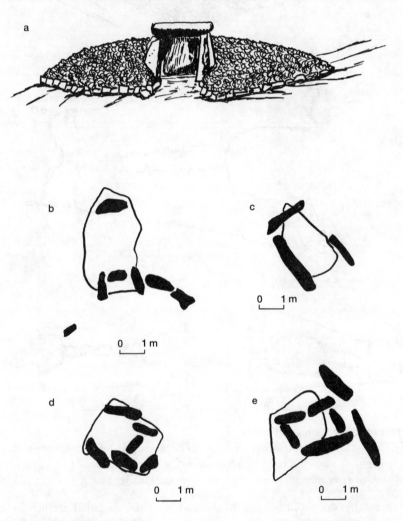

FIGURE 2.2 Portal dolmens
a Conjectural reconstruction of a 'typical' portal dolmen; *b* plan of Pentre Ifan (Dyfed); *c* plan of Penrhiw (Dyfed); *d* plan of Trethevy Quoit (Cornwall); *e* Zennor Quoit (Cornwall).

centuries. In the far north of Scotland and the Orkneys, passage graves were accompanied, perhaps from the beginning, by stalled cairns: long chambers divided into sections by slabs jutting from the walls, within long or oval mounds.

By 3800 BC, as the mid-Neolithic began, more local variations were evolving. In the Shetlands the people built kidney-shaped mounds with small stone chambers. In the Cotswold hills and south-east of Wales, the so-called Cotswold–Severn group appeared: long, often trapezoidal, mounds with forecourts set into one end (see figure 2.3). Sometimes the forecourt gave on to a long chamber with up to three, and perhaps more, pairs of side-cells. In other cases, apparently of the same period, the forecourt had only a dummy entrance and the long chambers, without side-cells, were entered from the flanks of the mound. In south-western Scotland, small chambers in round or oval mounds, entered from openings flanked by stones, grew into the so-called Clyde tombs. These had long mounds and large forecourts, with imposing façades of megaliths. Upon the hills surrounding Kent's river Medway appeared an isolated group of rectangular stone chambers, each entered from the side of a rectangular mound, sometimes sharply defined by a wall of boulders. All over the British Isles as the fourth millennium advanced, the earlier styles were rebuilt or copied with an increase in size and grandeur. In Britain, from the Scottish Highlands to the Cotswolds, several older tombs were given long instead of round mounds, and pronounced forecourts. At Carrowmore in Ireland's County Sligo, a set of simple passage graves was expanded not in individual size but in numbers, until it became the biggest megalithic cemetery in Europe. About a hundred small tombs were clustered around the mighty isolated outcrop now called Knocknarea, the Hill of the King. At the same time, in south-eastern Ireland between Dublin and Counties Kilkenny and Carlow, communities demonstrated that capacity for ignoring the norm which was to be a feature of the prehistoric human record. Instead of building the tombs, from 3700 BC onward they placed bodies in massive stone chests, or 'cists', generally of polygonal shape and set in a round mound. The result was very like a box dolmen, save that the chamber shape was more like that of a passage grave and the upright stones all sloped inward. The style spread west into Counties Tipperary and Clare, mingling with the more complex tombs, but remained very thinly scattered: less than a dozen certain examples are at present known.

The fashion for long mounds may, as already mentioned, have derived from the eastern British earthen long barrows, which were themselves

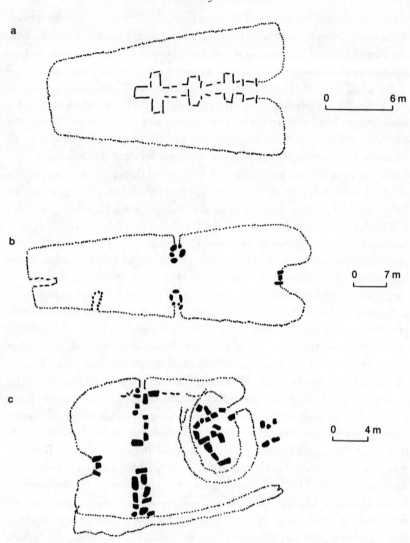

FIGURE 2.3 Some varieties of Cotswold–Severn tombs
a Stoney Littleton (Avon); *b* Belas Knap (Gloucestershire); *c* Ty Isaf (Powys).
There is nothing regional about these styles: types *a* and *b* are found all over the
Cotswolds and south-east Wales and type *c* is an example of the sort of individual
variation which abounds in all tomb-building areas.

every bit as early a form as the first British stone monuments. A count of these is impossible, because so many in the number would be uncertain, represented by crop-marks untested by excavation. Essex, for example, may prove to have either twelve or none. The proven survivors are scattered from the hinterland of Aberdeen to Dorset, the greatest concentration being the sixty-nine on Salisbury Plain. The long mounds, broadening towards one end, vary greatly in size, the largest upon Salisbury Plain being seventy times as big as the smallest. Many began as timber mortuary houses, which often stood for many years before being buried within the mound, just behind a forecourt or a flat façade. In several cases, recorded over the whole extent of their range, the mortuary house was burned before the mound was added, but in others, equally widespread, it was not. Often the wooden hut was built upon a stone platform, and sometimes there was a pit instead of any building. In some regions, such as Wessex, the earthen long barrows were being constructed and used within sight of the chambered long barrows with their stone tombs, apparently by people with the same culture. It is impossible to account for their preferences, or for those at Wayland's Smithy in Oxfordshire, Lochhill in Scotland and Gwernvale in south-east Wales, who converted an earthen long barrow into a chambered one.[7]

If some readers find this description complicated, it must be added that it conceals several subdivisions to the styles. Furthermore, there is a large number of surviving tombs, one sixth of the total in Ireland, which are either so idiosyncratic that they fit into no category but their own, or so badly ruined that they cannot now be identified. But was this variety balanced by a greater uniformity of ritual and burial practice? Answering this question is far more difficult than classifying the tombs, for which their empty shells can suffice. The task is complicated in respect of England by the fact that so many of the tombs were roughly dug over by nineteenth-century antiquarians who unwittingly removed the evidence upon which modern archaeology depends. Several important Irish sites have been ruined in the same way. Scotland, on the other hand, may well prove to have the best-preserved collection of Neolithic tombs in Europe, but there has only been time to make a few full-scale excavations there. In Ireland fewer than forty court cairns have had any recorded investigation, of which just seven have been properly excavated. Most proved to contain the cremated remains of a single person, but some had larger numbers of burials: seven at Ballyalton in County Down, seventeen at Cohaw in County Cavan and thirty-four at Audleystown in County Down. All the bones at Cohaw and most at Audleystown were unburnt, and had been

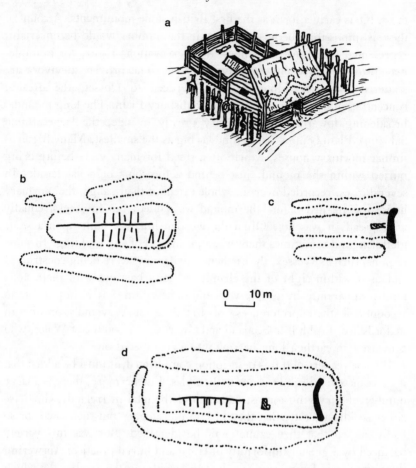

FIGURE 2.4   Earthen long barrows
a Conjectural reconstruction of the timber mortuary house at Nutbane
(Hampshire), burned down before the long barrow was heaped up (it is assumed
that the various pieces of timberwork would have been decorated); *b* Beckhampton
Road, (Wiltshire); *c* Willerby Wold (Yorkshire); *d* Giant's Hills (Lincolnshire).
In *b–d* the dots indicate the mound and its flanking ditches, the solid lines hurdle
fences to contain the chalk of which the mound was made, the solid black shapes
the timber façade and the hatched areas the position of the original mortuary
house.
Source: all after Castleden, *The Stonehenge People*. Rodney Castleden deserves a special
acknowledgement for the generosity with which he answered my enquiry.

brought in after the bodies had decomposed elsewhere. Ballyalton and Cohaw had foundation deposits beneath the cairns, of black earth mixed with human and animal bones, charcoal and flints. It is as if refuse from an abandoned village had been brought to consecrate the tomb–shrine. Gravegoods were few, but included pots or potsherds, animal bones (including those of sheep, goats, dogs, cattle and pigs), arrows, flints, ornaments and balls of clay. Most of the court cairns examined, however, had no foundation deposits, no goods and only the one cremated human – usually a young male, suggesting the burial not of a respected leader but of a token representative, perhaps a sacrifice. To call such monuments tombs at all is stretching the meaning of the word, the shrine component being more or less all-inclusive. Sites like Audleystown really belong to a different tradition within the same architectural form, and it is frustrating

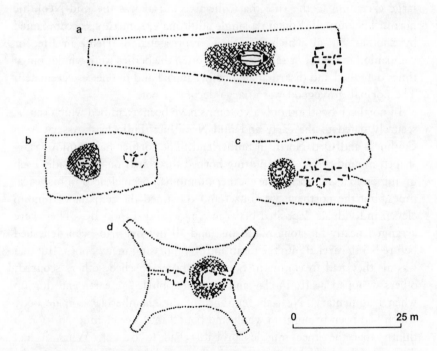

FIGURE 2.5   The transformation of early tombs into long cairns
a Wayland's Smithy (Oxfordshire): earthen long barrow; *b* Dyffryn Ardudwy (Gwynedd): box dolmen/rotunda grave; *c* Notgrove (Gloucestershire): box dolmen/rotunda grave; *d* Tulloch of Assery A (Highland): simple passage grave.
Source: after Corcoran and Darvill.

that we do not yet have enough data to determine if one was later than the other.

The score of Irish portal dolmens which have been examined give the same impression of token deposits. Only thirteen had any contents (though the others might have been cleared out), and these consisted of small quantities of cremated bone, with occasional unburned pieces of skeleton and flint tools or weapons, and potsherds. Three of the simple passage graves in the Carrowmore cemetery have been thoroughly excavated, and their contents ought to have been particularly interesting because they are so early, dating right back to the beginning of Ireland's megalithic tradition. Unfortunately, they remained in use until *c*.3000 BC, and were all then either re-used or disturbed in the Bronze or Iron Ages. As a result it is impossible to reconstruct their first burial patterns. The cist graves of the south of Ireland show a clear pattern which forms a large exception to the rule that collective burial was the mid-Neolithic norm. They usually contain a single adult male, sometimes accompanied by another burial which may have represented a friend in life, or companion in death, or sacrifice. Most often the bodies were whole, but at times defleshed and disarticulated before burial and in one case cremated. The normal gravegood was a large decorated pot.[8]

In northern Scotland only two tombs have been examined which can be securely dated to the early and mid-Neolithic: Tulloch of Assery A in Caithness and Ord North in Sutherland. The former has a unique star-shaped mound, created by putting horned forecourts on either side, each giving on to a chamber. The southern tomb had been cleared in historical times, but the northern was intact and contained the remains of nine to eleven individuals deposited between *c*.3800 and *c*.3600 BC. They were arranged neatly on stone platforms, and all but one had been defleshed before being carried into the tomb and were missing many bones. But that was all they had in common. Some had been scorched, others scoured, others wrapped neatly in clay and yet others buried in earth and dug up when fragmentary. Near the entrance of the chamber lay a male body which had been brought in whole and bound into a crouching position so tightly that the knee muscles probably had to be cut. When it had decomposed, somebody removed the bones of the jaws, spine and feet, perhaps because they were considered important and were required for rituals, or perhaps because they were considered unimportant and therefore not needed in the tomb. Thus the same chamber contained five different methods of burial for only twice that number of people. At some later time, another tomb was built next to this one and a third within sight of them. Neither resembled the first in design and both had methods of burial quite different from it and from each other. Ord North was a passage grave with the rather unusual feature of two antechambers. We shall never know who was buried there and how, because around 3400 BC the chamber was cleansed of bones and its floor carefully coated in a layer of soil holding potsherds. When the latter were examined, they were found to have belonged to seven vessels of totally different styles, only a couple of which resembled anything else found in Britain.[9]

The stone tombs of the fourth millennium in England and Wales have been so damaged by time and antiquaries that little can be learned from many of them. Nevertheless, the examples of the Cotswold–Severn tradition at West Kennett and Lanhill in Wiltshire, Hazleton North in Gloucestershire and Ascott-under-Wychwood in Oxfordshire, have yielded rich material to the modern archaeologist, and older excavations have produced some information for many others. The numbers of people placed in them varied enormously, from five or six at several Black Mountain and Cotswold sites, to about thirty at Hazleton North and at Ty Isaf in Powys, about forty at Belas Knap in Gloucestershire, and about fifty at Ascott-under-Wychwood and at Tinkinswood in Glamorgan.

The construction of the first of two chambered long barrows at Hazleton, Gloucestershire, as imagined by John Sibbick. The careful excavation of this site in recent years permits a quite accurate depiction of the monument when new. Mr Sibbick portrays it, as seems at present most likely, to have been a communal achievement, of a whole family group or clan. Reproduced by kind permission of the Corinium Museum, Cirencester.

Burial ceremony at the West Kennet chambered long barrow, Wiltshire, as imagined by Judith Dobie. The appearance and the animal sacrifice seem well-attested by archaeology, as does the crouched and complete condition of the body, although this last feature was the norm neither at West Kennet nor at most other Cotswold–Severn tombs. Other features are more controversial. It is not clear whether the great blocking stones of the forecourt, shown ready for erection, were added at a time when burial was still going on, but this seems unlikely. Ms Dobie has adopted Aubrey Burl's suggestion that ceremonies were nocturnal and moonlit. The identity of the male figure presiding, priest, chief or merely next of kin to the deceased, is left tactfully obscure. By kind permission of English Heritage.

Even these higher figures would have represented only some of the community which built the monuments and then used them for centuries, while many of these tombs clearly held only token burials, like most of the Irish sites and Tulloch of Assery A. At several of those which were entered from the side, the chambers contained either nothing or a few scraps of bone. Counting the burials is difficult because the bones were usually brought into the monument defleshed, disarticulated and often broken, and then mixed together. On the other hand, some bodies, especially in tombs entered through the forecourt and equipped with side-cells, were deposited whole. At times they were left in a crouched posture. When some of these, in turn, had decomposed, their bones were swept into a pile with those of their predecessors. At West Kennet all three treatments were apparently present in the same set of chambers. Several tombs had a few cremations in addition to all the unburned skeletons. Another common feature of these burials is that very few skeletons are complete. At Ty Isaf, for example, thirty-three people were represented by three thigh-bones, seven skulls and twenty-two jawbones. Two of the indiviuals counted at Ascott-under-Wychwood had left only a fibula and a scapula respectively. In many chambers skulls and long bones were missing, although in some, entered through the forecourt, there were too many of them in proportion to the other bones. Either bodies were brought incomplete from the places where they had decomposed or else bones were removed from the tombs for ritual purposes. The evidence suggests that both occurred, at West Kennet in the same monument. At several sites the skulls and long bones were stacked together in the chambers. Some attempts were also made to distinguish people by age or gender. As in Scotland and Ireland, both sexes and all ages were present, though while women or men could predominate, children were generally under-represented. Children were also usually deposited separately, and in some cases the sexes were divided. At West Kennet, mature men tended to be placed at the far end, while adults of both sexes, youths and old people were in different side-cells. Gravegoods tended to be relatively few and simple, including pots, tools and weapons, and could not be identified with particular burials. Cattle bones are often found in the chambers. They would seem to have acted as totems or emblems rather than simply as the remains of food offerings, because they were usually treated in the same way (cremation, decomposition, whole burial) as the human skeletons which they accompanied. The comparative rarity of pigs' bones in tombs, despite the fact that they were a favourite food item in the period, would bear out this idea.[10]

About a hundred of the earthen long barrows have had some recorded investigation, and they show a comparable variety of practices. At Fussell's Lodge, Wiltshire, almost sixty people were placed in the mortuary house. Their bodies had been exposed for at least two years before being brought to the hut and were stacked in piles containing an average of two individuals. But the scores of other earthen long barrows in southern England contained an average of six people each: as with the stone tombs, the monumental function was generally more important than the morutuary one. Indeed, this seems to have become more true with time, for at present the barrows with the most bodies appear to be the earliest. As in the English stone tombs, individuals were sometimes deposited whole, and in the earthen barrows these were overwhelmingly adult males. It was only these male bones which had gravegoods lodged with them. As at Tulloch of Assery, those bodies which had been stripped of flesh before deposition had gone through differing processes, some bones apparently exposed upon platforms or in enclosures, some temporarily buried and some scorched. Some were cremated, though the frequent custom of burning down mortuary houses makes it diffcult in some cases to determine which bones were brought to the house already burnt. Half of the total of bodies recovered from the great concentration of barrows upon Salisbury Plain were adult men; the remaining half were women and children in roughly equal proportion. The same sort of variation is found in the earthen long barrows of eastern England, of which those of Yorkshire are the best studied. Indeed, the only difference is that the proportion of men to women is nearer equality, although children are still under-represented. The same is true of this type of monument in Scotland, save that cremation was far more common there.[11]

All this information may be only a fraction of what further excavation will reveal, but it is sufficient to support certain conclusions. It is obvious that most (though not all) communities in the British Isles during the mid-Neolithic attached great importance to the building of impressive monuments in which the remains of some of their dead were deposited. It also seems to have mattered to many of them that the bones should be defleshed before deposition, though the number of exceptions makes one wonder if this was a matter of religion or of practical convenience. Both in architecture and in burial custom, the tombs varied so much that one can only assume either that these matters were considered unimportant or that people held strongly contrasting ideas. What does seem clear is that these monuments were not places in which to dispose of corpses, so much as religious centres which played a continuing part in the community – as did the dead, or at least the bones of some of them. Where sufficient material survives for analysis, it is clear that the tombs were used for a relatively long time after being built, in most cases for between one and four centuries. The condition of the bones, and at Hazleton North the architectural remains, indicate that the tomb entrances were completely closed up between burials and ceremonies. The latter have left the most obvious traces in the forecourts, which played an ever more significant part in the construction of the monuments as the fourth millennium wore on. Frequent finds of potsherds, the remains of fires and the bones of pigs (the most prized animal for Neolithic feasts) testify to festivity as well as to piety. The presence of pieces of skeleton indicate that human bones had a part in the ceremonies.

What is most difficult to determine is whom, in both human and divine terms, these monuments and rituals were intended to serve. The court cairns of Ireland, the earlier tombs of the Orkneys, and the stone-chambered and earthen long barrows of southern England, were all normally spaced out quite carefully, as though fulfilling the function of parish churches. In Wiltshire, which enjoyed exceptional advantages of both soils and trade routes, the 'parishes' were on average one and a half miles across. Elsewhere they were larger. It seems as if each tomb was the focus for a group of scattered farms or a settlement, bonded as a clan or a family. In the Orkneys they were placed upon the worst farming land of each territory, to free all the best for exploitation. One of the insoluble problems arising from this picture is that we do not know how many people were involved. Were these monuments built by many in a short time or by a few over a long period? Did neighbouring groups help each other out? The burial of people without distinctions of rank, and in a fashion which mixed their bones, appears profoundly egalitarian and drew some rash statments from scholars in the previous generation about the democratic nature of Neolithic society. But, as Michael Shanks and Christopher Tilley have recently reminded us,[12] profoundly hierarchical societies can enact communal rituals and in any case only a small percentage of people were selected for interment (or partial interment) in these tombs. In the case of single burials, as in Ireland, they could serve the same representative function as a sacrifice. But the most common custom was the cumulative deposition of a selection of individuals of all ages and both genders. Were they from a chiefly or a sacred family? Chosen for looks or talents? Drawn by lot? Why had their bones or bodies come to matter? And why were sexes or ages segregated in some tombs and mixed in others, apparently delivering different social statements? Were only a privileged few allowed to enter the tombs and to handle the bones? And what do we make of the fairly frequent occurrence of tombs in pairs or (occasionally) a trio? Were they used successively (as at Tulloch of Assery), or simultaneously? By the same community or by newcomers? Or were they a symbolic mixing of clans in death as in marriage? Did the mixture of bones within the chambers represent the same alliance of different groups? And what are we to make of the great cemetery at Carrowmore, which is an utterly different phenomenon from the well-spaced court cairns and long barrows? Was it the burial ground of an exceptionally large, stable and enduring community? Or a place of pilgrimage for many strangers? As yet we cannot answer any of these questions.

Perhaps we shall fare better when enquiring after the deity or dieties in whose honour the tomb–shrines might have been raised. One means of approach to this question is to examine the orientation of the tombs, for if they can be demonstrated to point towards the sun or moon, then a sky-cult of some sort is implied. At once it can be seen that many tombs are disqualified from inclusion. The earthen long barrows of Cranborne Chase, Dorset, are laid out along ridges, while those of the Yorkshire Wolds were apparently designed to overlook river valleys. The simple passage graves clustered at Carrowkeel, County Sligo, all face between north and north-west, and if they seem to be pointing at anything then it is the great cemetery at Carrowmore, nearby. At least one Orkney passage grave was sited to look towards a neighbouring tomb. A tomb of the Clyde tradition on the Isle of Arran faces the midsummer sunrise fairly exactly, but there are nineteen other specimens of the same style on the same island which point in quite different directions. So the one midsummer alignment may be accidental. But having said all this, a majority of the Irish court cairns, of the Cotswold–Severn tombs, of the earthen long barrows and of either the mounds or the passages of the northern Scottish monuments, face between north-east and south-west. Aubrey Burl, who has taken more interest in this aspect of the tombs than any other scholar, made a survey of the Wiltshire long barrows. He discovered that although most could be said to have faced the sun's span, a significant minority were aligned upon points outside it, but within that of the moon. He concluded that rituals in their forecourts probably took place by moonlight, conjuring up a wonderful picture of feasting around bright fires, the ghostly moonbeams glistening upon the bones being held in the rites. This may well be correct; but another significant minority of these long barrows, as of the Cotswold–Severn tombs, the court cairns and the Scottish sites, point outside the range of either sun or moon. Perhaps the ones within those ranges had individual ceremonies connected with either or both of the great heavenly bodies. Or perhaps they were just pointed towards the warmest and least windy direction. Once again, the people who built and used these great structures seem to have taken a positive delight in making exceptions to every rule which we try to discern in their behaviour.[13] So, sky-gazing has not achieved anything conclusive, and we have instead to turn our attention to the earth, and to confront the question of the Goddess.

'The great megalithic tomb builders of Western Europe were imbued by a religious faith, were devotees of a goddess whose face glares out from pot and phalange idol and the dark shadows of the tomb walls, whose image is twisted into the geometry of Portuguese schist plaques and the rich carvings of Gavrinis and New Grange.' So wrote one of the most respected prehistorians of this century, Glyn Daniel, in 1958 at the height of this deity's reign over the hearts and minds of scholars.[14] Her conception lay in an archaic Greek myth about the mating of a male sky and a female earth to make the cosmos. From time to time classical philosophers referred to Mother Earth, as an abstract concept based upon this old tradition. But no temples were raised to this being, people preferring to identify with specific goddesses and gods of the sort which will be discussed later in this book. Writers in the Anglo-Saxon and medieval periods who were schooled in the classics occasionally made the same reference as the philosophers, and the concept was taken up again by some of the authors of the eighteenth-century Enlightenment. But it was the world of late nineteenth- and early twentieth-century scholarship which extended the idea into the principle that prehistoric peoples had believed in such a universal deity. Once this decision had been taken, evidence was easily produced to substantiate it, by the simple device of treating any female representations from the Old and New Stone Ages as images of this being. Reference has been made in chapter 1 to the practice in the case of the Palaeolithic 'Venuses'. Any male image could be explained away as the son and/or lover of the Great Mother. During the mid-twentieth century, scholars such as Professor Daniel and the equally celebrated O. G. S. Crawford extended the Goddess's range by accepting that any representations of a human being in the Stone Ages, if not firmly identified as male, could be accepted as her images. Even a face, or a pair of eyes, were interpreted in this way. Because spirals could be thought of as symbols of eyes, they also formed part of the Goddess's iconography, as did circles, cups and pits. In the mind of a historian of art like Michael Dames, the process reached the point at which a hole in a stone signified her presence. Mr Dames was doing no more than summing up a century of orthodox scholarshp when he proclaimed that 'Great Goddess and Neolithic go together as naturally as mother and child'.[15]

As a matter of fact, when Dames published those words in 1976, they were about seven years out of date. In 1968 and 1969 two prehistorians directed criticisms at this whole edifice of accepted scholarly belief which brought it all down for ever. One was Peter Ucko, in his monograph *Anthropomorphic Figurines of Predynastic Egypt and Neolithic Crete*, which

also scanned the evidence for the Neolithic Levant in general. He pointed
out that in Egypt the earth was always considered to be male, that there
was no clear evidence of a female deity in Crete before *c.* 2000 BC, and
that the only unequivocal evidence for a mother goddess anywhere before
that date is found in relatively late texts in Sumeria, while the only certain
fertility goddess was confined to Anatolia. The Egyptian Isis was literally
a mother, but this was not her role with regard to the world. Professor
Ucko reminded readers that a large minority of Neolithic figurines from
the near East were male or asexual, that few if any statuettes had signs of
majesty or supernatural power, and that few of them had accentuated
sexual charactistics (the 'pubic triangles' on many of the females could be
loincloths). He warned against glib interpretations of the gestures
portrayed upon figures; thus, early Egyptian figurines of women holding
their breasts had been taken as 'obviously' significant of maternity or
fertility, but the Pyramid Texts had revealed that in Egypt this was the
female sign of grief. In pursuit of sounder explanations, Professor Ucko
studied the function of similar statuettes among primitve agriculturalists
of the present world. He found that all over the globe clay models very
similar to those of the Neolithic are made as children's dolls. Just as in the
modern West, most are intended for girls and are themselves female.
Another widespread use of such figures is in sympathetic magic, to draw
illness or danger from a person. Just as in the Stone Ages, many portray
pregnant females, as without modern obstetrics childbirth is one of the
greatest dangers women have to face. Some tribes, like the Baluba, use
them in mourning rituals. Professor Ucko concluded that Neolithic
figures may have had just as many different functions, and that if they
apparently portrayed supernatural beings there was absolutely no need to
interpret them everywhere as the same female or male deity.

The second attack was made by Andrew Fleming, in an article in the
periodical *World Archaeology* uncompromisingly entitled 'The Myth of
the Mother Goddess'. He pointed out the simple fact that there was
absolutely no proof that spirals, circles and dots were symbols for eyes,
that eyes, faces and genderless figures were symbols of a female or that
female figures were symbols of a goddess. This blew to pieces the accepted
chain of goddess-related imagery from Anatolia round the coasts to
Scandinavia. He was helped by the revolution in the carbon-dating
process, which disproved the associated belief that megalithic architecture
had travelled from the Levant with the cult of the Great Mother. It also
revealed that the gallery graves of Brittany were among the youngest
megalithic tombs there, not among the oldest as had been thought: they

dated from the very end of the Neolithic. This mattered because they are the only prehistoric monuments in western Europe to bear the figure of an unmistakable female, the shape of a woman carved upon one of the uprights of the chamber. This now had to be reinterpreted as evidence for a late-developing local cult, which the radiocarbon dates could trace spreading into the Paris Basin and the Gard region. It could, of course, merely have been making explicit an allegiance to a goddess whose worship had been implicit in the tombs all along. But that was now only one possibility among many, and not even the most likely.

There was no answer possible to Ucko and Fleming, and during the 1970s the scepticism which they embodied proceeded to erode more of the Mother Goddess's reputed range. Ruth Whitehouse considered the statue pillars of Italy, Sardinia and Corsica, which had been treated as part of the deity's icongraphy, and found that only a few had any female characteristics; many, indeed, carried weapons. Even Malta, long considered one of the most obvious centres of Neolithic goddess worship, fell before David Trump. He pointed out that although some of the Maltese statuettes were certainly female, many of the large cult statues were kilted, flat-chested and generally androgynous. The plans of the temples, traditionally thought to represent the female body, have been proved by Dr Trump to be the result of a long experimentation with different circular forms which settled for the 'hourglass' one as the most symmetrical. Thus the deities of Neolithic Malta are also now an open question among academics.[16]

However, the same mood of iconoclasm in the late 1960s which inspired Peter Ucko and Andrew Fleming brought into being a women's movement bent upon challenging patriarchy in both society and religion. Professor Ucko's book was an academic monograph with a forbidding title, while Dr Fleming's essay was lodged in a scholarly periodical; the old popular works on prehistory were still lining public library shelves (and indeed being reprinted), and they provided some radicals with precisely the universal female deity they had been seeking. At the very moment that the concept of the Neolithic Great Mother crumbled inside academe, it found more enthusiastic adherents among the general public than ever before. This tendency was enhanced by the appearance in 1974 of Marija Gimbutas's beautiful book *The Goddesses and Gods of Old Europe*. It won deserved praise for two great achievements: it established that the Neolithic cultures of the Balkans had left a huge trove of figurines, statues and painted ceramics, and it provided a feast of new images for historians of art and indeed for artists themselves. Yet

Professor Gimbutas's interpretation of those images caused much scholarly concern. She had accepted Peter Ucko's work to the extent of speaking of different goddesses and gods instead of one. But she completely ignored his other criteria by regarding a very large range of human representations, especially among the statuettes, as divine, and proceeding to classify them confidently with no other justification than her own taste. She explained the significance of geometrical symbols in the same fashion, and in subsequent works went on to complete her portrait of a goddess-worshipping, woman-centred, peaceful and creative Neolithic Balkan civilization, destroyed by savage patriarchal invaders. There is good archaeological evidence to cast doubt upon this, but Professor Gimbutas has refused to recognize it.[17] The mixture of affection and frustration which her work inspires is neatly summed up by her Festschrift, the collection of essays by admiring colleagues customarily presented to a distinguished scholar who is approaching the formal age of retirement. That delivered to Professor Gimbutas is characterized by both deep respect for herself and profound dissent from her views. Her most famous book, and the popular works of Michael Dames about the British Neolithic, which are based firmly and innocently on the academic texts, have become staple sources for the Mother Goddess's new host of followers. In the canvases of a painter such as Monica Sjöö, the 'golden age' view of the Neolithic is translated into a visionary world with a tremendous power to comfort or to inspire. If the revised ideas of academe concerning the Goddess were made available to her modern worshippers, the latter would probably reject them. There *is*, of course, a chance that such a being may have been venerated in the Neolithic, but it is beyond doubt that she would not now possess so many followers had not scholars like Professor Daniel proclaimed her existence with such certainty. It is a delicious irony that these establishment figures, themselves no friends to radicals or to 'alternative' archaeologists, may unwittingly have been the founders of a new religion.

But is it at all possible to recognize the nature of a religious cult in the New Stone Age? Here the test case must be Çatal Hüyük[18] in Turkey: the largest Neolithic settlement yet known, it has yielded a large quantity of apparently religious art, consisting mainly of wall-paintings and figurines. It was discovered by James Mellaart in the 1950s, and one eighth of it was excavated by him in 1961–3. He published his interpretation of it in a textbook for the general reader, *Earliest Civilisations of the Near East*, in 1965, and in the monograph *Çatal Hüyük*, which appeared two years later. The comments in the monograph are slightly more cautious than those in the textbook, but they amount to the same thing. In harmony with the prevailing orthodoxy, he declared that the female figures were all aspects of the Mother Goddess and the males were all images of her son and consort. But he went further, suggesting that the fact that the females were represented with an emphasis upon breasts and pregnancy, rather than upon genitalia, indicated that they were created by women. He based upon this the proposal that the whole religion of the community was devised and conducted by women. The celebrated artist Alan Sorrell produced a picture of vulture-masked priestesses serving in a shrine at Çatal Hüyük, which was published in a newspaper and then again in James Mellaart's textbook. Mr Mellaart returned to the subject once more, in a detailed text for students, *The Neolithic of the Near East*, published in 1975. By now Peter Ucko's warnings had made their impact upon academe, and Mr Mellaart scrupulously avoided any interpretations of the kind which he had made earlier. He now spoke only of 'female figurines', 'male statuettes' and 'ex-voto figures', and raised the possibility that some were dolls. When he wrote of the Balkans, in the wake of Marija Gimbutas's book, he carefully declined to repeat any of her interpretations of the finds there. But this dry, densely written academic text made no impression upon the public, whereas his own popular book of ten years previously had now been reissued in paperback. Read with the work of Professor Gimbutas, it produced strong and escalating interest in Çatal Hüyük among the same sort of feminist writers and artists who were taking up the Mother Goddess. By the time the feminist philosopher Riane Eisler published in the mid-1980s,[19] the settlement was confidently believed by them to have been matriarchal in its society as well as its religion, and also – or rather, 'therefore' – a peaceful community requiring neither weapons nor defences (a claim contradicted in Mr Mellaart's original textbook).

What was almost lost in this process was the point that the images at Çatal Hüyük *are* trying to deliver a powerful message. The female figures are often shown in association with animals, almost always predators such as leopards or symbols of death such as vultures. They appear upon walls in the act of giving birth to horned beasts. Female breasts are modelled to project from other walls with the jaws of predators (a fox, a weasel), or the beaks of vultures, protruding instead of nipples. Yet women are also modelled holding and comforting a child. Ian Hodder has recently taken a fresh look at this evidence and the context in which it is set.[20] He notes that women were buried with ornaments and cosmetic boxes, men with weapons of war and hunting and implements of agricultre; that women were portrayed far more often in the figurines, usually nude, while men were portrayed most often in the wall-paintings, clothed and usually engaged in hunting; that the art placed a great emphasis on wild nature and little upon agriculture or domestic tasks; and that the living spaces around the hearths and the cooking-pots were never decorated like the rest of the house. He concluded, convincingly, that all this argues for a considerable tension between the sexes, the female being viewed alternately as comforting, producing and nurturing, and (more often) as predatory and threatening. We cannot tell from this whether the women of Çatal Hüyük were powerful, feared and honoured, or suspected, feared, constrained and subordinated. Despite this wealth of information, we have no entry to the system of thought and worship which it represented. And if we cannot find one at Çatal Hüyük, where the images are so abundant, what hope do we have elsewhere in the Neolithic?

Are there any obvious contrasts among the images yielded by New Stone Age sites in different areas of Europe and the Near East? There is one which does emerge very clearly. The sites in south-eastern Europe and the Levant produce a large number of figurines, most of which are female. This does not mean that male iconography is comparatively slight: it generally takes the form of erect phalluses, of varying sizes and carved in a range of materials, which occur in great numbers upon many of the same sites. Though they have attracted far less attention than the figurines (in Marija Gimbutas's famous book, the female statuettes are dealt with in scores of pages, the phalluses in two), they were obviously of great importance. In north-western Europe the phalluses are also abundant. They occur at several different types of British Neolithic monuments, normally as a portion of ritual deposits in ditches. Associated with them in these deposits are often pairs of chalk balls, and the proximity presents a possibility that these were intended to portray testicles. By contrast, however, the British Isles only furnish two undoubted human statuettes which are possibly from Neolithic contexts. Crudely shapen chalk blocks from the ditches of some sites are occasionally interpreted as female, but so far this is in the eye of the beholder. One of the two certain figurines came from the Somerset Levels, from beneath a portion of the New Stone Age wooden pathway called the Sweet Track. The latter has been dated to about 3800 BC, so that the figure is itself almost certainly from the fourth millennium. It is a little block of wood, carved with two large breasts and a huge erect penis, and is generally taken to be a hermaphrodite (the suggestion that the 'penis' is actually a remaining leg seems refuted by the absence of any

a

b

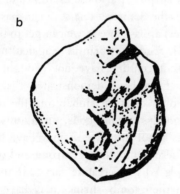

FIGURE 2.6   British Neolithic statuettes
a The Somerset Levels 'god dolly' or hemaphrodite; *b* the Grimes
Graves chalk spirit or goddess.

mark where another was snapped away). The experts upon the
archaeology of the Levels, Bryony and John Coles, suggest cautiously that
it might have been a lost toy, a piece of gross Neolithic humour or a
potent ritual object placed beneath the track to strengthen it spiritually.[21]

The other figure is a lump of chalk crudely carved into the shape of an
obese or pregnant woman, found in one of the flint mines at Grimes
Graves, Norfolk. As these mines began to be exploited at the end of the
fourth millennium and reached their height of production halfway

through the third, if the statuette is contemporary then it seems most probable that it is about a thousand years younger than the Somerset find. The miners in that pit had worked a promising seam only to find it give out in a disastrous fashion. The chalk woman is said to have been set up on a ledge with a heap of flint beneath her capped with a set of antler-picks. The picks may have symbolized regrowth as well as the business of mining, for they were mixed with the chalk balls often fround with phalluses. The chalk lady is supposed to have been seated upon one side of a tunnel with, on the other side, another pair of these balls, but this time with the more usual companion of a chalk phallus.[22] The sympathetic magic of the assemblage seems obvious: the chalk was to be made fertile and to bring forth flint. But, ever since the announcement of this discovery in the 1930s, there have been persistent rumours that the female image is a hoax produced by the girlfriend of the discoverer, a sculptress. After this amount of time has elapsed, it seems unlikely that we shall ever know the truth; a question mark must remain hanging over the status of the finds in that pit. And these examples of male genitalia and these two little figures (the Somerset one seven inches long, the Norfolk one less than five inches) are as close as we can get to the divine beings of British Neolithic ritual. Studies of primitive agriculturalists and hunter−gatherers in the present century have not brought a solution to the problem any nearer. They have demonstrated that such peoples can believe in a large number of spirits inhabiting the natural world, in a varying number of goddesses and gods, in a universal deity, or in differing combinations of all three. So it may have been with the New Stone Age peoples. There is moreover a strong and obvious possibility, that groups which displayed such creative variety in the local architecture and burial customs of their tomb−shrines may have had a comparable complexity of local cults.

It is time to return to the development of the monuments themselves. As the earlier Neolithic gave way to the mid-Neolithic, around 3800 BC, another type of structure became common in north-west Europe. It consisted fundamentally of a circular ditch, interrupted by causeways to form a broken ring and thus called a causewayed enclosure. Normally there were at least two of these rings, arranged concentrically, and often some of the outer ditches were incomplete, forming semicircles. Their range overlapped with that of the tombs, extending from Poland and Czechoslovakia to Britain, north into Denmark and south into France. Throughout this zone certain features were repeated in addition to this basic form, such as the placing of human bones in the ditches, the digging of pits for the reception of special deposits, and the evidence in many cases that the enclosure was used for ritual purposes rather than for settlement. In most areas there existed alongside the causewayed enclosures others with continuous ramparts, like that at Carn Brea, which were apparently intended for defence. In Britain there are a few isolated early dates for the causewayed enclosures, such as that of 4300 BC at Briar Hill in

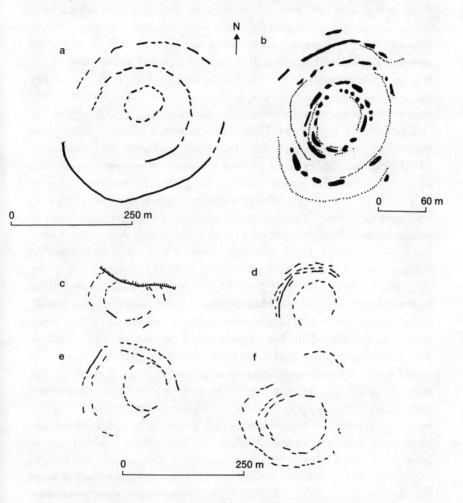

FIGURE 2.7   Plans of causewayed enclosures
a Windmill Hill (Wiltshire); *b* Whitehawk Camp (Sussex); *c* Coombe Hill (Sussex); *d* Orsett (Essex); *e* Briar Hill (Northamptonshire); *f* The Trundle (Sussex).
Source: after Mercer, Bamford, Hedges and Buckley

Northamptonshire: as in the case of tombs, these may indicate genuine forerunners, or accidents producing false dating. Certainly, from 3600 BC these monuments appeared all over southern England and the Midlands, south and east of a line drawn between the mouths of the Severn and the Humber. At present a possible sixty are known, some still trailing low banks across hillsides, some now only crop-marks. Of these, twenty-one have now been excavated, most to a high standard.

The reason why these structures have received such a large amount of attention from modern archaeologists is that until recently there was no agreement upon their purpose. It is now becoming clear that they did, in fact, vary considerably in use and that the broken ring of ditches was just the way in which Neolithic people in many areas defined an enclosure which was not intended primarily for defence. At Abingdon in Oxfordshire, Crickley Hill in Gloucestershire, Etton and Great Wilbraham in Cambridgeshire, Hembury in Devon and Staines in Middlesex, the ditches seem to have enclosed settlements. Yet a ritual element was present in some of these, as though to consecrate the enclosure. At Etton and Staines careful deposits were made at the ends of ditches beside the causeways. The objects laid at the former site included heaps of animal bone, a complete pot on a mat, hazel nuts, twine and a folded length of birch bark. Flints were very carefully kept out of the ditches. At Staines, piles of pottery, flint and animal bone were concentrated at the ditch ends. The enclosures of Briar Hill, Bury Hill and Offham Hill in Sussex, Orsett in Essex and Haddenham in Cambridgeshire had similar deposits in ditches but an interior almost free of refuse and lacking either post-holes or pits. This last feature could be due in some areas to destruction by deep ploughing, but the lack of large quantities of charcoal would appear to confirm the impression given by the unploughed sites of assembly places for occasional use. The same is true of the causewayed enclosures of Wessex, but these are distinguished from the others by the very large quantity of human bone found in the ditches. Skeletal remains from three sites represented a total of 344 individuals. Isolated human bones are found as part of the deposits in the ditches of most causewayed enclosures. The inner one at Offham Hill contained a crouched male burial while the interior of the Staines enclosure had two such interments, plus a cremation, placed in pits. A broken-ditched precinct near Eynsham in Oxfordshire contained pits in which cremations had been placed. But the number of human remains at the Wessex sites, collected over quite a long period, is remarkable. That at Hambledon Hill, Dorset, had skulls set at regular intervals along the ditches as well as many stray bones lying

Causewayed enclosure at Staines, Middlesex, as reconstructed by the late Alan Sorrell. The view from above nicely portrays the 'broken ring' pattern of the ditches. It also, wisely, prevents any too precise indication of the nature of the buildings or activities within, although the presence of fires is indeed indicated by archaeology. Staines is more likely than most such enclosures to have been a settlement. By kind permission of the Museum of London.

in them. Its excavator believed that the interior of the structure had been a
place where bodies had been exposed after death, some of the remains
later being taken to long barrows. It would have been a great charnel
enclosure. At Windmill Hill, Wiltshire, the site may have had a
relationship with the tomb–shrines even before the huge enclosure was
built there. The body of an adult man was found there in 1989, laid in a
grave which had apparently been left open until the flesh had decayed,
whereupon it was filled in. It may have been thus, rather than upon
platforms, that the corpses intended for the tombs were reduced to
bones. This body lay under part of the enclosure, and so pre-dated it, but
the fact that the great structure was itself partnered with the chambered
long barrows is absolutely obvious. Some of the bones found there
represented missing portions of the bodies deposited in the tomb at West
Kennet.

Also in the ditches at Windmill Hill were examples of the kinds of
stone used in the construction of the mound at West Kennet, complete
skeletons of pigs and goats but only skulls of oxen, flints, pieces of local
and imported pottery, antler-picks, mysterious cup-shaped chalk objects,
equally puzzling chalk plaques with incised lines, stone discs with shaped
edges, chalk phalluses, fifteen pairs of chalk balls and pieces of shaped
chalk with etched vertical lines which may possibly have been intended to
represent female figurines. This assumbly suggests a gathering-place of
considerable ceremonial importance, complementing the great tomb
nearly three miles to the south-east. The human remains at all the Wessex
causewayed enclosures, in fact, suggest a complementary relationship
with those chosen for entombment. Whereas children are always in a
small minority in the tombs, they are far more numerous in the enclosure
ditches. Skulls and long bones are over-represented in the ditches as in the
chambers. All this suggests that mid-Neolithic religion was bound up
with a continuous dialogue with the dead, or with death itself. To speak of
a cult of ancestors is perhaps to ignore the continuing deposition of human
bones at both sorts of monument, rather than a sealing up of an initial set
of burials. Yet outside Wessex, with the possible exception of Sussex,
human remains were a far less prominent feature of the ditches' content,
being just one element among many. Finally, when surveying the
possible uses of the causewayed enclosures, it must be added that
Hembury, Crickley Hill, Hambledon Hill and Whitehawk Hill, and
the Trundle in Sussex, were all turned into fortified strongholds by
c.3200 BC. The enclosures of East Anglia and the East Midlands usually
had continuous palisades added within the ditches, which may have been

intended to provide shelter and privacy for gatherings, but might equally have been defensive.

So, it seems as if many or most of the causewayed enclosures were places of occasional or seasonal assembly, raised at a time when the population and the number of farms appear to have been increasing. Whether they assembled primarily for religious purposes, or for the exchange of marital partners, artefacts and information, and for the settlement of disputes, we cannot say. Common sense, and the examples of local assemblies in early historical times and among tribal peoples in the modern world, would suggest a mixture of all of these. What they certainly were not were fairs where objects and livestock were bartered, for the finds in the ditches do not include a high proportion of unworn exotic goods or animal carcasses. The ditches themselves were usually too shallow and wide to pen cattle or sheep effectively; but they do contain evidence for the consecration of many of these sites and of feasting at them. Still, though, they raise more problems than can at present be solved. Why did mid-Neolithic societies in Ireland, Scotland, Wales and northern England share the tradition of tomb-shrines but apparently reject that of causewayed enclosures? Even inside their restricted range within England, no two of these enclosures are exactly alike, any more than any two of the tombs. There are also regional differences. Those of Wessex, apart from being distinguished by the large quantity of human bone present, are much bigger than those elsewhere. Hambledon Hill was the largest monument of its time in what is now Dorset, and half a millennium was to pass before another was built there to rival it. The outer ditch at Windmill Hill was three quarters of a mile around, fifteen

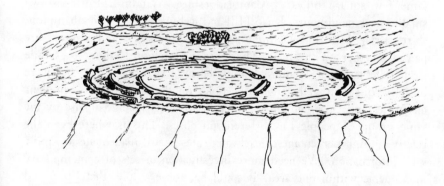

FIGURE 2.8 Conjectural reconstruction of a chalkland causewayed enclosure

feet wide and seven feet deep, representing the removal of 13,000 tons of chalk. By comparison, the enclosures of the Thames Valley, of the Cotswolds, and of eastern England from Sussex to Cambridgeshire, are small and slight. In some cases they were also apparently short-lived, the banks being pushed into the ditches after deposits had been made in the latter. The classic broken-ringed pattern is itself intriguing. In many ways it represents a circle of elongated ritual pits. Was it, as has often been suggested, made up by a set of different social groups (families or clans) working together, each digging a section of ditch? Perhaps this would explain why it was apparently more important to have the lengths of ditch dug than to enclose the space within. It has been stated earlier that some of the rings of ditch are only about half completed, and it may be that in many of these monuments they all were. The Orsett and Staines examples were definitely left open upon one side, and indeed, only six of those which have been excavated were proved to have been completely enclosed: the practice of modern excavation, of taking sections through monuments instead of exploring the whole, tends to leave such problems unresolved.

The working hypothesis that these enclosures were assembly places also poses as many questions as it answers. It is logical to suggest that they were used by the occupants of scattered farms in the neighbourhood, for communal activities. But these farmsteads, which exist so persuasively in theory, have yet to be discovered on the ground. Nor are the enclosures divided neatly among territorial units, but rather are often bunched together. Those of Sussex are gathered in two groups at opposite ends of the South Downs, unless all those in the central section have been utterly destroyed. Etton, Great Wilbraham and Haddenham are all within the same few square miles of Cambridgeshire. Windmill Hill has two smaller near neighbours, Knap Hill and Rybury Hill. In Northampton-shire, Briar Hill and Dallington Heath, Southwick and Tansor, are paired together on the map. There are six enclosures along a 15-mile stretch of the upper Thames. It must be suggested that either they were built by different gatherings of people, on the frontier between their territories and close enough together to allow parleying, or else by the same group of people for different purposes. This is where even the relatively high percentage of excavated sites is still inadequate to supply vital information. We need more investigation of sets of contemporary monuments within one area. It could be, for example, that Etton and Great Wilbraham contained settlements whose peoples gathered in the palisaded enclosure at Haddenham for ceremony or for refuge or for both. Knap Hill and Rybury Hill may have been forts to guard the passes northward from the Vale of Pewsey to the area around Windmill Hill. Likewise, did the Windmill Hill enclosure itself have a ritual relationship with the West Kennet tomb alone? Most of the other burial chambers nearby, such as the Milbarrow, have been destroyed, but the huge mound at East Kennet seems to cover an intact chamber and deserves the same careful investigation as its famous neighbour. Finally, further investigation of groups of monuments should relate each to the environment as well as to the others in the group. Causewayed enclosures often seem to be placed at the boundary of different types of soil and of farming. Some seem to have been placed near sites of more than local economic importance: Maiden Castle (Dorset), Hambledon Hill and the Windmill Hill group are all near flint quarries, and Bury Hill and Offham are right next to them. We have as yet only fragments of interwoven prehistoric complexes.[23]

The fortification (and destruction) of causewayed enclosures around 3200 BC has been taken by some prehistorians to represent one aspect of a period of instability at the end of the southern English mid-Neolithic. In Norfolk, the Somerset Levels and the Windmill Hill area, pollen analyses have revealed the abandonment of exhausted field systems at this time. Areas of the Cotswolds, the Marlborough Downs and the Sussex Downs were forsaken by many of their people, who moved slowly into the adjacent lowlands. It may be that these changes were too gradual and undramatic to deserve the name, which some have accorded them, of 'crisis'. The decline of the southern English uplands was only relative, and in some cases temporary.[24] Yet the years around 3200 BC do represent a significant watershed, and the late Neolithic was going to be a different cultural phenomenon. In Ireland and Scotland the existing monumental traditions were to reach their apogee, while in England and Wales they were to be altered beyond recognition. The achievements of the previous millennium were to be eclipsed by what is generally considered to have been the most glorious period of British and Irish prehistory.

3

The Coming of the Circles
(c.3200–c.2200 BC)

In many ways the circle might seem an obvious unit of sacred space for human beings. It mirrors the sun, the full moon and the bounds of the horizon. It can be profoundly egalitarian, if the people define the ring, or profoundly hierarchical, if there is a number of concentric rings or a single person in the very centre. Yet these advantages were forgone by many of the communities of the British Isles before about the year 3200 BC, which preferred trapezoidal, rectangular or heel shapes for their tombs which would enhance the geometric importance of the forecourts. One of the changes which set in around that date was an increased interest in circular shapes for monuments throughout the whole archipelago. This was just part of a process which was to make the transition from the mid-Neolithic to the late Neolithic as fundamental as that from the Mesolithic had been.

In Ireland, and on those coasts of Britain which faced it directly, this alteration initially took the form of the developed passage grave. This had in common with the simple passage grave a round or oval mound and a chamber entered by a passage, but the mound was now much larger, the passage proportionately increased in size and length and the chamber extended by a number of side-cells or recesses. The tendency of the simple graves to occur in cemeteries was reproduced to provide two great concentrations of these magnificent monuments in County Meath, as well as many individual examples. The cemeteries are those of the Brugh na Bóinne, along a low ridge in a bend of the river Boyne, and at Loughcrew, on twin spurs of a high hill. In the Brugh stand the three huge tombs which are the most famous prehistoric monuments in Ireland: Newgrange, Knowth and Dowth. Each has its satellite passage graves, no less than eighteen at Knowth. It was probably also around this time that

FIGURE 3.1   Tomb no. 7 in the Carrowmore cemetery (Co. Sligo)
An early and simple example of a passage grave. In the background is the hill of
Knocknarea, perhaps the focus for the cemetery, and visible upon it the huge
cairn of Miosgan Méadhbha, possibly a developed passage grave.

Knocknarea, the hill dominating the old Carrowmore passage grave
cemetery, was crowned with a huge circular cairn now called Miosgan
Méadhbha, the tomb of Queen Medb. It may contain a chamber like
those in County Meath, and certainly the cemetery around it was still
used, and probably multiplied, at this time. Ten miles to the south is the
Carrowkeel cemetery, of passage graves intermediate in size between
those of Carrowmore and those of Meath, which may date from anywhere
in the fourth millennium. In addition, there are a number of solitary
examples of the developed passage grave scattered across Leinster and
over the Irish Sea in Anglesey and Lancashire. Of these, Newgrange,
Knowth, Tara and Fourknocks in County Meath, and Bryn Celli Ddu
and Barclodiad y Gawres in Anglesey have been excavated to a satisfactory
standard. Indeed, Knowth, which has been under continuous investigation
since 1962, may turn out to be the most extensively excavated megalithic
complex in the world. In addition, some finds survive from the looting of
Loughcrew, Carrowkeel and Carrowmore by earlier investigators. Only
two dates have so far been obtained, from Knowth and Newgrange, which
show that both were constructed around 3300–3200 BC.
     Like their predecessors, these greatest of all the Irish and British
Neolithic tombs display considerable individual variety within the
general architectural theme. The chambers are usually cruciform, but
·sometimes polygonal and sometimes mere tunnels. Most mounds have

only one passage and chamber, but some have two. The number of recesses is generally three or four, but this also differs, ranging up to the eight in Loughcrew Carn L. The mode of burial is more consistent, cremation being the rule everywhere with the single exception of some disarticulated unburned bones at Tara. At Newgrange, Knowth and Loughcrew there were large stone basins thought by many to have contained the burnt remains during rituals (though this is pure supposition). Certainly at the time that the tombs ceased to be used, the remains were in the recesses and the basins empty. The gravegoods are standard, consisting of necklaces of bone and shell, pendants and bone pins, all cracked from the funeral pyres upon which they were burned with the dead owner. In addition there are potsherds, animal bones and mollusc shells, the remains of ritual meals, offerings to spirits or nourishment for the deceased. Pointed stones, possibly intended to be phallic, were found just outside the entrances of Newgrange and Knowth. But there remains as many discrepancies between sites, and as many mysteries, as for earlier tombs. At Knowth, the eastern chamber contained the remains of about twenty people, who were apparently

FIGURE 3.2　The entrance to Newgrange (Co. Meath)
Arguably the most famous developed passage grave in the world, as restored by O'Kelly.

deposited as a group, after which the tomb was sealed. The picture emerges of a huge monument, which must have required years of labour, being completed, 'inaugurated' with a burial ceremony, and then closed up and left to decay. At Fourknocks, where remains from at least sixty-five individuals were deposited, each recess in the chamber seems to have been given a group of cremations at one particular time, and then sealed. The Tara passage grave held remains from over 100 people, the burned bone spilling out of the chamber into the passage, and they seem to have accumulated gradually by a process of successive burial as in most British tombs. The same is apparently true of the inmates of the Carrowkeel chambers, which contained an average of over thirty individuals each. Newgrange had been disturbed by various intruders since the early Middle Ages, and held only five or six people. But (according to the excavator) these had all been buried in earth after cremation and then dug up to be brought to the tomb, a procedure which does not appear to have been followed elsewhere. The most peculiar rite detectable in one of these monuments, however, came not from Ireland but from the Welsh passage grave of Barclodiad y Gawres. The builders had made what virtually all who write upon it cannot help but describe as a 'witch's brew': a stew containing oysters, limpets, a winkle, two fish, an eel, a frog, a snake, a mouse and a shrew. This was poured over the cremated bones of two young people laid in the chamber, which had themselves been mixed with the bones of sheep.

Of all the features associated with these tombs, two probably stand out above all. One is the sheer size and magnificence of some of them. The mound at Knowth is almost 330 feet across and almost 36 feet high, covering one and a half acres. Its eastern chamber and passage are just over 130 feet from end to end, making it one of the longest Neolithic passage graves in existence. The chamber's ceiling is beautifully corbelled, each stone jutting out from on top of one below. Newgrange's mound is the largest of all, 340 feet across and over 40 feet high, and contains a passage and chamber supported by sixty upright stones. The ceiling of the chamber is 20 feet from the ground, and beam-ended, each stone resting upon the joint of two below. If the Brugh na Bóinne monuments did not exist, then the Loughcrew would be the finest prehistoric cemetery in Ireland, while the two Anglesey examples are arguably the most impressive prehistoric tombs in Wales.

The other celebrated feature of these passage graves is that they contain the best examples of British Neolithic art. It is concentrated in eastern Ireland and western Britain, Ireland supplying 576 decorated stones from

'Shaman/priestess sleeping within New Grange listening to the voices of the Otherworld', by Monica Sjöö and reproduced here by her own kind permission. This is not intended as a straightforward reconstruction of the monument and should not be regarded as such. The 'buckler' motif on the left is from a Breton tomb, and the other stones are not decorated exactly as shown. The picture is instead an evocation, entirely possible given the available evidence, of a female-centred Neolithic religion.

fifty-one sites and Britain twenty-one from seven. Some monuments have many such ornaments while some have only one or two, but all are overshadowed by Knowth, whose 250 surviving carved megaliths represent almost half the passage grave art of Ireland, and over a quarter of that of all Europe. The motifs are invariably abstract, and four different classificatory schemes have been claimed by as many experts. The simplest division is that made by George Eogan, who is excavating Knowth, into curvilinear (circles, dots, cup-marks, U-shapes, spirals and radials) and rectilinear (parallel lines, offsets, chevrons, zigzags, lozenges and triangles). Of all these the spiral is the most common design, found throughout Leinster and upon the British examples. But local differences in taste are just as obvious in decoration as in architecture and burials. At Knowth the favourite form is the circle, at Loughcrew rays and stars abound, and at Newgrange there are many lozenges. Fourknocks, Knowth and Loughcrew Carn L all have stylized human faces, placed in passages or chambers at points where they will strike fear or awe into an unwary person approaching. Some designs are unique to particular tombs, Knowth having three of its own. Altogether, there are about 130 different motifs.

So what does this art mean, and where did it originate? The answer to both questions must once more be a confession of ignorance. We can only guess, according to our own whims and prejudices, at the identity of the being represented by the stylized faces. The spirals, circles and rays have all been interpreted as eyes, but they occur singly, in triples or in groups more often than they do in pairs. Among the native Australians and Americans, as among the ancient Egyptians, such abstract designs are maps of spiritual progress. The temptation is to apply the same notion to the megalithic decoration, but not only have we no legend for the map nor any cipher for the code before us, but we may be investing the symbols with a profundity which they did not possess. On the question of origins we have a little more evidence. The developed passage graves of Spain and Portugal seem to be earlier than those of Ireland, and although their stones are bare of art, some of the pots and plaques found in them are decorated. The same sort of monument also occurs in Brittany, where the megaliths are carved with designs similar to those of the British Isles. So it may be argued cautiously that the whole fashion for the tombs and their associated artwork came north up Europe's Atlantic coast. But even if that were true, each region still evolved its own set of symbols. The paired eyes which occur most often in the Iberian art are unknown in France, Britain or Ireland, and altogether the tombs of Spain and Portugal have only five basic designs in common with those further north. Brittany has only four motifs which are found in Ireland or Britain (circles, cups, wavy lines and U-shapes). It lacks the spiral, while its yokes, crooks, crosses, axes and 'buckler' shapes are unknown in the British Isles. Of all the countries named, it is Ireland which has preserved the most variety as

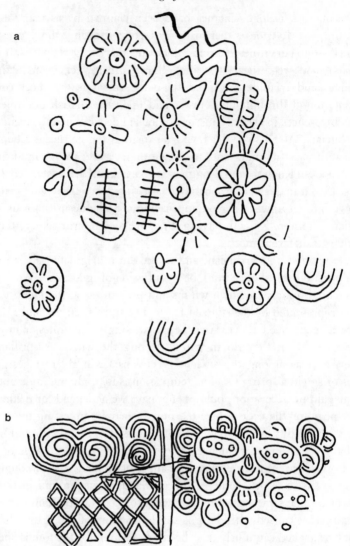

FIGURE 3.3   Passage grave art: spirit maps or megalithic doodles?
a From the rear of the chamber of Cairn T at Loughcrew (Co. Meath); *b* from
kerbstone 52 at Newgrange (Co. Meath).

well as the greatest abundance of this art. Why this should be, we do not know. Nor do we understand the social and political basis for the religion practised in these tombs. Were the three great monuments of the Brugh na Bóinne built by successive rulers, like Egyptian pyramids? or by competing clans? Or for different ceremonies? We cannot tell. We do not even know what they actually looked like. Michael O'Kelly, the excavator of Newgrange, faced this problem heroically when he restored the tomb on behalf of the government of Eire. He not only ensured its future as the most celebrated and most visited prehistoric monument of his country, the Irish Stonehenge, but provided the best opportunity in the world to view the original appearance of a developed passage grave. To those used to smoothly curving mounds grown with grass or trees, the massive, flat-topped, sheer-sided tumulus, like a great drum, can come as something of a shock. The shape is certainly correct, as is the striking placement of the large decorated stone in front of the entrance. But are all the details accurate? What, for example, of the quartz crystals and banded stones found on the ground outside the entrance? Professor O'Kelly decided that they had once decorated the walls above and around the opening, and there they are now. But at Knowth, George Eogan found the same rocks and wondered whether they had not been strewn upon the ground outside the entrance in order to provide a spiritual barrier. There is a possibility that at times the statements made by the tomb-builders (to spirits as well as to posterity) may be getting scrambled by their most careful interpreters.

But Professor O'Kelly must certainly be thanked, in particular, for restoring one aspect of Newgrange to its old glory. The passage of the tomb was precisely aligned on the point upon the horizon at which the sun rises for the time of the winter solstice, three or four days around 21 December. The original builders had constructed a small rectangular opening above the entrance to admit the rays, which then creep slowly up the passage until their eerie red glow falls upon a stone bearing a triple spiral at the far end of the chamber. Since the restoration of the monument, modern observers can once again appreciate this remarkable effect. What gives particular pause for thought is that the rectangular aperture should have been necessary at all. Why was the entrance not simply made high enough to catch the sunlight itself? The only conceivable answer is that the small opening was necessary if the sun was to get into the chamber while the entrance was blocked to exclude humans. The beautiful appearance of the rising solstice sun was not intended for the rituals of the living. It was for the dead. But why, then, were the dead of the other big Irish passage graves not also in need of it? For none of these other tombs has the same alignment. The entrances to Knowth's passages seem to have been trained upon the sunrise and sunset at the equinoxes. Those at Dowth face no cardinal points. Nor do those at Fourknocks, Tara and the Carrowkeel cemetery. The many tombs of Loughcrew have entrances which between them face north-west, north-east, east and south. No other site than Newgrange has an aperture for the sun above the opening of the passage. The bold attempts of Martin Brennan to combine the orientations, the art and the settings of the County Meath tombs in order to explain the theology behind them have produced no more than conjectures. His confident tone and refusal to recognize the limitations of his evidence reduce the value of his declarations in the eyes of prehistorians as they may increase it in the estimation of a less wary public. Certainly, the wonderful phenomenon of the solstice at Newgrange at present offers us puzzles, not answers.[1]

The region around the Boyne was the 'core area' of Ireland at the end of the fourth millennium; the Orkneys enjoyed the same status in northern Scotland. Developed passage graves appeared there also, and the style culminated in the building of Maes Howe, probably the finest British megalithic tomb. The passage is 54 feet long, to a chamber 15 feet square, of polished stones fitted neatly together and rising 20 feet to a corbelled roof. Some of the slabs in the ceiling are 8 feet long and weigh 3 tons each. Around the circular mound is a feature missing from the Irish tombs, a rock-hewn ditch 35 feet across. It is often suggested that the developed passage grave reached Orkney along the trade routes from Ireland, and two factors strengthen this possibility. The first is that the entrance of Maes Howe, like that of Newgrange, is aligned upon the movement of the sun at the winter solstice. But the effect is the precise opposite: it is the sunset which reaches into the chamber. Instead of building a special aperture as at the great tomb on the Boyne, the Orkney people left a gap at the top of the huge stone blocking the entrance. The other factor is the presence in the islands of art like that found around the Irish Sea. In Maes Howe a carving of interlocking triangles and chevrons appears to be contemporary with the tomb. A developed passage grave at Pierowall Quarry, on Westray, yielded three stones covered in linked spirals. Both these motifs have been found in stone-built houses in the islands, dated to c.3200 BC. But they are only faintly similar to the patterns incorporating the same designs in Ireland and Wales. If the culture of the great passage graves of County Meath was indeed transplanted to Orkney, it shed the emphasis upon cremation and upon cemeteries in the

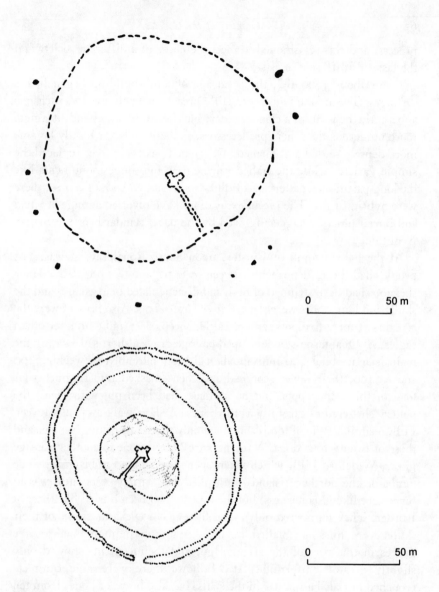

FIGURE 3.4   Plans of the greatest developed passage graves of Ireland and
Britain
a Newgrange (Co. Meath), showing the passage and chamber, the ring of
megaliths defining the mound, and the incomplete stone circle around the
monument, apparently begun much later: could there be another passage grave
still hidden in the mound? *b* Maes Howe, Orkney, showing (from the centre)
the passage and chamber, the mound, the ceremonial area around the monument,
the broad ditch and the narrow bank.
Source: Newgrange redrawn after O'Kelly.

process, and was refashioned to meet the needs of a different society and the tastes of different artists.

From about 3400 BC, the great age of tomb-building began in the Orkneys. The monuments were still spread out fairly evenly, each one apparently the focus of a clan territory, but they were larger and, it seems, more numerous than their predecessors, as the islands apparently became more densely settled and farmed. Developed passage graves replaced the simple variety, while the stalled cairns grew into huge monuments like the long partitioned gallery of Midhowe on Rousay. And, of course, there were hybrid forms. The recent excavations have revealed a range of ritual and burial practice staggering even by the usual standards of the British Neolithic.

At the hybrid tomb of Isbister, upon South Ronaldsay, at least 312 people had been deposited between *c*.3150 and *c*.2400 BC. Their skeletons had been stripped of flesh and disarticulated beforehand, and the skulls and long bones were stacked in separate areas. Also present were the remains of forty-five pots, and of cattle, sheep, deer and a number of sea eagles. At Quanterness, a developed passage grave a short sail away on the main island, about 400 individuals had been entombed between *c*.3400 and *c*.2400, their bones scorched and then smashed into fragments. A total of thirty-four pots, but no animals, had been put with them, the pottery shattered as carefully as the bones. A short walk away at Cuween Hill, a similar style of tomb contained only the skulls of five humans and those of twenty-four dogs. A further stroll brings one to another passage grave, Wideford Hill, which when opened was found to be empty. The tombs on the northern islands multiplied this variety. Quoyness was in form very like Quanterness, but the inmates had been buried like those at Isbister. They numbered only about fifteen, however, and some of their skulls were missing. Stalled cairns were more common than passage graves in this part of the archipelago, and their contents showed only slightly greater uniformity. At Midhowe there were nine complete crouched burials laid neatly in the stalls, but also heaps of bones from ten other individuals piled elsewhere and skulls alone from six more. A pigeon's egg had been put in the armpit of one of the crouched bodies. Holm of Papa Westray contained three crouched and four disarticulated bodies. Korkquoy had almost seventy individuals, some crouched and most disarticulated. Burray had bones from about twenty-three people, mixed with each other and with those of seven dogs. Knowe of Yarso had untidy heaps of bones from thirty people, mixed with parts of thirty-six red deer, while twenty-six of the human skulls had been set apart and stacked neatly together. There were no ceramics at Knowe, but a very similar stalled cairn called Unstan had over thirty-five pots, in pieces, together with parts of about five people. But for sheer elaboration, the prize must go to yet another tomb of this style, called Blackhammer, which held not only human bones but also those of twenty-four sheep, plus oxen, deer, gannet, cormorant and pink-footed goose.

What does all this mean? A popular suggestion has been that the principal animal represented in the tombs was the totem of the clan which built it. Thus Isbister is known in the Orkneys today as the Tomb of the Eagles, and by analogy the people who built Cuween Hill and Burray ought to have been Dog Clans, with the burials at Knowe of Yarso from the Clan of the Deer. But this does not explain why no animals were found in so many chambers, and so much pottery in some; and Blackhammer's people can only have been the Clan of the Menagerie. An alternative suggestion, that individuals had spirit guides in animal form which were placed with them in the tombs, begs the question of why some groups had nobody with a guide in them and why those at Cuween Hill had so many. The most recent work in and upon Orkney has only served to raise some fundamental doubts about the data themselves. John Barber's excavation of the tomb at the Point of Cott produced bones from thirteen humans, sheep, dog, otter, cattle, deer, rodents, birds and fish. But he noted that some of the animal remains were certainly modern, and that otters had recently been using the chambers as a holt. He realized that it was possible that during the millennia since the tomb ceased to be used by humans, it may have acted as a refuge to most of the animals represented in it when it was excavated, while some of the bones may have been dragged in as carrion or as kills by carnivores living there. As a result, he was completely unable to judge whether any were deposited with the burials during the Neolithic. This problem must apply to all the other monuments in our sample. Colin Richards has recently re-opened the question of why a few tombs contained such enormous numbers of individuals while most had small totals and some were empty. He suggested that specimens such as Quanterness may have been used as charnel-houses for bones brought from several other monuments when a change in society or politics demanded a concentration of the dead. If this is true (and at present it is impossible to verify) then the present pattern of burials bears little resemblance to the original one, and we are yet further away from reconstructing the funeral traditions of the Neolithic Orcadians and the beliefs which inspired them.

The only demonstrable distinctions between categories of burial deposit in the Orkney tombs raise questions instead of answering them. The stalled cairns were mostly built on the northern islands, and the pottery in them is of a style confined to northern Scotland, called Unstan Ware. The developed passage graves are mostly found on the large island, and the pottery in them is Grooved Ware, a type which was used throughout Britain. This would suggest that the stalled cairns were associated with people of more parochial customs and restricted horizons, while the passage-grave builders had extensive connections overseas. Yet the two styles of monument occur close to each other and there is no sign of fortification or warfare in Neolithic Orkney. And, as already noted, the differences of burial practice within each category are as great as those between them. Maes Howe seems to have been built last of all the tombs, upon rich agricultural land right in the centre of the main island. It must have required the labour of several, if not all, of the islands' clans in unison. Did it represent a political and religious unification of the archipelago? Or a place for communal rituals and token deposits by a still fragmented society, which felt the need for displays of mutual strength? Or a prestige monument built by the islanders to attract traders and pilgrims of the sort who might have gone to marvel in the Brugh na Bóinne? The Vikings who occupied Maes Howe removed our slim hope of finding evidence for any of these suggestions. All that remained from the Neolithic was a little unburned human bone. One Viking graffito boasted of the finding of a treasure in the chamber, but nothing ever dug out of a Neolithic tomb could fit that description. We can only assume that it was booty hidden shortly before by another party of invaders.[2]

New local styles of megalithic tomb continued to evolve in Ireland and upon the fringes of Britain. In northern Scotland, around the Moray Firth, appeared the Clava Cairns, passage graves covered in circular mounds of piled rock which were in turn surrounded by a ring of standing stones. All those which have been examined contained only scraps of bone from one or two people: token burials. None has been dated, but their form would point to a time around 3000 BC. In west Cornwall, the Scilly Isles and eastern Ireland are found entrance graves, small circular mounds with a chamber consisting of a single broad passage in each. They often seem to have contained deposits of earth mixed with potsherds, flint and bone instead of human burials, and although (again) undated appear to belong near the end rather than the beginning of the tomb-building tradition.

The most important and long-lived new style was the Irish wedge tomb, a rectangular chamber inside a wedge-shaped mound (as we shall

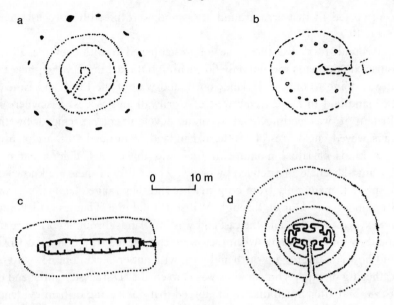

FIGURE 3.5   Plans of some late megalithic tombs
a One of the Clava Cairns, Balnuaran: the passage and chamber are set within a piled stone cairn, upon a circular terrace, within a stone circle; *b* the developed passage grave of Bryn Celli Ddu (Anglesey): the open dots indicate the stones of the henge-circle replaced by the tomb; an ox was deposited in the pit shown in the front of the entrance; *c* Midhowe stalled cairn, on the island of Rousay in the Orkneys: the entrance to the long partitioned chamber was blocked by two great stones; *d* the developed passage grave of Quanterness, in Orkney: the elaborate chamber was surrounded by a cairn held by four successive rings of revetment walls.
Source: *d* redrawn after Renfrew.

see, the people who built them employed the circle for related monuments). About 400 remain, making them the most common variety of prehistoric tomb found in Ireland. Most are in the western counties, but they are fairly well scattered over all other parts. Twenty have been excavated, revealing that the usual burial rite was cremation, as in the great Irish passage graves, that often only one or two people were buried in each tomb and that pottery and arrowheads were also deposited. Although this variety of monument began to be built before 3000 BC, it continued in Counties Cork and Kerry long after megalithic tombs had gone out of use everywhere else in the British Isles. They were still being constructed in that area around 1700 and were possibly used as late as 1000 BC.[3]

Around 3000 BC then, the long-established tradition of megalithic burial monuments was not only flourishing but reaching new heights. Yet it was doing so only in Ireland, north and west of the Highland Line of Scotland and in the extreme west of Cornwall and Wales. Elsewhere in Britain it was ending, and separate developments, presaged by the causewayed enclosures of southern England, continued with a clutch of new kinds of ritual monument. One was the cursus, a long narrow, rectangular enclosure defined by banks. About fifty of these are known or suspected, many only from crop-marks, and they range diagonally across England from Dorset through Wiltshire and the Thames valley into Essex, East Anglia, and the east and west midlands through Yorkshire up into Scotland. We know when they were constructed (c.3400–c.3000 BC) and how (mounding up earth and rock with antler-picks) but not why. A gathering of experts on cursuses was convened at Dorchester at the end of 1988, and after much discussion agreed that not a scrap of firm evidence survived to testify to their purpose.

We do know that different regions had different attitudes to these monuments, as to causewayed enclosures. The people of south-east England ignored them, and built none. Those of Wessex built huge examples and used them for a relatively long time. The biggest, in Dorset, runs for nearly seven miles. It was constructed upon land not previously used for anything, and the deposits put into its ditches were identical to the remains already so familiar from those of the causewayed enclosures: potsherds, flints, human bones and portions of wild and domestic animals. Inside the monument flints were grouped with particular care, worked specimens buried in one place, cores in another, burnt flints in yet another. Another Wessex cursus, on Salisbury Plain, is almost two miles long, and there are others spread out across the region. In the Thames Valley and Yorkshire, they tended to be smaller (though still at times up to a mile in length) and to occur in groups. At Dorchester-on-Thames a cursus was built in about 3000 BC with a circle of pits and an enclosure of posts inside, and in about 2700 BC the posts were burned down. In Yorkshire some of the cursuses form patterns: at Rudston four of them intersect near a single great megalith. At Springfield in central Essex, deposits were found in the ditches similar to those in Dorset; inside, a concentration of pits and a circle of posts were uncovered similar to those at Dorchester-on-Thames. Into the pits had gone animal bones, flints and potsherds, all burned before deposition.

Interestingly, unlike the monuments at Dorchester and in Dorset, the Essex example seems to have been built, used for this single ritual, and then abandoned. At Maxey in Cambridgeshire, a cursus was dug in sections over a long period, with such low banks and slight ditches that the previous portion must have been decayed and invisible by the time that the next was made. It could never have been used as a complete monument, just piece by piece.

These regional variations aside, cursuses differ individually. Most occur on the terraces of river valleys, but there are some in uplands. Their ends can be round, convex or sharply rectangular. Some contained cremation burials, others one or two complete bodies, others stray human bones in ditches and yet others none of these. It is an obvious supposition that their shape would have lent itself to processions, but aside from this the present scholarly consensus is to conclude that cursuses, like causewayed enclosures, were sites with a range of possible functions. The great examples in Wessex may have been essentially a different sort of monument from the smaller specimens elsewhere.[4]

The enclosures recognized as cursuses are just one example of a variety of Neolithic earthworks put up at this period, of virtually every shape. One kind, which often occurs in the vicinity of cursuses, has been given the name of 'long mortuary enclosure'. These are elongated rectangles in shape; as human bone has been found in the ditches and precincts of some, it has been suggested that they might have been places where bodies were exposed before some bones were taken to the long barrows. However, the discovery of equal quantities of human skeleton in and around cursuses and causewayed enclosures has removed the argument for a special function for these earthworks. In form they are identical to small cursuses, and may soon be added to the latter category.[5]

All these types of monument were closely associated with the last earthen long barrows. The great Dorset cursus incorporated one barrow into each end and ran parallel to another. The large cursus on Salisbury Plain ended upon a long barrow. Others occur in the immediate vicinity of most late Neolithic enclosures. But the barrows themselves were changing, even the existing welter of individual variations upon a common theme starting to break down further into a range of novelties. In Wiltshire and Dorset long barrows like Beckhampton and Thickthorn Down were built, of classic size and shape but covering no burials at all. The former had three ox skulls planted along the summit, the latter had one ox skull and some cattle bones interred within it. It may be remembered that cattle bones had often been mixed with those of humans in earthen and chambered long barrows. It seems that they were considered necessary after even token human burials had ceased. Yet single human burials, mostly complete and unburned, and mostly male, were still put under other late long barrows. In several areas of the old earthen long barrow range, oval, rectangular and oblong mounds either appeared or became more common, often covering one or two human burials but sometimes with none or just with flakes of human bone in the ditches. In Dorset bank barrows appeared, huge rectangular mounds like cursuses which had been filled in and raised. They cover neither burials nor deposits and seem to have been platforms for ceremonies or focal points around which processions could turn.[6]

Three principal explanations have been offered for these developments. One is that the formerly egalitarian and communal atmosphere of the earlier Neolithic was being eroded by the rise of elite individuals and groups. Accordingly, fewer and fewer people were allowed the privilege of burial under the long barrows, and great monuments were raised to the glory of those elites as a fragmented society was drawn together into chiefdoms. The second explanation is compatible with the first. It contends that during the fourth millennium the descent of authority through generations had been legitimized by the ancestors resting in the long barrows and chambered tombs; but as the third millennium began rulers started to derive and display power in terms of their own talents, wealth, trade connections and possession of prestigious goods, and the authority of the ancestors was overthrown.[7] The trouble with both theories is that burial under the great mounds had always been selective, and that those who recieved it had therefore always been either an elite or representatives of their people. The numbers buried under the long barrows of Wessex during the fourth millennium declined from an average total of six to one or two. The evidence for successive deposition in the chambered tombs or mortuary houses over a period of some generations indicates also that more was involved than the honouring of an original set of ancestors. The scale of the new monuments might argue for a more participatory sort of religious and political ceremony, in which greater numbers could be concerned than in those located in the forecourts of barrows. So we need to take account of the third sort of explanation: that whatever function was ascribed to the human remains in the tombs, the builders believed that fewer and fewer additional remains were required to perform it, until the monument was seen as sufficient in itself.[8] But if this was so, a long barrow with one burial or name was on the way to becoming obsolete, its purpose being displaced to other monuments or regarded as having lost any importance. Earthen long barrows were still being raised after cursuses appeared, but none seems to have been built after 3000 BC. Nor does any megalithic tomb in England (except perhaps west Cornwall), Wales or southern Scotland. Nor any causewayed enclosures, nor any of the cursuses themselves, nor the bank barrows which had so recently appeared. In most of Britain the ritual monuments of the future were to be of another kind, which had quietly appeared beside the other monuments of the end of the fourth millennium.

The new structure was a set of circular or oval enclosures, sometimes defined by a ditch, sometimes by a bank, and in most cases by both. The first type are now generally called ring ditches, the second best described as ring banks, and the third as henge monuments. Of the last – the most important – variety, 90 per cent have the ditch inside the bank as if to proclaim that they were ceremonial, not defensive, precincts. Indeed, it is likely that the remaining 10 per cent would not be considered henges at all, were it not for the awkward semantic fact that one of them happens to be Stonehenge, which first gave the name to the whole class of monument. The earlier dates yielded by henges come from as far apart as Arminghall in Norfolk, Llandegai in North Wales and Barford in Warwickshire, all from around 3250 BC. We thus have no means as yet of pinpointing the origins of a development which was to set Britain apart from the rest of Europe, with which it had until now shared all its main categories of monument. Late Neolithic enclosures did abound upon the Continent, but they tended to be rectangular, not round like the henges. At present some 324 British sites are recognized as henge monuments, many (like so many other prehistoric remains) visible only from the air. They are found from the Orkneys to Cornwall, showing a distinct tendency to be positioned in valleys and therefore near water. Within this huge range, large regions have few or none of them, including the three south-eastern counties, the Welsh Marches, the Yorkshire Wolds, East Anglia and much of the south and west midlands. Others, notably Cornwall, the Thames valley, north Wales, Cumbria and central and north-east Scotland, are full of them. A dozen have also been identified in eastern Ireland, notably around Kildare and on the Boyne, showing that this fashion travelled across the Irish Sea just as developed passage graves had done in the opposite direction. Most henges had two entrances, to allow a procession to enter and leave in a continuous line, or to permit two processions to converge, or for use at different ceremonies. A few had only one, while a Northumberland site had three. They range in diameter

from 13 feet to 1700 feet, and all which can be dated were constructed
between 3000 and 2200 BC. They are thus the 'classic' ritual monument
of early third millennium prehistoric Britain. Wherever a cursus existed,
it was usual to find a henge built near one of its entrances, though the
henge generally continued in use long after the cursus was abandoned.
Sometimes henges were grouped together, like the three in a row at
Priddy in Somerset, or Knowlton in Dorset, or Thornborough in
Yorkshire. Twenty-two of the British examples and three of those in
Ireland have now been excavated.

The adoption of the henge monuments in Britain seems to have been
extremely rapid: the examples which have been dated in eastern Scotland
and the Orkneys are only slightly younger than the earliest English
examples to be excavated. As with every previous type of structure,
regional traditions resulted in a diversity of size and form. The peoples of
Wessex constructed huge specimens, indulging a taste for grandeur which
they had shown in previous centuries. In the Thames valley there were
several small examples. Those of the midlands also tended to be small,
those of Somerset larger; and Yorkshire has a mixture of sizes. In Sussex
no henges appeared and causewayed enclosures continued to be built. In
west Wales small henges were raised, with stones lining their banks and
flanking their entrances. In the Orkneys the great henge at Stenness was
built at the same time as the great passage grave of Maes Howe, while in
England those who constructed henges seemed simultaneously to stop the
construction of chambered tombs or earthen long barrows.[9] In addition
there is the possibility that henges, like cursuses and causewayed
enclosures, had various functions, so that some may not have been sacred
sites at all.

Even so, the henges show a greater uniformity in design and in traces
of ritual than the tombs. The wide distribution of the circular ditch
within a bank, broken by two entrances, is impressive. The usual deposits
made inside these monuments, either in the ditch itself, or in pits, or
both, are already familiar from causewayed enclosures and cursuses. They
may be termed 'ritual rubbish', the assortment of odds and ends which
might normally be expected upon a Neolithic kitchen midden: pieces of
animal bone, bits of pottery which had been broken some time before,
and flints. Were the people who brought them to the henge consecrating
it, after a fashion, with portions of their daily activities so that their whole
lifestyle was represented in it? Or were they imprisoning evil spirits
within the charmed circle, brought out of their homes in the trash, as
people still do in present-day Indonesia?[10] Were the henges territorial

centres for unified clans or tribes? Or meeting places for different groups, as could be indicated by the fact that the ditches were first dug in segments like those of causewayed enclosures? As might be expected, there was still some individual variation in the nature of the deposits. At Stenness in the Orkneys, the builders put their 'ritual rubbish' in the centre and then covered it with seaweed, the local fertilizer. The ditch contained burned and unburned bones of wolf, dog and ox, a slate disc, potsherds and some pieces of human skeleton. At Llandegai in North Wales a henge held axes from the neighbourhood and from Cumbria, and a human cremation. From that at Barford in Warwickshire came quernstones. At Gorsey Bigbury in Somerset, a woman, a child and a man were buried together in a stone chest or 'cist', placed within the ditch beside an entrance. After a while this was opened and the bones scattered in the bottom of the ditch, leaving the male skull inside the cist. At Moncreiffe, Perthshire, nine pits were dug inside the henge and then left empty.[11]

Another of the structural variations between henges was that some had one or more rings of stones or timber posts within the ditch and bank. This would seem to be the origin of a form of monument which at the present day appears to be the 'classic' ritual centre of the late third millennium and the beginning of the second: the stone circle. These seem to have been built first as part of the henges and then separately from them, and they continued to be erected after henge monuments had become obsolete. It is as if the ring of stones took over the ritual function of the bank and ditch. Some 702 are known to survive in Britain, and 261 more in Ireland, almost half of which are concentrated in Counties Cork and Kerry and the rest well scattered.[12] The stones of which they were constructed have survived where the monuments of earth or timber have vanished above the ground, giving them a rather exaggerated impression of importance. For example, at the present day many visitors to the Rollright Stones, the famous Cotswold ring with its outlying King Stone, believe it to have been the greatest prehistoric monument in that part of England: but when first built it was dwarfed by the great henge at Condicote a few miles to the west, which has been levelled. It was also overshadowed by older tombs, a Cotswold–Severn chambered barrow just to the north and a portal dolmen nearby to the east. Both would have required twice the effort sufficient to build the circle, but one vanished completely in the eighteenth century AD and the other is reduced to a clump of megaliths, the Whispering Knights. In fact, one of the attractions of the stone rings must have been the relative ease of their construction: thus, with late Neolithic antler-picks, wood sledges and leather ropes, twenty adults should have been able to raise a circle of 200 stones, each weighing about a ton, in three weeks.[13]

Dating these monuments is difficult because only thirty-six in the British Isles have been scientifically excavated and of these only eight produced datable materia. The earliest from a stone ring inside a henge comes from Orkney in *c.*3000 BC, while artefacts indicate that independent stone circles were being constructed by *c.*2500 BC. The variety in form between individual sites was, of course, considerable. Some had large stones, some had small. In some the megaliths were well spaced while in others they crowded together. Some had their stones embedded in low banks. Only occasionally were the rings true circles, most being eggs or ellipses. Some had a stone in the centre, while others had one or two outside the ring. Some had two concentric rings. Generally, the larger and more perfectly circular rings seem to be earlier, dating from the late Neolithic.

Is there any regional pattern to this variety of form? It seems clear that there is, although it is as complex, roughly defined and full of overlaps as the distribution of styles of megalithic tomb had been. In the far north of Scotland and the Orkneys, the rings were made of large but few stones. All along the west coast of Britain, from the Hebrides to Cornwall, are found examples with equally large stones, but more numerous and less regularly spaced. In north-eastern Scotland, especially the Mar district, are the 'recumbent stone circles', close-set rings carefully graded in

FIGURE 3.6   The Nine Maidens, Boscawen-Un
A famous ring in the West Penwith district, much loved by modern earth mystics. The size, number of stones and modern name are all fairly typical of west country stone rings: the central pillar is not.

height, with a single horizontal slab positioned in the southern arc. In Scotland there are settings of four stones, often almost square rather than circular. On Dartmoor are small circles of close-spaced stones, usually with a central feature. In addition, there are forms which are scattered widely throughout Britain. Perfect circles are found in south-west England, Wessex and north-east Scotland. Egg-shaped and elliptical rings with large, well-spaced stones of regular height are distributed around Cornwall, Devon, Wales and Scotland. Small and irregular rings and rings with the stones set in a bank are found in many parts of Britain. Most of these varieties are also found in Ireland, although the great concentration in Counties Cork and Kerry are almost all small, with their tallest stones at the entrance and a recumbent stone in the south-western sector, very like those of north-east Scotland.

The distribution of the rings within regions reveals pronounced differences indicating contrasting social or political needs. In Wessex they tend to be huge, like the henges with which they are often combined, and well spaced across the region as if forming centres for large territories. In north-east Scotland and south-west Ireland they appear to be scattered at random and are often closely packed in the areas of the most fertile soil, as if every family put one up. The people of East Anglia and south-eastern England, by contrast, though numerous and concentrated, did not trouble to put up any stone rings, even where stone was available, just as these areas contain few or no henges. They apparently did not require these great ritual monuments. As with the megalithic tombs, long barrows and henges, stone rings sometimes occur in groups of two or three.[14] Were these concentrations of circular monuments, like the two Grey Wethers rings on Dartmoor or the three henges in a row at Priddy, Somerset, intended for dedications to different deities, or for different seasons, or for different tribes or clans, or for different groups within a clan? We cannot tell.

The possible significance of the rings, like their dates, is made more difficult to determine by the lack of systematic excavation, the frequent absence of finds, and the fact that many deposits which are found had been made after the stones were erected, and perhaps by people with different beliefs. Thus, what had been built as a temple might have been turned into a cemetery centuries later. Apparently no material survives from Neolithic circles which is clearly contemporary with their construction, except in the case of those combined with henges. There are other problems connected with this sort of monument. One is a version of that perennial archaeological headache, the matter of timber. Wood rots; stone doesn't. The art associated with developed passage graves might have been unique to those tombs, or it might have been minuscule in quantity compared with woodcarvings which have perished. With their disappearance we may have lost the context, and so the true meaning, of the megalithic engravings. Similarly, we know that upon a few sites stone rings replaced earlier wooden posts, and it is possible that we have failed to notice the traces of timber circles in places where no stone examples existed. Then there is the riddle of the 'coves'. These are settings of three giant stones, to create a box shape with one side and the roof left open. At present five examples survive, along with the site of one more and three other monuments which appear to be variants upon the cove form. All are associated with exceptionally large and important stone circles or henges, and none was used as a burial place or a hearth for great fires: in fact the space which they define is generally bare of finds. This would suggest a unity of purpose, but we do not know what that purpose was. Aubrey Burl, who has thought harder about this problem than anyone else, has suggested that they may have been a symbolic imitation of the forecourts of chambered tombs, and used for ceremonies transferred from these monuments.[15] This is an intelligent guess, but does not explain why coves are a feature only of these few great sites and not of most henges or circles. Moreover, the nine sites concerned are scattered from the Orkneys to Dorset, and there is a small chance that they had a different function in each region and that their similarity is superficial. Finally, there is the matter of the folklore attached to the stones. Many of the rings are traditionally described as dancers or players of sport, petrified for breaking the sanctity of the Sabbath by performing upon that day. It has been suggested by some writers that this may be a distant memory of actual ritual dances or games performed there by the builders. The idea is tempting, and the monuments would have been ideally suited to circle-dancing. But nobody who has studied the late Tudor and early Stuart campaign against profanation of the Sabbath can doubt that the sheer intensity of this may account for all the stories.

Across the whole range of henges and henge circles, the great sites of Wessex stand out. Indeed, some of them are among the most famous prehistoric monuments in the world, and modern prehistorians have usually placed them in a category of their own, as 'henge enclosures', or, more simply, 'superhenges'. They deserve an extended treatment not just because of their fame and their bulk, but because the richness of the finds made at them to some extent compensates for the difficulty of isolating primary deposits at the Neolithic stone circles. They were spaced out in a

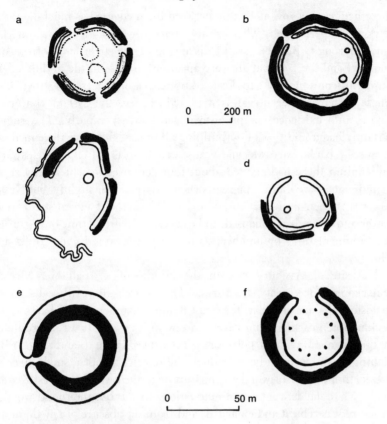

FIGURE 3.7   Henges and superhenges
a Avebury: the dots indicate stone rings; *b* Durrington Walls: the circles represent the two 'roundhouses' so far excavated; *c* Marden, with its river: the circle indicates the great mound; *d* Mount Pleasant: the circle represents the round structure; *e* Llandegai henge A; *f* Stenness, in Orkney: the dots indicate surviving or former megaliths. Dark shading represents banks; light shading represents ditches.
Sources: *a–d* redrawn after Wainwright; *e* redrawn after Houlder; *f* redrawn after Ritchie.

great gentle curve from Avebury in a hollow of the Marlborough Downs, to Marden in the Vale of Pewsey, Durrington Walls in the Avon valley, and Maumbury Rings and Mount Pleasant together around the river Frome. Their low-lying situation is typical of henges in general, expressing perhaps the importance of water or fertile ground in their rituals, or maybe just a desire for a sheltered place. To an extent, their great individual size was only one among several ways of using space: the three henges in a row at Priddy between them covered as much land as a Wessex 'superhenge'. This is also true of those at Knowlton and Thornborough. But the careful distancing of the superhenges from one another, and the fact that all were apparently in use in the middle of the third millennium BC, supplies additional reason for treating them as a single system of territorial centres. Moreover, the system concerned sprang into existence, in prehistoric terms, very rapidly. The region certainly had a tradition of outbuilding all others, but since the enormous cursuses, bank barrows and causewayed forts of the late fourth millennium there had elapsed about four centuries in which only small monuments were built. The superhenges were not slightly but vastly larger than their immediate predecessors.[16] It was as if a great structure of power and belief had collapsed, to be succeeded, after a time of confusion and fragmentation, by another, as in the histories of Egypt, India and China.

The site of Avebury was in the middle of a small area already remarkable for great structures. The Windmill Hill causewayed enclosure was just above it, the West Kennet chambered long barrow and Beckhampton earthen long barrow a few miles away. It was surrounded by burial monuments of both sorts. Yet between c.3250 and c.2700 BC nothing seems to have been built in the district except a small circular wooden hut or pair of wooden rings a mile to the east of the West Kennet tomb. Many fields went out of cultivation. In c.2700, the round wooden structure was rebuilt and enlarged, and from the absence of any domestic debris upon its site appears to have been intended for a ritual purpose. But what that was, we do not know, the only clue being lumps of burnt stone found in the post-holes. On the strength of these, Aubrey Burl has suggested that it was a mortuary house where bodies were 'cured', burned or disarticulated before the bones were deposited in nearby tombs. From modern ethnographic parallels, one might add the possibilities that it was a sweat-lodge of the native American sort, a place for dream visions or a place where women segregated themselves during menstruation. Michael Dames's belief that it was a place where girls underwent puberty rites is based upon nothing other than his intuition, but may by chance be correct. This is all that can be said about the early story of the site which was to become known in historic times as 'the Sanctuary'.

At about the same time that this mysterious monument was being rebuilt, an equally enigmatic but infinitely more spectacular one was raised in the valley of the Kennet a mile westward. This was the largest prehistoric mound in Europe, Silbury Hill. It began as a hurdle fence encircling a heap of turves covered with earth sprinkled with antlers, stone, bones and twigs. Fence and deposit were then covered by a mound of earth and gravel. Upon this were piled seven successive drums of chalk rubble. The method of construction consisting of partitioning sections of the growing mound and then filling them in, was the same as that used to raise the earlier long barrows. Twice the monument was almost finished, and then altered to enlarge it still further. At last the builders were satisfied and filled in almost all the steps of the terraces to present a smooth slope. Yet the topmost step was never completely filled, either for some ritual or practical purpose, or simply because Silbury never was finished. The result is 520 feet across the base and 130 feet high, and contains about 35 million baskets of chalk. Although this bulk is unique, there were other great mounds of similar sort nearby at Marlborough, within the Marden henge ten miles south, at Knowlton, at the Derbyshire henges of Dove Holes and Arbor Low, the Ford Hall stone ring in Derbyshire and the Strathallan henge in Scotland. The Marden and Arbor Low examples covered the same sort of deposit at Silbury.

This distribution pattern is almost as wide and sparse as that of 'coves', and even more puzzling. Why is there no henge near the Marlborough mound, and why do most henges, including superhenges, have no trace of these structures nearby? They can hardly be observatories, as most (including Silbury) have no clear alignments with heavenly bodies and are too low-lying. So, either they were platforms for rituals which we cannot now reconstruct or they were emblems in a thought system which we cannot recapture. The foundation deposits are virtually the same as the 'ritual rubbish' found at henges and causewayed enclosures, so tell us little. Perhaps they were intended to echo the large round mounds of the Yorkshire Wolds, which will be described later in this chapter. Perhaps they were intended to represent developed passage graves, just as the Beckhampton and Thickthorn Down long barrows represented their sort of monument without requiring mortuary houses or burials. The largest mound in the Loughcrew passage grave cemetery in Ireland was a dummy, containing no chamber, and Miosgan Méadhbha at Carrowmore may prove to be the same. The consensus among prehistorians is that Silbury and related monuments are at present inexplicable.

Into this vacuum has leaped the visionary writer Michael Dames. His answer is that they were at once sculpted representations of the Neolithic Great Goddess and platforms for the celebration of the later Celtic festival of Lughnasadh, the opening of harvest. This is arrived at by linking the former orthodoxy concerning the Goddess with the historic Irish custom of gathering on hills to feast at Lughnasadh, the historic Scottish custom of building mounds for parties at this time and the fact that the foundation deposit at Silbury was made in late July or early August, near the time of Lughnasadh. But the links will not hold. The evidence for the Great Goddess has been considered. The Irish gathered at Lughnasadh beside lakes, rivers and wells as often as upon hills, while the Scots youth defended their artificial mounds in mock battles in a very un-Irish manner, making them castles rather than just platforms. Moreover, the Scottish mounds were only raised in the least Celtic part of the country, while the Irish gatherings were held in the most Celtic part of theirs. As will be shown, there are difficulties in presuming that the Iron Age held the same festivals as the Stone Age, and it may be doubted how important the harvest was around Silbury in the mid-third millennium, when the evidence suggests a pastoral economy in place of the earlier arable one. And in any case, the fact that a structure was begun at a certain time of year does not mean that it was to be completed and used then. All told, Mr Dames has supplied an explanation which is possible but somewhat unlikely.[17]

About a mile north-east of Silbury, and about two or three generations after it was constructed, work was begun upon the greatest circle-henge in the British Isles: Avebury Ring. Only 6 per cent of it has been excavated so far, and so any account of its development must be conjectural, but upon present evidence the sequence suggested by Aubrey Burl is the most likely. According to this, the people first put up a wide stone ring, with a gigantic megalith in the centre. Probably just afterwards, they built a second ring to the north, with a large 'cove' in the middle. They seem to have started a third one, north-north-west of that, to make a row like the Priddy henges, but instead changed their minds around 2500 BC and enclosed both the existing circles in a bank, ditch and ring of stones. The latter contained about 100 megaliths, amking it the greatest ring in the British Isles; the ditch 35 feet deep, was also the largest of its kind. Antler-picks, mysterious stone discs and many human bones were placed in it. The first may have been symbols of regrowth, or may simply have been discarded when the work was done. At about the same time, the wooden structure at 'the Sanctuary' was replaced by two massive concentric rings of timbers.[18]

At Marden a large horseshoe-shaped henge was built with the great mound inside it and one side open to a river. At about the same time, c.2500 BC, the biggest monument in this class was put up beside the Avon. Now called Durrington Walls, it is 1680 feet across, defining an

A harvest ceremony inside the 'cove' at Avebury, Wiltshire, as imagined by Judith Dobie. She manages to provide a wonderful image of a flourishing late Neolithic society, based upon the current archaeological evidence, without venturing any suggestions as to the precise nature of its religion or its political and social structure. By kind permission of English Heritage.

area even larger than Avebury, but contained roundhouses or multiple wooden circles, some 100 feet across, instead of stone rings. A fraction of the interior has been excavated, revealing some pits filled with 'ritual rubbish' and the sites of two of the wooden structures. One had more pits with ritual deposits, but the other had middens full of odds and ends discarded without any careful arrangement. It looks, therefore, as if Durrington was both a sacred site and a settlement, perhaps a gathering-point at which councils were held or even (as Euan MacKie has suggested) a 'monastery' or 'university' for a religious and intellectual elite. The same may be said of Mount Pleasant in central Dorset, where around 2500 BC a henge-style enclosure almost as large as Durrington was put up with a similar roundhouse or multiple wooden ring within it. The usual 'ritual rubbish' was deposited in the ditch, including eleven antler-picks, a chalk phallus and ball, and a human skull.[19]

Insignificant beside these huge monuments was an average-sized round enclosure with a bank, external ditch and two entrances, put up somewhere in the period *c.*3200–*c.*2800 BC, opposite the southern entrance of the biggest cursus on Salisbury Plain. It was one of a pair, the other being on Coneyburgh Hill nearby, with the same bank and ditch and the same main entrance facing north-east, apparently towards the midsummer sunrise. The one nearer to the cursus had apparently had a megalith upon each side of that entrance and some kind of wooden structure in its centre. A few centuries after its construction, around 2600 BC, a total of fifty-six pits were dug in a ring inside the bank and made the receptacles for successive deposits, being covered with earth between each. The material put in consisted of the usual medley of objects, but grouped with great care, flint never put with antler and animal bones never with the long bones of humans. At each entrance were placed potsherds, long flint knives, chalk balls, antlers and the cremated remains of a single adult, perhaps the mother of the small child placed beside. Then the whole monument was abandoned, possibly as the activity in the district became concentrated at Durrington Walls. It would not merit such attention now were it not for the fact that it was to be rebuilt very differently later on, and eventually named Stonehenge.[20]

Elsewhere in Britain giant monuments similar to those of Wessex appeared in isolated contexts. One such was constructed at Forteviot in Tayside, opening on to a river upon one flank, like that of Marden, and with smaller henges inside and outside it. At Meldon Bridge near Peebles, a massive timber palisade crossed the neck of a peninsula between two streams. It may have been a ceremonial centre or simply a fortress, depending upon whether one thinks that the courses of the streams were deep and steep enough at that time to present an effective barrier. However, it was not these structures which were to exert a decisive effect upon British cultures, but some which had already been erected upon the Wolds of eastern Yorkshire. Shortly before 3000 BC the building of earthen long barrows there had come to a decisive end, and was replaced immediately by the construction of large round burial mounds. Perhaps these were inspired by the news of the developed passage graves of the far north and west of Britain, or perhaps they reflected a purely local change of taste. Certainly, they suggest the emergence of a clear social elite. As already stated, the individuals placed under the long barrows had been selected from the population and may have represented some kind of chosen people themselves; but the high status of the people in the principal graves made in the great mounds is unmistakable. The majority of human remains from this district in the late Neolithic consist of cremations without any mounds or accompanying goods. Those in the central portion of the round mounds are almost all adult males, laid out unburned with jet beads, arrowheads, antler maces and boars' tusks, all symbols of prestige. They sometimes had human companions as well. At Duggleby Howe in the valley of the Gypsy Race, people piled up a mound of packed chalk. Within it they built a wood mortuary hut like those in the defunct long barrows, and here laid a man with a pot, some flints and red pigment probably used for body-painting. Then they built up the mound further to produce a shaft above the hut, and started to fill this in. Halfway up it, they put the skull of a youth, with a suspicious-looking hole in it. At the top they placed the skeleton of a child aged about three. To the side of this little corpse a hollow was scooped out, to recieve a man of about fifty years, with arrowheads, knives, ox bones, beavers' teeth, a bone pin and boars' tusks. In the filling of his grave were put the bodies of another young child and another youth. A man of about seventy years was put beside the original shaft, his head laid as if looking down into its packing and one hand holding a piece of semi-transparent flint, like a crystal ball, up to his face. At some time later a man of about sixty was buried near the others, with another youth and child above him and an axe, arrowhead and macehead with him. The mixed bones of ox, roe deer, fox, pig, sheep or goat, and human being were placed in four piles around the graves, as offerings, totemic emblems or spiritual recipes. Soon after, a further layer of chalk was piled over everything, and over fifty cremations buried in it. A layer of blue clay and more chalk rubble completed a round monument containing 5000 tons of material.[21]

This was collective burial, but of a kind radically different from that practised in the previous millennium. The whole structure was intended to glorify a few old men, almost certainly to the point of sacrificing other humans in their funeral rites. And the finished product, the great round white mound in the valley, made a very different image from the long white spine of a chalkland long barrow. These two characteristics, the round mound and the privileged burial, were to spread slowly across central and southern England during the next thousand years. But even in the Yorkshire Wolds, where it probably began, the process was not uniform. There are two other great circular mounds in the valley of the Gypsy Race, Willy Howe and Wold Newton, and although they contained many skeletons there was no elite grave in the centre of either. They may have been communal burial grounds, or cenotaphs for important people who for some reason could not be interred there. As suggested, these monuments may possibly, by some transfer of symbolism, have inspired the slightly later and much bigger solid mounds of the south, such as Silbury. Nor were all the richly endowed burials of the late Neolithic Wolds put into big mounds. Some were under small humps of chalk, others in circular precincts defined by a single ditch, the 'ring ditch'.

The practice of individual burial with gravegoods under round mounds seems to have spread next to Derbyshire and into the Thames valley, and so eventually to Wessex. So far, eighty-eight of these 'round barrows' in England and Wales have been identified as Neolithic. The fashion for burial in ring ditches seems to have travelled with them from Yorkshire, and before the end of the New Stone Age it was found as far afield as North Wales and Cumbria. News of these developments would have travelled along trade routes such as the ridgeway of the Chilterns and Berkshire Downs. In England north of the river Tees and in all of Scotland, no late Neolithic burials have been identifed save a small cremation cemetery within a henge at Cairnpapple Hill south of Linlithgow, and the addition of more bones to a few Orkney megalithic tombs. On the other hand, prestige goods like antler maceheads and jet ornaments, associated with elite burials further south, do appear in Scotland at this period. Along the Thames, individual burial within round barrows began while long barrows there were still in use, and multiplied while the long mounds were gradually abandoned. The circular mounds reached Dorset's Cranborne Chase later than that, and the people there never took to the notion of individual burial. In Wiltshire, between the two, long barrows were being forsaken before the round variety appeared. Both in that county and in the Cotswolds, the earliest round barrows contained quite large numbers of people: up to forty-four were placed in a pit beneath the Soldier's Grave in Gloucestershire. The idea of individual interments and of rich gravegoods arrived later than the form of the mound: indeed, in many areas the first round barrows contained more bodies than the last long barrows had done.[22] Yet the rule which had been constant since the beginning of the Neolithic still obtained: most people in most communities do not appear to have received any formal burial. What had altered was the conduct of funerary ceremonies, which now, like all other rituals were in most of England and Wales contained within the charmed space of a ring.

So far this chapter has laid out the skeleton of late Neolithic religious activity, that is, the apparatus of monuments which sustained it. It is now time to try to flesh out the picture by taking account of how these structures related to each other in chronology and in the landscape, and how far they were a part of a general exchange of ideas and objects. By 2500 BC what might be termed the main 'industrial areas' of the British Neolithic were all in operation and exporting their wares. Mines in Wiltshire, Sussex and Norfolk produced flint for much of England. Factories at Great Langdale in Cumbria, Craig Lwyd in North Wales, Mounts Bay in Cornwall and the Cheviot Hills of Northumberland all produced stone axes. Clusters of axe-heads from all these areas, and from Ireland and Scandinavia, have been found in the estuaries of rivers in Essex and Suffolk, indicating the presence of 'merchant shipping'. Certain areas adopted fashions in these artefacts: in Wessex, for example, the Cumbrian axes replaced the Cornish kind. Several different regional varieties of pottery were in use in the British Isles between c.3400 and c.2400 BC, but two came to dominate all others: Peterborough Ware, which was developed in southern England and soon covered almost the whole country, and Grooved Ware, which probably originated in the Orkneys and also quickly spread through almost the whole of Britain. The interaction of these two styles indicates something of the complexity of the relationship between long-distance contact and local traditions in this period. In England, Grooved Ware tended to be collected wherever the people were already fond of Peterborough Ware, as if those who appreciated the latter were attracted to another decorated ceramic in an exotic style. Whereas the Peterborough pots had formerly been deposited at sacred sites in Wessex, the people seemed now to lodge either kind, but not both, at ritual monuments. Generally the Grooved Ware was placed at the most important, such as the superhenges of Marden and Durrington. But there remain puzzling exceptions, such as Avebury where the builders never showed much interest in the new style. In the Thames valley, both styles together were placed at ritual monuments, while in East Anglia and the east midlands both together were put into ceremonial deposits, although Grooved Ware was preferred. What really marks off these eastern counties is that here ritual deposits were made without requiring the sacred monuments which featured so prominently elsewhere. In east Yorkshire, apparently so influential in the development of burial traditions, neither kind of pottery was placed at sacred sites. Nor did either appear in west Wales, which seems to have traded exclusively with Ireland. But in Scotland and the Orkneys, as already described, Grooved Ware is found at the most impressive of the ceremonial centres.[23]

Whatever the regional differences in the nature and pace of change, it seems fairly certain that the great alterations in the nature and use of monuments after about 3200 BC took place among an existing population. Nobody has argued for an invasion of Britain during the early third millennium BC. Not only do artefacts develop locally, but after a style of monument had ceased to be built it was still used for a period and still reverenced for a period after that. Potsherds, flints and human bones were deposited in the crumbling ditches of some abandoned Wessex causewayed enclosures during the first centuries of the third millennium. The West Kennet long barrow was possibly abandoned for some centuries around 3000 BC, but some cremation burials and pieces of Peterborough and Grooved Ware were added after that date to the by then ancient fill of bones and deposits within the chambers. Offerings which left behind potsherds and animal remains were still apparently made outside other Cotswold–Severn tombs in the same period, after they had ceased to be used for burial. In the Orkneys bones were still added to a few tombs until about 1700 BC. All over eastern and southern Britain, the new round barrows often clustered around the older long mounds. Indeed, in places late Neolithic monuments of different sorts and ages cluster so thickly that the relationships between them must have been important. The large Cumbrian stone circle of Long Meg and Her Daughters, for example, had a large circular embanked enclosure by its side, with two others of similar sort nearby and also a semicircular bank with a single standing stone, and a small stone ring. A few miles to the north was a henge, and another henge and a ring bank stood an equivalent distance to the south. However, no evidence has yet been obtained to suggest what these relationships, or those of similar sites, actually were.[24]

Having said all this, the evidence for abandonment of old customs and edifices during the late Neolithic is as striking as that for measures to preserve some continuity with them. The megalithic tombs and earthen long barrows may have been forsaken in slow stages, but forsaken they were. It appears that by 3000 BC the construction of both sorts of monument was over in the whole island of Britain and all its offshore islands except the Orkneys and Scillies, and that by 2500, over the same area, no more offerings were made at them. In Orkney the only tomb which may have been built after 3000 was the great Maes Howe, and at all but a few burial ceased around 2400. Across most of Britain after 3000 BC, the old tomb–shrines were not merely no longer used for burial but deliberately blocked up to make further use as difficult as possible. In the Orkneys, by 2500 the tombs at Quoyness, Pierowall Quarry and perhaps Maes Howe itself had been closed up in the same way and surrounded by a paved area for ceremonies. At Isbister and Midhowe the capstones were wrenched off and the chambers filled with rocks, as if to prevent these sites from competing with those at which rituals were still conducted. Others may have been cleared of their burials before blocking, presenting modern excavators with the puzzle of an empty tomb. These may have been the actions of clans choosing to end their local cults in order to concentrate upon joint rituals with others which seemed more effective. Or it may have been the work of a growing central authority intent upon annihilating local foci of faith and power. Likewise, we cannot tell whether, upon certain sites, monuments were in combination or competition. In Anglesey one of the early henges was razed, only to have the spectacular developed passage grave of Bryn Celli Ddu built on top of it. Was this to pool the ritual force of both sorts of structure? Or were the passage-grave builders crushing the henge beneath their tomb as they may have crushed those who had constructed it? At Callanish on the Scottish island of Lewis, people erected a circle of tall stones with a central pillar, an avenue of megaliths approaching the circle from one side, a short stone row running up to it upon the other, and another row running into it halfway along each of the sides between them. It looks as if it had been intended to turn the row opposite the avenue into another avenue, but this was not done. Instead, a small passage grave was built inside the ring, between the central pillar and one side. Was this carried out by people who had prevented the completion of the great cruciform monument and placed an older style of religious structure inside to reconsecrate it to a better, more traditional faith? Or had the builders of the ring run out of enthusiasm for elaboration of its complex, and added the tomb instead so that burials might be placed inside doubly sanctified ground? At the big henge of Arbor Low, Derbyshire, holes were dug for the erection of a stone circle within it, and all the megaliths dragged to them ready to be put up. But instead they were left lying there. Did the builders change their minds or were they themselves destroyed?[25]

a

b

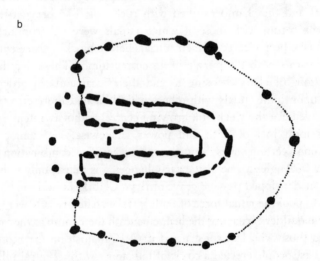

FIGURE 3.8   An Irish Wedge Tomb: at Island (County Cork)
a Conjectural reconstruction (redrawn after E. M. Fahy); *b* plan (redrawn after Michael O'Kelly). At the time of excavation the cairn had slipped over the retaining ring of megaliths, and most of the latter were missing, leaving only their sockets. There was a cremation in a pit within the chamber.

Prehistorians in the 1980s naturally gave much thought to the problem of why selective, successive burial in tomb–shrines was replaced in the course of the Neolithic by ceremonies in open circular enclosures and burial of selected individuals under sealed round mounds. However lengthy the funeral ceremonies at round barrows, once the burials were in them they were never re-opened as the old tombs had been. Nor were the bodies mixed together as in the tombs, and prestigious goods were buried with them in a way previously unknown. As mentioned earlier, some have suggested that the authority of lineage was being overthrown, to concentrate reverence upon the living figures of rulers who were, in death as in life, set apart by symbols of wealth and power.[26] Conversely, it has been suggested that the tombs were blocked to limit the number of the ancestors who conferred power and mediated with the divine. Thus the privileged dead became a closed body, like a ghostly senate, conferring a permanent authority upon the current leaders.[27] Or it has been proposed that religious traditions may have altered, directing attention away from the dead.[28] Certainly, any explanation for the change must take into account the undoubted evidence for the glorification of leading individuals in late Neolithic burial patterns. But it is virtually impossible to draw any convincing conclusions, because we do not know either what the cult of the tomb–shrines actually signified or how mid-Neolithic society was ruled. Was the ritual role of the bones deposited in the old tombs later represented by the bodies interred under round barrows? Or by the pieces of skeleton dropped into the ditches and pits of the henges? Does the presence of those bones around the henges mean that the ceremonies conducted within them were focused on or through the dead as those at the tombs must have been? Or were the human remains now just one ingredient among many, along with the potsherds, flints and animal bones? Had a religious tradition altered, or simply the way in which it was expressed, rechannelled by the changing needs of rulers? Why did regions in which each family seemed to put up its stone ring, as in the Mar district of Scotland, abandon the tombs in the same way as English areas in which power appears to have been concentrated in large regional centres? Why did the farmers of western Ireland still raise tombs in the old way? Why did the people of the east midlands, East Anglia and south-eastern England, who seem to have been as numerous and as fond of the new prestigious possessions as those of Wessex, erect only a few, not very impressive monuments? Once again, the recent discoveries of prehistorians have served only to raise questions. It remains to be seen whether the provision of answers becomes easier as the most celebrated age of British prehistory moves towards its climax, and disintegration.

4

Into the Darkness (c.2200–c.1000 BC)

One of the principal changes which the past decade has made to our view of prehistory has been to render the traditional system of ages redundant. It used to be thought that the New Stone Age, Bronze Age and Iron Age each had their own monuments, their own culture and their own mentality, which set them off from one another. Now it is clear that the truly great changes occurred halfway through each of the first two periods and (subject to an argument about definitions) the third. But until the 1980s scholars who were abandoning the classic divisions still believed in the vital significance of an invasion which was said to have happened towards the end of the Neolithic, that of the Beaker People. These newcomers were given most of the credit for the major developments of that time, including the appearance of henges, stone circles and round barrows. They were supposed to have been a new race, crossing over from the Netherlands and bringing with them a collection of new personal possessions. The most celebrated of these were the large, broad-waisted drinking-vessels which gave the hypothetical owners their name, but there were also barbed arrowheads, stone wristguards (to catch the whiplash recoil of a bow string), buttons, gold jewellery and copper daggers. Some writers credited them with bringing a new religion, with a cult of the sky, to replace the Neolithic Mother Goddess.

Around 1980 it became obvious that at least some of this had to be wrong. The improvement in dating methods revealed that the appearance of the new types of monument was a gradual process, which took place centuries before the new goods were adopted. The latter could thus be accounted for in terms of an importation of continental fashions by an existing population. The adoption of these possessions in area after area of

Europe might be related to the emergence in these places of elites, which created a demand for prestige goods. Certainly, these goods now seem to have been adopted in Britain only gradually, some appearing before 2500 BC and continuing to spread until about 2000. By 1988 some pre-historians were declaring roundly that the Beaker People had never existed. Some scholars even felt that the assertion that a colleague still believed in them was a condemnation in itself, not needing further elucidation. Others cautiously allowed of the possibility of a little immigration, while Aubrey Burl was still prepared to argue for the probability of this, based upon evidence from the Stonehenge area. It must be said that his portrait is so much at variance with that presented by other regions that either Salisbury Plain was a special case or there is something amiss with his argument.[1] When considering ritual and funerary monuments, the weight of the evidence is against the idea of the sharp break with the past which would favour the notion of a 'Beaker People'. What does emerge is a picture of rapid development of existing sites and traditions.

This may be considered first of all in the case of the Wessex 'superhenges'. At Avebury the characteristic beakers seem to appear as the huge circle-henge itself was being completed and extended into a wider ceremonial complex, around 2400 or 2300 BC. The wooden rings upon the site of the Sanctuary were replaced by two concentric stone circles, and the body of a young adolescent, probably female, was put beside one of the sockets intended for the megaliths. Her position strongly suggests a human sacrifice; this was certainly a foundation deposit. An avenue of stones was constructed to link the new rings with the Avebury henge itself, and more burials spaced along it. A second great avenue was extended from the henge, about a mile to the south-west. A deformed woman, virtually a dwarf, was interred by the henge's south entrance, where the avenue arrived from the Sanctuary. Like all the other burials, this one was accompanied by beakers. A young woman with bones warped by malnutrition who was put into the ditch by the north entrance of Marden superhenge seems also to have been interred at this time. Now, too, the entrance to the West Kennet megalithic tomb was finally blocked up, not merely filled in with earth (mixed with beaker sherds) but shut off with gigantic stones. It is as if, with the completion of the whole Avebury complex, the now ancient tomb was not only redundant but considered to be either a competitor with, or harmful to, the ceremonies now in progress around the henge. The destruction or lack of excavation of the other tombs in the vicinity leaves us unable to determine at present whether the one at West Kennet was uniquely favoured or feared during the late Neolithic.[2]

The women buried by the entrances at Avebury and Marden may have carried moral authority despite (or because of) their physical disabilities, and been honoured by interment in this fashion. On the other hand, there is a strong and nasty possibility that their communities were getting rid of their more expendable members by offering them as sacrifices. The young person at the Sanctuary probably fell into this category, and at Durrington Walls the evidence is unequivocal. Around 2300 BC a separate henge monument was built to the south-west of the enormous one, with a large round wooden structure, almost certainly a roofed building, inside it. Christened 'Woodhenge' by prehistorians, it was probably a shrine used by the people of Durrington. Pits were dug in it and filled with 'ritual rubbish', and the foundation sacrifice was put near its centre. It was a three-year-old child, whose skull had been cut in half with an axe blow. The pattern continued when, within two centuries of the construction of Woodhenge, both it and Durrington Walls were suddenly abandoned. Attention shifted to one of those two decayed henges on the nearby plain. Its bank and ditch were restored and an avenue dug out from the north-east entrance, pointing towards the midsummer sunrise but also, roughly, towards Durrington. In the ditch near that entrance was dumped the body of a young man still dressed in one of the wristguards associated with the beaker culture. He may have died close by and been buried there for the sake of convenience, or he too may have been a sacrifice. Whichever is true, there is no doubt about the cause of death. The points of three arrowheads were still sticking among his bones. In this manner the construction began of the monument which was to achieve enduring glory as Stonehenge.[3]

The superhenge at Mount Pleasant in Dorset was also rebuilt around 2100 BC as part of a large complex. Its decaying wooden structure was demolished and replaced by a 'cove' of four megaliths open to the south. Beakers, Grooved Ware and animal bones were put into the ditch to join the centuries-old ritual deposits already there. At the same time a palisade of 1600 huge oak posts was erected inside the ditch, a fortification of such strength that it was probably intended against human enemies rather than to define a sacred enclosure. Yet it was given spiritual strength as well by a large number of objects deposited in the post-holes. They included arrowheads, a polished axe, thirty-eight antler-picks, thirty chalk balls, some carved cylinders and blocks of chalk, animal bones, beakers and both Peterborough and Grooved Ware. It is possible, though unlikely, that the enemies were based only a couple of miles away, on the site of modern Dorchester where part of a huge circle of wooden posts with a ditch has been found under Greyhound Yard. To the south of this, at the same time as the reconstruction of Mount Pleasant, was built a henge monument which would be considered large were it not for the proximity of the superhenge and the timber circle. Known now as Maumbury Rings, it may have functioned as a satellite to the circle. The ritual deposits grouped carefully in its ditches were, again, lavish. They included bones of wild and domestic animals (especially stags' skulls), pieces of human skeleton, chalk balls, chalk phalluses, potsherds, tools, and drums and grooved blocks of chalk. These were laid in a total of forty-five pits dug through the ditch's bottom, some 35 feet deep. The less mundane objects, such as the bones and worked chalk, were laid nearer the top. In this way the whole monument seems to have been charged with power for those who built it.[4] The traditions being followed date back to the mid-Neolithic, if not earlier, but like the monuments they accompanied, the deposits were on a lavish scale.

Everywhere the people who used beakers and the other new goods emphasized their continuity with the past by imitating or honouring structures or traditions from preceding centuries. In the upper Thames valley, the first large henges were constructed at this time. The inhabitants of East Anglia and the east midlands adopted the new prestige goods without altering their habitual disinclination to construct large or numerous monuments. At Ty Newydd in Anglesey, Tinkinswood in Glamorganshire and Sale's Lot in Gloucestershire, burials accompanied by beakers were inserted into megalithic or earthen tombs built in the previous millennium. In Wessex, beakers were at first placed in obsolete long barrows and causewayed enclosures more often than in the relatively new henges. Their sherds are found in the ditches of henge monuments and the mounds of Neolithic barrows in Scotland. They turn up, often with unburned or cremated burials, in and around stone rings across the whole island of mainland Britain which, on the evidence of other deposits, appear to have been constructed at an earlier period. In Ireland the pattern of intrusion into older tombs and circles is repeated. The most spectacular case of the veneration of an archaic monument seems to have been at Newgrange, where people using beakers put up a flimsy timber settlement against the huge passage grave. It was apparently they who began to raise a ring of megaliths around the crumbling mound, but the work was left unfinished.[5]

Nevertheless, for all this pious antiquarianism, the evolution of funerary customs in Britain continued steadily. Indeed, the 'beaker burial' has long been a classic component of British prehistory. It consists of a single crouched inhumation in a rock-cut or rock-lined grave or a stone chest, sometimes below a round barrow but with the ground above usually flat. Such burials occur in small cemeteries or individually, and each is accompanied by the new goods, especially a beaker. Most are of men, but a significant minority are female. In northern England the males tend to have heads to the south and facing east, while the women have heads to the south looking west. In Wessex, men had heads to the north looking east, but women still to the south facing west. In both regions, only the men were accompanied by weapons: the bow, flint arrows and copper dagger which were the standard military equipment of the time. But the people of that period were no more immune than any others to the prehistoric tendency to make exceptions to every rule which archaeologists have tried to identify. Most graves still contain bodies but not goods, such as eleven of the twenty-one excavated in a cemetery at Eynsham, Oxfordshire, and eleven out of fifteen at Barnack in Cambridgeshire. At Dorchester in Oxfordshire the bodies were burned with their ornaments, tools and weapons and then the remains of humans and goods together were put in leather bags and taken to ring ditches dug in the old cursus monument. But the same cemetery included two rectangular enclosures, one containing another cremation and the other an unburned skeleton which had been crushed almost to powder, perhaps before burial. The owner may have been punished for some misdeed, or may have been a foundation deposit.[6]

Upon the western fringe of Britain and in Ireland completely different courses were followed. In Anglesey facsimilies of the old tombs were constructed at the end of the Neolithic. In Ireland the British pattern was completely reversed: beakers have often been found on settlement sites but so far in only one grave in the whole island. Indeed, except in the west, where wedge tombs were still constructed, it is difficult to identify burials from this period.[7]

Around 2000 BC the British Isles passed into the Early Bronze Age – a transition utterly without meaning for the purposes of this book, as ritual monuments of the late Neolithic continued to evolve at the same pace. During the next five centuries settlements spread across Dartmoor, Bodmin Moor, the Welsh mountains, the north Yorkshire Moors, the Scottish Highlands and south-west Ireland. In all these areas the forest was felled and first grazing and then cereal agriculture introduced.[8] With farming came the monuments from the lowlands, mutating to adapt to poor and perhaps more dispersed communities and to stonier ground. Smaller stone circles were built, though sometimes as part of elaborate ritual complexes. The round barrows of the lowlands were turned into cairns of piled rocks. In the older areas of activity, henges ceased to be built and eventually to be used, but round barrows multiplied and in southern England they diverged in form. As well as the familiar shape of an upturned bowl, there appeared a type with a broad kerb, giving it the silhouette of a bell. This often covered unusually rich burials, while female graves were sometimes placed under a small round mound surrounded by an area of level soil bounded by a circular ditch (now called a disc barrow). Beakers were demoted to the status of household accessories, to be replaced as a favourite gravegood by another kind of ceramic, a tapering pot called a 'food vessel'. These were succeeded in turn by different varieties of urn. By the end of the early Bronze Age, these pots very often contained the burial rather than accompanied it, for cremation had replaced inhumation as the most common mode.

These were the general developments of the period (greatly simplified). A proper examination of them would best be done region by region, trying to relate the monuments to each other and to their societies. Nevertheless, there is not space for such an exercise in this present book so a more general overall view must be attempted. By the early second millennium, several areas which had been notable centres of ritual activity, such as the Boyne Valley, the Orkneys, the Cotswolds and the Avebury area, were turning into cultural backwaters. Instead, the granite uplands of south-west Britain and of Wales, the Kilmartin Valley of Argyll, Counties Cork and Kerry and the Curragh plain in County Kildare were crowded with ceremonial monuments, while a few areas which had already been notable for the construction of such centres, notably Mar, continued to flourish. An absence of megalithic structures or large earthen enclosures did not mean a lack of people, for round barrows of this period cover the Yorkshire Wolds, and 1403 others (surviving or destroyed) have been identified in Norfolk, Suffolk, Cambridgeshire and Essex.[9] None of these places has ceremonial centres of the same age, and as yet there is no apparent reason for their absence.

Bodmin Moor, Dartmoor and south-west Ireland are all examples of regions which had been cleared and farmed only a few centuries before being thickly studded with stone monuments in the early Bronze Age. All three contain rings and rows of stones, spaced out so carefully that they seem to mark territories. A notable feature of these is their small size, for on Bodmin Moor and in the two Irish counties they define areas far smaller than a medieval parish and indicate either a very large population or division into very small groups. The relationship between the rings (ideal for gatherings) and the rows (ideal for processions) is quite mysterious. Their social function as family, clan or tribal centres may well have been the same, but the ceremonies could hardly have been so. Yet some communities wanted rows and others wanted circles. In the Irish case the situation is further complicated by the presence of a third type of contemporary monument, the wedge tomb. These tombs, the last variety of megalithic burial shrine to be erected in the British Isles, are spaced neatly between the rings and lines as if all three were alternative monuments. All are aligned upon, or have entrances facing, the south-west, apparently towards the setting sun or rising moon. And the three rings and the wedge tomb which have been properly excavated contained identical deposits, a single cremation like a foundation burial or sacrifice. We seem to have here a uniform local cult, but one which required three different types of structure. On Bodmin Moor and Dartmoor a hierarchy of monuments can be discerned as well as alternative kinds. At the lowest level were cairns and single stones, and perhaps the houses themselves, many of which reproduce the shape of the circles. Then would come the carefully spaced rings and rows, and finally large complexes of circles, lines, avenues or cairns (one on Bodmin Moor, four on Dartmoor) which were probably major gathering places, 'cathedrals' to the 'parishes' of their districts.[10]

Excavation has added little to our knowledge of the purpose of the stone rings during this period. Fires were burned in many of them, across the whole of their geographical range. Quartz, the crystal already used prominently at Newgrange, apparently retained arcane associations, for it was scattered or buried within certain rings in Dyfed, Mar and south-west Ireland. Human burials, mostly cremations, have been found in the Druid's Circle, Gwynedd, and seem to have been common in those of Mar, Cork and Kerry. At Longstone Rath, on the Curragh, Bronze Age people erected a pillar of limestone next to the mingled burned bones of a man and a woman, and dug a henge around it. It seems more likely that the couple were interred to add power to the monument than that it was constructed to honour them. In the middle of another henge on the same plain, excavators found a pit aligned with the two entrances, containing the contorted body of a young woman. A pathologist concluded that she had been buried alive, though his verdict, reached at a time when both his science and archaeology were in their infancy, might be challenged by some today. An indication of how complex the rituals could be is provided by the Broomend of Crichie complex, in Mar. There a ring of six megaliths was put inside a centuries-old Neolithic henge next to a more recently completed recumbent stone circle. A body was cremated in its centre and a deep pit dug through the pyre. At the bottom was built a stone chest or cist into which were put the burned remains, along with the skull and long bones of a man who had been buried elsewhere years before. We cannot tell whether two bodies were needed, one burned and one not, or whether either corpse was believed to require a companion.[11]

Early Bronze Age cairns, distributed thickly in the stony areas of the British Isles, display all the now familiar prehistoric dislike for exact similarity. In a relatively small area such as Bodmin Moor, they occur in many sizes and locations, some with kerbs, platforms, central spaces or central mounds, and some with none of these features. In Wales those composed of rings of piled rocks may have represented solid stone circles. The sense that they might have been shrines rather than graves is reinforced by the fact that most contain deposits of charcoal rather than burials. On the other hand, the kerbed cairns, those on platforms, and some which have a surrounding stone ring all tend to have prominent sites, and the few which have been excavated have yielded human remains with rich goods. Lesser burials have been found in simple cairns, sometimes with an encircling ring of wooden stakes.[12]

In eastern Britain north of the river Tees, most early Bronze Age burials were under flat graves, but further south round barrows were the rule. The sheer number upon the Yorkshire Wolds permits a proper comparative study of funerary practices. In addition to cremations in urns, some 636 unburned bodies have been discovered. These reveal that, although there were fashions, nobody felt constrained to follow them. Some burials were of groups, and some mixed burned with unburned corpses. The most common alignment was east to west, the second favourite position north to south. But only a fifth of the total were in the east–west position, and the majority were scattered around the compass. The most common posture was crouched, but many bodies were laid out straight and some squatted. Some were accompanied by goods but most were not.[13]

Two sites in different countries must suffice to give some notion of the complexity of burial rites in a few remarkable cairns or barrows. One is on a hilltop in Fife, where people lit fires and dug eight pits. In these they placed cremations and the severed human heads of both children and adults, put together with the burnt bodies or by themselves. Three cists were built among them, and into these were put crouched unburned

Part of the long and elaborate burial ceremonies at Pond Cairn, Glamorgan, as imagined by the late Alan Sorrell. Ceremonial maces of the sort shown have accompanied richly furnished male burials from the period, but whether such a figure would have presided over these rites we cannot say with any certainty. By kind permission of the National Museum of Wales.

bodies, cremations, beakers, food vessels, a necklace, pebbles, antlers, beads and an awl. Three graves were dug in the earth beside the cists and a mixture of burned and unburned bodies put into these too. Then a low round mound was raised over all.[14] Just as elaborate, and disturbing, were the rituals reconstructed from the site at Pond Cairn near Coity, Glamorgan. First, in early spring, people cremated a man and placed the charred bones in an urn. They dug a long pit and threw in pebbles mixed with a flint flake and the burnt bones of a child. The pit was then filled with clay and paved over, so that the urn could be put on the top and covered with a small slab. Just to the north a new pit was dug with a trench leading into it. Into this was thrown charcoal mixed with bits of bone and a sheep's tooth. Rocks were piled around the urn and then the whole site covered in a round mound of turves. During the summer a high ring cairn was built around it, ash thrown on to the mound and the earth between mound and ring stamped flat, perhaps by dancers. That autumn the people made a breach in the ring and dug a pit in front of it, beside the mound. A fire of twigs was kindled next to this and dropped or pushed into it, followed by sheaves of wheat and barley which burned in turn, and a small grey stone. Sir Cyril Fox, who carried out this marvellous excavation, posed the unanswerable question of whether all this was to honour the man buried in the cairn or whether he (like the child?) was a sacrifice to commence a chain of seasonal rituals.[15]

The most famous British edifice of this period is, of course, Stonehenge. To prehistorians it is probably the most tragic monument in the entire world, for its very fame has ensured the destruction of the evidence which might have permitted us to know its story. In the 1620s, workmen employed by the Duke of Buckingham gouged out the entire centre, looking for treasure of the past, and threw away the deposits which would have meant so much to the modern scholar. Other equally pointless private excavations followed in the next two centuries, and rabbits were introduced to the monument, driving their burrows through surviving remains. Between 1919 and 1926 over half of the site was dug into by Colonel William Hawley, a patient worker who recorded his finds but did not possess the resources either to notice or to interpret features available to modern archaeologists. During the 1940s and 1950s Richard Atkinson set new standards of investigation at Stonehenge (and several other sites) and subsequently produced what has long been the definitive study. Unfortunately, contemporary historians are increasingly of the opinion that he was making a gallant attempt to interpret something which had been damaged beyond the point at which such an attempt was still practicable. As a result, his careful periodization of Stonehenge I, II, IIIa, IIIb and IIIc must now be abandoned. We can trace the perimeter, but cannot determine what happened in the centre. All we can say for certain is that a wooden structure of some sort existed around the end of the fourth millennium and that a large number of stones were erected from *c.*2100 onwards, to achieve their present pattern by *c.*1500 BC. We can also be certain that the Heel and Slaughter stones were set up, outside and inside the entrance, when the first henge was built. But nobody can now say with certainty when the four Station Stones were erected between the bank and the inner precinct where the great megaliths stand, or how they relate to the rest of the complex.[16]

As things are, the more we do know about Stonehenge, the odder it seems. The problem is not really with the great uprights which form the facade of the inner precinct, capped with the remains of their ring of level stones, nor with the three huge 'trilithons' like door-frames standing clear, which defined the innermost sanctuary. We know that they were dragged from Marlborough Downs near Avebury, about twenty miles to the north. Nor is it difficult to surmise why it was that these great blocks became the only components of a stone circle in the British Isles to be tooled to shape and fitted together in the celebrated trilithon pattern. The technique is that of a woodworker, indicating that some native original genius, accustomed to making timber frames with mortice and tenon joints, dared to transfer this trick to the medium of stone. Though successful, it was a unique experiment, without imitators inside or outside Britain. All this is plain. But now the problems begin. The fact that people decided to abandon the superhenge of Durrington Walls and construct a ceremonial centre of unprecedented splendour nearby indicated that they wanted a fresh start. But the associated fact that they did not start completely afresh, but reconstructed an obsolete henge monument, indicates that this particular site had especial significance. All that we can now make out to justify this is that the old henge had a stone-flanked entrance facing north-east. This may have been crucial, but a dynastic memory, or a vision, may have accounted for the choice instead. Since the precise sequence in which the structures were built and then rebuilt has been lost, we cannot account for the curious mixture of skill and wanton carelessness shown in the construction. The stones were given their tenons and mortices, bevelled along the edges, and hammered smooth, with an expertise remarkable in view of the novelty of the medium. The lintels were made to curve slightly to make the circle, and when fitted made an almost level line (the variation is never more than six inches). Yet it also shows signs of carelessness and haste. One upright in the outer circle was badly erected and so soon fell and broke. Its pieces were piled on top of each other and the lintel replaced, whereupon they subsequently collapsed again, this time permanently. The biggest of the central trilithons eventually toppled and broke because one of its uprights had been embedded in far too shallow a hole. The completed monument was visually stunning, but rickety in places. Nor was it, in a sense, ever actually finished. Two concentric rings of holes (known on modern plans as 'Y' and 'Z') were dug around the facade as if to receive more stones, or posts; but they never did.[17]

The most curious feature of the monument is the set of small uprights called 'bluestones' which now form a circle within the great façade and a horseshoe within the central trilithons. It has long been known that at the present day they occur nowhere closer to Stonehenge than in the Presceli Mountains at the west end of Wales. The logical conclusion to the question of why they appear on Salisbury Plain is that they occurred there, in an isolated outcrop which was worked out when they were extracted. As they weather badly and are not well suited to service in megalithic structures, it would make sense to visualize them simply as the closest and most convenient source of stone. This view would appear to be supported by the occurrence of a bluestone boulder inside a much earlier Neolithic long barrow on the western fringe of the Plain. But the argument is betrayed by geology: there is such a total lack in the area of any stratum which might have produced an outcrop of this sort that scientists are inclined to term it impossible. So we are left with the apparently far less sensible idea that the 'bluestones' were moved at least 200 miles from Presceli to Stonehenge and that they had possessed special significance in the latter area for at least a millennium before. Yet they seem to have possessed it nowhere else, for no other stone ring (including those in the Prescelis themselves) is made of this soft and corrodible material. By every other test, such as styles of artefact and monument, west Wales was not closely associated with Wessex at this time. It is also very difficult to understand why the bluestones were not hammered into shape at the quarries, thereby shedding half the weight that would have to be shipped and dragged to Wessex: the quantity of detritus from them makes it indisputable that they were worked upon when they arrived at Salisbury Plain. They were apparently first intended for setting in or near the old Stonehenge cursus, where much of the discarded material from them has been found. It was also intended that some at least would be set up as jambs and lintels like the huge Marlborough Down stones, for one bears a mortice hollow. Why the builders of Stonehenge should have considered these stones, of such low practical utility, to be of such compulsive arcane significance at present defeats the imagination.

This problem summons up the related one of the nature of the community of early Bronze Age Salisbury Plain and its relationships with the rest of southern Britain. Unquestionably, the people in the vicinity of Stonehenge had not only the most spectacular monument but one of the riches social elites of the contemporary British Isles. Their round barrow cemeteries line the ridges within site of the stones, and form more clusters around the old long barrows further out on the plain. Stonehenge itself appears to be a very elitist monument, for the space at its heart is about half the size of a modern tennis court and the great stones would have blocked off the view from outside. It looks as if only a few people could have participated in the mysteries within, although as we do not know the nature either of the rites or of the terms upon which individuals were admitted to them, this remains only a supposition. Certainly a relatively large number of people must have been involved in the construction of the complex, as a minimum of 100 men would have been needed to erect one of the great uprights. Certainly also the surrounding graves testify to the existence of a privileged few, individuals who were laid there with some gold and bronze goods of great beauty. They have the appearance of members of ruling dynasties, both sexes treated with truly royal honours. If one is tempted to think in dynastic terms, then there were two 'ruling houses', the first from $c.2100$ to $c.1900$ and the second from $c.1600$ to $c.1400$ BC, for the rich burials occur between those dates.[18] On the other hand, it would be more in harmony with current fashion among prehistorians to think in sociological terms: to ask why the society concerned was more inclined to express wealth and power by burying their symbols with its honoured dead at those times. This question is no more open to resolution, as yet, than the others hanging over Stonehenge. It seems that people worked on the monument and made rich burials $c.2100-c.1900$, worked on the monument $c.1900-c.1600$, and made rich burials $c.1600-c.1400$. Nevertheless our lack of a precise chronology for Stonehenge makes it possible that from $c.1900-c.1600$ was a period of stagnation in which nothing much was built or deposited.

The place of Stonehenge in the ritual structure of Wessex is easily discerned: its building was part of a process which extinguished all the other ceremonial centres. Marden was apparently abandoned at about the same time as Durrington. The gigantic complex at Avebury seems to have been completed around 2200 BC, but there is no evidence of activity within it after about 2000. Instead, its vicinity, as just mentioned, was the source of the megaliths dragged to build Stonehenge. Its neighbourhood retained sanctity, for large round barrows were built to overlook it during the early Bronze Age, but their burials were poorly equipped in comparison with those of Salisbury Plain. At the end of the period a field wall was built across the avenue joining the henge to the Sanctuary, proving total lack of respect for it, let alone sacred use of it, by then. Either the worshippers at Avebury had been tempted away by the greater reputation of the site of Stonehenge, or else they had been conquered and forced thither.[19] The fate of the last of the old superhenges, at Mount Pleasant, indicates either a dramatic repudiation by its own community or ruthless destruction by its rivals: in about 1900 BC the massive defensive palisade was burned down and the site deserted.[20] In the course of the next five centuries the dominance of the area centred upon Stonehenge becomes all the more apparent in the archaeological record. Two quite different cultures were formed. Upon Salisbury Plain were the great monument and the great barrow cemeteries full of treasures. To the south, in parts of

Wiltshire, Hampshire and Dorset, were farming settlements which buried their cremated dead in simple urns, placed in fields or in older round barrows. They represent what is called the 'Deverel–Rimbury' culture. Clearly the two had some kind of relationship with each other.[21] Were the southern farmers working to support the political and religious elite of the plain, as well as themselves, and travelling to Stonehenge to worship? Were the ruling individuals of both regions brought up to the cemeteries of the plain for burial? Or were the leaders of the plain an increasingly isolated and reactionary society, striving to assert the old importance of their area with an even greater ostentation than before? Did the prosperous, hard-headed independent communities of the south contemptuously reject such a flamboyance in religion and in personal ornamentation? The sheer wealth of the graves around Stonehenge at the beginning of the second millennium, and the human resources mobilized to build the monument, would argue for one of the first two explanations. But the third may have come to operate at a later date. Certainly, the isolation of Stonehenge as a great sacred monument had an ominous as well as a grandiose aspect. Just as long barrows without burials were on their way to becoming obsolete, so an island which possessed only one ceremonial centre was soon to be capable of doing without any.

Before dealing with that story, it is necessary now to ask whether any generalizations can be made about early Bronze Age religion in the British Isles. From a survey above, one is immediately obvious: that the number, identity and combination of monuments varied so much between regions that it is scarcely possible to conceive of the situation in County Cork and that in Suffolk as existing in the same millennium. Furthermore, there were in some areas one or two sites which have left evidence for dramatic or elaborate ritual practices. The problem with these is that, even allowing for the destruction of so much evidence and the potential for further discovery, such practices appear to have been exceptional. They show what was possible to the early Bronze Age imagination, not what generally went on. To select one aspect of an unusual site in (say) Ulster, find the same phenomenon among different aspects of equally atypical sites in (say) Fife and Cornwall and describe it as 'Bronze Age religion' would be appalling prehistory. We need to proceed much more cautiously.

Previous generations of scholars and enthusiasts have handed on to us different models. As already said, in the first half of this century there was a vague but widespread notion that the Bronze Age British practised sky-cults from stone circles, doing away with the worship of the Great

Goddess carved upon megalithic tombs. This is reflected in the work of writers of the 1970s such as Michael Dames, to whom a peaceful, egalitarian, goddess-centred, earth-loving Neolithic was succeeded by a warlike Bronze Age, patriarchal in both politics and religion. This view is of course paralleled in the writings of Marija Gimbutas, whose attractive Balkan Neolithic society could have been at best a distant memory by the second millennium. On the other hand, prehistorians have traditionally accepted that the religions of early Bronze Age Crete, the Cyclades and (perhaps) Greece were centred upon goddess worship. Indeed, writers who have dreamed of ancient societies led by women have drawn heavily upon the early Bronze Age Aegean for their material. In Egypt, Syria, Anatolia and Mesopotamia at the same period there existed powerful communities whose writings we can decipher, and we have long understood the nature, if not the details, of their religions. They had pantheons of deities of both sexes, usually put together by associating a number of local divine patrons. But the general assumption has been that the peoples dwelling in Europe, being more 'primitive' in their culture, had also to be so in their theology. From the last century onwards, linguistic historians made efforts to reconstruct the religious beliefs of Bronze Age Europeans and Asians. It was (and apparently still is) generally accepted that the Indo-European group of languages derive from a common tongue spoken in a homeland from which its speakers fanned out as far as India in one direction, and the Atlantic in another, by the late Bronze Age. By examining the primitive Indo-European words for sacred things, it was long believed possible to reconstruct the concepts that lay behind these things. The problem was that as a theoretical game it was too easy for a good linguist to play: by the mid-twentieth century a number of different schemes had been produced, all logically convincing, all mutually incompatible and all impossible to prove.[22]

So much for the models. To illustrate what may be learned of the beliefs of an early Bronze Age society, it is interesting to try a good test case. Just as Çatal Hüyük served for the Neolithic, as the site richest in evidence, so Crete is almost certainly the best choice for the second millennium. It is prehistoric to us, not because it had no writing but because we cannot read the script. But the evidence for religion, in structures, reliefs, sculptures, ceremonies and engraved seals, is copious. Female figures appear, standing with gestures of command, associated with animals such as snakes; staring aggressively, they were placed in shrines or sanctuaries. At times one of them appears upon a height, with female figures worshipping or dancing at her feet. There are also male figures, some young and very handsome. From this one can conclude with some confidence that these Cretans believed in both female and male deities but that the former were more important in their religious life. Perhaps there was one goddess who appeared in various guises, perhaps there were several. Perhaps the young male figure was a goddess's divine consort or priest, or perhaps quite independent. It is also practically certain that women took part in religious rites, though whether on behalf of all the people or on their own is more difficult to say. Females in sacred dress are portrayed dancing before crowds, but whether they were priestesses or goddesses, one cannot state. There may have been priests as well, and some of the male figures accorded special status in the art may be these religious leaders. But this is no more than a possibility, and nothing conclusive can be said about the role played by gender in Cretan political life, nor about their politics, save that they had a palace-dwelling monarchy.[23] None the less, compared with the evidence from Çatal Hüyük, that from Crete does tell us a good deal. The last megalithic tombs in Brittany also carry a plainer religious message than the earlier. Many of the 'gallery graves' of the late Breton Neolithic have uprights bearing an obvious female figure, sometimes just symbolized by a pair of breasts. It is placed in a commanding position and deposits of pots and flints placed underneath may have been offerings to the personality which it represents. It is tempting to call her 'the gallery-grave death goddess', but that is running beyond the evidence. Still, there is more proof of goddess worship (or indeed any kind of worship) in the late Neolithic and Bronze Age of Europe than in its earlier Neolithic.

What of the British Isles? Irritatingly, there are no images from an earlier Bronze Age context which are unequivocally religious. Instead, we have more abstract motifs. Goldsmiths working around Ireland's Wicklow Mountains were especially fond of one which has endured right up to the present day. It is the so-called Celtic Cross, a simple cross within a circle. In its origins there was nothing Irish, or British, or 'Celtic', about it. It developed in the western Carpathian region around 3000 BC, upon pottery. During the next millennium it spread slowly across Europe, being especially popular upon metalwork of the so-called beaker culture. Traditionally it has always been regarded as a sun symbol, and the particular frequency with which it appears upon prehistoric gold objects would perhaps strengthen that supposition. It became virtually a brand-mark for the Irish work, which was traded far and fast enough to appear in a beaker burial at Mere, Wiltshire, in the form of a gold-coated button now in the Devizes Museum. Otherwise the art of the early

Bronze Age is hammered or carved into stone, whether on monuments or on natural outcrops. In Ireland it is well scattered, but most common in the south-west. In Britain it is mainly confined to the northern uplands. Although much of it, by its nature, is undatable, every certain context in which it appears is Bronze Age. Whereas the Neolithic art was confined to developed passage graves, this was fairly ubiquitous within the ranges stated. We lack any dossier of the Bronze Age carvings, probably because in comparison with the passage grave motifs they seem limited and repetitive: but that impression might be corrected by more systematic research. Most common are cup-shaped hollows scraped out of stone, and concentric circles. Sometimes they are combined to make the cup-and-ring mark which is the most celebrated Bronze Age motif. Some of the cups-and-rings have a straight line drawn vertically across the rings from the central hollow to the edge. The symbolism intended by these designs, if any, is of course as inscrutable as that of the Neolithic patterns. Suns, moons and eyes are obvious interpretations, and often made, but the context never allows us to make any firm association in any one case. Cup-marks are found upon the stones of cists and of megalithic rings, as well as upon natural boulders and rock faces, yet their position is never consistent, either with features in the sky or with parts of the monuments. The other design especially favoured is of an axe-head, this one found more upon human sites than upon natural features. The axe was not only a favourite tool and weapon of the three Stone Ages and early Bronze Age, but clearly possessed a powerful symbolic value. Replicas of axe-heads in materials of no practical utility (such as chalk and clay) are often found deposited upon late Neolithic sacred sites. Miniatures in bronze were personal decorations in the next millennium. The image has obvious connotations of power, the ability to destroy trees, beasts and humans alike, but it may have had a more arcane symbolism which is now lost. In addition to these most common designs there are also wavy lines, spirals, footprints and individual geometric shapes, including a wavering swastika upon Woodhouse Crag, Ilkley Moor, Yorkshire, the first known appearance of this sign in Europe.

Again, a foreign comparison may be of use: this time we need to go to Scandinavia, which has the finest Bronze Age rock art of the northern half of Europe. Here the 'Celtic Cross' symbol recurs, together with the many-spoked wheel. Both appear being carried aloft by humans or upon the shields of warriors, indicating that they were images of power. The Celtic Cross sometimes appears being borne in boats, or in chariots or carts, or drawn by horses, and once a ship appears to be bowling along on

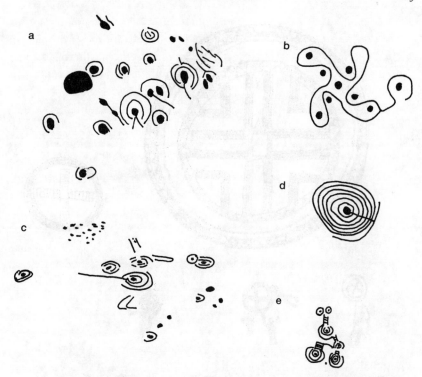

FIGURE 4.1 Early Bronze Age art: religion or decoration?
a Patch of cups and rings from the Badger Stone boulder (West Yorkshire);
b carving from Woodhouse Crag (West Yorkshire), usually, for convenience,
described as a swastika; *c* pattern from part of a rock outcrop at Baluacraig and
d cup and ring from a rock face at Achnabreck, both in Argyll's Kilmartin
valley; *e* cups, rings and ladders from the Panorama Stone boulder on Ilkley
Moor (West Yorkshire). Even the dating of some of these designs to the early
Bronze Age is conjectural.

top of it. There is an almost irresistible temptation to regard it as an image
of the sun, making its daily passage, and when coupled with the solar
associations of the same symbol in the British Isles, this identification
becomes virtually certain. In fact it may very probably be a simple
wheel, the cross being the four spokes and the whole representing the
turning of the sky. Why many-spoked wheels were also depicted at times
is a mystery, and may mean that the usage of the Celtic Cross was very
specific. Axes are also frequently brandished on the Swedish rocks,
confirming the impression of their importance as symbols of authority or

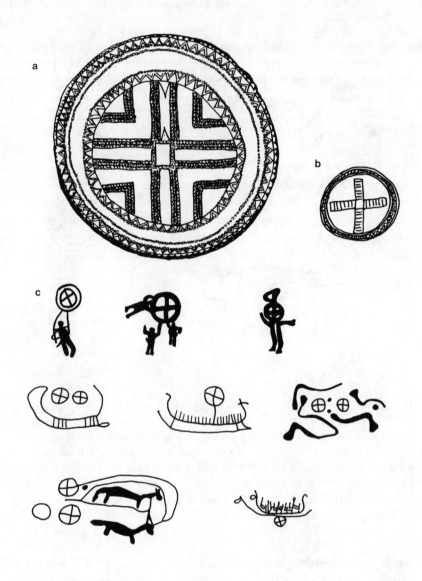

FIGURE 4.2   The first centuries of the 'Celtic Cross'
a Disc from Tednavet (Co. Monaghan), now in the National Museum of
Ireland, and *b* cap for a button, found with a beaker burial and now in the
Devizes Museum (Wiltshire), both of Irish gold; *c* figures from Bronze Age
Swedish and Danish rock art.
Source: figures in *c* redrawn after Gelling and Davidson.

potency.[24] The Scandinavian carvings also show the concentric-circle design so common in Britain, but much more rarely and without any context which might clarify its meaning. Nor do the even more common British and Irish cup-marks have any Scandinavian parallel.

Neither set of artwork includes the labyrinth or maze, a design which appears in the British Isles cut into rocks, or built in turves or stones upon the ground so that humans can tread it. These images and structures are usually impossible to date, but there is no proof of any belonging to the Bronze Age or Neolithic. Their range, scattered across these islands, bears no resemblance to that of the cup, ring and axe art. They have yielded no prehistoric artefacts, some were certainly constructed within historic times, and they do not appear in prehistoric ritual complexes. The most famous to its devotees is also the least convincing: the putative maze upon the slopes of Glastonbury Tor. To archaeologists, the terraces upon the hill look like perfectly normal medieval or Iron Age hillside field systems, and their name, upon estate maps, indicates that the identification is correct. They are called the 'lynchets', meaning fields. But in the 1930s, the mystic Violet Firth ('Dion Fortune') had a vision of a processional way around the Tor, constructed and used by refugees from Atlantis. Her idea was taken up in 1969, when Glastonbury was filling with people seeking the arcane and the supernatural, by Geoffrey Russell. He suggested that the terraces were a sacred way of the Neolithic or early Bronze Age, and mapped out the presumed route, winding up the hill in a flattened spiral. As a result, modern pagans and earth mystics can have the immense satisfaction of following this path in the belief that they are participating in a genuine ancient ritual.[25] To say that this belief is tenuous is to understate things in the gentlest way. Even the assumption that Glastonbury itself was a major Celtic or pre-Celtic holy place is dubious. In 1964–5 Philip Rahtz excavated the crest of the Tor and found ample evidence of occupation in the sixth century AD but none of any prehistoric structures. But then, the terraces themselves remain uninvestigated. Perhaps it would be a simple and worthwhile matter to put a few sections through them and enquire after their date and purpose, treating the putative maze as a Somerset Shroud of Turin. Or perhaps in this case the faithful are best left to their faith.

For the purposes of this book it is more interesting to examine the relationship of the early Bronze Age art to religious complexes, by taking two major examples. One is the Kilmartin valley of Argyll. The southern defile into the vale is flanked by outcrops covered in carvings, as though to watch, to warn or to consecrate those approaching. One bears over 130 cups and twenty-three cups-and-rings. Within the valley, the third cairn northward in the line, Ri Cruin, contained a cist with axes etched into one of its slabs. Another carried a form like the head of a rake, interpreted by many to represent one of the ships, with banks of oars, which feature so commonly in the Scandinavian art. Ship of the sun, ship of the dead, or ship at all? There are no clues. To the south-east are the Ballymeanoch stone rows, in which half of the surviving megaliths are almost covered in cups-and-rings. North of Ri Cruin were three pairs of standing stones within a stone ring. The surviving monolith of the central pair has many cups and a few cups-and-rings. Beyond them is a Bronze Age cairn with two cists. The smaller had a cup on one slab. Did cups signify the moon and the rings the sun? Were cups more associated with night and death? We do not know, and nor do we know why the little megalithic ring just to the west has a double spiral on its northernmost stone. Nor why the next cairn to the north contained a large cist with forty-one cups and ten axe-heads upon the underside of the capstone. They were apparently intended to give comfort or status to the occupant. Did the cups signify the longevity of the deceased and the axes wealth or military power? Or did each confer a spiritual benefit? It seems that only the dead can tell.

The other site is Stonehenge itself. The barrows around it contain objects clearly influenced by the fashions of Brittany, such as cups with knobbed decoration and gold-studded dagger hilts. One of the great trilithons inside (stone 53) bears a famous carving of a dagger and two axe-heads, the association of weapons being found in the Breton gallery graves and the axes being identical to Breton forms. Upon stones 29 and 57, on the western side of the inner sanctuary, are two outlines which may be images of the so-called 'death goddess' found on the western side of the same Breton gallery graves. From this, Aubrey Burl has speculated that the monument was concerned with funerary rites, associated with a goddess, as at least part of its functions.[26] Some might wonder even further, and ask whether the trilithons were not intended to be the thighs of this deity, from between which light is born. Such thoughts are justified, but unhappily not conclusive. The faint shapes on stones 29 and 57 do not look very like the images in the Breton tombs. One seems to be like a child's bib, perhaps reflecting the 'buckler' motif long used in Brittany but not in the British Isles. The plainest is a narrowing rectangle with a semicircle on top of the narrower side, like a briefcase seen from its end. It may just be taken as a stylized human, but there is not even a trace of breasts. Thus a fascinating line of enquiry has to be left as no more than an unsubstantiated proposal.

Another line of approach might be to ask whether, in an age so conscious of prestigious objects, the burials show any trace of a religious elite, distinguished from political and military leaders and from commoners by their trappings. Again, it is Aubrey Burl who has collected the available evidence. The most celebrated is from Upton Lovell in Wiltshire, where a round barrow covered an adult male skeleton with rows of thin, perforated bones about his neck, thighs and feet. They had almost certainly hung in fringes from his clothes. With him were fine stone axe-heads, boars' tusks, white flints and pebbles of a stone not found in the area. A similar mound at Youlgreave, Derbyshire, held a man with the teeth of a dog and a horse under his head and a round bronze amulet on his chest. With him were an axe, quartz pebbles and a piece of porphyry. The ashes of another burial from Rockbourne Down in Hampshire were mixed with four stained rectangular bronze tablets, one plain and the others incized with a cross or a star or a lozenge (Bronze Age tarot cards?). All these suggest the presence not so much of a priesthood as of shamans or medicine people, familiar in the tribal peoples of the modern world. Danish graves of about the same date contained individuals who could have been little else, their wallets filled with pieces of animal skeleton and dried plant without practical value, which could only have been for the working of magic.[27]

It is a little irritating that the English graves do not contain such certain evidence. Although the general import of the finds appears to be the same, the individuals concerned may have been given the items as charms, or prestigious possessions, or to assist their passage beyond death, rather than as signs of office. Some of these burials could have been those of political rather than of religious dignitaries, and indeed it is not clear that the distinction existed. Such problems are well illustrated by a round barrow at Garton Slack on the Yorkshire Wolds. It contained the skeleton of a youth with two quarts pebbles in the left hand, a joint of pork by one elbow and two boars' tusks in front of the face. Behind the head was a clay die, nearby were two balls of yellow ochre, and a tiny pot containing an animal, perhaps a rodent, was placed in the mouth. It seems likely that this lad was being given a large helping of culinary and magical equipment by a loving family or friends.[28] Another difficulty is posed by those Bronze Age burials which were placed in boats (really timber canoes) or boat-shaped graves. Examples are few, but spread across the whole island from Fife to Glamorgan and Gloucestershire.[29] It is natural to wonder whether these craft were not intended to carry the occupants into the next world, and the graves hewn into the forms of boats fit this idea especially well. On the other hand, the canoes may just have made convenient wooden coffins of the sort relatively common in areas without supplies of stone, and the small number and scattered distribution of 'boat burials' do not suggest a common belief. Boats do not occupy the same place in British rock art as they do in the Scandinavian. The gravegoods pose similar questions. Were boars' tusks prized ivory ornaments, hunting trophies and political insignia (as emblems of strength)? Or did they have a sacred significance?

So, we have strong but not conclusive evidence of a religion or religions in early Bronze Age Britain and Ireland, mediated by figures like tribal shamans and containing a cult of the sun and perhaps of the moon. An obvious way to trace this cult further is to examine the monuments for alignments upon heavenly bodies, and to this large subject we must at last proceed. It would be very odd indeed if such alignments had not existed. After all, as shown above, a large percentage of the mid-Neolithic tombs appear to have been built to face either or both the moon and the sun. Around 3200 BC, when round monuments came so markedly into fashion, wonderfully precise orientations were achieved at Newgrange, Maes Howe and the first structure on the site of Stonehenge. Modern anthropology adds weight to the supposition that the ancient British and Irish carried out astronomical observations. The Trobriand Islanders of the western Pacific were, by the standards of 'developed' nations, a very simple society in the 1920s, but they had an elementary astronomical calendar based upon the moon. Some of the world's most underdeveloped hunter–gatherer communities, such as the San, the native Australians and native Tasmanians, have regulated their year by similar observations of the heavens. The Pawnee tribe of North America kept charts of the stars. The Thonga of South Africa, the Mandaya of the Philippines and some native Brazilians all farmed in response to the movement of the Pleiades, as did (according to the Roman Pliny) the ancient Mediterranean peoples. The Mursi of Ethiopia, the Bafioti of Angola, the South African Xhosa and the North American Blackfeet all mixed a stellar and lunar calendar. In North America the Kawakiutl, Thompson and Haida tribes had one based upon moons and solstices, and the Zuni, Tewa and Hopi all carefully compiled solar calendars. In the Gilbert Islands of Polynesia the position of the sunrise was checked every ten days. But having said all this, anthropology also warns against making easy assumptions in the matter. The Trobriand Islanders did not ask questions about the sky or fit its bodies into their religious practices. The Andaman Islanders, Ibo of Nigeria, Abaluyia of Kenya and Fijians are all cases of tribal peoples who totally ignored the heavens. Nor does the existence of a lunar, solar or stellar calendar imply the existence of a group of astronomer--priests. The Polynesians had such people, but most of the different native American tribes cited did not. And none of them employed stone or timber circles for its observations.[30] So the expectation that the Bronze Age British and Irish were concerned with the sky is powerfully reinforced but not confirmed by modern parallels, and the nature of the concern is made no clearer.

Research into the question might have carried on in this cautious manner for a long time had it not been greatly accelerated, and perhaps wrenched out of context, by the work of Alexander Thom in the 1960s. This splendid Scot, a retired professor of engineering, carried out a large number of detailed surveys of stone circles and rows in the British Isles and France. He concluded, first, that the builders had used a standard unit of measurement, the 'megalithic yard', and had laid out the eggs, ellipses, true circles and other forms represented by the stone rings with deliberate and careful intention. Second, he asserted that virtually every site had functioned as an astronomical observatory, with stones aligned against natural or human features of the landscape to synchronize with the movements of the sun, the moon or individual stars. The association between Stonehenge and astronomical observation had been made by writers since the beginning of the century. Thom's own major publications were directly preceded by the work of Gerald Hawkins, who suggested that the great monument had (among other things) been used to predict ellipses. But the sheer scale of Professor Thom's investigations gave them an immense impact. Their implications were built upon in the 1970s by a fellow Scot, Euan MacKie, who suggested that the observations had been carried out by an intellectual and religious elite of the sort which had been possessed by the ancient Mayans. He speculated that the 'superhenges' might have been their monasteries or colleges and that they were part of an international prehistoric intelligentsia. Furthermore, at Kintraw in Argyll, where Thom had considered a standing stone to be aligned upon the midwinter sunset behind a mountain peak, Dr MacKie claimed to have found the observation platform. It was described as a stone terrace upon the hillside opposite to the mountain, which permitted a perfect alignment between megalith and peak.

Alexander Thom's assertions were received in silence by most mainstream prehistorians. This was mainly because they did not feel competent to reply to them. To do so required a training in archaeology, astronomy and statistics, and the specialists in the monuments concerned usually had only the first of these. On the other hand Professor Thom actually had none of them, and as a result made some obvious gaffes: the most celebrated was at Stonehenge, where of three sighting-mounds which he identified as being crucial to the alignments one was natural and two were modern. There were in addition certain problems with his theory which could be identified without expertise. A stone ring was a natural ceremonial precinct but a very unlikely mechanism for observations of the sky, for which a row or a few individual stones are better suited. There was moreover an utter lack of uniformity among alignments claimed for neighbouring monuments, which were held to be directed towards a great variety of different heavenly bodies at different phases. As soon as these were published, some people commented that if you pointed anything at the sky then it would hit a star or phase of the sun or moon sooner or later. Very often single stones in complexes would be declared to be markers, calling into question the purpose of all the other megaliths, or cairns, present. As for Dr MacKie's astronomer-priests, it was striking that societies which had possessed them, like the Mayans, also possessed writing, enabling them to record the observations made. Bronze Age Britain most certainly did not. Nor did the notion of monuments laid out with sophisticated geometry consort well with the apparent reality of many sites. A glance at the plans of Wessex superhenges will reveal that the classic shape is that of a battered car tyre. Either the builders of these vast enclosures could not produce something more symmetrical or else they were not bothered about the matter. Since the eighteenth century AD, mystics have been excited by the fact that the avenue from Avebury to the Sanctuary ripples like a great serpent. So it does, but it was constructed by driving forth a straight line in the general direction of the Sanctuary, stopping to check on progress, building another straight line to get on course again, and so forth. Most of the stone rows and those henges or rings which lie in a sequence are only very roughly in a straight line. Either this was a society of very slapdash surveyors, or else (more likely) precision of this sort was simply not important to those who raised the monuments.

By the end of the 1970s, the collusion between archaeologists, astronomers and statisticians necessary to consider Alexander Thom's work had begun. By now he was dead and unable to answer his critics, but perhaps it was just as well that he was thereby spared what ensued. John Barnatt and Gordon Moir noticed that rings which Professor Thom's surveys had revealed to be eggs or ellipses actually looked circular to the eye. Dr Barnatt experimented by getting students to lay out circles purely by eye, and found the result was a set of shapes which appeared perfectly round to the builder but turned out to be eggs or ellipses when surveyed. The builders of the prehistoric rings, far from using pegs and ropes with marvellous precison, may in most cases not have used them at all, but set up rings which looked like circles and been happy with the result. J. D. Patrick and C. S. Wallace ran a statistical analysis of this problem, and concluded that it was 780 times more likely that the rings which were not true circles had been laid out by eye than not. Meanwhile the mathematician Douglas Heggie tested Thom's geometry and pronounced it faulty. He left the possibility that there had been such a unit as the 'megalithic yard', but thought that the odds were against this. A further count against the Thom view was that there was no trace among any British prehistoric finds of anything like a measuring rod, even among the wooden objects preserved in bogs. Indeed, this was true of all western and central Europe, save for one single and doubtful case, a notched stick from peatland in Denmark.[31] As a result of all this, only a few faithful enthusiasts, virtually none of them academic scholars, still accept the reality of Alexander Thom's sacred geometry. A more fruitful line of approach appears to have been that of Aubrey Burl, who suggestd that long barrows and stone rings in different areas were constructed upon different counting bases. These, he proposes, altered over time as well as space. Thus, the last long barrows in the Avebury area were built by piling chalk within twenty-one and twenty-seven small enclosures of hurdle fences respectively, suggesting a counting base of three. The early stages of the Sanctuary, over a mile away but half a millennium later, seem to have been built on a counting base of four.[32] This theory would correspond better to all that we now know of the intense regionalization of monument-building in the prehistoric British Isles.

The evidence for Thom's argument that the rings and rows were observatories for scientific astronomy rested upon the alignments which he had drawn from them to the moon and to the rising of specific stars. By 1982 these, too, had been subjected to detailed criticism. Because stars move around, to prove that one was in alignment with a megalith when the latter was raised it was necessary to know the exact date of the stone's erection. This is, of course, impossible to fix by any current or foreseeable methods. Thom's own estimations were all wildly wrong because they preceded the great revision made in the rough dating of prehistoric monuments following the correction of the Carbon 14 process. Thus all his stellar alignments have to be rejected, and nobody is anxious to replace them because of the impossibility of proof. As for his lunar alignments, the whole body of them was considered by the scientific astronomer Clive Ruggles, who found half to be either dubious or impossible and most of the rest unprovable. He noted that as Thom selected his monuments, his ways of surveying them and his foresights, it was very easy for him to come up with alignments, as a typical set of megaliths in hills or mountains would have hundreds of features on the horizon which could coincide with lunar movements. Douglas Heggie considered this problem from the point of view of a statistician, and declared that it made all Thom's lunar sightings inadmissible. Gordon Moir added valid but by now almost superfluous comments to the case for the prosecution, noting that Thom had misreported the features on the horizon of certain sites, ignoring those of no value to his case and including some which could not be seen with the naked eye.[33] As a result of all this, Alexander Thom's belief in the existence of scientific astronomy in British and Irish prehistory is now only shared by his family, by Euan MacKie and by a handful of admirers outside academe, most of whom do not seem to be aware of the case against it. Dr MacKie's own claims for the site at Kintraw foundered in an argument over whether the 'observation platform' was not in fact a natural feature, and whether the midwinter sunset could be seen from it.[34]

In 1988 three of Thom's defenders staged a gallant rearguard action by suggesting that the famous gold lozenge found on the chest of a male burial at Bush Barrow, near Stonehenge, was actually a long-term astronomical record. They interpreted its markings as representing the directions of significant solar and lunar events, and a direct reply has yet to be published.[35] At the risk of impertinence, it might be considered easy to predict the form of such a reply: that their reading of the markings is susceptible neither of proof nor disproof, but that all the other counts against the Thom thesis make it extremely unlikely. Nevertheless, any prehistorian has reason to be grateful that Alexander Thom lived and worked. It is not merely that he was a magnificent personality, nor that he greatly stimulated interest in this aspect of prehistory. It is also because he was, pre-eminently, a first-rate engineer, and most of the plans which he made of so many monuments are not merely excellent, but in many cases the only such surveys that we have.

So what *can* now be said about the relationship between early Bronze Age ritual monuments and heavenly bodies? Most stone rings and rows and all surviving 'coves' do not provide any obvious alignments upon either moon or sun, and the problem of determining whether they referred to stars is insuperable. The tribal peoples of the present century who made stellar calendars were in any case all interested in constellations, not individual stars. The two greatest stone rings of all present precisely opposite difficulties in this respect. At Avebury too many megaliths have vanished to provide modern investigators with experimental sightlines, and the great bank blocks off the horizon around much of the circuit. Those who have tried to determine its astronomical significance have been discouraged by the problems presented. At Stonehenge, by contrast, far too many astronomers have found alignments to their own satisfaction: at least 112 have been identified, by various people, from the centre of the monument. Some theories can be invalidated from the archaeology; Gerald Hawkins's proposal that the Aubrey Holes were used to predict eclipses was made on the assumption that they were contemporary with the great stones, whereas in fact they are much earlier. But far too many cannot be tested, and many are mutually incompatible. Was the Heel Stone a backsight for an alignment through the post-holes now under the car park (as Peter Newham says)? Or a foresight for the full moon-rise nearest to the winter solstice (as Jack Robinson says)? Most authorities accept that it formed one of a pair which flanked the entrance and between which the midsummer sun was framed just as it cleared the horizon. But now Aubrey Burl has thrown this too into question, by suggesting that the empty socket on the opposite side of the original entrance contained not the twin of the Heel Stone but the Heel Stone itself, which was moved to indicate more accurately the rising of the moon, not the sun. In Dr Burl's scheme, the total of fifty-four post-holes found in front of the entrance once held temporary markers aligned with the various points at which the moon rose in successive months. He suggests that the southern entrance pointed towards the place at which it was highest in the sky. There is now not a single astronomical aspect of the monument upon which scholars are firmly agreed.[36]

Something which *has* commanded general agreement in the 1980s has been the suggestion that it is best to study the celestial alignments of monuments of a particular type or grouped together in particular areas. Most complete has been the study made by the ubiquitous Aubrey Burl, of two successive groups of monuments in north-east Scotland, the Clava Cairns and the recumbent stone circles. The passages and entrances to the former, tombs roughly contemporary with the developed passage graves, virtually all face the south-west quadrant. The span which they represent is too wide for sunsets at significant times such as solstices and equinoxes, but covers the major and minor lunar standstills. The stone rings, built perhaps a millennium later, all have their recumbent stones in the south-

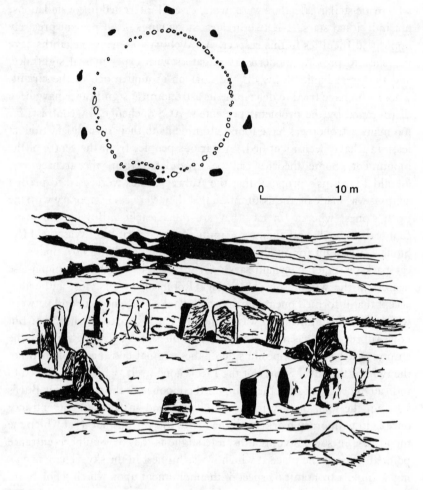

FIGURE 4.3   Recumbent stone circles
a Plan of Loanhead of Daviot (Grampian): the black shapes mark the uprights
of the ring, the white shapes mark the periphery of the ring cairn within it;
b Drombeg Circle (Co. Cork) at the present day.
Source: a redrawn after Kilbride-Jones.

south-east to south-west sector. None was aligned upon the midwinter
sunset, but they do all cover the moon's movements and the moon's orb
would have been framed between the two flanking megaliths as it passed
over the recumbent stone. Dr Burl suggested from these data that the
ceremonies might have been monthly, and nocturnal. He went on to

speculate that the similar stone rings in south-western Ireland could have been constructed for the same purpose, while the entrances of the wedge graves, which face a narrower sector in the south-west, could have been aligned upon the sunset at the opening of winter. If the rings in Counties Cork and Kerry were for lunar rituals, and the wedge graves for solar rituals, an explanation would be provided for the co-existence of those two kinds of monument.[37]

What emerges from this splendid piece of imaginative deduction is that these groups of monuments must have been built to incorporate some features of the sky into their symbolism or rites. But Dr Burl's suggestions, intelligent and carefully considered as they undoubtedly are, present only considerable possibilities. Rodney Castleden has pointed out that the recumbent stones may have been facing the sun at the warmest time of the day. It must be a matter of preference whether one wants to believe in a lunar or a solar orientation, or both. The moon is easier to contemplate, undergoes more dramatic regular changes and is associated with the night and so (arguably) with mystery and with the dead; the sun is far more obviously in these latitudes the bringer of comfort and life. Likewise, the Clava Cairns may have faced either particular phases of the moon or else the sunset (in general, rather than at particular points of the year). Ann Lynch has made a separate study of the stone rings of Counties Cork and Kerry, and come up with another set of answers. According to one set of criteria, eleven of the thirty-seven surviving rings might have been aligned upon the sky; three on the southern lunar maximum, three on the midwinter sunset, one on the northern lunar maximum, one on the midsummer sunset and so forth. But a different set of critera yielded twenty-three possible alignments, thirteen upon lunar standstills and ten upon solstice sunrises or sunsets.[38] It may be that studying groups of monuments is not going to yield very much more conclusive data than Alexander Thom's methods.

One is left with a sense that celestial events were important in the design as well as the use of a great many stone rings, and that the south-western quadrant was particularly important. Long Meg and her Daughters (in Cumbria) has one entrance in line with the midwinter sunset. Ballynoes (in County Down) has an entrance to the west-south-west, as do the Druids Circle in Gwynedd and the Stipple Stones on Bodmin Moor. Several Cornish rings have their tallest stone at that point, as does the Beltany Ring in County Donegal. The Lios circle in County Limerick has two huge megaliths framing it, opposite the entrance. It has been suggested that what lies at this point may be the sunset

on 31 October, commencing the greatest festival of the Iron Age Irish
year and perhaps that of earlier periods.[39] But the individual alignments
are rather imprecise and we may be in danger of repeating the technique
condemned in Thom of grouping together widely scattered sites, ignoring
the other rings in their respective regions and making the observations
from a range of features within the selected monuments. After such an
enormous amount of work, it appears that the early Bronze Age ritual
monuments can only be related to the sky with as many qualifications,
exceptions and puzzles as the Neolithic tombs can be. None of them displays
any synchronization of earth with heaven as stunning as that at Newgrange.

The ideas of Alexander Thom and Euan MacKie, however transient in
their effect upon academic prehistory, did have a more enduring impact
and win less critical followers in the parallel world of 'alternative
archaeology' or 'earth mysteries'. It is with the late Neolithic and early
Bronze Age, the time of the stone circles, that the writers of this world are
most concerned, and thus it is most appropriate to accord them full
consideration at this point. Professional prehistorians find the beliefs of
'earth mystics' at best irrelevant and at worst completely misguided, and
they have been rather at a loss in knowing how to cope with them. Some
attempt to refute their assertions, but too often this is done with a few
contemptuous phrases, thrown out in consideration of other matters and
doing no justice to the ideas involved. One or two scholars, like
Christopher Chippindale, prefer to state the views of 'alternative' writers
in a separate section, politely and without further comment. 'Earth
mystics' therefore deserve some sympathy for their claim that orthodox
prehistorians do not attempt to engage with them directly, even though
many academic scholars may believe that this neglect actually stems from
tact and from charity. But as the purpose of this book is largely to portray
and to criticize, to a wider audience, ideas and data often only known so
far to specialists, it would be disgraceful not to accord the same privilege
to the 'earth mysteries'.

As they themselves are often at pains to point out, 'earth mystics' and
'alternative archaeologists' hold a wide range of beliefs. Yet it is still
possible to identify certain common characteristics. One is an intense
sense of the romance and beauty of the prehistoric past and an equally
profound impulse to identify personally with it. A passage from Paul
Devereux and Ian Thompson is entirely typical:

During the fieldwork for this book, we camped alongsde a tumulus on a ley
in idyllic countryside. A full moon rose, silhouetting the mound. Such was

the sense of primordial power and kinship with our remote ancestors that there could not be a moment's doubt concerning our work. While mathematicians and certain archaeologists baulk at such reactions, others will recognise the validity of our experience.[40]

But then, most academic prehistorians have had that sort of experience too: it is one of the reasons for their choice of career. What marks off the 'alternative' researchers is that they tend to couple this love of the past with a distaste for the present world, or at least for many features of it. Messrs Devereux and Thompson refer elsewhere in the same work to the pernicious and spiritually debilitating 'urban consciousness' of current society. Michael Dames laments 'the modern primitivism of false alternatives'. John Michell has written that 'the history of our era is one of continuous defeat for those groups and individuals who have attempted to reverse the flowing tide of ignorance, superstition and arbitrary violence'.[41] The essence of 'earth mysteries' lies in the belief that by gaining access to the wisdom of an older world, one can redeem the shortcomings of the present. Indeed, some think that the past may contain the means to save our planet from military and ecological destruction. On this I may quote Nigel Pennick and Paul Devereux: 'The need to examine the fundamentals of geomancy for the wisdom they impart has never been more relevant than now, at the end of the twentieth century, as we face increasing ecological, social and environmental ills.'[42] Or Michael Dames: 'Uneasy about a rationale which can glibly justify poisoning the planet for the sake of a brief spasm of "peaceful" nuclear energy, we start to hanker after stability and wholeness not least because we want to survive. Therefore walking the avenue [to Avebury], we may come across the ancient circular reality again.'[43] Or John Michell: 'As everybody knows, the earth is slowly dying of poison, a process whose continuation is inevitably associated with many fundamental assumptions of the modern technological civilization. . . . Through the rediscovery of access to divine law, revealed in the processes of natural growth and movement, the principles of true spiritual science may be re-established.'[44]

Another common trait among 'alternative' archaeologists is an antipathy towards orthodox institutions and social norms. Some have particular detestations, common targets being the Christian Church, patriarchy and capitalism. Indeed, many belong to a 'counter-culture', most notably that associated with the intellectual wing of the youth movement of the late 1960s. A great many prefer an 'alternative' lifestyle in general, and a great many earth mystics are mystics in a broader sense. While they tend in the main to have clearly defined dislikes, there is also a great eclectism in their work, arising from an instinct that humanity is fundamentally a whole. Thus there is often very little sense of historical distance in the way in which earth mystics relate to prehistoric peoples, and the careful distinctions of place and period made by scholarly prehistorians mean little to them. Equally, they are likely to group together beliefs and practices associated with peoples dispersed over the globe as well as in time, as if they possessed natural affinity. 'Alternative' researchers often express impatience with the reluctance of modern orthodox scholars to make leaps of the imagination, and their tendency to announce that a problem is insoluble in default of better evidence.[45] To most 'alternative' archaeologists, it is absolutely correct to offer imaginative interpretations of an apparently insoluble problem: indeed, many would, therefore, not see that there was a problem. The preferred interpretation for each group is that which appears most beneficial to humanity as its needs are conceived by that group. It is the one which appears most logically and instinctually correct: in New Age parlance, the one which 'works'. After all, if a large part of the point of searching for the ancient wisdom is to reactivate it, 'working' can be taken quite literally. In comprehending the impact of Michael Dames's book about Silbury Hill in 'alternative' circles, it is important not merely to understand that he provides an interpretation of Silbury and a portrait of Neolithic society which tells those circles, confidently, all that they most want to hear. It is also that he sets forth his vision of the ritual performed upon Silbury with an invitation to his readers to try it for themselves. And so, to great personal satisfaction, many have done.

Nevertheless, despite these common characteristics, earth mystics do differ considerably in their interests, and not all are amenable to a dialogue with orthodox scholarship – or, indeed, with anything else. Those in this latter class are wedded to ideas which are demonstrably wrong, or which depend upon personal beliefs belonging to the sphere of religion rather than of archaeology. They include people who insist that prehistoric ritual monuments were raised by Phoenicians, Egyptians, or the inhabitants of Atlantis or of outer space. Even reckoned together there are now very few of these. But there are also those who believe that ancient people speak to them directly, and such individuals are rather common in the 'New Age' sector of 'alternative' archaeology. Most of the views held by people who consider themselves to be earth mystics, however, are susceptible to discussion. Broadly, they fall into three overlapping groups. There are those who believe in the golden age of the Goddess, discussed earlier. There are those who believe that prehistoric peoples devised a system of wisdom which descended to historic times and is discernible in ancient mystical literatures. Some credit groups such as the Gnostic writers, the Cathars, the Knights Templar and the 'Culdees' of the early Christian Church as being bearers of this secret knowledge. And there are those concerned with earth energies, especially those embodied in the alignments known as 'leys', or, more popularly (though, it seems, incorrectly), 'ley-lines'.

The idea that old sacred sites migh have been constructed in alignment with each other probably goes back to the Revd Edward Duke, who wrote in 1846 that medieval churches and prehistoric monuments seemed to form straight lines upon the map. The idea resurfaced at times in England during the late nineteenth and early twentieth centuries, and appeared in Germany in 1909, but its systematic propagation began with Alfred Watkins in 1921.[46] Watkins, a Herefordshire businessman, conceived the notion of the Old Straight Track, a network of completely straight roads used by traders and travellers in early England and aligned through a variety of prehistoric, Roman and medieval monuments. To these he gave, with some doubts, the name 'leys'. His writings inspired a small band of enthusiasts, who spent much time drawing lines between a great variety of old sites upon maps to discover more of these putative roads. But the logical and practical difficulties of imagining medieval traders trundling straight through swamps, rivers and a host of other obstacles, and a natural weariness with a spent enthusiasm, brought about a virtual demise of 'ley-hunting' by the 1950s. Its revival in the next decade came as a result of the enthusiasm of a group of people primarily concerned with flying saucers (flying saucers, not Unidentified Flying Objects, as most of these individuals were quite certain that UFOs were visiting spacecraft). These took up the idea of Watkins's leys as magnetic paths for the spaceships and gave it a wider currency, but there seems little doubt that the great popularity of the concept of alignment among the 'counter-culture' resulted from the publication of John Michell's book *The View Over Atlantis* in 1969. Indeed, this work was almost the founding document of the modern earth mysteries movement. Mr Michell is an admirer, and to some extent a reincarnation, of the free-thinking English gentleman-scholars of the eighteenth century. That a notion is rejected by mainstream scholarship is in itself a recommendation to him, and a man who gives his books titles like *The View Over Atlantis* or *Flying Saucer*

Vision is deliberately not bidding for the attention of academics. The former work lay in the tradition of those seeking to reveal a lost wisdom of the ancients, and his particular service to the development of ley ideology was to equate leys with the Chinese dragon-paths or *lung mei*. These were also 'old straight tracks', but made by greater forces than Watkins's human surveyors and for greater purposes. They were believed to carry divine spiritual energy across the face of the earth. By suggesting that the alignments which Watkins and his followers had drawn between British monuments were actually energy-flows of the Chinese sort, John Michell made 'geomancy' a central feature of 'alternative' archaeology in Britain and America.

The idea developed rapidly all through the 1970s. Almost simultaneously with *The View Over Atlantis* appeared the posthumous work of the dowser Guy Underwood, who claimed to have found a 'blind spring', of water welling up from deep in the earth, concealed under the centre of every stone circle which he tested. This news became blended with the idea of *lung mei* to reinforce the notion of prehistoric sacred sites as meeting places for great natural forces, and added the idea that the energy flows, like water, could be traced by dowsing. One such dowser was Tom Graves, who borrowed another Chinese concept, this time that of acupuncture, to suggest that the megaliths of prehistoric sites were actually stone needles designed to regulate the energies. By the end of 1970s it was widely accepted among earth mystics that dowsing could be used as a tool for 'spiritual growth' and the 'raising of consciousness' and that this process was enhanced if carried out at prehistoric sacred places.[47] In the mid–1970s John Michell published a detailed local case study intended to prove the existence of alignments between prehistoric monuments. He chose the West Penwith district of Cornwall, the westernmost peninsula of Britain, and produced an interlocking web of leys representing dozens of sites. It was certainly the finest piece of surveying work hitherto undertaken by an 'alternative' archaeologist, and made a case worth answering by others.[48] And the books of Alexander Thom and Euan MacKie greatly encouraged earth mystics, because their vision of a prehistoric society guided by sophisticated astronomer-priests harmonized with the dream of ancient wisdom which the mystics pursued.

During the 1980s, 'alternative' archaeology has continued to flourish under the momentum of the earlier publications. But there are signs of an alteration of mood among some of its practitioners. The decisive academic rejection of scientific astronomy in prehistory has destroyed earlier hopes that mainstream scholarship would look more indulgently upon the earth mystics. The Dragon Project, founded in the 1970s to demonstrate beyond doubt the energy-channelling nature of ancient sites, has produced data capable of impressing only the converted. An important development was signalled by the publication in 1989 of *Lines on the Landscape* by Nigel Pennick and Paul Devereux. This is by far the most well researched, intelligently written and beautifully produced work yet published on leys, and it has two major objectives. One is to attempt, once again, to offer orthodox prehistorians a case which is so soberly and thoroughly argued that it is at least worth contesting. The other is to dissociate the authors' branch of the 'earth mysteries' from those whom they describe rather brutally as '"New Age" cultists, would-be gurus, "soft" or popular theoreticians and journalistic hacks'.[49] In particular, this means that they reject the notion of leys as energy lines, because the only way to demonstrate the reality of such energies is through the rods of dowsers who are themselves believers. As a result, they argue, the way is open for people to impose all manner of personal prejudices upon monuments which need to be studied objectively if anything is to be learned from them. How far the enunciation of such views indicates a genuine split in 'alternative' archaeology, and the end of its former easy-going camaraderie, cannot yet be decided.

Such, then, is the modern study of earth mysteries. Before assessing its value, it is worth briefly tracing its intellectual origins. To a very great extent it is bound up with the romanticism of the late 1960s, and may be characterized as the archaeological dimension of that counter-culture. But it draws upon a heterogeneous group of traditions, some considerably older. One is that of the 'pseudo-Celticism' to be discussed in the next chapter. Another is academic archaeology, although as so few earth mystics have access to copyright libraries, university departments or archaeological institutes, their notion of mainstream scholarship is often as hazy as the latter's notion of them. Another seems to begin with an Austrian academic called Joseph von Hammer-Purgstell, who was employed to write propaganda by the reactionary Chancellor Metternich. In 1818 he published a book purporting to expose a link between the Gnosts, the Cathars, the Knights Templar, the Freemasons and the French Revolutionaries, whom he claimed to represent the same conspiracy to subvert Church and state, extending over two thousand years. A minimum of research on the part of Hammer-Purgstell's enemies, the early nineteenth-century political radicals, would have destroyed his chain of argument. But they found it easier and more effective to hijack it, turning all the groups he condemned into heroes, bearing the creed of liberty through centuries of persecution. A further elaboration of the same myth was made by a Frenchman in minor religious orders, one Alphonse-Louis Constant, who wrote under the name of 'Eliphas Levi'. His contribution was to assure readers that what these same groups were handing down was not simply an ideal of liberty but a pre-Christian mystic wisdom rooted in Egyptian and Hebrew occult practice. It was this creed, together with the system of magic developed by Levi and passed off by him as 'ancient hidden wisdom', which was further elaborated by the late nineteenth-century occult groups such as the Golden Dawn and the Theosophy Society. Through them it survived to become part of the inspiration of modern writers such as John Michell. But the methodology of these writers draws heavily upon yet another source, represented by those scholars of the late nineteenth and early twentieth centuries who must be reckoned among the founders of the science of anthropology. Sir James Frazer may be accounted the most celebrated at one end of this time span, and Claude Lévi-Strauss at the other. To these authors, there existed certain rules of primitive religion which applied equally to tribal peoples at all places and times. Thus it was perfectly intellectually respectable to select customs recorded in Ireland, Borneo and Canada and to consider them to be part of the same phenomenon and contributing in turn to our knowledge of places and periods from which no such records survive. This technique eventually died out in British academe, but has survived to the present day in America, in the work of such very different authors as Joseph Campbell and Mircea Eliade.

Clearly, then, the intellectual antecedents of 'alternative' archaeology include traditions which are part of the heritage of orthodox scholarship itself. So why is the academic establishment so hostile to the modern earth mystics? The brief answer is that the overlap is only partial, and the elements of the past which both have in common are precisely those of which modern academics are most ashamed and which they are most eager to reject. The current scholarly world contains many people who share the earth mystics' fears for the modern world, and a few who are members of the same counter-culture, but none who *set out* to impose their world-picture upon the past; rather, they seek instead to work with scholars of all ideologies to achieve knowledge which is based upon evidence acceptable to all. If leaders of academe within living memory can, in fact, be seen to have made pronouncements which far outran the evidence (as in the matter of the Mother Goddess), then their successors are the more anxious not to repeat the fault. Part of the new rigour towards evidence consists of a strong sense of the very different ways in which superficially similar monuments and rituals can operate, given different societies. It is the separate and distinct nature of peoples, places and periods which has been emphasized by mainstream scholarship of late, thereby striking both at a fundamental principle of the earth mysteries and at an important part of the methodology of 'alternative' archaeologists. This may be compared to a solution to the problem of what to do with a jigsaw puzzle from which most of the pieces are missing. The modern academic scholar has simply to accept the fact that most of the pattern has probably gone. The 'alternative' researcher will very often take pieces from many other jigsaws, usually snipping them into shape and daubing them into shade if they do not make an immediate fit with that being 'reconstructed'.

An example of this technique which has already been considered is Michael Dames's interpretation of Silbury as a Lammas 'harvest hill'. Another which can be quickly appraised was devised by Alfred Watkins and copied by John Michell: 'Hermes, known to the Egyptians as Thoth, to the Gauls as Theutates, the name surviving in numerous Tot or Toot hills all over England'. In this way Mr Watkins 'uncovered' the name of the deity who presided over the leys.[50] Now, the identification of Hermes with Thoth was indeed made in antiquity. And Teutates (to spell it correctly) was a Gaulish divine name which one commentator thought might be identified with Mercury (the Roman equivalent of Hermes) or with Mars. But forty-four other Gaulish deities were identified positively with Mercury, and Teutates seems to have been not a personality but the title given to the various protective gods of the tribes of eastern France. Toot is just a Saxon dialect word meaning a small hill, evolved by Germanic peoples different from the Gauls who coined 'Teutates'. The three words have, in fact, nothing on common except their sound. By an equally simple means one might conflate Thoth, Thor, Tor and thorn to 'prove' that Glastonbury and much of Dartmoor were once the scene of ancient pan-European rites, involving tree worship on hills. But here I am in danger of being accused of delivering one of those contemptuous asides which I have already described as being an unworthy response from orthodox to unorthodox scholarship. A more extended case study is required, and for it I am going to concentrate upon the attitude of modern earth mystics to dragons.

The English word dragon is a translation of a Latin term, used in the Middle Ages to describe the fire-breathing, flying reptilian monster of Scandinavian and Germanic myth. In that myth, these creatures feature as

threats to humankind, to be slain by heroes, and they entered the pan-
European medieval imagination in that guise. They did not exist in
ancient Celtic, or Roman or Greek mythology, although human-eating
serpent-like monsters (often dwelling in water) did. Nor were they found
in ancient Egypt, where the closest equivalent, the crocodile, had positive
sacred associations. But in the Babylonian creation myth, the earth
goddess Tiamat assumed the form of a mighty lizard (usually translated as
'dragon' by English writers) and in that guise was killed by the hero
Marduk. The Chinese, by contrast, have always believed in great lizard-
like winged beasts very similar in form to the north European dragon and
therefore described as 'dragons' by English-speakers. Their legendary
function, however, is quite different, for they are viewed as vessels of
great spiritual power, very often beneficial to humanity. When John
Michell transplanted the tradition of *lung mei*, 'dragon-paths', to the
English landscape, he had to reckon with the fact that in English tradition
dragons were regarded as destructive monsters. He did so by superimposing
Chinese upon English myth so that the English dragon-slaying heroes
were turned into villains, striking symbolically at the sacred forces
represented by the *lung mei* or leys. Feminist writers and artists among the
earth mystics brought in the myth of Tiamat and Marduk to suggest that
both Babylonian and Germanic dragon-slaying stories were folk-
memories of the destruction of matriarchal religions and societies by
militaristic patriarchical brutes. By the mid–1970s it was a widespread
creed among 'alternative' archaeologists that wherever dragons were
mentioned, across the world, they were the symbol of the Earth Mother
and her energies. Thus, when contemplating statues, paintings or stories
of medieval heroes who rid a countryside of a dragon, the sympathies of
the onlooker had to be reversed. This well-rounded picture draws upon
Scandinavian, Germanic, Chinese and Babylonian myth. But it would not
have been recognizable to the Vikings, or the Germans, or the Chinese,
or the Babylonians, let alone to other ancient peoples. It is a modern
mythology, constructed by a process which may be compared to the
looting of stonework from ruined buildings of several different kinds and
ages in order to put up a brand new cathedral.

    This then, is one major aspect of the methodology of much 'alternative'
archaeology which is quite unacceptable to orthodox scholarship. Another
consists of straightforward perversion of truth or statements of pure
untruth. Both occur even in work by a distinguished earth mysteries
writer like John Michell, who informs his readers that traces of a great
prehistoric sea wall survive upon the coasts of Essex and Kent. He states

this as a well-known fact requiring no evidence, and thereby escapes the reality that no evidence for it seems to exist. He likewise states that excavators of Roman roads have found roads beneath which are equally fine or even finer. Who these excavators were is not mentioned, and they appear, again, to be a poetic invention.[51] It is well known to historians that Richard Whiting, last Abbot of Glastonbury, was executed in 1539 on a trumped-up charge of trying to conceal abbey treasures from the Crown. The evidence was a goblet said to have been found hidden by him in a chest. Mr Michell distorts this celebrated story by telling his readers that Whiting died for refusing to give up the ancient mystical treasures of the abbey, which have been concealed ever since.[52] But all this, disturbing though it may be to more conscientious scholars, does not justify rejecting all John Michell's work out of hand. It might still be that moments of mere tale-spinning do conceal others of genuine insight. I would say at once that I am not wholly qualified myself to determine how far this is the case, because Mr Michell's enthusiasms are too wide-ranging to be the province of any one specialist. For example, I lack the mathematical ability to comment upon his long passages on systems of sacred numbers. All I can say is that virtually all his work within my own provinces of history and prehistory is as unacceptable to an academic as those examples I have cited – even that most admired by his followers for its apparent objectivity, namely his study of the monuments of West Penwith. Within the 98 square miles of the area which he selected for his study are or were eighty standing stones and 300 barrows, in addition to several chambered tombs and several stone rings. There is thus already a high probability that somebody could draw straight lines through a map of this district and hit a large number of prehistoric sites with each, purely by chance. But Mr Michell compounds this chance by admitting to his sample all the 150 medieval crosses recorded in West Penwith. Many of these are now considered to date from between AD 1300 and 1500, a thousand years after the Christianization of Cornwall, but Mr Michell admits them all upon the grounds that any might mark a pagan holy place or be itself a reworked prehistoric standing stone. So it is unsurprising, and impressive or instructive to nobody but devoted earth mystics, that he came up with a large number of 'alignments'. A pair of statisticians subsequently ran a computerized study of them and equally unsurprisingly came up with the possibility that many of them could have been produced by chance. But to a conscientious prehistorian the whole study was inadmissible from the start, for John Michell had not considered all the prehistoric monuments of West Penwith, or even all those in the area dating up to the sixteenth century AD, but a selection of sites, from many different periods, which happened to fit his theory best.[53] But then, in doing so, he had only been following the practice of most 'ley-hunters'.

There are lots of reasons why orthodox scholarship is hostile to the concept of 'leys'. Even the word itself seems irritatingly inappropriate, and Watkins was well justified in having qualms about its use. It is perfectly plain, from both place names and literature, that ley is the Anglo-Saxon word for a significant cleared space. The early English would never have employed it to signify a line, and Watkins only adopted it because it occurred in names along his Old Straight Tracks and he needed a handy term for the latter. The concept of a series of perfectly straight tracks of uniform kind running across the prehistoric landscape is also unlikely to a person steeped in what is known about prehistory. Much of the picture built up in this book, of intense local regionalism, profound changes in tradition over time and rough-and-ready surveying methods, suggests a world in which the great ley system would have had no place. When prehistoric ritual monuments were put in a line, it was generally a straggling one. But then, nobody who believes in leys has ever been able to base a case upon prehistoric sites alone. It is so blatantly obvious that most megalithic tombs, stone rings, barrow cemeteries and henges are not in alignment with one another that the whole concept depends upon bringing in monuments of other ages. The classic ley recognized by *The Ley-Hunter* and similar publications consists of one or two Neolithic or Bronze Age monuments of very disparate kind and often minor importance, plus one or two Iron Age forts and a string of medieval parish churches. Indeed, once the churches are subtracted virtually all such alignments disintegrate.

In trying to cope with this problem, those who believe in leys have suggested two very different answers. One is that the churches (and medieval cathedrals) were built by people who still understood the prehistoric system of wisdom regarding earth energies and chose deliberately to put their sacred places upon leys.[54] According to this school of thought, this understanding was systematically destroyed in the course of the late medieval and early modern periods by persecution carried on by the leaders of the church and state. In this way most knowledge of leys and of 'spiritual dowsing' was eradicated as those who held this knowledge were accused of witchcraft and heresy. Nobody with any real knowledge of early modern or medieval history can sustain this view. There is not a single mention of leys among the thousands of documents left by the highly literate people who ordered the building of medieval churches or who accused, tried and interrogated heretics or presumed witches. Nor is there among the many heretical writings, or works upon magic, which have survived. Significantly, those proponents of leys who are read most widely, such as John Michell, Paul Devereux and Nigel Pennick, prefer a second explanation. They suggest that the knowledge of leys was lost before the end of prehistory but that medieval churches were positioned upon spots which had been sacred in prehistoric times, and thus conformed to the ley pattern. To test this hypothesis, all that is required is to excavate beneath those Iron Age and medieval structures which sit on presumed leys and to see if anything from an earlier period lies beneath. As this has not yet been done with sufficient regularity, the question of the existence of leys is ultimately an open one. But the likelihood that such a test would confirm the existence of such alignments seem small. The great majority of those Iron Age forts and medieval churches which have been excavated across Britain were not built over earlier structures. The citation by the three writers named above of several cases of the Christianization of pagan holy places fails to conceal the fact that these cases are exceptional. Nor will it make much impression upon orthodox scholarship to point out, as these three gentlemen do, that long straight tracks and sacred alignments did undoubtedly exist among the Chinese or different groups of native Americans. The fact that these structures, planned in widely separated places at very different dates, can be identified so easily makes it all the less likely that the British leys, which fail the tests of evidence passed by the foreign tracks, are imaginary.

But then, ancient earth energies have passed so far into the religous experience of the 'New Age' counter-culture of Europe and America that it is unlikely that any tests of evidence would bring about an end to belief in them. I have spoken to people who have been cured of medical ills by contact with prehistoric stone rings, who have felt physically or psychically attacked by ancient megaliths and who have endured crises and rebirths of faith in such places. Everything that Messrs Pennick and Devereux have recently written about the subjectivity of the concept of energy-bearing leys and its lack of utility to the advance of knowledge must be endorsed by any academic prehistorian. But I must suggest, perhaps presumptuously, that the sort of people whom they condemn, the '"New Age" cultists, would-be gurus,' etc., are precisely the natural constituency for those who believe in leys. It was the concept of these lines as bearers of energy-currents which made them so very attractive to many 'alternative' archaeologists. The stand taken by these two writers was based upon high moral probity and considerable common sense. It remains to be seen whether it has lost them a great many allies without winning them any new supporters.

At this point, many of my academic readers will be weary with me for having devoted so much space to writers to whom they attach no importance; and if any of my readers are earth mystics, they may well have given over the book by now. One could make a very good case for the statement that orthodox and 'alternative' prehistorians have nothing to say to each other. To many of the latter, academic scholars seem to take an unforgivably desiccated, limited and selfish view of the past. They appear in some ways to behave like priests who, quite incapable of saying anything conclusive about the nature of the past, persecute anybody else who ventures an idea about it. At least priests tend to follow a consistent line, whereas prehistorians are repeatedly proved wrong in both major and minor respects but then proceed simply to alter the orthodoxy without any sense that their right to crush unorthodoxy has been diminished. For their part, academic and institutional scholars can reply that at least they clean up their own mess. Each time an orthodox prehistorian has been exposed as wrong, it has been by a colleague or successor. Not a single idea from the earth mystics has succeeded in toppling an orthodoxy, not because the ideas of academic prehistorians are so powerful or well defended but because those of the earth mystics are so weak. Indeed, it is precisely as mystics that they can be said to have failed most. During the last twenty years thousands of hitherto unsuspected prehistoric monuments have been rediscovered by means of geophysical surveys and aerial photography. Not one has been found by all the psychics and dowsers who abound in 'alternative' archaeology. In most cases they have been content to focus upon more spectacular ones identified by scholars long ago. In a few, such as that of Glastonbury Tor, they claim to have recognized monuments which have so far not been confirmed by subsequent excavation.

And yet, it may still be suggested that the exchange has not been completely barren. 'Alternative' archaeologists, obviously enough, depend upon academic scholarship for their fundamental knowledge of prehistory. Conversely, a few facts may be gleaned from the earth mysteries. One of John Michell's alignments in West Penwith, through the Boscawen-Un stone ring to five other standing stones, does look convincing. So does the rough line in Yorkshire made by the Thornborough henges with that at Nunwick and the Devil's Arrows standing stones, first recognized by another ley-hunter.[55] More important is the fact that Mr Michell's work in West Penwith produced an excellent survey of the district, with an account of the monuments present and destroyed, which must of use to anyone studying the area. Likewise, a more recent book on the same district, by the artist Ian Cooke, though prefaced with an account of prehistory which is pure New Age fantasy, is a good guide to the sites themselves.[56] Nor can dowsing be completely written off by the academic. Archaeologists have successfully used dowsers in the past, while being reluctant to admit the fact in print. When Philip Rahtz admitted to employing one at Old Sarum in the 1960s, the Council for British Archaeology sent a sharp letter to the Ministry of Works (which sponsored the dig) deploring the use of such 'unscientific' devices. But a book by two eminent academics and a dowser, published in 1988, argues sensibly from case studies for the efficacy of dowsing in church archaeology; and it has produced some sympathetic responses in academe.[57] It would be not only ironic but very sad if the technique of geophysical survey were to render dowsing redundant just as it begins to become respectable.

But the most precious gift that earth mystics have to offer others may be that very capacity for fantasy which can be such a liability in the eyes of academic scholars. If prehistory is a time of which we do, in fact, know very little, then the more imaginative reconstructions which we possess of how things *might* have been, the better. To be of real value, such reconstructions need to be based upon the latest archaeological data and to make clear precisely where the data end and speculation begins. It is a difficult but not impossible set of rules for 'alternative' archaeologists to follow. A classic case which comes to mind is that of the first 'earth mysteries' writer to be considered in these pages, Michael Dames. Some of what Mr Dames writes is factually wrong because of misreading of the archaeological sources, such as his beliefs that the ditch at Avebury contained water and that the floor plan of the Sanctuary formed a winding pattern. A large part of his interpretation of the Avebury complex is based upon an application of the fourfold Celtic system of festivals, anchored on an identification of Silbury with Lughnasadh which has been criticized above. The climax of his vision is the discovery of a great figure of the Mother Goddess delineated by the Neolithic monuments and natural features of the Avebury area.[58] The trouble with this is that it is a matter of joining dots selectively upon a map. So many Neolithic sites and natural features have been recorded in this district that a great many different patterns can be 'discovered' by the same technique. I myself produced a perfectly nice unicorn by it, and thank Mr Dames warmly for

the sheer childish pleasure of that experience. But, when all is said, there
is about a one in a hundred chance that his vision is correct. This means
that if we had ninety-nine other reconstructions of the purposed design of
the Avebury complex, all based upon the available evidence, there is a
very good chance that one would be correct – even if we could not know
which. Unhappily, human nature being as it is, what we are likely to have
instead are ninety-nine followers of Mr Dames's vision.

Having now considered the early Bronze Age ritual monuments from
every angle, it is time to face up to the question of why they ceased not
merely to be built but to be used. The break which occurred in the course of
the Bronze Age appears to have been very dramatic. After about 1500 BC
there is no evidence that ceremonial centres of any kind were built
anywhere in the British Isles. By 1200 BC virtually all the existing ones
seem to have been abandoned, and even round barrows were ceasing to be
constructed. An attempt was made around 1350 BC to extend the avenue
which ran out of the north-east entrance of Stonehenge, but the work was
never completed. Shortly afterwards even this greatest of all British
monuments seems to have been deserted. In Ireland, the complex at
Beaghmore in Tyrone and the megalithic monuments of County Cork and
Kerry were still used, until c.900 BC, but these were the very last old-
style temples to retain respect.[59] After about 1500 BC any round barrows
that were still built became smaller and less impressive, all over the
British Isles. Urn cremations were regularly added to the existing
barrows, or buried in flat cemeteries. Both practices were carried on for a
very long time. At Kimpton, Hampshire, cremated bones were added to
what had begun as a late Neolithic cemetery around some great stones, to
achieve eventually a continuous use of the site from c.2100 to c.600 BC.
Within the Middle Bronze Age urn cemeteries, gravegoods were few and
poor and the burned bones pulverized, but distinctions were still possible:
some burials were upright or inverted, some sealed with a slab and some
marked with a post. The classic southern English pattern is a cluster of
ten to thirty urns with one among them marked out by goods or other
special treatment. The natural guess at the meaning of this is that they
were family plots, established around a founder. But after 1200 BC even
the urn cemeteries begin to vanish. In the British Isles, the late Bronze
Age, from c.1100 to c.600 BC, is a period apparently entirely destitute of
ceremonial monuments and almost without burials of any kind.[60] Over
3000 years of continuously developing tradition had, it seems, come to an
end. Society was neither poorer nor less industrious. The beauty of the
bronze and gold objects made in or imported into these islands between

c. 1500 and *c.* 600 BC is remarkable. In the first half of that period settlement sites and field walls were constructed which must have required just as much labour as henges, stone rings or barrows. Between 1200 and 1000 BC the first of the 'hill forts' which were to be such a notable feature of the Iron Age were built. It seems that the British and Irish had simply turned their backs upon the old sacred monuments, and perhaps upon the old sacred ways.

What we are looking at is something familiar to prehistorians and ancient historians, under the name of a 'systems collapse'. This is the phenomenon, found among early civilizations across the globe, of the rapid and complete disintegration of a long-lived and apparently formidable political and cultural bloc. It used to be attributed to invasion by outsiders, but in recent decades much more credit has been given to the capacity of prehistoric and early historic civilizations to fall to pieces as a result of internal stresses. In the case of the early Bronze Age British Isles, a number of different explanations have been offered for the great cultural changes which occurred. One is that the centres of population and of economic activity shifted to new regions as soils became impoverished in the old 'core areas' and as trade routes moved. This certainly happened. In the course of the Bronze Age many great traditional cultural centres, such as the south-western British uplands, Wessex, the upper Thames valley, the Cotswolds and the Norfolk Breckland, turned into backwaters. In their place, formerly peripheral areas, such as the south-western and southern coastal strips, the lower Thames valley and the Fens, became the most important centres of human activity.[61] But this shift in itself is no explanation of cultural change. Why did the new 'core areas' not reproduce the ritual monuments of the old, as when similar shifts of population occurred into the Upper Thames valley around 3200 BC or into the Welsh and south-western uplands around 2000 BC? A second current theory is that a change in the nature of society made monument-building obsolete. One version of this is that between *c.* 2600 and *c.* 1700 BC the focus of prestige switched from glamorous buildings to glamorous personal possessions.[62] Another is that more intensive agriculture, the result of growing population pressure and worsening farming conditions, consumed the human energy required for monument-building. This suggestion ascribes the apparent egalitarianism of the middle Bronze Age urn fields, with their lack of social or gender distinctions, to the construction of a 'group identity' appropriate to highly-organized farming.[63]

Both explanations beg more questions than they resolve in the matter of religious belief. Prestigious goods and prestigious monuments are not necessarily alternatives for flamboyantly self-assertive societies. Most have had both. The pioneers of agriculture probably faced as heavy a task in land clearance as their Bronze Age successors did in maintenance, but their priority in many places was to put up a great tomb–shrine. Indeed, one of the theories of explanation for the megalithic tombs, it may be remembered, is that societies under pressure tend to put up monuments. Nor were the people of the middle and late Bronze Age especially 'democratic': the quantity of contemporary weaponry and ornamental metalwork suggests a warrior elite of the sort which emerges into history a few centuries later.

Clearly we need to consider other sorts of explanation. One is that the Bronze Age suffered an ecological disaster profound enough to destroy faith in the traditional deities and rituals. Such a disaster certainly occurred. From about 1800 BC the climate of these islands began, very slowly and unevenly, to deteriorate. By the early Bronze Age it was probably still slightly warmer than it is today, having during the early Neolithic been more like that of the modern south of France. But from about 1400 BC the trend grew radically and consistently worse, the weather getting cooler and wetter until about 700 BC, beginning to recover again from *c.*500 BC onwards. The populations upon which this blow fell were relatively large, having by then cleared the woods from most of southern England, Wales, the northern uplands and much of Scotland and Ireland. Their farming methods had removed the roots which were needed to anchor the soil and to regulate the water table. By about 1400 BC the North Yorkshire Moors, which had only been settled a few centuries before, were already denuded of soil. By *c.*1200 BC the Cotswold valleys were collecting alluvium washed off the fields above. By 900 BC the south-west of Ireland was showing a steep decline in human activity and by 700 it had largely been abandoned. The compound effect of bad weather and bad farming turned large areas into heath, moor, bog and marsh equally useless to agriculture. Dartmoor, Bodmin Moor, the Pennines, the uplands of much of Wales and Ireland, the Fens, the Breckland, the Wessex Downs, the heathlands of Sussex, Hampshire and Dorset and much of the Scottish Highlands all assumed their later barren appearance at this time. In the case of the Highlands, the long-term problems were considerably worsened by a short-term disaster, the eruption of an Icelandic volcano in 1159 BC which showered ash over northern Scotland, sterilizing fields and further depressing the temperature by blocking out sunlight.[64] Many of these areas were precisely those which had been most given to the building of ceremonial monuments. Except in the case of the Highlands, the process of decline was too gradual for us to imagine crowds of demoralized and panic-stricken refugees streaming into less vulnerable districts. And our dating of it is as yet too imprecise (again, with the exception of northern Scotland), to judge whether the abandonment of the old ritual centres came before or after the change of climate. Over much of England, it undoubtedly began earlier. But the ecological factor is one which demands to be taken into consideration. So does another which, ironically, has been little considered for this period, when it might justly demand more attention than in others where it has been over-emphasized:[65] that of invasion. Between 1200 and 1000 BC, most of the civilizations of south-eastern Europe and the Near East collapsed violently, with much evidence of population movement. In central and northern Europe there are many archaeological traces of armoured warriors in these years, given increased striking-power by technical innovations such as the hafted spear and the sword. Both appeared in the British Isles at this time, along with defensive enclosures and copious proof of close cultural contacts between southern England and France. All this is no more decisive than the other evidence for and against prehistoric migration and invasion, and it occurs too late to explain the abandonment of monument-building in many regions. But it may, like the changes in the environment, have played a part. So, we are left with a clutch of possible reasons which are inadequate individually and even in total may not give us the whole picture. A large part of our problem is that many more of the early Bronze Age ritual centres have been surveyed than properly excavated in the past few decades. If we could discover when more of the stone rings were last used, then we may find that they, like some in Ireland and many round barrows and cairns, were still centres of attention until the time of climate change and possible invasion. Then we should be closer to an answer.

All this, of course, is to beg the question of whether the religions of the Iron Age British Isles were not substantially the same as those of the early Bronze Age and Neolithic, having shed the monuments formerly associated with them. Such a view has been advanced by Paul Ashbee and Aubrey Burl.[66] The former points out that the great Irish ceremonial centres of the first millennium BC, such as Tara, Emain Macha and Dún Ailinne, all contained round enclosures with ditch inside bank, exactly like the henges of the third millennium. The latter adds that at Tara the site was used for ceremonial purposes from the time of the developed passage graves until the early Christian era. He suggests that the whole of prehistory has in common a cult of the head, foundation deposits and a preoccupation with the symbolism of heavenly bodies. There are faults in these arguments. The great Irish Iron Age centres may resemble henges in some respects, but differ in the other portions of their structure and also in the nature of the traces of ritual found at them. Tara certainly spans about four millennia of occupation, but in that respect appears so far to be unique among the Iron Age complexes of its type: it may just have been upon a very attractive site. The same may be true elsewhere, when Iron Age and Neolithic monuments occur together. And the practices cited by Dr Burl are too common in tribal religion to provide a foundation for such an argument. As the nature of Iron Age beliefs is to be the subject of the next chapter, it would be premature to consider the opposing case here, and therefore unjust to those scholars who presented the case which is being opposed. But something of the strength of the argument for a break in tradition can be indicated.

Most stark is the fact that the great majority of the earlier ceremonial centres were never used again, even where their stones made them very conspicuous and where settlement endured or returned. The abandonment of monuments during earlier millennia was, as shown, a very gradual process involving deposition of offerings long after the structure was in decay, and respect for the site long after that. Later monuments were built close to those used earlier, and the evolutionary line from one to the other is often discernible even if the reason for it is not. By contrast, the older ritual and sepulchral edifices were from the middle Bronze Age onwards not merely forsaken but treated without respect. As already mentioned, a field wall was built across the avenue of megaliths leading from the Sanctuary to Avebury, and by the Iron Age the great henge monument itself seems to have been completely overgrown. In that latter age, also, the setting of stones in the Mount Pleasant superhenge was demolished in order to clear the ground for agriculture, while a henge monument at Hanborough was levelled for the same purpose. At Moncrieffe in Perthshire, a Neolithic henge was turned into a ring cairn during the early Bronze Age: but during the Iron Age the site was converted into a forge, and when the cremation urns were uncovered, they were smashed. A systematic study of this process in southern England has now been made by Richard Bradley. He found that in the later Bronze Age there began a pattern which continued right through the Iron Age into the Roman period and beyond, of farming first encroaching upon, and then removing, the monuments of the earlier cultures. By the Iron Age, barrows and henges were being destroyed wholesale wherever settlement was dense. They survived best upon the hills simply because these were less heavily farmed after the middle Bronze Age, but even there considerable damage was done. To those cases mentioned above may be added the partial demolition of the Dorset Cursus, the bank barrow at Maiden Castle and several round barrow cemeteries. Nor is there a single case of continued ritual use of a site in Professor Bradley's survey.[67]

The evidence for discontinuity can be multiplied. Celtic mythology regarded the prehistoric monuments as the work of another race. Humans were encouraged to avoid them, especially the great tombs. Prehistoric stone axes were commonly carried to Romano-British temples, especially those associated with Jupiter. According to the Roman Pliny, this was because they were believed to be thunderbolts once used by the god as missiles, indicating that the people of his time were already as detached from prehistory as those of the Middle Ages who thought that the same artefacts had been the weapons of fairies.[68] Late Neolithic and early Bronze Age temples were circular and of stones, but Iron Age temples were rectangular and of wood. Occasional burials were put into prehistoric mounds from the time when inhumation was revived at the end of the Iron Age until the adoption of Christianity. It seems, however, that the ancient barrows were simply convenient dumping grounds or memorials for bodies. The seven henges which were used as burial enclosures by pagan Anglo-Saxons cannot have stirred any folk-memories in them, any more than the Saxon or Viking who was interred at the top of Silbury Hill could have known more of its purpose than we do.[69] At Newgrange certainly, and at Maes Howe probably, we have evidence of the importance of the winter solstice around 3200 BC. Some stone rings appear to have been aligned upon it in the early Bronze Age, but the Iron Age British and Irish do not seem to have celebrated it at all. The evidence is not conclusive, but it is very suggestive. As far as the scholar is concerned, the spectacular monuments of the prehistoric British Isles end as mysteriously as they began. The rift that seems to lie between the evidence for religion before 1400 BC and after 600 BC is almost absolute.

This chapter may end with a cautionary tale. One of my favourite Cornish folk-stories concerns a wizard who dwelt on the Cheesewring Rock in the south-eastern part of Bodmin Moor. He offered refreshment to passing hunters, in the form of wine contained in a marvellous golden cup. His enchantments ensured that no matter how thirsty his guest was, there always seemed to be more wine in the vessel. One day a huntsman came who was determined to defeat the sorcerer by draining the cup.

When he failed to do so, he threw the wine in his host's face and rode off with the vessel in his hand. He fell over some rocks and was killed, being buried beneath a cairn where he had fallen with the cup still beside him. I have read in various modern sources[70] that this story was told for centuries before 1818, when the cairn, known as Rillaton Barrow, was excavated. It was found to be a burial monument of the early Bronze Age, containing the skeleton of a man, a bronze dagger – and a wonderful gold cup. The latter is now in the British Museum. For years I told myself (and others) that, incredible as it might seem, the people of eastern Cornwall appeared to have preserved the memory of an event which had occurred nearly four thousand years before. But then, in 1976, Leslie Grinsell published his researches into the folklore of prehistoric monuments. It turned out that the story of the wizard and the cup is a popular old international story, particularly associated with Scandinavia. The earliest trace of the association of the story with Rillaton Barrow is in 1899, generations after the well-publicized discovery of the cup.[71] It seems probable that the wizard of the Cheesewring represents not an astonishing proof of the length of folk-memory, but an illustration of the genius of nineteenth-century Cornish 'drolls' or travelling entertainers, in linking new information with old tales to improve the latter. It is a reminder of the treacherous nature of the oral tradition as a historical source. But it also refutes one of the remaining arguments for continuity between the world of the early Bronze Age and that which came later.

5

The People of the Mist
(c. 1000 BC–c. AD 500)

When the British Isles emerge, part by part, into the records of history, they are found to be populated entirely by members of the pan-European family of peoples called Celts. In these islands they are divided into two linguistic groups, Gaelic and Brythonic, but this apart they share an apparently similar political, social and cultural order. Any trace of pre-Celtic populations has vanished. Until the past couple of decades it was widely believed that the Celts were relative newcomers who arrived in three waves during the first millennium BC. This idea has gone the way of all firm assertions of belief in prehistoric invasions, many scholars now preferring to believe that 'Celticization' represented the slow importation of a set of cultural traits by the existing inhabitants of these islands.[1] Thus, the first Celts must be consigned to the same ideological limbo as the Beaker People and the Neolithic pioneers, their existence to be neither proved nor absolutely disproved. For our purposes, the most important single fact about the Iron Age British and Irish is that they are semi-historic. Unlike all their predecessors they left some trace of their culture in written records.

Unfortunately, those records are precisely the sort of material which presents many problems, conceals others and solves few. One of the greatest for the innocent is that of modern forgery, principally for Wales and principally attributable to Edward Williams (1747–1826), who assumed the name Iolo Morgannwg.[2] Williams was a man of considerable talent and a major influence upon Welsh culture. By trade a stonemason and a (failed) small businessman, he was also the co-editor of the basic grammar of modern Welsh and a good original poet, songwriter and hymn-writer; and he amassed one of the finest collections of medieval and early modern Welsh manuscripts existing in his time. Williams's trouble was that he was a reckless romantic, imprudent in his attitude to the truth as he was in his politics, his financial habits and his consumption of laudanum. As a young man, he attempted, quite understandably if less respectably, to get a better market for his poems by passing them off as hitherto undiscovered work of the fourteenth-century master Dafydd ap Gwilym. Unfortunately, he applied this same inventive ingenuity when, during a spell in a debtors' prison, he discovered a mission to reveal to the Welsh the lost wisdom of their ancestors. He emerged from gaol, went straight to his manuscripts, and found that neither they nor the collections in the British Museum contained the information which he required. So he used his own power of inspiration to supply it, lifting a line here and there from an original text. Williams went on to 'revive' the medieval Order of Bards to teach the prehistoric system of mystical belief which he proclaimed. He specified the ceremonies, costumes, regalia and hierarchy which the Order had known in Druidical times, and the first 'Gorsedd', or assembly of the new Bards, was held on Primrose Hill, London, in 1792. Williams set it within a stone circle, having brought the stones along in his pocket. In old age he devoted himself to two tasks. One was the continual rewriting of his autobiography, embellishing it with more and more fantastic episodes. The other was the continual elaboration of his system of 'Druidic' philosophy. His addiction to laudanum had by this time taken such a hold that it is doubtful whether he could himself any longer distinguish fact from fiction. But by the time of his death, he had achieved the romantic's highest goal, of having his dream taken as reality by others.

Williams was just one of a number of writers between 1760 and 1840 who also set out to 'reconstruct' the principles of a noble and natural religion worthy to be associated with prehistoric philosopher-priests. The others included Rowland Jones, John Cleland, William Cooke, D. James, Edward Davies and the famous William Blake. What distinguished Williams was partly the direct appeal which he made to the contemporary Welsh patriotic revival, and partly the fact that he provided a ritual as well as texts. The Welsh living in London revived the medieval institution of the eisteddfod, or national competition of the arts, in the early 1790s. When an eisteddfod was held in Glamorgan (or Morgannwg) in 1819, Williams included his Gorsedd ceremony in it, and this later became an integral part of the gathering. This self-conscious association of his ideas with Welsh nationalism rescued his Order of Bards from the fate of the Ancient Order of Druids, which was 'revived' by the London carpenter and builder Henry Hurle in 1781. That too survives to the present day, with ceremonies as confidently enacted, and as impeccably eighteenth-century, as Williams's. From the late nineteenth century until 1989, they were allowed to perform them within Stonehenge, a more spectactular setting than that achieved by any Gorsedd. But Hurle's Order has remained the preserve of a small number of relatively obscure people, subject at times to schism and refoundation: Williams's Bards are now the cultural elite of a nation, and number among them our monarch herself.

That all this was possible was due to the appalling state of genuine Welsh studies at the time. During the nineteenth century this situation improved, but it is difficult to eradicate a myth once it has become the property of a nation. Furthermore, conscientious scholars were unable to find any system of pre-Christian religion in the old Welsh texts to render the impostors superfluous. So the work of the latter was elaborated and multiplied. At the national eisteddfod at Llangollen in 1858, the promoters appealed for further evidence of the 'Bardo-Druidic' faith, offering a prize. What they got, sent in by an anonymous donor, was the unpublished portion of Edward Williams's work. This was handed over to the perfect editor, the Revd J. Williams ap Ithel, whose carelessness and credulity in handling real Welsh manuscripts has aroused the irritation of modern scholars. He duly issued it as part of the Welsh Manuscripts Society series, under the title *Barddas*, thereby providing the new Bards with their 'definitive' account of ancient Celtic mystical belief.

During the twentieth century most came to accept that *Barddas* was not the authentic voice of their remote ancestors, and to perform the Gorsedd ritual with tongues firmly in cheeks. But Williams's work has continued to exert great influence upon British mystics, largely thanks to the influence of Lewis Spence. To historians and scholars of old literature, the story of this man is a sad one. He was a good folklorist, some of whose work will be used positively in the present book. But he was also a tremendous romantic, who presented *Barddas* to the public as the central text of the 'Celtic mysteries'. Spence did not read Welsh himself: indeed, he rather prided himself upon the fact. Space does not permit the presentation here of those long passages in which he declares that the possession of Celtic blood confers powers of intuition which outweigh all the knowledge of scholars. Himself a Scot, Spence based his own claims upon the remarkable assumption that the whole Scottish nation, from the Isles to the Borders, was of Celtic origin. He listened to 'ancestral voices' and felt 'magic in his blood', leading him into 'the cavern of Celtic profundity'. In view of all this, his publications were really quite restrained, merely presenting the work of Williams, Davies and others, simply and attractively, to the general reader.[3] It was largely through him that the system of initiation and the ascent through spheres of spiritual being towards God, set out in *Barddas*, reached modern mystics such as John Michell.

No serious scholar now believes Williams or anybody else who has claimed to reveal the religion of the ancient Druids. But the notion of a home-grown system of very old wisdom, matching those of the East, still holds a considerable attraction for many people in the British Isles today. Whereas in the eighteenth century the key words for such a system were 'Druidic' and 'patriarchal', since the nineteenth century the adjective 'Celtic' has been crucial. This is a result of the belief in the importance of national characters, racial identity and folk-memories which was one product of the Romantic Movement which began towards the end of the eighteenth century. It was French writers like Amedée Thierry, Henri Martin and Ernst Renan who evolved the concept of the imaginative, dashing, sensitive and cultured Celt, as opposed to the practical, dull, brutish Teuton. The intention was, of course, to match the 'Celtic' French against the 'Teutonic' Germans and English. In doing so, these writers were drawing upon a statement by Julius Caesar, that the peoples west of the Rhine were Celts and that those east of it were Germans, which (as will be discussed later in this book) is itself dubious. They also ignored the fact that the kingdom of France was itself founded by Germanic rulers. But their model had an obvious propaganda value, and was taken up in turn for their own purposes by English authors, notably Matthew Arnold. It was he more than anybody else who defined the Anglo-Saxon peoples of the British Isles as the embodiment of progress, industry, sobriety, utilitarianism, science, materialism and 'masculinity'. The Celts of the archipelago, by contrast, were archaic, emotional, mystical, creative and 'feminine'. This argument both justified England's domination of the islands and turned Welsh and Gaelic culture into an intellectual holiday camp for English people jaded with their own civilization. It was also rapidly turned against its composers by separatist movements, notably in Ireland, who could claim that it awarded the Celts a moral superiority.

The Second Romantic Movement of the 1960s gave a new impetus to the concept of 'the Celts'. It extended local separatism to involve all the areas in which Celtic languages survived past the Middle Ages, so that 'Pan-Celtic' gatherings and journals were launched in unprecedented numbers. It also mightily increased the number of English who were dissatisfied with their parent culture and sought alternatives with a greater spirituality. As a result, the past twenty-five years have seen a proportionate boom in the publication of books upon 'Celtic magic', 'Celtic mysteries' and 'the inner Celtic world'. The best of this sort of writing is probably represented by the popular works of Caitlín Matthews. She is clearly highly intelligent, her style is fluent and lively, she reads both Welsh and Irish and she uses a full range of published primary sources. She has no time for the fantasies of Edward Williams and his successors. A lovely personality shines through her work. Yet she still falls below the standards required of a professional historian. She makes no attempt to distinguish between the relative value of sources, so those from the seventh century and from the seventeenth are put together with no sense of context. She assumes that the 'Celtic world' formed a whole, from Ireland to the Alps, and consequently mixes data from all over this vast area without raising the possibility of local variation. Thus she plucks her material from all over time and space and arranges it to suit her taste and that of her audience, on the assumption that Celts are always and everywhere much the same. A swift example of this process at work may be seen in her consideration of 'the Celtic year'. She states that the quarter days 1 February, 1 May, 1 August and 1 November were important festivals. This is perfectly true for Ireland and Scotland, but it is a Gaelic system which may not have operated further afield. She also refers to them as 'fire feasts', upon the grounds that they were formerly associated with fire. There is no source-reference for this, and in fact the term is a common one among modern pagans, appearing first in the work of the very popular Victorian folklorist, or anthropologist, Sir James Frazer. But Frazer did not apply it to all these quarter days, only, quite correctly, to two of them which were associated with customs involving fire; and he included these two with a number of others which make no appearance in the scheme presented by Caitlín Matthews. On to these four Gaelic feasts she superimposes the solstices and equinoxes, which do not feature as feasts in any of the early Celtic literatures. But they are celebrated by modern pagans, and these eight festivals together, which make up her 'Wheel of the Celtic Year', turn out to be simply those of the modern witch cult. To these she adds a lunar calendar from the first century AD which was dug up on the far side of France. It was made under Roman rule and in Roman characters, and kept in a temple to the Roman god Apollo. There is no sign in the Welsh and Irish texts that anything like it was used in the British Isles. But she includes it with her 'Wheel' as part of the system used to reckon 'the Celtic year'.

Some of this can be ascribed to the simple fact that unacademic writers of history do not usually work with the same rigour as present-day professionals. Most of the approach adopted by Ms Matthews can be found in scholarly books upon the Celts produced before the 1970s, when the new care in textual criticism and mutual appraisal came to be adopted in universities. But her work is also conditioned to the needs of her audience. To a great extent, the world of the modern 'Celtic mysteries', like that of the 'earth mysteries', is self-contained. Thus, her bibliographies are filled on the one hand with old academic works and on the other with writings of the contemporary Celtic mystical movement right up to 1990. What are missing are the scholarly publications of the 1980s, many of which have radically altered existing news of the sources for our knowledge of the ancient Celts. But then any 'movement', or 'tradition', tends to build upon itself, and is not much given to questioning its basic texts. Caitlín Matthews and her colleagues are not really concerned with the past, so much as with the present and the future. They are creating a mystical tradition out of old materials but suited to modern needs. One aspect of this is her imposition upon Celtic lore of a lot of native American religion, such as the totem, the spirit-quest and the shamanic vision. There are actually no precise parallels for any of these in ancient Celtic culture. Comparison and contrast between peoples is a valuable ethnographic device, and the obvious cultures for comparison with the Celts are those of the Germanic and Norse tribes, who were contemporary and neighbouring societies of a similar kind. But the plain fact is that an interest in native American culture is very marked among the sort of public at which Ms Matthews's books are aimed. 'Shamanic' now ranks with 'Celtic' as a buzz-word among that audience, following the impact of Carlos Castañeda's publications and those of native Americans such as Sun Bear. By contrast, to the present Pan-Celtic Movement, early Germanic culture is presumed to be that of traditional enemies. This accounts for the importation of what would otherwise be considered utterly foreign traditions. The result is perfectly sound theology, and gives immense pleasure and is of great practical utility to many people. Like the earth mysteries, it 'works'.[4] Only from the narrow point of view of one interested solely in the ancient Celts can there be said to be something wrong with it. But from this point of view it *is* a pity that writers as able as Caitlín Matthews have not given themselves over more to a quest for objective truth, whether the result has utility or not. There remains even now a lot of unpublished early medieval Irish material, and the latest scholarship has reminded us of how much we have still to find out about the society which produced it. The gulf between the modern Celtic mysteries and academic scholarship is just the same as that between the latter and the earth mysteries. Both sides can accuse the other, within their own very different terms, of being irrelevant and irresponsible.

Another major, and separate contribution to the confusion surrounding the Celts was begun in 1944 by one of the greatest modern English poets and historical novelists, Robert Graves. In three weeks during that year he completed the first draft of a book which was to become *The White Goddess*, drawing upon images culled from Celtic and Graeco-Roman literatures and fusing them within his own tremendous creative inspiration to provide a personal religion to accompany his poetry. The result is a sustained metaphor, a vision of the sort of past that the writer thought ought to have existed. His friends have maintained that in private he himself did not believe that his vision *had* existed in reality: he was expressing a state of creative longing which made what he wrote poetically, not literally, true. But nowhere in the book itself did he warn his readers that they were to take it as metaphor or myth. As a result, it was taken as history by a large number of unscholarly readers. His confident statements that ancient societies were ruled by women has made him a hero of many modern feminists. He presented those who wanted a matriarchal religion with a Celtic Great Goddess, appearing in the three aspects of maiden, mother and crone, who is still believed to be historical by many who do not worship her themselves. He devised what has become known as the 'Celtic Tree Calendar' to people who do not realize that it was an invention of Graves, which would have amazed the Iron Age Celts even more than the Triple Mother Goddess. And he firmly associated goddesses with the moon in a way which he made to seem natural but was not so to many ancient poeples, including the Celts. His bluntest retrospective comment on the work, written to a stranger, was: 'It's a crazy book and I didn't mean to write it.'[5] But it still has great influence in shaping the view of Celtic paganism held by unscholarly readers.

What must be obvious from all this is that the genuine sources for Celtic religion either contain too little for that religion to be reconstructed or testify to something which people like Williams rejected as unpalatable. So to the nature of these sources we must now turn. They fall broadly into two categories: those written by the Celts themselves and those written about them by other ancient peoples, namely the Greeks and Romans. The latter texts are at first sight relatively numerous, representing between them a dozen authors, some of whom quote others.

But their value diminishes considerably upon closer inspection. Virtually all were written between about 150 BC and AD 100, when the Celtic world was in the process of alteration and adaptation. Most referred only to the tribes of southern Gaul, modern Provence and Languedoc, which were the most affected by contact with the Mediterranean civilizations and may have been very atypical. Only one author had any first-hand experience of Britain, and none was primarily interested in the Celts themselves. One group, based originally upon Alexandria and including writers such as Timaeus, Timagenes and Polyhistor, attempted to portray the Celts as noble savages whose example exposed defects in Graeco-Roman civilization. Timaeus was copied by the Greek historian Polybius, who in turn was copied by the Roman historian Livy. None had much detailed material. Another set of authors is defined by their determination to prove that the Celts were barbarians who required the civilizing influence of Greece and Rome. Some, notably Athenaeus, Strabo and Diodorus Siculus, relied heavily upon a lost writer called Poseidonios. This individual only knew southern Gaul, and to him and those who followed him the west coast of that region, and Britain, seemed remote and mysterious. He had a marked bias against the Celts and was an exponent of Stoic philosophy, which may have caused him to exaggerate the sophistication of barbarian religious beliefs. Of rather different sort are the accounts written by historians such as Tacitus, Lucan and Dio Cassius, of military campaigns against Celtic tribes. None had personally taken part in these campaigns, and in some cases the writers were dealing with events generations before their own time. In a class of his own is Julius Caesar, who himself conducted the operations in France and Britain of which he was writing. But he devoted very little space to describing his enemies, and when he did so he had a powerful motive for disparaging them in order to justify his aggressive warfare against them.[6]

So we must turn to the Celtic sources in the hope of finding fuller representation and less distortion: and at once we hit a different problem. The Graeco-Roman writers, whatever their imperfections to the modern historian, were at least contemporary with the pagan Celtic world. The British and Irish texts were all written down after the islands had become Christianized, and referred to a vanished system of belief to which the authors themselves were perhaps hostile. Nevertheless, for the first half of this century there remained a great deal of faith in them among scholars, as products of an ancient oral tradition which, however bowdlerized by Christians, preserved glimpses of a pagan society. One of the achievements of the last thirty years has been to reduce that faith considerably. This process needs to be considered first for the literature in Welsh. By about 1900, experts had rejected both forgeries such as *Barddas* and the mystical writings of the High Middle Ages (which will be considered later) as sources for pre-Christian British religion. They were left with some of the Triads and some of the tales collected by Lady Charlotte Guest in the nineteenth century under the title of *The Mabinogion*. In 1961 the great Celticist Kenneth Jackson pointed out that many of the motifs in the latter, far from deriving from a lost world of 'Druidical' magic, were actually popular international tales with their origins in Egypt, India or China. The spread of these across Asia and Europe could be traced in a number of early medieval and older sources. In the stories of *The Mabinogion*, they are mixed with Irish and British myths and committed to their final form in the late eleventh century AD by a courtly entertainer. By the time he got hold of them they were already confused and incomplete, but probably not more than a century or two old. They contain a few very faint memories of pagan deities and beliefs, but all are too far removed from their sources to be useful in reconstructing the original religion.[7]

During the 1980s specialists' belief in the antiquity of Welsh literature declined still further. Until the past few years it was accepted that certain poems, associated with the bards Taliesin, Aneirin and Llywarch Hen, dated back to the beginning of the Welsh poetic tradition in the sixth and seventh centuries AD. It now appears that there is no good evidence that any of them is older than the ninth century, and that they refer to people and events which were not contemporary but already semi-mythical. There is increasing reason to believe that early medieval Welsh poets wrote under the names of illustrious predecessors, holding that they were inspired by the spirits of these bards. None of the original work of people like Taliesin may survive, if indeed they ever existed. There is no longer any reason to suppose that the earliest surviving verses had any career as oral poetry before they were committed to writing, or to assert that any of the tales which appear in them belong to a pre-Christian age. All the personalities who feature in these oldest poems are not deities but warriors, and it may indeed have been the function of those who composed them to extol human heroism rather than treat of religion. In brief, what little value the Welsh vernacular texts may once have been thought to possess for our quest has now largely evaporated.[8]

But then, it has always been the Irish, and not the Welsh, sources which have been recognized as the best literary evidence for the pagan Celtic world. They are much more numerous and have been thought to be both older and less contaminated by foreign material. Professor Jackson, who dealt such a blow to accepted opinion of *The Mabinogion*, himself described the Irish tales as 'a window on the Iron Age'.[9] Yet he stated in the same work that these sources were less valuable for scholars of religion than those of society. The earliest extant versions of them are from the twelfth century AD, and although some of the stories were presumed to be about a thousand years older, all were transcribed by Christian monks who may not merely have been hostile to the earlier paganism but actually ignorant of it. The texts contain the personalities of former deities but not the beliefs or forms of worship associated with them. So even in the 1960s, when trust in the antiquity of the Irish literature was still firm, doubt had been cast upon its utility to students of paganism. Then, starting in the mid–1980s, came a devastating series of attacks upon that very antiquity which the scholarly world had deemed valid. The law codes, thought to have been archaic compilations rooted in pagan oral techniques, were dated to the eight century AD and attributed convincingly to Christian churchmen who were part of the Latin literary world. Irish poets and historians were shown to have been expert in dressing up contemporary issues and contexts in ancient forms right up to the seventeenth century. Archaeology suggested that the earliest literature was a window not upon the Iron Age but upon the early Middle Ages in which it was composed. The authors could remember where the great pagan centres had been, but turned them into royal halls filled with warrior aristocrats instead of showing them as the complex ceremonial sites which they were. The heroes in the tales fight with swords from the Viking age, not the Iron Age. They ride in chariots, which are well attested in the early Christian centuries but not from those before.[10]

The idea that the earliest written tales represented literary versions of a much older oral tradition was so dear to scholars that it was not until the late 1980s that anybody pointed out clearly that all the evidence suggested the opposite. The tales do not show any of the classic techniques of an oral tradition. They are in prose, not verse. They lack a formulaic structure, key phrases often repeated, alliteration, rhyme, rhythm, metre, assonance and other devices used to commit works to memory. The earliest notes upon the stories, from the ninth century AD, suggest that they were told orally by bards who had also known them as literature. By the early eighth century some of the tales were in existence, but as short episodes instead of the epics which appear later. The language of these epics suggests that they were produced around AD 750, by the same monks in Ulster who were writing lives of local saints.[11] Furthermore, those authors would have been acquainted with the Greek and Roman classics, which we know were much admired in early medieval Ireland. It is impossible to tell how much an imitation of these foreign texts, conscious or unconscious, conditioned their reworking of native traditions. It has often been pointed out that a custom of the Gallic Celts recorded by Poseidonios, that champion warriors contested the honour of having the first portion of a feast, is also recorded in the Irish tales. This has been used to demonstrate the fundamental unity of the Celtic world, and also the accuracy of both sets of sources. But what if the composers of the tales were familiar with Poseidonios (or rather, with the classical authors drawing upon him)? Could they have actually taken the idea from the Greek? So the earliest Irish literature does not, after all, seem to be much older than the earliest in Welsh, and both date from a period of at least two centuries after their societies had become Christian. They are therefore of limited utility for our purpose, although they *do* supply names of deities and details of a few rituals.

The equivalent Scottish sources, consisting of a few king-lists and chronicles (most of the latter actually kept by the Irish), have not featured much in the work of those interested in the Celts. But they were used to support a scholarly belief which, like that regarding the ancient Irish oral tradition, lasted about a hundred years until it was shattered in the 1980s. This one concerned the Picts, and stated that these northern Scottish tribes were remnants of the pre-Celtic population of Britain and that as part of this greater antiquity they were matrilinear, passing on kinship through the female line. Late Victorian scholars were enthused by the idea that women had possessed more power in early societies. They expected to find evidence that the early British were matrilinear, and in the case of the Picts they thought that they had discovered it. From this sprang the notion that these people were pre-Celtic and preserved customs older than the Iron Age: which, if true, is of obvious importance to the student of religion. But in the 1980s it required only a brief re-opening of the question to reveal that the belief in matrilinear succession probably rested upon a misunderstanding of a few entries in early medieval texts.[12] It now seems that the Picts were probably another set of Celts, indistinguishable in their culture from the other tribes of Britain.

All this notwithstanding, it remains true that the literary sources for Celtic paganism do yield some insights which can be reinforced from the findings of archaeology. Good recent work has been done in this field, among which that of G. A. Wait is outstanding. For the purposes of this book, an attempt has been made to separate the religions of the pre-Roman southern British and the pre-Christian Irish and northern British, from those of the Roman province of Britain. There is obviously a considerable overlap between all, but the Roman rule of Britain as far as the Forth created a synthesis between native and foreign traditions, which will be the subject of the next chapter.

Having entered all these warnings, and made these exclusions, we can now proceed. The first step is to enquire into the nature of Celtic deities. For non-Roman Britain and Ireland almost the only source for these consists of the early Irish literature, with all its attendant problems noted above. Dr Wait has made a useful threefold classification of the divine beings in these tales into the Tuatha de Danaan, the tutelary goddesses and the miscellaneous deities.[13] The first, the children or subjects of Danu, were the Irish pantheon, a divine society of beings associated with each other and dwelling in a parallel world with its own politics and customs. They had individual functions, such as healer, smith, wheelwright, metalworker, harper and poet, suggesting that they may have functioned as patrons of people engaged in these activities. But there were also two who were multi-talented and occupy a higher status in the stories. One was Lugh, known as 'the many-skilled', 'the long-armed' or 'of the long spear'. The first epithet gives away his nature. He was the sophisticated, inventive, brilliantly clever and handsome god, the favourite deity in the stories. He was the particular patron of heroes, and gave his name to the most joyous Irish festival, Lughnasadh. He seems to have been a very widespread deity in the Celtic world. His name appears in a Welsh tale, as Lleu Llaw Gyffes, 'The Bright One of the Skilful Hand', although the character concerned is not a god. It also forms the basis of the names of the Roman cities which were the ancestors of Carlisle in England, Leiden in Holland, Laon and Lyon in France and Leignitz in Silesia. In its plural form, Lugoves, it is recorded in Roman inscriptions in Switzerland and Spain. It would be easy to imagine how such an attractive divine personality could have a very widespread appeal, but we do not know whether he had exactly the same identity upon the Continent as in Ireland. There is some suggestion in the Irish Book of Invasions (*Leabhar Gabhála Éireann*) that he was a late arrival among the deities of the island, but this, again, cannot be substantiated. The other outstanding personality among the Tuatha de Danaan was the Daghda, the 'good god' or 'great father', the patron of the Irish in general and of priests in particular. His insignia were his club, which gave protection, and his cauldron, which gave plenty. He had an exact counterpart in Gaul (modern France, Belgium and part of Germany) in the popular god Sucellus ('the good striker'), who was associated in his images with hammer or club and pot. But there is a dissimilarity between the two: Sucellus often had a consort, the goddess Nantosoelta, while the Daghda, though mating with goddesses, stood alone. Nor was the distribution of this figure as wide as that of Lugh. Sucellus is found in eastern Gaul and Provence, especially along the Rhône. His cult was very much sparser further west and it hardly seems to have existed in Britain, where his name appears only upon one ring from York. A large expanse of geography therefore separates him from the Daghda.

A glance at a few other personalities among the Tuatha de Danaan illustrates further the difficulty of speaking of 'Celtic deities' as if the same figures existed across the whole Celtic world. Nuadha Airgedlamh ('of the silver hand') appears in the *Leabhbar Gabhála* as their original leader. His name features in a Welsh tale, as Nudd Llaw Ereint, but like Lugh's it is applied to a human figure: one wonders whether he was a memory of a home-grown Welsh deity or imported in an Irish story. There was a British god called Nodens, but he was identified with healing, not a special attribute of Nuadha. The divine smith among Danu's people was Goibhniu, who appears in a trio with Luchta, the wheelwright, and Creidhne, the metalworker. His very name means 'smith' and it reappears in early Welsh literature as Gofannon, though again not attached to a god. But in several Irish texts he features as a healer or a host of great feasts instead, while in others he is an all-round craftsman and in folk-tales a mason. Either his identity is varied between regions or storytellers or he is a compound of different gods. Then there was Ogmha, who had a dual role as both a warrior and the inventor of writing. In Gaul there was a god called Ogmios, who was associated with strength and eloquence. It is possible that the two were fundamentally the same, but whether they were two variations on the same source, or whether the cult was brought from one country to another, we cannot say. A still worse tangle exists over the identity of Oenghus, the handsome young god of the Tuatha de Danaan. He has been related to Maponos, the divine youth honoured in parts of Gaul and Britain whose name features in a Welsh story as Mabon. But Oenghus was a wilful and witty trickster, the Gallic Maponos a healer associated with springs, the British one a musician, and the Welsh character a hunter. This seems to be a classic case of the identification of deities with similar names or characters creating more problems than it solves. It is interesting to turn the picture round, and see what happens to the cults of Continental Celtic gods as they are traced westward towards the British Isles. A good study is that of Belenus, the favourite deity of the Celts of Noricum, modern Austria, whom they regarded as the god of the sun. Dedications to him are also found in northern Italy and southern France, and occasionally in Britain. But either the latter were made by Roman immigrants from Europe or else Belenus had changed his character, for there is no trace in the Irish or Welsh literatures of any deity associated with the sun (or moon). Attempts have been made to detect the presence of Belenus in the British Isles from names for gods, places and festivals with the prefix Bel or Bal. But this is the common Celtic word for 'bright', so the exercise is a pointless one.[14]

From all this it may be seen already that there is a strong possibility that the whole concept of the Tuatha de Danaan was invented by storytellers, perhaps working in the early Christian era and influenced by the Graeco-Roman myths. They may have brought together various international and local deities to form a literary pantheon which bore no relation to the way in which the pagan tribes had conceived of and worshipped these divinities. This possibility is increased when one considers the relationship of the deities concerned with the second category defined by Dr Wait, the tutelary goddesses. These appear most clearly in a different category of Irish literature to the heroic tales: the so-called Dinnshenchas, which are accounts of the origins and names of particular places. It seems very clear from these that many mountains, rivers, districts and clans were regarded as being under the patronage of specific female deities. This tradition is reflected in the number of rivers which preserve their names (Boinne and Sionna for Boyne and Shannon) and the number of mountains in both Ireland and Scotland which are called 'of the old woman'. But they were all individuals, and there is no trace in the early Celtic texts of that Great Mother or Supreme Triple Goddess so popular in modern romances. None the less, some goddesses do feature in the heroic tales as other than local patronesses. Three, the Morrigan, Badhbh and Nemhain, were terrifying attendants of battle, exulting in slaughter even though they never fought themselves. The tendency to honour female deities as sponsors of war is found beyond Ireland and may be a feature of Celtic religion. The name of a goddess from south-eastern Gaul, Cathubodua, means 'crow of battle', which is exactly the significance of the Irish word 'Chatha', applied as a nickname to the Badhbh. The British warrior queen Boudicca dedicated her spoils of victory to Andraste.[15] Goddesses rarely feature in the Irish literature as maternal or nurturing, being more often aggressive and voracious in both their sexuality and their bloodlust. Whether they represented role models for self-assertive Celtic women, or the fantasies of pagan Celtic male warriors, or the nightmares of the Christian monks who wrote the stories, is an open question.

There are a few female deities who appear in the tales as representatives of the whole of Ireland, but again one wonders how much they have been created, or their importance inflated, by storytellers. In the *Leabhar Gabhála* the Tuatha de Danaan arrive in Ireland to find it represented by three goddesses, Eriu, Fódla and Banbha, who married three of the newcomers. It is impossible to say whether they were actually once worshipped or were literary inventions to provide a symbolic role in a creation legend. The Danu who gave her name to the Tuatha de Danaan is presumably the same as the 'Ana' described in *Sanas Chormaic*, Cormac's Glossary, written around AD 900. There she is called the mother of all deities, a further inflation of status from being the founder of her great Tuatha. But another text, *Cóir Anman* ('The Fitness of Names'), calls 'Anu' the tutelary goddess of the province of Munster, where indeed twin mountains are still said to represent her breasts. If Danu, Ana and Anu are the same then it is possible that a local goddess grew into a generalized one, perhaps aided by the fact that Cormac was a Munster leader.

A similar but yet more complex problem surrounds the figure of Brighid, Bríg or Bríd, the Christian Mother Saint of Ireland. A superficially easy case could be made for describing her as the patron of Leinster, later given national status as Danu may have been. The centre of her cult was in that province, at Kildare next to the Curragh plain which had been such a centre of prehistoric ritual activity. Here, until the Reformation, a sacred fire was kept burning in her honour, a feature generally agreed almost certainly to have been a surviving pre-Christian custom. The medieval Leinstermen regarded her as their special patron, and told how at the battle of Allen in 722 she appeared above their army like an ancient war goddess, routing the forces of Tara. But the Munsterman Cormac, while stating that she was indeed once a goddess, called her the patroness of learning and prophecy, with twin sisters of the same name, one overseeing healing and one metalwork. He followed this statement with a passage which translates as either 'from whose names a goddess was called Brighid by all the Irish', or 'from whom all the Irish recognized Brighid as a goddess'. The former sense was accepted by Graves, and upon it he founded his myth of the Triple Mother Goddess, although he remodelled her as maiden, mother and crone rather than as teacher, doctor and craftswoman. But an early medieval inventory of identically named female saints lists a total of ten different Brighids, twelve Brígs and three known as both. Other sources supply two more former goddesses, Bríg ambue, patroness of jurisprudence, and Bríg briugu, the provider. Some modern writers identify all as one pan-Celtic deity, worshipped in Britain under the name Brigantia and being associated with the rivers Braint and Brent. But the names of the rivers are probably coincidental, while Brigantia was specifically the tutelary goddess of the Brigantes tribe. Upon this evidence it seems impossible to say with confidence whether we are dealing with various forms of the same mighty goddess, or genuinely separate local deities with the same or similar names, or the most important deity of Leinster who was later given more general roles in mythology.

Then there is the goddess Macha who was associated with Ulster, her name being given to its ancient ceremonial centre, Emain Macha, and its medieval one, Armagh (Ard Macha). In one tale she appears as the wife of the leader of an invasion of Ireland, in another one as the ruler of the whole land and wife of King Cimbaeth, and in yet another as a supernatural visitor to Ulster who cursed its warriors. It looks as if the authors knew nothing about her except her name, and were inventing stories to go with it.[16]

Tutelary goddesses do not feature in the Welsh literature, but then, nor do deities of any sort. In *The Mabinogion* there does appear a family called 'the children of Don', a name which is an exact parallel to the 'Tuatha de Danaan'. But Don is never identified, the personalities of the family are quite different and they are earthly rulers with supernatural powers, not deities. We cannot know if they were based upon home-grown Welsh tales or some imported from Ireland. Rhiannon, who is the main female character of the story of Pwyll, Prince of Dyfed, is clearly a figure from the Otherworld: she rides a magical horse and her very name means 'divine queen'. She may be a literary memory of the Romano-Celtic equestian goddess Epona, or of the tutelary goddess of Dyfed. But the inscriptional evidence from the Roman provinces of Britain and Gaul does more firmly indicate a belief in female protectors of places or tribes, similar to those so well attested in Ireland. Brigantia has been mentioned, as has Andraste who seems to have been unique to Boudicca's people, the Iceni. Female deities were certainly associated with the springs at Carrawburgh in Northumberland (Coventina) and at Bath (Sulis) and with the source of the Seine (Sequana), as well as with other waters to be listed in the next chapter. It is notable that male deities in those provinces were often given additional names relating them to Roman gods, whereas goddesses retained only their Celtic names. Perhaps this was because the gods had functions which permitted some comparison with those of Rome, whereas the female divinities were inseparable from the land.[17]

The process by which pagan deities were transformed into characters in early Christian literature is made still plainer when one considers Dr Wait's third category, the miscellaneous divinities. Some, like some of the tutelary goddesses, appear in the same tales as the Tuatha de Danaan, while clearly being separate from them. Others, like others among the goddesses, have their own stories. Yet more are slowly integrated into the people of Danu. The classic case is Manannán Mac Lir, who features as the major divine figure in the tale called *The Voyage of Bran*. In later stories he is also an important god, often associated with the sea, until by the High Middle Ages he has become one of the Tuatha de Danaan, even though he was not associated with them before. His name appears in a Welsh text, as Manawydan fab Llyr, but (again) given to a human character. Another 'stray' deity in the stories is Cui Roi, the god who gave his name to County Kerry. Had we possession of any early tales from western Munster, it would be easier to find out more about him and his relationship with the local goddess Danu, or Anu. But he features as an interloper in the Ulster cycle. Then there is Donn, who is an important character in the folklore collected by nineteenth- and twentieth-century researchers, where he is protrayed as god of the dead and sometimes as ancestor of the Irish. But although he is present in the early literature, it is as a marginal character with little relevance to the plots and no relationship with other deities. In the oral folk traditions, another major character is Chrom Dubh, a dark and sinister being personifying hunger, cold and night. He appears in an early twelfth-century text, so he is at the latest medieval in origin. His role in the folk stories is to be defeated and converted by St Patrick. But he never features in the early tales. Either he was a former god whom the composers of those tales failed to 'employ' or else he was never actually worshipped but was a folk spirit representing general nastiness. He may have been overlaid by, or even inspired by, notions of the Christian Devil.[18]

Thus there is considerable evidence that the Celtic vernacular literatures preserve memories of genuine pagan deities, but that many if not most of these were originally local figures who were given wider roles, and perhaps functions and relationships with one another, by early Christian authors. A very few, notably Lugh, seem to have had an international status in the pagan Celtic world, but the sources do not permit us to know whether that world conceived of a pantheon like the Tuatha de Danaan or how, indeed, it made connections between its different divinities. The impression of an intensely localized religion, with deities peculiar to districts or to tribes, is strengthened by a glance at Gaul, the Celtic region of the Roman Empire which has left the greatest number of religious inscriptions. These name a total of 375 gods, of whom 305 appear only once. Their functions overlapped enormously, the most popular personality being a warrior and the second most popular an artist and trader. There were a few honoured throughout a region and a very few known across most of the province. There was no divine hierarchy. One of the striking functions of these archaeological data has been to show how misleading are the few Roman authors who dealt with Celtic deities. Caesar said that the people of Gaul worshipped Mercury, Apollo, Mars and Jupiter, which means only that the local gods whom he encountered shared characteristics with these Roman divinities. Lucan, in a passage which was quoted uncritically by some historians and classicists as late as the 1970s, stated that the Gallic gods were Teutates, Esus and Taranis. Now Taranis is known from just seven inscriptions. Teutates, as mentioned in chapter 4, was not an individual but a title for the protective god of a tribe, and was applied to several. And Esus has only one inscription credited to him. The Roman writer fails to mention all the hundreds of others worshipped in Gaul; so his famous passage may now be considered worse than useless.[19]

Did the pagan Celts worship forces or elements as well as humanized deities? Evidence of any kind exists for only one aspect of this question, their attitude to the sun, and it is confusing. In his *Confessio*, St Patrick declared that all in Ireland who adored the sun would perish eternally. This is the only reference to a specific cult which he (or any other early Irish Christian) made, and as it was written by somebody contemporary to the activities described, it must be taken seriously. In Cormac's Glossary there is a statement that the solar symbol was carved upon certain altars. From the iconography of the Celtic provinces of Rome, to be discussed in the next chapter, it seems fairly obvious that the image concerned was the wheel, or 'Celtic cross'. Yet, as mentioned above, the earliest literature contains no trace of a cult of heavenly bodies, or of divine figures associated with them. As things stand at present, the matter is a mystery: it may be that the sun was venerated without being made the concern of any specific deities, and that adoration of it was deliberately left out of the early medieval stories. Or it could be that this aspect of the old religions was one of those forgotten by the time that the stories were composed.[20]

What images did the British and Irish Celts make of their deities? The answer is disappointing, on two counts. First, it is increasingly obvious that the Iron Age inhabitants of these islands did not consider it necessary to portray the beings whom they worshipped. Second, virtually all the human figures which have been assigned to the Iron Age may equally well

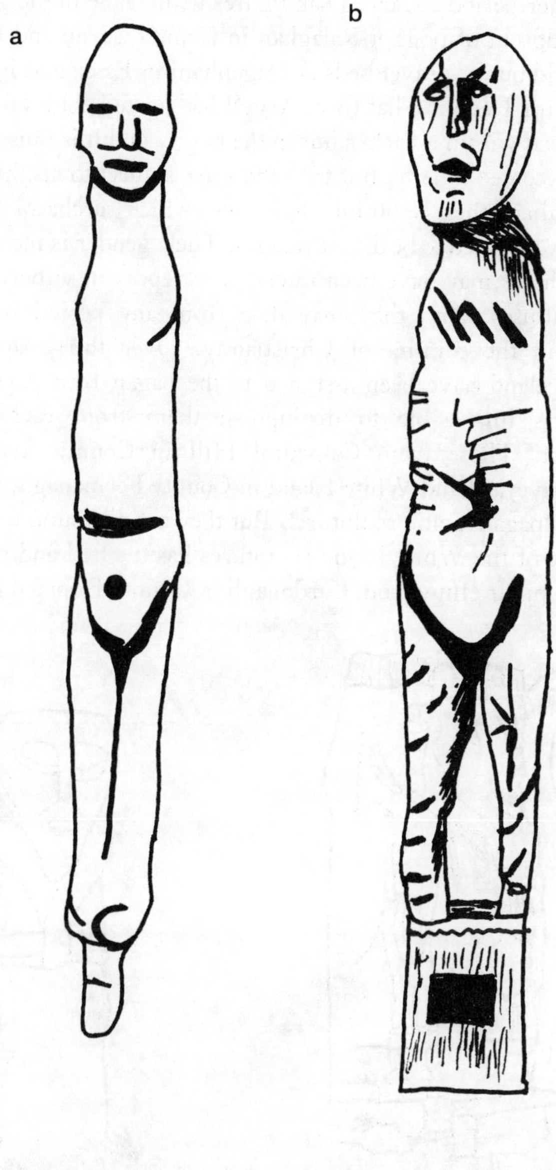

FIGURE 5.1   Iron Age images?
a Wooden idol found in a bog at Ralaghan (Co. Cavan): certainly prehistoric, but from what age, and of what gender? *b* Wooden statuette once mounted in a wicker hut in a bog at Ballachulish, Argyll, now in the National Museum of Antiquities of Scotland: usually called an Iron Age goddess, but the dating is only probable and the gender hardly emphasized.

belong to other periods. Carved oak figures with a hole in the genital area
have been dug out of bogs at Ralaghan in County Cavan and Ballaculish
in Argyll, and out of gravel beds at Dagenham in Essex and in the lower
Teign valley of Devon. That from Argyll had agate pebbles for eyes and
may have stood within a wicker hut in the bog,[21] and it is thus very likely
to have represented a deity; but the others are subject to all the questions
levelled against the Neolithic figurines which archaeologists once
automatically assumed to be divine images. Their gender is indeterminate,
because the holes may have been intended to represent vulvas or to hold
wooden phalluses. And they may date from any period between the
Neolithic and the coming of Christianity. Over thirty stone human
images in Ireland have been assigned to the pagan Iron Age. But it is
more or less impossible to distinguish them from early medieval
Christian art. Those from Cathedral Hill in County Armagh, and
Caldragh graveyard and White Island in County Fermanagh, are famous
examples of 'pagan Celtic sculpture'. But they are all found on Christian
sites and one of the White Island sculptures has the bell and crozier of a
bishop. The pillar effigy from Cardonagh in County Donegal looks like a

a

b

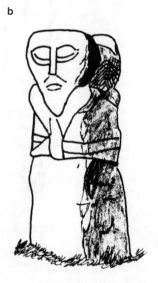

FIGURE 5.2   Pagan gods or Christian holy men?
Figures *a* on White Island and *b* in Caldragh graveyard (both in Co.
Fermanagh).

fearsome deity and has a horned figure holding two discs and a hammer upon one side of the 'body'. But on the other side is a crozier and the main image holds a bell and a book, so it is certainly Christian. A head from Beltany in the same county has often been described as pagan because it has nicks in the neck as if to represent a torc, one of the neck ornaments so familiar from Iron Age hoards. But faces upon a Christian cross at Killnaboy in County Clare have identical neck-markings. A triple head found at Corleck in County Cavan has been compared with busts of triple-headed gods who were worshipped in Roman Gaul and Britain. But the isolated Irish example may be a medieval joke.[22] The *Tripartite Life of St Patrick*, composed in about the ninth century, speaks of Maigh Slecht, 'the plain of adoration', in County Cavan, where a ring of stones contained twelve stone idols and one of gold, the latter being called Chrom Cruach. According to this tale, the pagan Irish offered a third of their healthy infants every year to these images. One might be tempted to dismiss the account as the product of over-active Christian imaginations familiar with the Old Testament, were it not for the vivid circumstantial detail with which the *Tripartite Life* describes the remains of the sanctuary as still visible. It speaks of the stones being buried up to their heads in earth, with the mark left by St Patrick's staff still upon the top of the biggest. Some explanation of the story was provided in the early years of this century, when the site was excavated and remains found of a stone decorated with abstract motifs. It may well be that a set of these, denoting a genuine pre-Christian sanctuary, was faintly visible in the early Middle Ages and generated the vivid fable.

That decorated stone is one of a small number recorded in Ireland, which from the style of their carvings can be assigned to the Iron Age more satisfactorily than the images. Four are at present known, at Turoe in County Galway, Castlegrange in County Roscommon, Killycluggin in County Cavan (Maigh Slecht), and Mullaghmast in County Kildare. There is a possible fifth built into the gable end of a church at Derrykeighan in County Antrim. All have spiral or foliate motifs similar to those found upon pagan Celtic metalwork. But their relationship with religious practice is impossible to determine. All of them seem to have been moved in historic times, so that we cannot know the position which they occupied on Iron Age sites. Nothing like them is known in Britain and nothing quite like them in Europe. The significance of their abstract decoration is open to as many different interpretations as the passage grave art, and their form and purpose have been the subject of much speculation. The most famous, the squat white Turoe Stone, has been

FIGURE 5.3   The Turoe Stone (Co. Galway)
Almost certainly Iron Age, but what was it for?

described variously as a stylized head, a phallic symbol, a sacrificial altar and a piece of art representing the union of earth and sky.[23] To the prehistorian, these stones are a classic case of a piece of jigsaw with no setting into which it can confidently be fitted. The same is true of the 'Pictish stones' of north-east Scotland, slabs beautifully carved with images of humans and animals. Some must date from before the coming of Christianity, but we have no conception of the system of belief to which their pictures refer.[24] We do have some evidence that the pagan Celts had cults which involved stones, from the well-known medieval story of St Samson of Dol, said to have found villagers venerating a megalith in Cornwall and converted them. But the pagan context of the tale, if it is not a fable, is lost as completely as that of the Irish and Scottish carved pillars.

A different category of image is represented by the figures carved into the chalk hills of southern England. Three of these have been considered to be prehistoric: the Long Man of Wilmington in Sussex, the White Horse of Uffington in Oxfordshire, and the Cerne Abbas Giant in Dorset. The first of these has been attributed to every age since the Neolithic, the second usually to the pre-Roman Iron Age and the third to

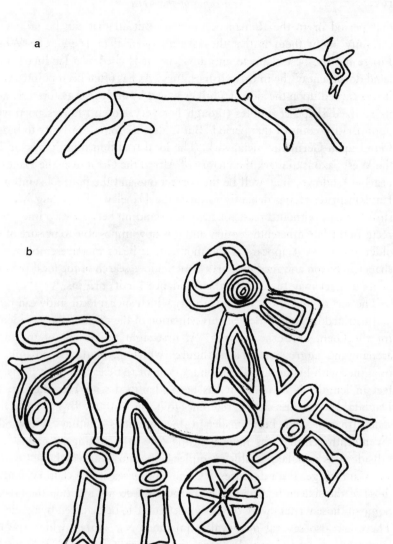

FIGURE 5.4 Horses – Celtic or Saxon?
a The famous White Horse cut out of the chalk and turf above Uffington: its stylized form could easily be Celtic, but still more easily Saxon, or even later in date; *b* this splendid and more ornate prancing horse is certainly the work of pagan Celts, specifically the Dobunni of modern Gloucestershire upon whose coins it appears. Horses were favourite motifs in Celtic metalwork: that of the Dobunni was distinguished by its three tails.

that period or to the Roman occupation. But all that can be said with certainty about them is that they are all older than 1742. The White Horse has the best claim to antiquity, for it is cited as a landmark in a legal document of the mid-twelfth century. As has often been pointed out, it was carved upon the side of a hill crowned by an Iron Age fortress, and its stylized shape resembles (though not very closely) horses portrayed upon British coins of that period. But it also has some similarity to beasts found upon Germanic metalwork. The local tradition, that it was cut by the West Saxons to mark the victory of Alfred the Great over the Danes at nearby Ashdown, may well be the correct one and the figure a symbol of English pride facing defiantly towards the Danelaw. The Long Man, a slim human, without breasts or genitals, standing between two lines, was recut in the late ninetenth century and it is now impossible to be sure of its older form. As it appears at the moment, it bears most resemblance to shapes in Saxon and medieval art. A meticulous search of the local records of its district may turn up further evidence for its origins.

The sort of uncomfortable possibility which such a local study can raise is illustrated by Joseph Bettey's investigation of the documentary evidence for the Giant of Cerne Abbas.[25] At first sight this is one of the most archaic and aggressively pagan figures which it would be possible to imagine, with his upraised club, huge pair of testicles and erect penis 30 feet in length. No wonder it has been identified with Hercules or the Daghda. But the first certain reference to it was in 1742. In 1751 a writer stated that it had been made in the previous century. Now, the seventeenth century was indeed a time when the cutting of giants into hillsides was popular, notable examples being those carved above Oxford and Cambridge. But references to Cerne in sources of that century, and in those of the sixteenth are fairly numerous and do not mention the Giant. Some of those writers were certainly not people to be deterred by prudery. There are also several medieval inquisitions *post mortem* which specify landmarks around Cerne. In them, the modern 'Giant Hill' is 'Trendle Hill', named after the old earthwork, apparently Iron Age or early medieval, on the top. None mentions the great carving. Medieval authors do speak of a god called Hel or Helith as having been worshipped around Cerne before Christianity, but none relates this to the spectacular figure. It may turn out to be that the story of the deity helped to inspire the later carving of the Giant, not vice versa. It used to be thought remarkable that such an erotic work of art could exist within sight of the great medieval abbey of Cerne and be kept in good repair. This was taken by some as a sign of the continuing strength of paganism in the medieval Church. It

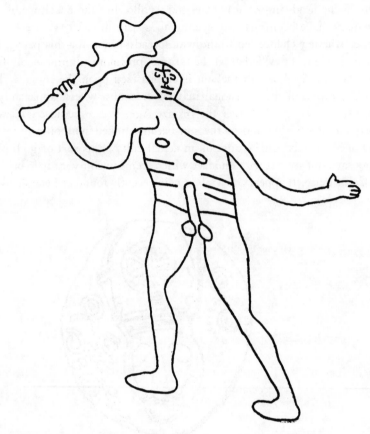

FIGURE 5.5   Pagan god or early modern humour?
The Giant of Cerne Abbas (Dorset).

may be instead that the Giant simply did not exist in the Middle Ages, and is a gross piece of late seventeenth-century humour.

One possible further source of representations of deities is the coins which were minted by the kingdoms of south-eastern Britain from about 50 BC onwards.[26] But the result is (again) very disappointing. Heads of rulers and figures of animals abound upon them, as indeed do the faces of divine beings. But the practice of striking coins was copied by the British from the Romans across the Channel, and the images were often copied with it. Imitations of that common Roman design, the head of Medusa, appear occasionally, and other figures have been taken as crude copies of deities upon the Empire's money. But the most common of all such images, found upon the coins of all eight of the British tribes which set up mints, is the head (in profile) of the god Apollo. For these Celtic realms, it seems to have been virtually synonymous with money. We are left to wonder whether chance led to the widespread fashion for this particular Roman design, or whether it had some profound significance. The association of Apollo with the sun is emphasized upon the coins by his radiant crown and the occasional juxtaposition of a wheel, apparently a heavenly or solar symbol since the Bronze Age. Was it because gold was the colour of sunlight and so the sun became linked symbolically to all coins of all metals? Or because of an actual cult of this sort of god? We cannot say, and are left with one face which seems unequivocally to be that of a Celtic deity. It appears on a silver coin recently found at Petersfield in

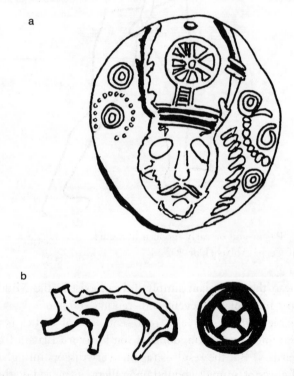

FIGURE 5.6   Iron Age images: the wheel
a Silver coin dated to *c.*AD 20, found in Hampshire and now in the National Museum of Wales: this striking face is the only certain image of a deity yet known to survive from the non-Roman Iron Age of the entire British Isles; *b* the wheel again, probably a symbol of the sun or of the whole heaven, this time modelled in metal; found with miniature boars at Hounslow, Middlesex, now in the British Museum.

Hampshire and dated to around AD 20. The features are of a bearded male with antlers and a crown bearing a wheel, again a form evocative of majesty. This single, though very powerful, image is the only one from the British Isles which can at present confidently be said to portray a divine being of the non-Roman Iron Age.

We should turn now to examine the formal structure of pagan Celtic religion in these islands: its temples or shrines, its priests or priestesses and its festivals. The holy places are notoriously hard to identify. Whereas the settlement sites and fortresses of the Iron Age are usually very conspicuous, the timber buildings within them have left only groups of post-holes which often conceal more than they reveal about the activities once associated with the structures. Shrines can only be identified by deposits of votive offerings or by the fact that the building concerned was set apart from others and had no obvious domestic or agricultural purpose. On this basis, some twenty-four have now been identified in England, at sixteen different sites. Of these, 70 per cent were rectangular or square, and the rest a variety of other shapes. A few were

The Iron Age temple at Heathrow, Middlesex, as imagined by the late Alan Sorrell. The ground plan and the bull sacrifice are well-attested by archaeology, but the upper part of the building is drawn speculatively. By kind permission of the Museum of London.

large enough to contain about fifty people, but most were only intended for a dozen and a quarter of the total could have comfortably accommodated only a single worshipper at a time. In their structure they resembled the other huts and halls of the time. Virtually all had doors facing between north-east and south-east, towards the sunrise. Over 90 per cent were isolated from other buildings within an open space and almost half had an enclosure to set them off further. Just over half were inside settlements or forts, but the rest stood in open countryside, reached only by special journey. In every case, if the site continued in use during the Roman period then the Iron Age shrine was rebuilt as a Romano-Celtic temple. Just over half of them produced votive objects when excavated. Brooches were found at seven, coins at six, animal bones at four and real or miniature weapons or horse harness at three. Pots were deposited at Uley in Gloucestershire and currency bars at Hayling Island in Sussex. It is very likely that offerings of food, drink or cloth were made at some, or all, but these leave no trace in the archaeological record. The presence of weapons at two sites indicates that a war deity was worshipped at them. But the identity of those venerated at the other shrines remains a puzzle.[27]

The fact that relatively few pre-Roman Celtic shrines have been identified in Britain does derive in part from a problem which has already been stated, that they are hard to spot. But there is also evidence that the pagan Celts often worshipped outside formal structures and did not require them. Some of this will be considered later in this chapter, in the section upon cult practices. Here it is necessary to note that certain natural sites also featured as holy places, in a way in which they may or may not have done earlier in prehistory. The Roman authors Lucan and Pomponius Mela wrote of the Celts of Gaul as worshipping in groves of trees, and Tacitus and Dio Cassius attributed the same practice to the British. Dio recorded that Boudicca's sacrifices to Andraste were made in such a grove. The word used by the Romans for these places was 'nemeton', and they incorporated it into the names of forts and towns in their province of Britain such as Vernemeton near Leicester, Nemetostatio in north Devon, Medionemeton in West Lothian and Aquae Arnemetiae (modern Buxton in Derbyshire).[28] Such sacred stands of trees may well have surrounded some of the shrines mentioned above and some of the pits and shafts to be dealt with below.

Then there are the famous Celtic holy wells. The veneration of natural springs of water for their sacred and medicinal value is so much a feature of Ireland, Cornwall, Wales, Scotland and western England that its association with the Celts seems natural. Similar cults were, however, found over most of the ancient Mediterranean world and of Europe. It is equally natural to speak of the 'Christianization' of these holy wells, whereby their rededication to a saint permitted their use for over a thousand more years. Indeed, Adomnán's *Life of Columba*, from the late seventh century AD, tells how the holy man concerned (who lived a hundred years before) reconsecrated one such holy well in Scotland. Furthermore, there is evidence from Roman Britain of the veneration of certain springs, which were believed to be homes to local deities. But, frustratingly, there is virtually nothing to testify to the use of these places in the non-Roman Iron Age. They do not feature in the early Irish or Welsh texts, and only the spectacular hot spring at Bath has yielded any pre-Roman votive offerings (in the form of some coins). Of the stone structures built over the wells, the oldest which can be dated with confidence was at St Cleer in Cornwall. Although it was destroyed and is known only from drawings, both from these and from local records it can be attributed to the late thirteenth century. A few others, such as that surviving at Perranzabuloe, also in Cornwall, may be a little older, but this is impossible to determine. Not a single structure, not even a basin or retaining wall, can be convincingly dated back to the early Middle Ages, let alone to pre-Christian times. Most of the surviving stonework seems to be late medieval, a period when there is ample evidence for a flourishing cult of these wells as holy and healing places.[29] We are at a loss to know which of them were venerated by pagan Celts as well as pious (and sickly) Christians, let alone how those pagans conceived of them or what they did there.

Thus far, the impression has been given that very little trace now remains of the sacred sites of the non-Roman pagan Celts. But there is a spectacular exception to this rule in the great ceremonial centres of Iron Age Ireland. *The Martyrology of Oengus*, a Christian text composed around AD 800, named four sites as pagan Irish capitals: Tara and Dún Ailinne in Leinster, Cruachain in Connacht and Emain Macha in Ulster. In the epic literature, Tara, Cruachain, and Emain Macha feature as residences for royalty and for warriors, while the Dún is described as a fortress, cemetery and royal residence in Orthanach's poem to St Brighid, which dates to around AD 830. None of this is corroborated by archaeology. Nothing at Cruachain (now Rathcroghan) and only one mound at Tara has been properly excavated, but the forms of the enclosures at each do not suggest permanent residences. Some of them are very large with low walls or banks, suggesting places for open-air assemblies or games. Others are small with ditches inside banks, and at Cruachain form rings and ovals without discernible entrances. They do not seem suited to the roles of strongpoints or residences, but rather of seasonal or occasional meeting-places. This impression is borne out by the palpable evidence produced by the excavation of the other two sites. At Emain Macha (known in modern times as Navan Fort), a group of huts was replaced around 100 BC with a massive circular wooden building 130 feet across, surrounded by a ditch and then a bank. That it was not a residence is suggested by the lack of domestic debris and the fact that after a short period it was carefully immolated: its outer posts were burned and it was buried in a big cairn coated with turf, a process suggesting that it was being rendered ritually redundant rather than simply destroyed by enemies. Dún Ailinne had an almost identical history, though it may have consisted of rings of posts open to the sky rather than a building (and the same might just be true of Emain). It seems to have survived until the fourth century AD as a freestanding circle of timbers in which occasional feasts were held.[30] All this suggests that the Iron Age Irish had regional ceremonial precincts which were as impressive in their way as almost anything from earlier in prehistory. Nothing like them is known in Britain. It also suggests that the early Christian writers who composed the epic literature knew nothing about these structures save the location of their sites.

The Irish centres provide a magnificent conclusion to those types of place and building which can more or less confidently be stated to have been used for sacred purposes in the non-Roman Iron Age in these islands. But there remains to be considered a group of structures which may, in some areas, have been religious in purpose, and which are at present controversial. They are found widely upon Iron Age settlements and fortified sites in Ireland and Brittany, where they are known to archaeologists as 'souterrains', in northern Scotland, where they are traditionally called 'earth houses', and in the far west of Cornwall, where they have the local name of 'fogous' (meaning caves). They are completely absent from the rest of Britain, which is a puzzle in itself. They consist of underground chambers with passages leading to them, often with a restricted point or points through which a person has to crawl. Most have rough-hewn walls with roofing slabs, and sometimes with masonry lintels and jambs or pillars to support the ceilings. In Ireland there is very little doubt as to their purpose, for the early literary sources spell it out: they were temporary refuges for people and their valuables if raiders broke into their village or fort. The inhabitants would crawl into a 'souterrain', leaving the enemy to seize the livestock and whatever else had been left above before moving on. Excavation has confirmed the message of the texts. The structures were ideal for defence, few warriors being foolish enough to try crawling, one by one, down a tunnel which had armed foes at the end waiting for their assailants' arms and heads to emerge. Concealed air-vents made it difficult to smoke out those inside, who could only be starved or dug out. Few Celtic war bands would have the time for such an operation, given the fact (amply revealed by the epic literature) that their campaigns consisted of hit-and-run attacks. The 'souterrains' are the wrong shape for the storage of goods in general, and excavation has revealed no deposits of dust from regular opening and no trace of storage containers. Instead the finds have been, as the literature indicated, of valuables, such as coins, a drinking vessel, a silver brooch, a bell and a skull once hung on a hook as a trophy.

The structures and archaeological data of the British and Breton sites offer very little reason to suspect that their purpose was at all different. Indeed, they would hardly merit a place in this book at all were it not for the common assertion made about the Cornish 'fogous' (though very seldom about the 'souterrains' or 'earth houses') that they might have been shrines. The evidence is, on the whole, overwhelmingly against this idea. Everywhere they occur, in the British Isles or in Brittany, these structures lack votive offerings or signs of animal sacrifice. They are mostly too large to be used for individual worship or vigil and mostly too narrow for assemblies. They do not seem to resonate impressively, were not burial places and almost always have ceilings too low to permit human beings to stand up. The fogou set in a beautiful glade within the grounds of Rosemirren House, Lamorna, Cornwall, has a faint carving at the entrance interpreted by earth mystics as a god or warrior. If both carving and structure are indeed Iron Age, then the refuge theory is not weakened. In Ireland, where that purpose seems proved, the souterrain at Rathcroghan has a slab bearing the names of two gods. But there again no trace of ritual activity was found and the carving was probably (as perhaps at Rosemirren) to appoint supernatural guardians for the refuge. The same consideration may lie behind the fact noted by the artist Ian Cooke, that the entrances of the Cornish fogous are or were almost always to the north-east, as if to face the midsummer sunrise. The only possible ritual deposit made at any of these structures anywhere within their range was at Rennibister in Orkney. The chamber of that earth house was scattered with human skulls, most of them taken from children: either the builders were head-hunters or they had chosen to preserve these parts of their family dead. So, overall, the belief that some of these underground constructions were religious in nature is very little supported by fact or inference. Indeed, the Irish evidence would be compelling for all, were it not for one large problem of chronology: all the structures in Ireland were apparently built between AD 500 and 1200, all those in Britain and Brittany between 200 BC and AD 200. The gap in time, as puzzling as the absence of these monuments from most of Britain, does raise the possibility that the Irish comparison may be a distorting one. And why would the Cornish need refuges during the first century of Roman rule, when peace ought to have obtained? Against pirates and Irish raiders in pursuit of the tin and copper mined locally for the emperor? Ultimately, there is still an enigma.[31]

This is probably all that can be said at present about pagan Celtic holy places. The 'problem of timber' may well operate here, for wooden images, altars and votives may have existed in large numbers and rotted away. But the lack of shrines in areas where the inhabitants built in stone is so striking that it must reflect a genuine aspect of their religion: that it did not greatly depend upon monuments and artefacts. How important, then, were its personnel? Did it have powerful professional mediators between deities and people? Here we face a situation opposite to that of the sacred places, for we depend heavily upon the literature, and archaeology can hardly help us at all. The Graeco-Roman writers agreed that the Celtic intellectual elite was divided into Bards, Druids and Vates, the last two categories being religious officials. The distinction between them was obviously difficult to make. The Druids were more prestigious and more concerned with philosophy and theology, while the Vates were more concerned with divination and sacrifice. But the Druids also undertook the same tasks as the Vates. Caesar states that the Druids had an assembly and a chief, met in the tribal territory of the Vates in Gaul and sent their pupils to learn from the source of their religion in Britain. But he had a vested interest in exaggerating the sophistication of the Gallic peoples to the Roman Senate, to support his assertions that they were a good prize if conquered and a threat if not. He saw Gaul at the height of its pre-Roman development. And, unfortunately, he was the only writer whose work survives to have had first-hand experience of the Gallic peoples before they became Romanized. He also recorded that the Druids were teachers, healers and judges and kept the calendar. Some of this is confirmed by the other Roman texts. Strabo and Diodorus Siculus agreed upon the judicial role of the Druids. Pliny confirms that they operated as healers. Lucan and Strabo state that they also cared for shrines. Much of this is neatly paralleled in the early Irish literature. Vates do not appear there, but Druids are shown as ranking before kings in assemblies. They sacrifice, prophesy, heal, teach, make magic and give counsel. There is also a glimpse of the same people at work in northern Britain, in Adomnán's *Life of Columba*. He writes of 'magi', who advised Pictish kings and 'magnified' their deities. The *Tripartite Life of St Patrick* contains further evidence concerning both the appearance of Druids, crediting them with the tonsure and white tunics, and their ceremonies, speaking of their baptizing children in water. Other early Irish texts also contain this last assertion, and the Roman Pliny portrayed Gallic Druids as donning white robes for the mistletoe-cutting rite.[32] But the *Tripartite Life* is a relatively late (eighth- to tenth-century) and wildly imaginative document, and in all these details it may be projecting Christian ways back on to the old religions. The same may be true of the other sources which mention baptism, and the description in Pliny may be coincidental.

All the various authors agree that these priests were male, and that the formal religion of the Celtic peoples was mediated through men. This did not mean, according to the same writers, that religious affairs were wholly the preserve of a priesthood. Other sorts of men, such as bards or physicians, and all sorts of women, feature in the Irish literature as gifted with prophecy, skilled in magic and capable of communing with deities. These people were essentially interlopers to the formal system of religion, but they were treated with great respect and their words were heeded. The appearance of the girl Fedelm before Queen Medb in the epic *Tain Bo Cuailnge* is perhaps the most dramatic among several examples. But the absence of priestesses is remarkable, especially as many other ancient peoples, including the Romans, had them. Tacitus records that when a Roman army prepared to attack the island which was later called Anglesey, the natives were encouraged by Druids and by black-robed women carrying torches. But whether the latter were religious dignitaries, prophetesses or just cheerleaders, we cannot tell. Strabo and Pomponius Mela repeat a story, old by their time, of an island off the west coast of Gaul which was a sanctuary staffed entirely by women.[33] The trouble with this report, which comes from Poseidonios, is that it was related when so little was known about western Gaul among Graeco-Roman authors that it was more or less over the edge of the world. It existed in the same sort of realm as India, which Roman geographers portrayed as having people with dogs' heads. The descriptions furnished of this island, where according to one writer the women could turn themselves into animals, and according to another they tore apart one of their number each year and carried her pieces around the temple, sound rather like the tall stories of travellers. Strabo himself thought them dubious. By the time that Roman rule, and Roman knowledge, reached the region concerned, no more was heard of them.

But then, the Irish Druids were properly speaking only regulators of the relationship between deities and people, there to conduct rites and interpret signs. In the last resort they seem to have been expendable. The indispensable figure, representing the true mediator between human and divine, was the local or tribal king. He had to be of royal stock, to be free of physical blemishes (the loss of an eye or limb disqualified him) and to prove himself favoured by the deities. An unlucky monarch, under whom the people suffered military defeat, sickness or dearth, had in theory to be deposed. The king was set apart from other humans by *geisa*, prohibitions which he dared not break for fear of forfeiting divine support. In *Togail Bruidne Da Derga*, King Conare has a total of nine *geisa*, including not being preceded into Da Derga's hall by three red-dressed men, not admitting a single person to a building after sunset, not interfering in a quarrel between two of his servants and not hunting in Cernae. There is ample evidence from the early texts that having served a period of 'apprenticeship' (which could last years) a king was regarded as having passed the necessary tests and could receive his *feis* or inauguration. At the heart of this was a ceremony in which he symbolically wed the tutelary goddess of his district or tribe. How this was done, we do not know. It seems to have involved a ritual nuptial banquet. According to Gerald of Wales, writing in the late twelfth century, the monarchs of what is now County Donegal were still given their *feis* in the old way. The king coupled with a mare which was then killed and boiled: while his subjects ate its meat, he bathed in water and then dressed in white. He stood barefoot in a footprint carved out of rock or sat on a stone to be handed his rod of office. Now, Gerald never went to Donegal, and the royal family which was supposed still to be practising this sacred bestiality had been Christian for at least six centuries and supplied (among other churchmen) twelve abbots of Iona. There is a strong possibility that the Welshman had been talking either to Gaels who decided to have some fun with him, or to Anglo-Normans who would believe almost anything of their native enemies. But bestiality apart, the ceremony sounds credible, and some details can be substantiated, as we shall see. It is clear that one of the important functions of Irish goddesses was to accept human leaders in marriage. In *Swift Chariots and Horses that Carried off the Prize*, an eight- or ninth-century poet celebrates the Christianization of his land by having its 'mother', 'the consort of kings', marry Jesus. *The Number of Medb's Husbands* lists the local monarchs who were said to have been wed to this great queen, the legendary ruler of Connacht. It is this, rather than her supernatural attributes (which include carving out valleys with her menstrual flows) which make one wonder whether she was not originally the divine patroness of the province.[34]

The inauguration sites of Irish kings are still among some of the best-remembered monuments of the island. Those of the O'Donnell and O'Neill in western Ulster were used until the end of the sixteenth century. The former, probably the scene of the rite described by Gerald, is a rock with the famous holy well Tobar an Duin at its foot. It was presumably in this well that the king bathed. The O'Neills were enthroned upon a great stone chair at the fort of Tullaghoge, which was destroyed by the army of Elizabeth I when the O'Neill's power was broken in 1602. The ritual of the bathing and the seating on a stone, described by Gerald, was still used by the fifteenth-century Macdonald rulers of the Scottish Hebrides, styled Lords of the Isles.[35] A spectacular case of the use of a footprint is supplied by the fort of Dunadd, in the Kilmartin valley of Argyll which has already been noted as a great centre of Bronze Age monuments and art. At the opening of Scottish history it was one seat of the kingdom of Dalriada, and upon the summit of the fortress the modern traveller can still find the carved footprint. Next to it in the rock surface is a bowl-shaped hollow and a splendid figure of a wild boar, perhaps the tribal emblem or perhaps an embodiment of kingly courage and fierceness. A ruler placing his foot in the print would be gazing north straight at the ancient row of megalithic monuments. No stone now exists there upon which a ruler might have been enthroned, but an unprovable tradition holds that one was used, and met with a glorious destiny. For this, the story holds, was the stone which was later (like the kings of Dalriada) moved to Scone and upon which all the kings of early medieval Scotland were crowned. It is now in the coronation chair in Westminster Abbey. Yet Anglo-Saxon monarchs were also first enthroned upon a rock, which survives in its original place at Kingston-upon-Thames in Surrey. Coronation or inauguration stones were also used for early medieval Scandinavian monarchs and German emperors.[36] Other aspects of Irish sacred kingship are even more widespread in time and geography. Virtually everywhere that monarchy has existed, it has been associated with a special relationship with deities and invested with a more than human aura. Any modern reader acquainted with the Old Testament or with ancient Greek drama will know how all-pervasive was the notion

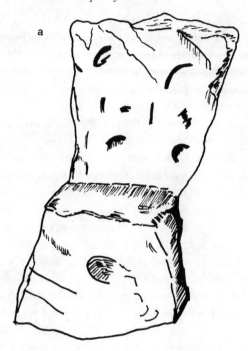

FIGURE 5.7   Relics of the Gaelic *feis*
a The only surviving stone inauguration chair, of the O'Neill of Clandeboy, now in the Belfast Museum; *b* an Irish inauguration mound, set round with stones: used by the O'Connors, it still rises from the landscape near Tulks (Co. Roscommon).

that misfortunes to the community meant that the king had offended a divine power.

So it is necessary to ask what was peculiarly Irish, or Celtic, about the system of kingship portrayed in Ireland's literature. A few features swiftly emerge. The footprint at the inauguration ceremony seems to be confined to Gaelic areas, and only appears in Scotland in places where Irish influence was very strong. Most important, the period of 'probation' for a ruler followed by his marriage to the tutelary goddess seems to have been unknown to Celts outside Ireland. The Graeco-Roman authors never mention it. Indeed, the whole tradition of royal inheritance employed by the Irish seems not to have been used by other peoples. It depended either upon tanistry, whereby a successor was recognized by the tribe during the existing king's lifetime and deputized for him, or upon a choice from within the royal family made by a Druid with divine inspiration. This would help to explain why the Irish do not seem to have had queens ruling in their own right, apart from the legendary Medb whose divine origin has been discussed. If only men are chosen to rule, the question of how a queen could marry a goddess if she happened to inherit the throne is rendered unnecessary. But it may not have applied to the British. Boudicca's rebellion began because her husband, king of the Iceni, had died, leaving his realm to the Roman emperor as joint ruler with his two daughters. Such a situation, whereby a tribe could be disposed of by a monarch's will or treaty, is very unlike that portrayed in the early Irish sources. We are left to wonder whether it had always been so, or whether the kingdoms of southern Britain had adopted Roman law as well as other traits of Roman civilization around the beginning of the Christian era.

It remains in this discussion of religious personnel to consider the status of heroes and heroines. So many scholars in the past have proposed that these figures in the Celtic tales are actually debased deities, that it is necessary to make an analysis of their role. And in some cases characters who appear to be human, such as Medb or St Brighid, probably were indeed once regarded as divine. But the warriors who are the main protagonists of the stories have the same status as those in the Greek myths, standing between the human and divine orders. To regard characters such as Cú Chulainn, Fergus Mac Roich or Conall Cernach as former gods turned into humans by a later storyteller is to misunderstand their literary and religious function. They are part of the human world and its affairs, are subject like other humans to the enchantments and machinations of deities, and perish as humans do. But they are marked off from the general run of humanity. Sometimes they have a divine parent and their births are accompanied by special portents. Usually they perform feats which are clearly impossible in the normal human world. Each of Cú Chulainn's cries could make a hundred warriors die of fright, and in his battle frenzy, apart from other unpleasant physical alterations, a column of blood would rise from the centre of his head. Fergus Mac

Roich was literally rather larger than life if, as one tale insists, his penis was seven fingers long and his scrotum the size of a sack of flour. So was King Bran in a Welsh tale, who could wade the Irish Sea and whose severed head could live on for years.[37] It will be clear from this why Medb's remarkable way of making valleys does not automatically mean that she is a goddess and not a queen. All this is the sort of half-serious exaggeration which audiences have enjoyed in heroic tales at all times and places. Cú Chulainn is no more a former god than Superman is. The religious function of Celtic heroic figures (and indeed most such figures in tales across the world) is to duplicate upon an informal basis what sacred monarchs and priests or priestesses do by nature of office: defend and inspire their people and mediate between the human and divine worlds.

So now to festivals. The four great points of the ancient Irish year are neatly set out in the Ulster tale of the wooing of Emer by Cú Chulainn. Among various tasks which she set him before he could wed her, was to go sleepless from 'Samhain, when the summer goes to its rest, until Imbolc, when the ewes are milked at spring's beginning; from Imbolc until Beltine at the summer's beginning and from Beltine to Bron Trogain, earth's sorrowing in autumn'.[38] This means, from 1 November to 1 February, from 1 February to 1 May, and from 1 May to 1 August. There are signs that the names of the festivals varied between localities just as deities did, though not as greatly. In the Yellow Book of Lecan, a high medieval text preserving some early medieval tales, it is said that the common people called Samhain 'the feast of Mongfind' instead.[39] Legend made Mongfind a witch-queen married to an early king of Tara, but the fact that the same source states that the people still prayed to her on 31 October indicates that we are dealing here with another goddess: queens and heroines were not prayed to, or given commemorative feasts. The August festival is called 'the first day of the Trogan-month' in the fourteenth-century *Colloquy of the Old Men*, echoing the word for it given by Emer. But the same line in the *Colloquy* refers to it as having a new title, Lughnasadh. It is by this name, meaning 'the feast of the god Lugh', that it is generally known to scholars. Lugh has been described above, but who or what Trogan or Trogain was is anybody's guess. The two names for the festival seem both to be ancient, as 'Lughnasadh' appears in the texts of the ninth and tenth centuries.[40] The spelling of all of them varies, Beltine being also written Beltain, Beltane, Beal-tine, Beltan, Bel-tien or Baltein. Sir James Frazer arbitrarily settled on one of the Scottish versions, Beltane, and made this standard among British scholars and modern pagans alike. But whatever the names, the pattern of the four quarter days was standard in early medieval Ireland. There is no sign of any celebration of the solstices or equinoxes.

Of the four festivals, there is no doubt whatsoever from the literature that Samhain, which began the year in November, was the most important. Tribal assemblies were held then, rulers and warriors conferred and laws were made. It was also the time at which humans were most susceptible to divine and supernatural interference. At Samhain heroic and royal figures met fated deaths or enchantments. Spirits, monsters or fairies attacked royal capitals, with physical destruction or with evil spells. Divine women allowed themselves to be wooed by human males. Supernatural beings fought or mated with each other, while warriors, gathered in royal halls, made important boasts or challenges. Magical gifts were presented to kings, or things stolen magically from them.[41] It is worth stressing that most of these occurrences took place in daylight, so the whole day of 1 November was regarded as exciting and perilous, and not just (as in modern times) the night before. After this feast, it was Beltine which features most prominently in the stories. Upon 1 May, according to the *Leabhar Gabhála*, the Tuatha de Danaan landed in Ireland. Other key events also occur at that date, but it is of minor importance in the tales compared to the great haunted festival which opened winter. Imbolc and Lughnasadh appear as feasts, but without much arcane significance attached to either.

The Irish pattern of festivals is so often taken as typical of 'the Celts', from Ireland to the Alps, that it must be pointed out that the available evidence on the matter is inconclusive. The early Welsh literature ascribes no importance to 1 November, 1 February or 1 August, and all the emotional investment made by the Irish writers in Samhain is attached instead to May Day (Calan Mai) and the night before it. Upon May Eve, according to the tale of Pwyll, a demon stole new-born children and animals in the land of Dyfed. During that night, in the tale of Lludd and Llevelys, dragons fought each other and terrified the people with their screeching. At Llyn Cwm Llwch, in the Brecon Beacons, a doorway into fairyland was said to have opened each May Day.[42] That festival features as the favourite one in the work of medieval poets such as Dafydd ap Gwilym, and indeed the first literary reference to a maypole in the British Isles is probably in a fourteenth-century poem by Gryffydd ap Adda ap Dafydd.

For the Celts of Scotland there is absolutely no literary evidence upon the matter, and that for Gaul is not very helpful. No Graeco-Roman author says anything about festivals. Caesar records that daily units were reckoned from sunset to sunset, so that each night was counted within the date of the following day. But he does not say which nights and days were important. His statement about the reckoning of the dates is proved by the Coligny calendar, an object engraved in bronze in the first century AD and dug up in France in 1897. Even this is only in some senses 'Celtic', for it was written in Roman characters, under Roman rule, and apparently kept in a temple of Apollo. It is certainly not the calendar of Rome, though, differing in the calculation of the months (from the full moon), their names, and the specification of lucky and unlucky days. But nor is it the same as the Irish calendar, it may not even have been generally used in Gaul, and it does not specify feasts.[43] Nor do the Graeco-Roman sources describe any seasonal ritual. Pliny's famous description of the gathering of the mistletoe by the priests of Gaul was not a regular custom. According to him it occurred only in the rare event of the plant being found on an oak tree, and then took place upon the sixth day of the moon. He did add that the same day began the months (which, again, is different from the Coligny calendar), and that these priests hailed the moon as healer of all things.[44] It is not clear from Pliny whether these statements were intended to apply to more than some of the Gallic tribes, and none of them is corroborated by the British and Irish texts.

But then the latter are themselves only slightly more helpful. In the seventeenth century a myth was concocted that the so-called 'Teltown marriages', trial weddings transacted for a set period at the fair of that name in County Meath, were originally ceremonies held at Lughnasadh and associated with the goddess Tailtu. In the 1950s this was disproved, it seems conclusively, and it looks as if 'Queen Tailtu, foster-mother of Lugh' was herself an early medieval poetic invention. Much more celebrated is the extinguishing of all fires at Tara at Beltine and their relighting from a single consecrated flame, recorded in Muirchú's seventh-century *Life of Patrick*. The point about Muirchú's description is that St Patrick defied the custom by kindling his Easter Eve fire, provoking a confrontation with the pagan priests which (of course) led to the triumph of Christianity. The obvious trouble with this story is that there is no way in which Easter and Beltine could fall on the same day. Other early sources for Patrick's life, and indeed his own autobiography, the *Confessio*, do not mention it and it is quite clearly a fabrication. There does, however, seem to be a real ritual involved. In the seventeenth century the antiquarian Geoffrey Keating noted that at Tlachtaga in ancient times the ceremony had been carried out at Samhain. Keating is not a very reliable source, but in this case his specification of time and place may be taken at least to signify a possibility. Much more important is the assertion by Cormac, writing around 900, that in every district at Beltine the fires were extinguished and the Druids lit two in honour of Bel. They canted 'numerous spells' over them and then cattle were driven between them, being thereafter divinely protected from disease.[45] The name of the deity looks suspicious: was the Christian Cormac remembering a real god, inventing one from the name of the feast or drafting in the Biblical one Baal? But the driving of the cattle is a rite which survived into relatively modern times, not just in Ireland but in other parts of the British Isles and at other festivals. The 'new fire' was still made on 1 May in Gaelic Scotland in the last century. Here we do seem to have evidence of a genuine and important ancient calendar custom, even if it is not absolutely certain that it occurred everywhere in Ireland and always at Beltine. We are also considerably less certain how far it extended into Britain.

The driving of cattle past fire was just one folk ritual which survived into modern times, and we need now to take a general look at the value of such practices for the study of ancient Celtic religion. There are some very large traps here for the unwary. A classic example is that of the Puck Fair at Killorglin in County Kerry, which, having been granted letters patent in 1613, is now the oldest fair surviving in Ireland. It is also distinguished by the presence of its 'king', a huge male goat who is hoisted on to a high platform from where he gazes down upon the proceedings for their full three days. This custom, and the fact that (at least before the adoption of the Gregorian calendar in 1752) the fair fell at Lughnasadh, has led some incautious modern folklorists to conclude that this was 'obviously' an ancient Celtic feast at which a goat was worshipped or sacrificed. Máire MacNeill, the historian of Lughnasadh, noted that in fact the presence of the presiding animal is only recorded from 1837 onwards, and doubted that the fair and the custom could have survived all the changes of Kerry's turbulent medieval and early modern history.[46] Also interesting is what the villagers themselves had to say when I asked them about the origins of their tradition. Some held that it was to commemorate a fleeing goat who gave warning that a group of Cromwell's soldiers were on their way to loot Killorglin. Others insisted that it dated from 1808, when a goat was first raised on a platform by the local landowner, Harman Blennerhasset, as a sign that goats alone were sold at the fair beneath it. This was because he was not entitled to levy tolls upon cattle, sheep or horse fairs, but the custom persisted even when the sale of those other animals was reintroduced. The first story is a version of an international popular tale, which counts against it. The second fits the known dates, and is so circumstantial that it may well be true. The only person present at the Puck Fair during my visit who was convinced that it had a pagan origin was a German tourist, who had been assured of the fact by his guidebook.

Then there is the case of Hinton St George, a Somerset village through which, upon the last Thursday evening of October, the children carry hollowed-out mangel-wurzels containing candles. The shells of the vegetables are carved with faces or designs, some of great beauty. They are called 'punkies', and the event bears the name 'Punky Night'. The popular books upon English folklore and calendar customs published during the 1960s tended to describe this as a vestige of the honouring of vegetation spirits at Samhain. At Hinton, as at Killorglin, I was given two explanations by the villagers for what they were doing. One lady told me that the word punkie came from 'spunkie', the word used in mid-Somerset for the little flames of ignited marsh gas known elsewhere as will-o'-the-wisps or jack-o'-lanterns. She went on to say that they were believed to be the souls of dead babies, and that the Hinton tradition was designed originally to honour and to placate them at the season of Samhain. Others among the villagers were quite irritated by her ideas. They agreed upon the origin of the name, but insisted that the punkies were first carved as genuine lanterns, to guide the men of Hinton back from a fair held in late October at a nearby village. Their families would turn out to welcome them home, and the procession and merrymaking became a festivity in its own right which endured after the feast ceased to be held. Nobody in Hinton that night had much time for the idea of vegetation spirits.

A third example is that of May Day at Padstow in Cornwall. This seaport probably celebrates the festival more vividly than any other place in the British Isles. Its streets are decorated with greenery, and through them dance, in separate parts of the town, two 'hobby horses' with ferocious masks. At times the 'horses' sink to the ground and then revive. If a woman is snatched momentarily under the cape of the 'horse' by the man dancing within it, she is thought to have good luck. It must be said that in Padstow upon this day there is an archaic atmosphere of such intensity as to impress almost anybody. The throbbing of the drums, the singing of the local May Song and the plunges and twirls of these monstrous mock-beasts produce an effect which is more familiar to me from tribal rituals in the tropics. But how archaic is it? The leaflet obtainable in the town suggests that it is an ancient British custom, perhaps 4000 years old. The earliest record of it, on the other hand, is in 1803.[47] None of the seventeenth- or eighteenth-century descriptions of Cornwall refers to the horses, and nor does that of the Elizabethan Richard Carew of St Anthony, who gave much attention to local customs. There is nothing especially Celtic about the Padstow festivity, which combines three old English traditions which were once widespread: Bringing Home The May, the Mummers' Play and the hobby horse dance. Only the snatching of the women by the 'horses' has no known exact parallel. Some of the more literary of the townspeople told me that the whole ritual was a memory of days in which the death and rebirth of a god, and the parallel sacrifice or symbolic resurrection of a sacred king, were enacted. I asked them where they had heard this, and those who could remember said that it was asserted by modern experts.

These three cases, which could be multiplied many times, are all inconclusive. They all leave room for several opinions, though at Killorglin and Hinton St George I wished that some folklorists would listen a little more carefully to the folk, and at Padstow I wished that the folk would listen a little less carefully to some of the folklorists. What can be stated categorically about them is that they furnish no good evidence for the nature of pagan Celtic religion. So, exercising a greater caution, what insights does a study of folk tales and folk rites provide on the subject? Such as there are can be obtained in two ways: by a close examination of one festival in the British Isles or by a general survey of calendar customs. Both present problems. The outstanding (indeed the only) example of the former is Máire MacNeill's famous book upon Lughnasadh.[48] She established that in the early medieval texts it was regarded as the celebration of the beginning of harvest. She then located 195 sites, usually on heights or beside water, at which Irish villagers had assembled in the eighteenth and nineteenth centuries in order to share this celebration. She discovered that many of these places were associated with a local myth in which a heroic newcomer (normally St Patrick) had defeated an established and unpleasant lord (normally Chrom Dubh). She found memories of similar gatherings at this time in the Isle of Man, Wales and Cornwall. From all this she argued that Lughnasadh had been a festival held all over the British Isles, at which people assembled to mark the safe arrival of the time of harvest and the season of plenty. She further suggested that these gatherings had enjoyed a ritual performance, a story or a piece of drama in which the god Lugh defeated Chrom Dubh, symbolizing the conquest of the old god of the earth and his surrender of the harvest. Now, one firm conclusion which can be drawn from this marvellous work is that popular assemblies were indeed held in pagan Celtic times all over Ireland and Western Britain, and perhaps elsewhere in Britain, to celebrate Lughnasadh. The rest of the author's reasoning is speculative, though legitimate and fascinating. What we lack is a basis for comparison, in two diffent ways. First, it would be helpful to know whether the local myths of the defeat of the old ruler by the newcomer were confined to sites associated with the August gatherings, or found in other places as well. Second, we need similar studies of the other great festivals of the Irish year, to isolate the distinctive traits of each. Unhappily, since Máire MacNeill's death nobody seems to have wished to undertake this work.

A general survey of folk customs in these islands provides some confirmation of the historical data.[49] There is ample evidence of the importance of Samhain in all the modern Celtic regions, namely Ireland, Man, the Highlands and Western Isles, Wales and Cornwall, though the focus has been shifted back on to the previous night, called in English Hallowe'en. The rites and festivities concerned revolve around feasting, bonfires and divination. By contrast, there were no comparable celebrations associated with that date in most of England and some of Scotland until modern America helped to transmit the Irish festival to Britain. So it really does appear to have been a feast known all over the Iron Age British Isles, with no equivalent among the Anglo-Saxon invaders. Imbolc (later St Brighid's Day) is also well attested in the folk customs of Ireland, and of the Western Isles and Western Highlands of Scotland: in all these places, the Eve was marked by the same belief, that households would be visited by the saint and that tokens of welcome should be put out for her. But it does not seem to feature in the traditions of most of Britain, including Wales, so may well have been more a Gaelic festival. Lughnasadh, as already pointed out, has left copious traces of outdoor gatherings in Ireland, and some along western Britain, though the latter are few compared with those of Samhain. The problem here is that the Anglo-Saxons had their own festival to open the harvest, Loafmass or Lammas, which fell on the same day and was celebrated with fairs and gatherings which sometimes make it very hard to distinguish from the Celtic feast. Beltine, as May Day, was commemorated enthusiastically across the whole British Isles, and the folk rites bear out the impression given by the literary texts, that in Britain it was even more important than Samhain. But then, May Day was a great folk festival from Ireland to Russia, with Slavs, Balts and Germans celebrating it as ebulliently as

Celts. It appears from the recorded customs that the maypole was more important in England, Wales, Cornwall and southern Scotland, and bonfires more important in Ireland and the Scottish Highlands. This may reflect an ancient division, or the spread of maypoles from the Continent during the Middle Ages. A similar problem attaches to the fact that, in historic times, the whole of the British Isles paid particular reverence to a non-Christian popular festival which is not mentioned in the early Celtic literature, nor does it have any place in the fourfold division of the Irish year. This is Midsummer, which like May Day was celebrated across the whole of northern Europe, and which was marked everywhere by the lighting of fires. From the Middle Ages until recent times it was kept with such fervour in all the Celtic regions of these islands that it was hard to believe that it was an importation by Anglo-Saxon and Viking invaders. But such it may have been.

To sum up: the records of folklore, combined with those of the early literature, suggest that the four great Irish quarter days were celebrated all over the Gaelic areas of the British Isles. Two of them, Samhain and Beltine, are well attested across the whole archipelago, although the former seems to have been more important in the Gaelic parts and the latter more so in the Brythonic parts. It is possible, though doubtful, that Midsummer was also commemorated by the pagan Celts of these islands. But there is no sign that they kept any feasts at the equinoxes, nor, despite the prehistoric wonders of Newgrange and Maes Howe, at Midwinter: they were interested in marking the opening of the seasons, not the range of the sun.

We should close this consideration of Iron Age religion with an examination of the evidence for metaphysical beliefs and for actual ritual. The former is, of course, entirely literary. The Graeco-Roman writers tended to agree that the Celts had some sort of theology, but they did not describe it in any detail and it may be that, as described earlier, they tended to exaggerate its sophistication because of the special preoccupations of Timaeus and Poseidonios. Caesar, Strabo, Diodorus Siculus, Pomponius Mela, Lucan and Ammianus Marcellinus all mention the belief of the Gallic Tribes that the soul survived death. Caesar and Pomponius were reminded of the Greek doctrine of Pythagoras, whereby souls were reborn in new bodies, but were shocked by the very literal way in which the people of Gaul believed that the human being transcended the grave. The Romans found something barbaric in the Gallic practice of burning or burying the favourite possessions of the deceased so that they could accompany her or him into the new life. How this habit could form part of a belief in rebirth is not clear, and the Celtic literatures do not resolve the puzzle. In most of the early Irish and some of the early Welsh tales, there is a divine Otherworld which is a superlative version of the mortal one. Its people enjoy eternal life in the sense that they do not grow old or fall sick, but they can, apparently, be killed. What happens to *their* spirits in that event is utterly unclear. This Otherworld can be entered from the human one by certain doors concealed in mounds, or islands, or hills, or in the floors of lakes or the bed of the sea. Royal and heroic humans may penetrate it and return. But what is not specified is whether the dead go there. Some of the tales refer to a country of deceased humans, the House of Donn, which is depressing and unattractive in comparison with both the divine and mortal worlds.[50] Sometimes the Irish stories seem to assume that body and soul both survive death. Sometimes there are traces of what could be a belief in rebirth, although set within a framework of magic. The heroine Etain is swallowed by a chieftain's wife and reborn as her child. The same fate befalls Lugh in one story, when he is eaten by the woman Dechtire and reborn as Cú Chulainn. And exactly the same tale is told of the Irish heroes Mongan and Tuan Mac Cairill and the Welsh poet Taliesin.[51] The theme may testify to a crude belief in the transmigration of souls to new bodies, but it is also an old international favourite, recorded as far away as China. In brief, if the pagan Celts did have a coherent theology of death and the afterlife, it has not survived.

But we can say much more about the physical traces of ritual. One category of these represents not only an important feature of Iron Age archaeology but arguably the principal trace of religious activity in the late Bronze Age. It is the casting of precious objects into watery places, such as rivers, pools and bogs. This may not have been a development of the first millennium BC, for so many Neolithic flints have been found in rivers that it is possible that some at least did not end up there accidentally. Five bone copies of daggers, found in the Thames, date from 1500–1400 BC. They seem to have been made by people who could not afford to throw in the real weapons, and so represent fairly clear evidence of ritual deposition. But from about 1200 BC the significance of the deposits becomes considerably more obvious. They consist of quantities of valuable weaponry and ornaments, in places separate from settlements, bearing little or no sign of use and including spears, which ought to have floated and been recovered if they had been dropped into water by mishap. The conclusion that many of them, at least, were thrown in deliberately seems inescapable, and that suggests a religious purpose. A distinct patterning emerges from the finds. The rivers selected in

England all flow eastward, being the Tyne, the Wear, and all those which empty into the Humber, the Wash and the Thames estuary. It seems that no others were so used. In part this distribution must reflect the fact that each of them has been subjected to dredging, which brings up finds, but others, like the Severn and the Bristol Avon, have been equally well dredged and supplied nothing. All of the rivers concerned flowed through areas in which wealthy settlement was concentrated in the period, and they were probably major trade routes. But they may possibly have possessed a spiritual significance as well. During the late Bronze and early Iron Ages (*c.*1100–*c.*600 BC), hoards were also put into rivers and bogs in Scotland's Tay Basin, in the Scottish Border country and in Ireland. There was, furthermore, a sacred lake, Llyn Fawr, in what is now Glamorgan, into which cauldrons, axes, sickles, harness and vehicle fittings were thrown around 600 BC. The only comparably important site from this period as yet found in Britain was excavated in 1989 at Flag Fen near Peterborough. It was used from the middle Bronze Age to the

The addition of another broken sword to the huge ritual water deposit at Flag Fen near Peterborough, as imagined by Robert Donaldson and reproduced here by his kind permission. In the background is the row of stakes, either a ritual alignment or a boundary, found at the site. The woman in the foreground wears ornaments of the sort found in the deposit. The helmet of the man presiding is also an authentic portrayal, and the warlike nature of much of the metalwork testifies to the importance of such military figures in the society.

middle Iron Age (*c.*1200–*c.*200 BC), although most deposition was made in the centre of that time-span. The total of objects recovered includes pottery, shale bracelets and 300 pieces of metalwork, including very fine weapons and ornaments. Most had been broken before being thrown into the marsh which existed there at the time, to render them incapable of further practical use, or to 'kill' them, or for both reasons. What makes Flag Fen unique, so far, was that virtually all this material was placed upon one side of a line of about 2000 great oak posts, driven into the marsh between an island and the nearby drylands. That this construction was sanctified is suggested by the presence of loose human bones, a boar's tusk, a bracelet and the skeletons of dogs around the bases of the timbers. But whether it could be described as a 'ceremonial structure' is open to doubt in view of the excavator's suggestion that it may have been a boundary marker akin to the walls and ditches known on Dartmoor and in Wessex during the middle and late Bronze Age. The people who went there may have been reinforcing their frontier rather than visiting a shrine. The whole catalogue of British water deposits made between *c.*1200 and *c.*400 BC displays certain conventions. Shields and vessels were almost always left in bogs and pools, while swords went into rivers. Neck ornaments were not found in either. Outside the areas in which hoards were deposited in water, they were sometimes put into the earth instead.

During the middle Iron Age (*c.*400–*c.*100 BC), the water hoards in England were much reduced in number, although they continued to be made in the same areas. Outside these, swords begin to appear on settlement sites, but they are never found on these in areas in which they are deposited in rivers: the claims of the water cults seem to have been too strong. It may be that there were two different ritual traditions in operation. The decline in the water deposits may be attributed to the fact that this was a time when trade was collapsing and many forts were destroyed, suggesting widespread disruption. Yet it was also the period in which use commenced of what was to be the most important sacred lake so far discovered in Britain, Llyn Cerrig Bach in Anglesey. From the second century BC to the first century AD, over 150 metal objects, mostly weapons and aristocratic ornaments with a few other items such as slave shackles, were cast into it, thrown from a low cliff overlooking the water. The wealth which they represent is apparently more than could have been dedicated by local rulers. It seems to confirm what the Romans said of Anglesey, that it was an island regarded as holy by many of the British. The known Irish equivalent is the so-called 'Golden Bog of Cullen', in

County Tipperary, where during the last century over 100 cauldrons, spears, swords, axes, gold bars, dress-fasteners, chains, discs bearing Celtic crosses and ear-rings were gradually discovered. The circumstances of the finding of this hoard, haphazardly and mostly by local farming folk, have destroyed any chance that we might know over what period of time it was deposited. Certainly, an unknown number of objects were lost or melted down by those who came across them, and the position of most was not recorded. But they seem to date from an earlier period than those of Llyn Cerrig Bach. During the late Iron Age (from *c.* 100 BC until AD 43 in southern Britain, and until *c.* AD 500 elsewhere), the great water hoard in Anglesey continued to grow, and more such hoards were left elsewhere in Britain. They were placed in the same districts which had been the centres of the custom in the early Iron Age, and in a slightly wider area around them. Cauldrons replaced swords as the favourite items to be dedicated. Many objects had been broken before deposition, whereas earlier they had been left whole, but others were not only complete, but of a very high quality, not known in the previous hoards.[52]

We seem to have clear proof here of a widespread and long-lasting ritual custom, but one none the less confined to specific areas. It seems to have become important as use of the old ceremonial monuments and burial customs came to an end, and so it would be helpful to our understanding of both the first and the second millennium BC if we could discern its meaning. One obvious interpretation is that it was a funerary rite, the goods being dropped into water with cremated bodies instead of being buried with them. It does seem to be true across late Bronze Age Europe that areas where weaponry was put into water, into hoards in the earth, or into graves, seem to be distinct from one another, suggesting that the customs were alternatives. At the beginning of the Iron Age (*c.* 700–*c.* 500 BC), most swords deposited in Europe were put in with burials, while most of those deposited in England were put into rivers. Evidence that some of the late Bronze Age British were returning to the Neolithic practice of stripping the flesh from corpses is furnished by the discovery around the settlement site at Wallingford, Oxfordshire, of stray human bones from excarnated skeletons, most of which may have been thrown into the Thames, which flowed past the village. That river and some of its tributaries have produced a large number of human skulls, and those from the Wallbrook, London, have been studied and dated to the period *c.* 1400–*c.* 700 BC.[53] It is possible, from the evidence, to construct the following theory: that as the climate grew rapidly wetter after 1400 BC, people became increasingly impressed by the power of

A later Bronze Age funeral beside the Thames, as imagined by the late Alan Sorrell. He makes the assumption, which seems increasingly likely, that the swords cast into the river in this period, such as the one shown on the left, had accompanied cremated remains. The helmets and spears are archaeologically authentic, the bare-breasted, hair-tearing women drawn from Greek parallels. By kind permission of the Museum of London.

Another ritual deposit of metalwork in the Thames, again imagined by the late Alan Sorrell. This time the period is the later Iron Age, and the offering accompanies no funeral. The object concerned is the 'Battersea shield', now one of the prize exhibits of the British Museum. The priests shown are drawn from Roman writings about Gaul, and the trumpets from the Gundestrop Cauldron, found in Denmark: neither may have been true of the British, although priests of some sort and black-robed women in Anglesey are mentioned by Tacitus. By kind permission of the Museum of London.

water and began to worship and placate its spirits and deities in particular; and that accordingly they began to give their own dead to this element, often equipping them with precious goods. And further, that the latter are found most frequently in parts of eastern England because the rivers of that region are better dredged and because the communities there were wealthier.

But the theory will not stand up. The regions which have not so far produced any water hoards from this epoch were not much poorer than the others and (as stated) do contain some rivers where dredgers have worked. But not a single such hoard has been found in them, be it small or large, of good or poor quality. It is difficult to explain why such a general deterioration in climate could have produced such a selective veneration of water. Also, while the custom of depositing objects in this way may well have had a funerary significance in the early part of the first millennium, it apparently did not have towards the end. No human bones were found, for example, in Llyn Cerrig Bach, where even burnt skeletal remains ought to have left a deposit if all that metalwork had accompanied bodies. Richard Bradley, who has done more than anybody else so far to link prehistoric remains to social developments, has noted that areas with water hoards and areas with fortresses tended to be separate in Iron Age Britain.[54] The Scottish Border country is the exception to this rule, but generally it stands and suggests a difference either in confidence or in ways of winning prestige. Professor Bradley points out that destroying riches in this way could keep high the value of prestigious objects, or impress observers with the wealth of the people who immolated them, or represent a competition between rival groups, or fulfil all three functions. But we cannot tell which, if any, of these notions applied to this case. The Graeco-Roman writers Strabo and Diodorus Siculus both state that the Gallic tribes cast the plunder of war into pools as offerings to their deities.[55] This is a neat confirmation of the religious nature of the action, but supplies neither the sacred nor the social context. Miranda Green has addressed the former question by pointing to the apparent importance of boats in late Bronze Age and Iron Age symbolism.[56] This theme has already been noted in Scandinavian rock art, and models of boats or ships have been found on first millennium sites in the British Isles. One from Caergwrle in Wales, made of shale decorated with tin and gold, has been dated to *c.*1000 BC, a gold one from Broighter in County Derry is attributed to the first century BC and a wooden example with a crew of five warriors, from Roos Carr in eastern Yorkshire, is also from the first millennium. They may have been symbolic vessels of the dead, important in an age in which the ashes or bones of the deceased may have been floated away into rivers or pools. But, of course, they may have had quite different meanings, or merely have been objects of art. With them we run out of further evidence for the meaning of the water hoards. It seems increasingly certain that they represented in part a late Bronze Age funeral ritual which replaced urn cremation and barrow burial in some communities. But they may well have had a greater significance, and by the Iron Age many, if not all, do not seem to have been connected with the disposal of bodies. They appear, as the Graeco-Roman writers said, to have been religious offerings. To whom, and why, we do not know. To war deities, to tribal patrons, or to tutelary goddesses of rivers? These are only some of the possibilities.

Mention has been made of the burial of hoards in the earth. Too often, it is impossible to distinguish items which were deposited for religious reasons from those which were simply hidden and never retrieved. The latter kind may be discounted if the goods were placed in a carefully prepared shaft, but if shallow the shaft may have been a storage pit and if deep it may have been a well: both, especially the latter, places where valuables and other objects could be lost or hidden. So the identification of 'ritual deposits' in the soil or rock is a delicate business, and a signficant problem in Iron Age archaeology, which ranks such deposits as quite important. They are, of course, probably as old as human religious activity. Some of the tools and pieces of mobile art dating from the European Palaeolithic may have been deliberately buried. Ritual deposits, as earlier chapters have shown, formed a major part of Neolithic ceremonial activity, and they are more prominent in the archaeology of the period after 1500 BC largely because they appear there without the ceremonial monuments of which they had earlier formed a part. When they did begin to be made upon their own is a vexed question. It currently seems impossible to determine whether the 100 foot deep Wilsford Shaft on Salisbury Plain, dated to 1600–1500 BC, is a religious construction or a well dug by cattle-breeders desperately trying to strike water. Experts upon the site are completely divided over its purpose. Towards 1000 BC the situation becomes a little clearer, for between 1600 and 1000 the Swanwick shaft in Hampshire appeared, which held a stake smeared with flesh and blood and is unmistakably a votive pit. Research into the use of such structures in the Iron Age has been vitiated by the fact that the first work upon them, though due all the respect merited by a pioneering study, was far too careless in distinguishing them from storage pits or wells. By 1985, scholars seemed to have agreed upon a total of twenty-one ritual shafts from the period. About half are concentrated in Kent and

Surrey, the remainder scattered across southern England as far as Exeter and Warwick. Only three of them contained the careful patterning of layers of offerings which indicates certain ceremonial activity, and most of the rest are included because they seem to have possessed no obvious practical purpose. Many of the south-eastern examples were uncovered by workers constructing railway lines, and the finds from them were sketchily recorded. But significant data do emerge. The shafts of Kent and Surrey contained more dog and bird bones and the others more bits of horse skeleton. Otherwise they held much the same material – a mixture of potsherds, ash wood and the bones of cattle and of human beings – and the majority which can be dated were made in the later part of the period.[57] So we seem to have here a more localized and generally less important tradition than the water hoards, with particular significance for a tribe or tribes living between the Thames and the Weald.

The animals who ended up in those pits were just some of a large number who were ritually interred in the British Iron Age. They were certainly important motifs to artists and rulers all over Europe in the period. Around the beginning of the Christian era horses featured upon the coins struck by four tribes in what is now southern England: the Atrebates, Catuvellauni, Dobunni and Iceni.[58] They, along with wolves, boars, bulls and stags, all appear upon metalwork from Ireland to the other end of the continent. But most of those which appear in deposits were of the domestic variety and represented offerings made for their sacrificial, as well as their symbolic value. There is an obvious potential difficulty in distinguishing their remains from the carcasses of animals which had simply been slaughtered and eaten in the course of normal living. Those ritually deposited tend to consist of only a few species, and sometimes only a few parts of the animal. They never seem to have been butchered for human consumption. Thus, in England and Wales the skulls of cattle and the skulls or bodies of horses and dogs are often found in the pits beside or beneath Iron Age houses and in the ditches or near the ramparts of forts. Sheep are rare in this context and pigs only found in the middle of the period. The frequency of such deposits in settlements gradually declined. Wild animals were almost never so used, apparently because a hunted beast was not a sacrifice: indeed, the sole exceptions known so far are the stag and six foxes carefully buried at Winklebury Camp.[59] In Scotland much the same pattern obtains, with the tally of wild animals being increased by the jawbones of red deer set round the hearth of a house on North Uist in the Outer Hebrides. One Pictish decorated stone, St Vigeans 7 in Angus, shows an unmistakable scene of the sacrifice of a bull.[60] Such finds have also been made upon Irish sites, although there has been no survey of the evidence there as yet. Certainly the literary sources refer to horse sacrifice, and the consumption of meat was also held to be an act of potential ritual significance: in modern terms, it 'raised the consciousness' of devotees. In *Togail Bruidne Da Derga* there is a description of a rite of divination which involved a man gorging himself upon the beef of a slaughtered bull and then retiring into a sacred sleep to await dreams in which the future king would be revealed. It would have been astonishing if the Celts had not practised animal sacrifice, for the entire ancient world did so. But the British evidence is still interesting, for it proves that the custom was carried on at all levels of society and not just by the elite. Nor was it standardized. Although there were clearly some generally favoured species of victim, in some cases the sacrificers dedicated only heads, sometimes only limbs, and sometimes whole carcasses, according to their own preference.[61]

The ritual slaughter of animals represented not only the offering up of wealth but also the most dramatic religious gesture known to humans: the destruction of life. The drama was greatly increased if the victim was human. Caesar, Strabo and Diodorus all asserted that the tribes of Gaul ritually killed people. All repeated the same story, that great wicker figures constructed to look human were filled with live victims then set on fire. Caesar added that this was only done in times of exceptional danger to the tribe, and that those burned were criminals. Strabo and Diodorus added another, equally nasty, story: that men were stabbed to death in the shrines of Gaul and Druids foretold the future from the pattern of their death throes. Diodorus also said that criminals or prisoners of war were employed. Strabo asserted that victims were shot full of arrows or impaled in Gallic temples. Dio Cassius recorded that Boudicca's Iceni hung up Roman noblewomen in the grove of Andraste, cut off their breasts and then sewed them to their lips and then passed long skewers through them. All these writers may be accused of 'black' propaganda against the Celts and all their specific stories may be fictions. It is significant that Pomponius Mela, writing in the first century AD, stated that the people of Gaul no longer sacrificed humans: but it is not clear whether his statement implied that they had ceased to do so because of Roman rule.[62] The early Irish tales themselves do seem to make coy references to the custom. When one of the southern Ui Niall married a strange woman, the Druids ordered the death of the son of a sinless couple in expiation (but a divine woman appeared leading a cow as a victim instead). The Desi were said to have defeated the people of Ossory because before battle they had sacrificed a Druid (but he magically turned himself into a cow for the occasion).[63]

The evidence of archaeology is also suggestive. Single human beings of both sexes were found buried under the ramparts of the Iron Age forts of Maiden Castle, Hod Hill and South Cadbury. It is hard to explain their presence except in terms of foundation deposits to lend spirtual strength to the walls above. It is not absolutely certain that they all died violently, but the famous discovery of a human body preserved in the peat of Lindow Moss, Cheshire, admits of no doubt. An adult male of the elite, with fingernails unworn by labour, he had been poleaxed and garrotted and his throat cut before his body was thrown into a pool. This procedure reminds one of the 'triple death' suffered by certain kings and heroes in early Irish tales. It is far too elaborate for a straightforward execution, and his final resting place in the bog seems to be an exact human parallel to the water hoards. The head of a woman turned up nearby may have been the remains of another victim. Although the dates provided for 'Lindow Man' vary between the laboratories which analysed the samples (a warning of the continuing problems of the Carbon 14 process), he is almost certainly Iron Age.[64] Other single bodies found in pits inside settlements or forts may also have been offered to deities. But we do not know anything about the ideology of the rite. Were those killed criminals or captives, as the Graeco-Roman writers held to be the case in Gaul? Or were they volunteers or chosen by lot, and treated with honour and gratitude until their deaths?

Moreover, there are cases where the evidence for human sacrifice is much more equivocal. One is represented by the young woman found at Salmonsbury Fort in Gloucestershire. Her body had been butchered and the bones smashed to extract the marrow. Clerly she was eaten by other humans. Was this for nutrition, in time of famine? Or by friends, as a bizarre burial rite? Or as a culmination to an act of sacrifice?[65] Then there is the matter of severed heads. Six of these were fixed upon the gate of the fort at Bredon Hill in Gloucestershire. The skulls of six men, a woman and a child were found in a pit inside Danebury Fort, Hampshire. Those found in the earth house at Rennibister in Orkney have already been mentioned. Others decorated ramparts at Stanwick in Yorkshire and Hunsbury in Northamptonshire, and individual human heads have been found in pits within other fortresses.[66] Our problem is to determine which of these, if any, had religious significance. Both the Graeco-Roman and the early Irish writers agreed that the Celts enthusiastically collected the heads of defeated enemies. Those stuck on gates and ramparts may have been dedicted to deities as well. Those found in pits ought, much more clearly, to have been ritually deposited. But were they initially trophies as well, or did they belong to human sacrifices, or to especially beloved members of a family or tribe, or to social outcasts not given normal burial, or to individuals who needed special help to get free of their bodies after death? We cannot tell, but it can now be said that there is no firm evidence of a 'cult of the human head' in the Iron Age British Isles, as was once asserted, and this plays no part in any of the possible explanations for the displayed or interred heads given above. As said earlier, no stone heads survive which can firmly be dated to the period. The frequency with which human heads appear upon Celtic metalwork proves nothing more than that they were a favourite decorative motif, among several, and one just as popular among non-Celtic peoples. And the story of the Welsh king Bran, whose severed head retained life long after his death, may be no more than a story about a semi-divine individual. As a working concept, the idea of such a cult should now perhaps be set aside.

The discussion of human sacrifice and of head-hunting has touched upon the subject of burial, which must be the last to be considered in this chapter. During the late Bronze Age, as explained previously, funerary monuments, tombs, cinerary urns and indeed datable human remains more or less vanish all over the British Isles. The story of the Iron Age, broadly speaking, is one of the reappearance of burial as a significant part of the archaeological record. But it was a slow and complicated process, and parts of it are still relatively obscure. The situation in Ireland, for example, is at present in a state of confusion. There is no form of burial there which can be called characteristic of the period. At Cush in County Limerick two early Iron Age barrows were put up next to an early Bronze Age specimen, perhaps in imitation of it. At Pollacorragune in County Galway and Carrowjames in County Mayo, Iron Age inhumations were dug into other early Bronze Age round barrows, while the same sort of monuments at Carrowbeg North in County Galway received some cremations. Over 100 empty stone coffins or 'long cists' are known, and may have been made in this period. But they pose the same problem as the stone heads, for they may well be early Christian.[67] In Scotland the situation is only a little clearer. In the north of the land, there survive twelve 'long cists' which contained extended bodies and were covered either by low mounds with ditches or by low cairns with kerbs. Five of these monuments were accompanied by 'early Pictish' carved stones, which seem to date them to the late pagan Iron Age. Otherwise the problem of distinguishing pagan from Christian coffins is as great in Scotland as in Ireland, and no pattern can be picked out.[68]

It is only in England that some kind of sequence may yet be discerned. The early Iron Age, as the late Bronze Age, has left very few identifiable burials of any kind. As noted above, some evidence survives for excarnation of bodies and for the deposition of human remains in rivers. The majority of burials detected on or near sites from the period 700–400 BC were individual interments inside southern English fortresses or unfortified villages. Most have been found in the forts and were of adult males. Often the deceased was represented only by a skull, or femur, or (on the contrary) a dump of small bones lacking head or limbs. The long bones were usually taken from the right-hand side of the body, suggesting that their selection was careful and deliberate. Sometimes pieces of skeleton were selected from different individuals and placed together. During the rest of the Iron Age, the number of such burials increased, the proportion of women grew and more people were interred in open settlements as well as in forts. The cumulative total of these deposits could be considerable: at Danebury, ninety-five bodies were found in a sampling of the site which suggested that there were about 300 there altogether, buried over 500 years. Of these, twenty-five had been put into the ground complete and shortly after death: most of them were crouched, most were adult males, many were covered in heavy stones and some were in groups. There was also a pelvis of a youth which had been hacked off and interred before decomposition. But the majority of the burials consisted of one or more bones from bodies which had already rotted. It might be argued from this evidence that the complete bodies were of sacrifices, or outcasts, or offenders, who were denied the usual rite. The weighting with stones does suggest fear or dislike. It might also be proposed that the normal ritual consisted of excarnation by exposure to the air, and that pieces of especially favoured people were brought back to the fortress as a mark of affection and for use in rites. All this is possible; none of it is certain. What we can say is that at most sites which have produced such finds, the number of people represented by them could not have come to more than about 5 per cent of the population of their community. Nor was it the elite 5 per cent, as none of the bodies was accompanied by marks of honour. What happened to the remaining 95 per cent we cannot say: there is, as has been suggested, some indication that they were exposed until they decomposed, rather like the dead of some native American tribes.[69] Some trace of the idea that buried bones conferred magical protection upon a site may be found in an early medieval Welsh saying, of the Three Fortunate Concealments of the Island of Britain.[70] One of these was the head of Bran (who has already cropped up twice), laid after much wandering at Tower Hill, London. Another consisted of the bones of Gwerthefyr the Blessed, interred at all Britain's seaports. Until they were dug up, recount the legends, they protected the island from invasion.

During the middle Iron Age (*c*.400–*c*.100 BC), not only did these sorts of burial increase in number, but more spectacular forms appeared in restricted areas. The people living on or around the Yorkshire Wolds began to construct huge cemeteries, within rectangular or square ditches, of mounds covering individual inhumations. The largest of these, the misnamed Danes Graves, consisted eventually of about 500 such structures. Most of the burials were crouched and laid out from north to south. Some were accompanied by pig bones, pottery and small ornaments. But a number of others, aligned east to west, had knives and swords as well, and a total of fifteen found so far were buried with two-wheeled vehicles which were either chariots or else carts which had carried the body to the grave. Fourteen of these 'royal' burials contained male skeletons, with all the goods found with other bodies, plus spears and shields. The fifteenth was female, with ornaments, a mirror and a workbox instead of weapons. This striking regional fashion was almost certainly imported from northern France, but why it only went to eastern Yorkshire is at present an insoluble puzzle. Nor can we tell why, during the same period, the people of the extreme south-west began to bury their dead in cemeteries of cists. So far two of these have been found in Cornwall, one in Devon and one in the Isles of Scilly, the largest (at Harlyn Bay) containing 130 bodies. Most burials were crouched, and there were a few poor gravegoods.[71]

In the course of the late Iron Age (*c*.100 BC–AD 43), the Roman conquest of Gaul stimulated trade across the Channel and greatly increased the wealth and sophistication of the southern British. This trend is reflected dramatically, in the burial record. Cremation once again became an important rite. It had never completely died out, as evinced by bundles of burned bone, accompanied by pots, found at sites in Sussex, Suffolk and Norfolk and dated to the sixth century BC. But in the first century BC it became the dominant fashion in Kent, almost certainly following Continental examples. Fields of funerary urns, similar to those of the middle Bronze Age, were buried in that county, while cremation bruials (with or without urns) were deposited across southern England as far as Gloucestershire. In the same period every existing type of burial, including the bodies interred in settlements and fortresses, the Yorkshire barrow cemeteries and the south-western cist cemeteries, increased in number. Mirrors and bronze bowls were now placed with women in the cists of Cornwall and Devon. In Dorset large inhumation cemeteries appeared, without cists. In Hampshire, the Isle of Wight, Dorset and Norfolk, male bodies were inhumed in isolated graves, accompanied by swords and spears. Very rich female burials of this period, yielding beautiful mirrors, bronze bowls and beads, have been found in Gloucestershire and at Colchester. In the first decades of the Christian era, powerful dynastic kingdoms were emerging in Britain, with proportionately magnificent burials. The wealthiest of the new states were

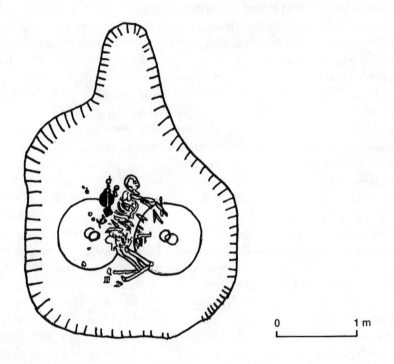

0   1 m

FIGURE 5.8   An Iron Age royal tomb?
Plan of cart burial no. 2 at Wetwang Slack (Humberside). It is by no means typical of the period, but is one of the richest graves in the barrow cemeteries of the Yorkshire Wolds, an exotic local burial tradition. In the past it has sometimes been described as the chariot burial of a warrior queen, but she has no weapons with her, her status in life is unknown and the 'chariot' may just have been a funeral cart: its wheels, and her mirror, are clearly visible.
Source: redrawn after Dent.

in the south-east, and in Essex, Cambridgeshire, Hertfordshire and Kent were dug deep grave pits furnished with imported wine-jars, drinking vessels and fire-dogs for spit-roasting. At Welwyn a young man was cremated in a bearskin and put into a pit with five wine-jars, Italian bowls of silver and bronze, and glass gaming pieces. He was clearly expected to entertain friends or hosts in the Otherworld. In this district, hierarchy was displayed in the positioning of burials as well as in the furnishing of the graves. At St Albans, 445 cremations were buried in the same cemetery, but many were put in groups around a central burial, like retainers. But then, this was the territory of the Catuvellauni, the most powerful and sophisticated of all the new tribal states. Elsewhere the burials were usually more simple, but the same signs appear of special honour paid to an elite. The 'cart graves' of Yorkshire, the warrior graves and the 'mirror burials' have been mentioned, and there were individual variations upon the theme. At Basingstoke, in the territory of the Atrebates, a young woman was inhumed in a pit with two sheep, two horses, joints of beef, four weaving-combs, two rings – and an older woman, who was buried crouched beside her with her head resting upon the younger's pelvis. Obviously one speculates that she might have been a servant sent to assist her mistress beyond death. By the first century AD it could almost be said that burial was once again a normal part of the archaeological record, but conducted according to a great variety of practices, apparently making different social and religious statements.[72]

A few other scraps of information about pagan Celtic belief can be gained by sifting through the early texts. It is obvious, for example, that like many ancient peoples the British and Irish believed that it was lucky to make a circle sunwise, in modern terms clockwise (or in Old Irish *deisiol*), and very malicious or foolish to proceed in the opposite direction or, as the English were to say, 'widdershins'. Also, colours played a great symbolic role. Red was associated with death, destruction and the more primitive deities. Green was the hue of the more sophisticated divine being, such as the Tuatha de Danaan, and of enchantment. White animals often feature in the stories as supernatural, especially if they had red ears. The presence of ash twigs in the ritual shafts is significant, for all over northern Europe it was regarded as the most arcane of trees, and there are more superstitions recorded about it in folklore collections from the British Isles than any other species.

But there remains a great deal that we do not know about the religion of the pagan Celts of these islands. In this respect they are like figures perceived through a mist and heard very faintly. We have no real idea, for example, whether their ceremonies were intended to ask the deities for favours, or to thank them for the continuing order of things, or both. We do not know what they believed about the afterlife, whether all religious activity had to be mediated through priests or rulers, or of what their ceremonies or prayers consisted. We do not know whether their religion had a mysterious element, requiring initiation. We do not know whether it embodied a system of ethics. All this is hardly surprising, in view of the fact that our evidence consists of badly remembered portions of mythological tales, based upon a paganism which had disappeared before most (or probably all) of them were composed, joined with an archaeological record which is actually rather less rich than that for previous millennia and which sometimes contradicts the literary sources. What the two types of evidence together do suggest is an intensely localized faith about which few generalizations can be made. Burial practices and most deities were regional, and the variation in the former makes one wonder whether religious beliefs themselves might not have altered from one area to another. Yet certain attitudes were found across the Celtic lands from the British Isles to central Europe, and holy places such as Llyn Cerrig Bach seem to have attracted worshippers from a much wider territory than that of the local tribe. In search of further insights, an obvious tactic is that tried at earlier junctures in this book: to consider a contemporary culture elsewhere in Europe and to draw comparisons. The obvious one for this period is the Roman Empire. But in this case the comparison is not so much desirable as compulsory. In AD 43 the Romans waded ashore in Britain and the similarities and contrasts between their beliefs and those of the natives became a matter of importance to both groups.

6

The Imperial Synthesis (AD 43–410)

The Romans were among the most profusely literate of ancient peoples, and they also delighted in stone architecture for their holy places, in stone iconography for their deities and in the carving upon stone of religious inscriptions. In brief, they have left behind them all the sorts of evidence which a student of ancient religion might require, and which have been deficient or absent for the earlier cultures examined in this book. It is no accident that in the short period since 1984, excellent studies have been published of religion in the Roman Empire in general by Robin Lane Fox, and of Roman Britain in particular by Martin Henig, Miranda Green and Graham Webster. This is not to say that serious problems do not remain. The greatest is that not a single work of literature survives by an inhabitant of pagan Roman Britain, or even of a visitor to it. This means that although a lot of physical evidence survives for the local cults, they are effectively prehistoric. Another is that the inhabitants of the Roman Empire themselves did not always understand what they were up to. Every year in February, at the festival of the Lupercalia, youths clad in goats' skins and stained with blood ran around Rome, striking at women, who were supposed to be made fertile by their action. Everybody in the city agreed that the rite was important and ancient, but nobody could say positively why it happened. Cicero, Varro, Virgil and Livy, who all tried to deal with the history of their own religion, were constantly hampered by a lack of sources. Cicero, writing of Bacchus, was forced to conclude that there were five quite different gods worshipped by that name, whose identities could not be reconciled and whose origins were mysterious. Nor could scholars of the first century BC agree upon the precise ingredients and attributes of Venus. By then the goddess was a compound figure incorporating a very old Roman spirit of vegetation, an

Etruscan deity of flowers and trees, and the famous Greek patron of romantic and sexual love, Aphrodite. This long and in parts mysterious evolution went some way towards explaining the striking anomaly whereby such a rampantly feminine deity bore a name which was itself a neuter noun.[1]

Still, the evidence from the city of Rome itself is abundant and unequivocal enough to permit some confident statements about Roman religion. The Empire was, of course, not so much a civilization as a patchwork of them, from Romano-Egyptian, Romano-Syriac and Graeco-Roman in one corner to Hispano-Roman. Gallo-Roman and Romano-British in the other. But the component in each which derived from Rome is clear, up to a point. If this is less true of religious beliefs and practices than of other matters, then the problem arises largely because Rome had in this respect much in common with the other cultures of the time. One striking aspect of this common ground was the concept of an almost infinite number of divine beings. To the Romans, every grove, spring, cluster of rocks or other significant natural feature had its attendant spirit. Generally the locals gave such entities personal names, but a stranger ignorant of these would refer to each simply as *genius loci*, 'the spirit of the place'. Especially awe-inspiring or beautiful spots possessed proportionately powerful *genii*. Furthermore, each human being had an individual divine opposite number, a *genius* for a man and a *Juno* for a woman. This divine entity came into being as the person was born and remained attached to him or her throughout life, functioning much in the way of the Christian guardian angel. It was thus a matter of practical common sense, and not the worship of a living human, that inhabitants of the Empire were required to honour and to encourage the *genius* (in this case generally called the *numen*) of the reigning emperor. In addition to individual spirits attached to places and persons, there were throngs who inhabited districts and buildings. The Fauni were found in the woods, and farms and houses had the Lares and Penates. The last two certainly had to be accorded honours by humans, to an extent much greater and more formal than those given by later Europeans to the fairies, pixies and elves whom these Roman beings resembled. Indeed, households were expected to offer food to the Lares and Penates at every meal.[2]

A similar complexity characterizes the deities themselves. Unlike the Greeks, the Romans were not interested in inventing myths about the nature, origins or family relationships of the beings whom they worshipped. Their goddesses and gods seem curiously intangible, often just names with functions attached to them. Very often the name of an important deity would be included in those of may lesser divinities, each a genuinely different entity with a responsibility within the broad sphere of competence associated with the great one. A few Neo-Platonist philosophers regarded them as aspects of the same personality, but the overwhelming majority of Romans believed them to be quite separate. Thus, the Imperial army was expected to sacrifice regularly to Jupiter the Supreme Ruler, Jupiter the Victor, Mars the Father, Mars the Victor, the goddess Victory, and a list of other deities, and woe betide the unit which decided that one of these was superfluous or merely an aspect of another. The great goddess of agriculture, it is often said today, was Ceres. But there were ten deities of that name, to protect each process. Ceres 'the Plougher' led off, followed by 'the Harrower', 'the Sower', 'the Fertilizer', 'the Weeder', 'the Reaper', 'the Raker', 'the Sheaf-binder', 'the Storer' and 'the Distributor'. And all of these had, strictly speaking, to be honoured with many others. They ranged from Tellus Mater, the goddess who quickened seeds in the soil, to Vercator, god of the ploughing of fallow land, Promitor, guardian of stored grain, and Sterculinus, god of manure. And the original responsibility of Mars was to protect and to nurture crops. Again, it is often considered nowadays that Pluto was the Roman god of the dead: but death also concerned Mercury, Demeter, Sabazios, Hercules, Orpheus, Venus, Minerva, Bacchus, Mars and Atys. The mighty Juno comforted women in labour, being the goddess with especial responsibility for women's affairs in general. But Lucina made the baby see the light, Levana helped the father acknowledge it as his own(!), Candlifera watched over the light in the birth room, Intercidona, Pilumnus and Deverra protected it and Cunina looked after the child in the cradle.[3]

This luxuriant polytheism had no boundaries. Not only did existing deities continue to multiply attributes or doubles, and new cults enter the Empire, but anybody could 'discover' a deity: and the new find, if approved by the Senate, would become the subject of an official Roman cult. All individuals were, in fact, free to define the nature of the divine as they wished, provided that they did not challenge existing practices and that their rites were decent. The result was that, theoretically, there were many more possible religions within the Empire than there were people in it. Even those who had a personal relationship with a particular deity, and were members of a cult requiring training and initiation, did not believe that their favourite goddess or god was the only one to exist. They just believed that this being was the best for their particular circumstances.

Indeed, even Christians did not claim that all pagan divinities were imaginary: rather, they declared that some were very real, but demonic. An enormous, indeed uncountable, number of greater and lesser supernatural beings was accompanied by a wide range of philosophies intended to account for the divine. Most of the principal human theories concerning the fate of the soul were to be found within the Empire, including oblivion, Heaven and Hell, reincarnation and transmigration. And although supernatural power was believed to be concentrated within deities and spirits, it was also thought to exist at large upon the face of the world, so that humans could invest places, objects, social relations or themselves with it through rituals.

Such a potential for choice or for confusion does not appear to have worried many people. Communities, families, friends or individuals employed the pattern which seemed to work best for them. Even the oldest rituals and institutions altered, century by century, to accommodate changing tastes. Furthermore, there was no penalty for a verbal attack upon the deities of others, for the divine beings concerned were considered to be capable of punishing insults to themselves. But there was a major addition to this rule: refusal to sacrifice to the *numen* of the emperor, the head of the state and of society, was tantamount to treason, and incurred terrible penalties. In practice, it was only the adherents of the new Christian cult who offended the state in this manner, and persecution of them was sporadic and initially local. Nevertheless, it became more widespread and intense during the third and early fourth centuries, and those who were convicted for their faith were often tortured to death for the amusement and edification of the public.[4]

A very significant point for the purposes of this book is that such a remarkable range of religious belief was contained within a much greater conformity of architecture and ritual. The temples and ceremonies of the Empire varied considerably less than the beings whom they honoured and the attitudes to the divine held by worshippers. This fact raises the strong but unprovable possibility that the prehistoric monuments surveyed earlier in this work, which showed a considerable local variety of form and traces of ritual, may themselves have embodied an equally heterogeneous range of religious attitudes. Within the Empire sacred architecture was fairly standard, normally consisting of an enclosure containing a platform bearing a temple conforming to one of a few principal styles, itself containing a cult statue of a principal deity. Some cults had small shrines, without enclosures or platforms. Within all these sacred spaces, at the heart of the ceremony was the principle of sacrifice.

Libations of alcohol, grain, fruit, vegetables, precious metals or works of art (like statuettes) were all permissible gifts, but most ranked far in value below the life of an animal. The great emotional centrepiece of a typical Roman ritual was the gush of blood as a beast was despatched. This last work required some skill, because the principle of sacrifice demanded a victim who was, in theory, willing: thus an animal stricken by fear was no fit gift, and the offering had to be kept content and docile to the moment of death. Once killed, it was butchered and only the inedible parts burned upon the altar, while the people present tucked into the rest: Roman rituals were generally part abattoir and part barbecue. In this readiness to eat the sacrificial animal, the Romans seem to have differed from the British Celts (to judge from the archaeological evidence), and they did so in another major respect. From 196 BC they made human sacrifice illegal throughout the Empire.[5]

Such actions embodied a sense of the function of worship which, again, was generally held despite the tremendous disparity in the beings worshipped. Any community considered it crucial to keep up the regular offerings to its principal deities upon their festivals in each year, as a sort of protection money paid to a divine Mafia. If these great beings were not honoured, then they would probably punish the community with disease, crop failure and other disasters, and failure to do so would certainly render it vulnerable to competition from outsiders who had properly enlisted the help of divine protectors. Hence the Christians represented a potentially terrifying menace, not merely because they threatened religious discord, but because by insulting gods and goddesses *en masse*, they invited catastrophe to strike the Empire. But individuals could follow a different sort of pattern of worship. While participating in the communal honouring of deities, they could also strike personal bargains. Somebody seeking a particular favour would promise an offering to a being if help were granted to achieve the desired end. If the need were desperate then the offering could be made in advance of any response. And there were people possessed of such a powerful wish for a perpetual and intimate relationship with the divine that this mixutre of community ceremonies and *ad hoc* individual approaches was not enough. Some would choose a particular patron or patroness, or set of them, according to their district or occupation, and pay a constant and loving devotion to these beings. Others would go further and join one of the 'mystery religions' which spread across the whole Empire, giving allegiance to one goddess or god, or divine couple, in the company of fellow devotees. These cults insisted upon spiritual training and initiation and often upon privacy of ritual. Some permitted, to the deeply religious, the joys of a structured personal progress, the sense of belonging to a select group and the ability to drop in at the local 'lodge' of fellow believers in most parts of the Roman world. This last advantage was one solution to a widespread problem of the time, that of personal mobility. The many soldiers, administrators and merchants moving around the Empire had at once to maintain respect for the deities of their homes and to honour those into whose territory they were transferring. One widespread method of doing so was just to worship both. Another was to identify local gods or goddesses with those already familiar, because of similar attributes, and to worship two beings under the same name. Both techniques were practised by individuals and by groups.[6]

How was this process applied in the Roman province of Britannia? The most recent authorities have had sharply divergent views. Miranda Green and Graham Webster have argued that only a thin veneer of Roman religion was applied to the flourishing native cults, while Martin Henig and Joan Alcock have proposed that British traditions and practices were thoroughly Romanized. That such fine scholars should disagree so fundamentally suggests that the problem may be insoluble. It is, indeed, likely that the degree of Romanization varied not merely between districts and communities but between individuals, so that generalization is fruitless. Let us take first the most complex aspect of the question, and the one for which most evidence survives: the identity of deities worshipped. Of those honoured at Rome, Hercules, Minerva, Jupiter, Mars and Mercury are all represented by inscriptions found widely in Britain, particularly in the east midlands, Essex, Suffolk, Gloucestershire and on the northern frontier. The last three gods were evidently the most popular, but then they covered between them most human concerns, including government, the weather, trading, soil fertility, death and war. Nor is their geographical distribution surprising, the southern districts being among the richest and most cosmopolitan and the northern zone having most of the province's garrison of soldiers. The god of healing, Aesculapius, is represented mostly by the dedications of military doctors, often Greek. There are also coins, reliefs and inscriptions to 'abstract' deities such as Virtue, Victory, Discipline and Fortune. Most are from the northern military zone, which accounts, for example, for thirty-seven out of the forty-four known appearances of Fortune. This is precisely what one would expect, given the especial cultivation of these qualities in the army. The cult of the Emperor's *numen* was also clearly well established. London, Lincoln and York have produced dedications by priests based in colleges paid for by local merchants. Others to the *numen* were left by officers in the military zone and by a 'policeman' stationed at Dorchester in Oxfordshire. Yet others come from Cambridgeshire and Colchester in Essex, and small bronze heads of individual emperors, perhaps from cult statues, have been found in eastern England. Many of the latter may attest to the belief that exceptionally gifted rulers became divine themselves upon their deaths and could be worshipped directly. The greatest monument to this idea erected in Britain was, appropriately, the massive temple built at Colchester to Claudius, the emperor who had launched the conquest of the province.

The 'mystery religions' also arrived in Britain during the second half of its Roman period. The characteristic rectangular shrines of the god Mithras have been found at London and York and upon Hadrian's Wall in the north. An image of the god Atys was found in the Thames at London, and near it a vivid reminder of the most sensational aspect of that cult, a bronze serrated clamp ornamented with busts of Atys and his mother Cybele. This (as is obvious from Continental sources) was used to castrate newly made priests, who surrendered their manhood to Cybele as part of their initiation. It is possible that the same cult was also present at St Albans and in Norfolk at Hockwold-cum-Wilton. An inscribed jug

FIGURE 6.1   Mithras
The famous relief now in the Museum of London: found in the Walbrook, it was dedicated by a veteran soldier who had been initiated into this most famous of mystery religions, dependent on a particular divine saviour.

from London and an amulet from a villa at Welwyn in Hertfordshire both testify to the presence of the goddess Isis, though these may have been personal possessions and do not prove the existence of a group of her devotees. But there was a temple of her consort Serapis at York and his image has been found in London. There is much more evidence of Bacchus, who under his Greek name of Dionysus was also the saviour-god of a mystery cult. Statues, figurines, incised vessels, decorated mirrors and mosaics proclaim his former presence in the cities of London, Cirencester, Bath and Wroxeter, up at Capheaton near Hadrian's Wall and in a villa at Spoonley Wood in Gloucestershire. The trouble with all this material, however, is that Bacchus was also the divine patron of wine and festivity, and it may have been nothing other than a general encouragement to merrymaking. Altogether, clear evidence of the 'mystery religions' in Britain is very slight, and occurs in situations marginal to the life of the province – army camps and the largest towns. There is a possibility that they were the preserve of foreign soldiers (mostly officers) and merchants who were resident in Britain. Nor did the worship of the more traditional Roman deities decline as the 'mystery religions' appeared in the island. They, rather than figures like Mithras, were the true representatives of the faiths of Rome in Britain.[7] What we do not know is whether they were worshipped by the native population as well as by the immigrants to the province, and this ignorance invalidates any attempt to specify the degree of Romanization which occurred.

Now we come to the hybrid deities, who bore both Celtic and Roman names, and those who were associated in inscriptions. Sometimes the process of association seems to be very much the work of individual people or groups. A centurion called Julius Secundus set up an altar to the Roman god of hunting and of the woods, Silvanus, upon Scargill Moor near Bowes, Yorkshire. But he also took care to honour the local god Vinotonus, placing his name upon the altar as well. He may have learned of the existence of this being from another, seemingly older, altar put up to Vinotonus in the same place by an officer called Lucius Caesius Frontinus. That individual had been an Italian from Parma, commanding Balkan soldiers. At Gallows Hill, Thetford, a hoard was found in 1979 which apparently consisted of the ritual impedimenta of a local cult of Faunus, Roman god of the countryside. Among the items were thirty-two spoons, upon which were inscribed Faunus's name with a range of different epithets in native Brythonic, translating as 'the Mighty', 'Long Ear', 'Fosterer of Corn (or Blossom)', 'Giver of Plenty', 'Protector' and 'Mead-maker'. The names of the local devotees were also inscribed on the

The shrine of Mithras at Carrawburgh, Northumberland, reconstructed by the late Ronald Ambleton. The shape, size and statuary are reproduced faithfully from the finds. As the ceremonies remain mysterious, none is shown. By kind permission of Frank Graham.

spoons, as if each were special to an individual. Here we have a case of a Roman deity being assimilated into the worship of a group of Britons.[8] But much more common was the addition of a Roman god's name to that of a local one. Several of the deities of Rome were employed in this manner. Jupiter, for example, was identified with Celtic gods who were, like him, associated with the sky. The main such coupling was with the deity Taranis ('the Thunderer') in the Rhineland, but the British evidence is much slighter. Across the Romano-Celtic world, from Britain to Czechoslovakia, the wheel was the symbol for the sky, representing either the sun alone, or the whole turning heaven. It may have kept the same connotation since it appeared in Scandinavian rock art during the Bronze Age. The presence of a wheel with the image of a god appears to have associated that deity firmly with the heavens. At Felmingham Hall, Norfolk, a small metal wheel was found with a head of Jupiter and a mask with solar rays spreading from it. And at Icklingham in Suffolk a similar

FIGURE 6.2   Universal symbols: the wheel again
Figure from Carlisle, now in the museum there: of unknown gender, it holds a horn of plenty in one hand and a wheel (symbol of the sun or the heavens) in the other.

wheel and wheel brooch were dug up with a statuette of Jupiter's symbol, the eagle. These suggestive associations are all the British evidence for the identification of the greatest Roman god with a local sky deity, and were it not for the abundant Continental evidence for the same thing, they might be dismissed altogether. There is not a trace of a sky god in early Welsh and Irish literature and neither does the name of an undoubted Celtic one appear to survive in any inscription of Roman Britain. The wheel symbol is certainly quite widespread, being found as gold miniatures in County Durham, on pots at Silchester, Hampshire, on gable ends at Caerleon in Gwent, and on altars in Gloucestershire and in three forts along Hadrian's Wall. But it may have denoted good luck or longevity, rather than being invariably associated with a specific cult. The East Anglian finds may just represent the addition of the Celtic wheel to the iconography of Jupiter rather than a native god. At Corbridge, a large fort near Hadrian's Wall, a mould was found for casting images of an armed male in a legionary's uniform with a club and a wheel. The Maryport fortress at the west end of the wall provided a headless figure with a wheel and a horn of plenty, while from Churcham in Gloucestershire comes a horned god in a long tunic accompanied by two wheels. But, again, these may have been images of Jupiter invested with Celtic divine attributes rather than actual British deities of the sky. The evidence for the latter at this stage is inconclusive.[9]

Jupiter may have been the dominant god of Rome and its legions, but the Celts tended to prefer Mercury, patron of traders and of culture, and Mars, patron of war and farming. In Gaul the name of the former has been linked with forty-five local gods and that of the latter with sixty-nine of them.[10] In Britain, perhaps because of a difference in economic life, the dominance of Mars in such pairings is even more obvious, even though the total sample of inscriptions is very much smaller. So far, twenty-one pairings of Mars with local gods have been found, together illustrating the range of attributes which the British perceived him to possess. Mars Camulos, Mars Thingsus and Mars Cocidius were warrior gods worshipped by soldiers on the northern frontier. Mars Lenus, at Caerwent in Gwent, seems to have been a healer, as was apparently Mars Nodens in Gloucestershire. Mars Olloudius, at Custom Scrubs in Gloucestershire, was a bringer of plenty. Mars Condatis, in Northumberland and Durham, and Mars Rigonemetis in Lincolnshire, were both associated with places, river junctions and sacred woods respectively. The names of others implied wider functions as protectors, such as Mars Loucetius ('the brilliant') at Bath, Mars Rigisamus ('greatest king') at West Coker in

FIGURE 6.3 Mercury and Rosmerta
Relief of the Roman god and his Celtic wife from Gloucester, now in the
museum there. He has a winged staff, a cockerel and a purse, symbols of his
roles as herald, messenger and protector of traders; she has a double axe, dish and
bucket, indicating her powers to protect and provide.

Somerset, and Mars Toutatis (echoing the Gallic name for a tribal
protector) in Hertfordshire. By contrast, there is only one British
inscription linking Mercury with a native god. But at Uley in
Gloucestershire a pre-Roman shrine was rebuilt as a temple with that
deity as the main patron, so that such an identification must have been
made. And at nearby Gloucester, Bath and Nettleton Shrub there was a
cult (probably imported from the Rhineland) which paired Mercury with
a Celtic goddess of abundance, Rosmerta. Her name means 'the good
bringer', and she carries a bucket, tub or purse (the Celtic equivalents to
the Mediterranean horn of plenty) while Mercury stands proudly by her.

A few other Roman deities found 'doubles'. Apollo was identified with
the young musician god Maponus on Hadrian's Wall, and appears as
Cunomaglus, 'the hound lord', in Wiltshire. Silvanus was linked to at
least three local deities in the northern military zone. And there is a single
example of a female identification, the pairing of Sulis, goddess of the hot
springs of Bath, with Minerva.[11] The process of identification was very
much a hit-and-miss matter, based upon personal taste. Cocidius appears

FIGURE 6.4   Minerva and her sisters

a The unblinking stare of Sulis-Minerva, patroness of the hot springs at Bath: this head from her great cult statue, now in the Roman Baths Museum, was probably crowned by a helmet, now lost; *b* bronze statuette of a typically Roman Minerva from Plaxtol, Kent, now in the British Museum: we know, from the survival of more complete specimens abroad, that she would have held spear and owl; *c* Brigantia, from a stele erected in the fort at Birrens near Dumfries and now in the National Museum of Antiquities of Scotland: were it not for the survival of her name beneath the figure, she might have been taken for Minerva or Victory; *d* a carving, still in the rock face of a Cheshire quarry, that retains the spear and owl lost by the figurine in *b*, suggesting that she is Minerva (though she might be a local goddess portrayed in like manner).

by himself in twenty-one inscriptions, is coupled with Mars in five and is paired with Silvanus in two more. Maponus was linked with Apollo in four dedications but stands alone in two others.

The attempt to determine the extent to which Roman religion affected that of the natives is further complicated by apparent introduction to Britain of cults which belonged to neither, but derived instead from other Celtic provinces of the Empire, especially from Gaul. The worship of Mercury and Rosmerta was one of these, as has been said, and so were Mars Loucetius and Mars Camulos, also cited above. Apollo Maponus was probably another. The greatest of all such importations appears to have been the cult of the Matres, or Mothers, which seems to have arrived with soldiers transferred from the Rhineland where they were particularly popular. At times they are called Matrones, Suleviae or the Campestres, but they remain recognizably the same personalities, three women in a row, usually seated. As will have been discernible at times in the last chapter, the Celts were greatly attached to the number three, and in particular liked to group three goddesses together. The Matres reflected this pattern, and it is important to emphasize that in absolutely no ancient sources are any of these triads of divine females regarded as aspects of one being. In both iconography and literature they are treated as three separate individuals who co-operate for an end and so treble the power at their disposal. The Romano-Celtic Matres were above all protectors of soldiers, for out of almost sixty dedications to and images of them in Britain, all but eleven have been found in forts or were made by the military. The remainder come from London, Lincoln and Colchester, unsurprisingly in view of the importance of these towns and the fact that all had Roman settlers, and also from an area around Cirencester and Bath, where they seem to have had a following among civilians. The extent of their popularity in the army gives them the distinction of being the most important dieties of the northern military zone: the units there had to sacrifice to Jupiter and the others in the official list, but they chose to honour the Matres. It is easy to imagine that soldiers would have an emotional need for female deities who nurtured and comforted as well as protected. The surviving images of the Matres bear out this idea, sometimes being associated with fruit or flowers, and almost always representing stately ladies. But, given the Roman penchant for multiplication, we cannot be sure that all the units were in fact worshipping the same three beings. The inscriptions include Matres 'of all nations', 'from overseas', 'of Italy, Gaul, Germany, Britain', 'of Africa, Italy and Gaul', 'of Italy', 'of the parade ground' and 'of the Household'. Yet in Africa they are

FIGURE 6.5   The three mothers
a On a schist plaque found at Bath and now in the Roman Baths Museum: we cannot tell what gifts, if any, they bear; *b* in a relief found at Cirencester and now in the Corinium Museum, apparently all carrying loaves; *c* on a slab found at Maryport and now in the Senhouse Museum (their nudity seems exceptional); *d* a set of sculptures found at Ancaster in Lincolnshire: less attractive matrons than most of the other Matres found in Britain but again seemingly carrying loaves.

unknown and in Italy they are so rare that they may easily have been taken there by Celts. It was when southern units came up into the Celtic lands that they acquired such protectors. Perhaps they also represented a transference of the tutelary function of local Celtic goddesses?[13]

Another probable importation were the enigmatic 'Genii Cucullati', 'the Hooded Spirits', figures shown standing in full face and wearing the cloak with the pointed hood which gave them their name. They are found across the whole Romano-Celtic region eastwards to Austria, but with a particular concentration (like the Matres, and Mercury and Rosmerta) in the Rhineland. They were especially popular around Trier, being found in temples and tombs and at sacred springs. Some from this area are shown carrying eggs, perhaps symbolic of life or rebirth. They tended, like the Matres, to occur in threes, and their distribution in Britain follows that of the Mothers, being confined to the northern frontier and to the Cirencester area. About twenty reliefs of them have been found. Around Cirencester they appear to be explicitly associated with the cult of the Matres, for they stand attendant upon a female figure looking very like one of the Mothers in the other reliefs. All their associations, in Britain or on the Continent, seem to be with protection, or fruitfulness, or birth: they appear to be spirits of general benevolence. Graham Webster has suggested that their hoods may have been intended to represent phalluses, and indeed they are very like the curved phallic stones which occur on Roman sites. But all this is no more than a possibility. As in the case of the Matres, we suffer very badly from the lack of literary sources from the Celtic provinces of the pagan Roman Empire.[14]

It is interesting to note those very popular European Celtic deities which apparently did *not* make much of an impact upon Roman Britain. There is no sign, for example, of the Rhenish thunder-god Jupiter Taranis. The mounted goddess Epona, patroness of Roman cavalry units

FIGURE 6.6　The Genii Cucullati
Three Genii Cucullati and a goddess, found at Cirencester and now in the Corinium Museum. Two of the Genii carry swords, presumably as protectors, and their characteristic hooded cloaks are very plain; the goddess looks like one of the Matres, but she is too badly weathered for us to tell what she is carrying.

along the Rhine and Danube frontiers, does appear, most frequently at northern British forts in which such units were stationed. Two carvings of such a figure occur upon 'Pictish' pillar stones, indicating that the British beyond the frontier may have taken over her cult from their enemies. But they may have employed the image to indicate somebody or something else. Certainly, the tiny amount of evidence for an impact by her upon civilians argues against modern attempts to associate her with the Uffington White Horse, or with the Irish goddess Macha, or with the mythical Welsh queen Rhiannon. And there is no dedication in Britain to the antler-wearing god of the Paris region, Cernnunos. There is, indeed a relief from Cirencester which looks exactly like him, and the fact that other Gallic cults put down roots in this city would argue for the identification. But it is unattributed, and may represent another deity, as could the coin from Petersfield in Sussex, mentioned in the last chapter.[15]

So we come to those apparently native deities whose cults were brought into the light of archaeology and history by the Romans. The density of military occupation along Hadrian's Wall, and the tendency of foreign soldiers to honour local divinities, has made the pattern there relatively if not absolutely clear. The most important local deity was Cocidius, mentioned above, whose worship was mainly concentrated in the Irthing valley. Belatucadrus, 'the bright beautiful one' is found in Cumbria,

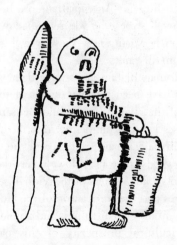

FIGURE 6.7 Cocidius
Looking rather like a budgerigar in armour, this is the local god worshipped by many soldiers along Hadrian's Wall: found on a silver plaque at Bewcastle, he is now in Carlisle Museum.

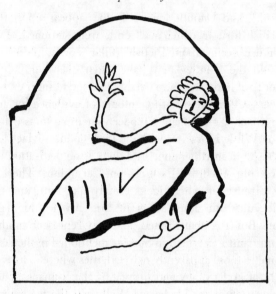

FIGURE 6.8   Coventina
The divine guardian of the spring at Carrawburgh, on a relief now in the
museum of Chesters Roman Fort (Northumberland).

where he was particularly popular with the civilian population, including
some who were semi-literate. Antenociticus has been found only at the
outlying fort of Benwell, where he was overshadowed by Cocidius. And
Coventina, who kept the spring near the Carrawburgh fort, attracted an
intense devotion from all ranks.[16]

   Across civilian Roman Britain are scattered the names and images of
goddesses who may have been tutelary deities of the Celts. Verbeia was
certainly the deity of the river Wharfe, and Belisama of the Ribble, but
no other watercourses can be confidently identified with divine patrons.
Most of those which have borne Celtic names in historical times have
derived them from words for water, flow, river, dark, swiftness, and so
on.[17] Around the Cotswolds, reliefs of individual goddesses, like those of
Rosmerta, the Matres and the companion of the Genii Cucullati, tend to
be associated with symbols of fruitfulness and abundance: this may reflect
the undoubted agricultural prosperity of this part of the province.
Especially common in the south-east, but found across southern England,
are little nude female figurines of pipe-clay, now often called 'pseudo-
Venuses'. They come from houses, shrines and graves, and we can only
guess at their function. The guess is an obvious one, that they were part of

a sympathetic magic or represented a protective deity to assist women to be fertile or to overcome gynaecological ailments. They are sufficiently small and cheaply made to have been kept by individuals. But, again, nothing of this is certain. And there are traces of divine female figures with attributes found as yet only locally: the lady with a key at Winchester, the one with a dog at Canterbury, and those with palms at Caerwent. And there are others who are described in such general terms that they could be native or Roman, very localized or widespread, such as the 'Celestial Goddess of the Woodlands and Crossroads' addressed by an officer's wife at a fort in Scotland. In general, men tended to dedicate to gods and goddesses, and women to goddesses alone. Yet too little evidence

A Roman lady adding to the enormous collection of votive coins dropped into Coventina's Well at Carrawburgh. The form of the rim and of the precinct are faithfully reproduced, as are the altars, though the triple relief of nymphs above the high altar probably came from another shrine nearby. Imagined by the late Ronald Ambleton and reproduced by kind permission of Frank Graham.

FIGURE 6.9   The 'pseudo-Venus'
An example from the Museum of London of the pipe-clay figures found
commonly on domestic sites and in tombs in the south-east; their purpose remains
mysterious.

survives in most cases to establish the nature of the people who venerated
particular deities, let alone whether those deities were home-grown, either
before or after the Roman occupation.[18]

Precisely the same is true of the gods whose anonymous effigies are
found across the province. The armed deities whose reliefs and statuettes
are found in the northern and Welsh military zones may all be native or
may all be Mars. Mars may also be the armed horseman whose image is
found across much of southern England, with a marked concentration in
the eastern counties. He seems to be called Mars Corotiacus at
Martlesham in Suffolk and Mars Toutatis at Kelvedon in Essex. But was
the equestrian figure a pre-Roman tribal emblem, or was it developed
under Roman rule? A non-Roman feature of many of the images of divine

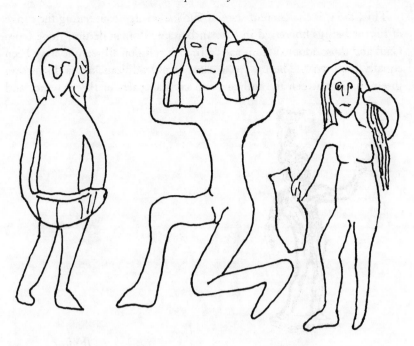

FIGURE 6.10   Goddess and nymphs
Relief of a goddess, probably Venus, taking a shower with the help of two nymphs: found at High Rochester (Northumberland) and now in the Museum of Antiquities, Newcastle upon Tyne.

males is that they wear horns, of bull, ram or goat. These are common all over the northern military zones, soldiers apparently being especially attracted to such aggressive figures. But horned gods (and some horned goddesses) are also found, though more rarely, across all of southern England, from Kent to Somerset and from Suffolk to Staffordshire. They are indeed, common acrosss northern Europe in both Celtic and Germanic areas and found on the Mediterranean in the shape of Pan and (in some incarnations) Faunus. Pagan iconography would hardly miss such an obvious symbol of power and pride. Those in Britain may all have been native personalities. But some may have been images of Roman deities such as Mars, upon whom horns were put by local artists used to conceiving gods in this way. Some of the icons of Mercury in Britain made his winged helmet into something uncommonly like a horned head.[19]

This, then, is the current state of our knowledge concerning the range of divine beings honoured in Roman Britain. Roman deities, those from Gaul and those adopted from native British religion all seem to have been equally important. There were marked local traditions, and a distinction in emphasis between the military and civilian parts of the province and

FIGURE 6.11   Mars and his brethren
a A classic Roman bronze figurine of Mars, missing his spear (the name of the god is on the pedestal below the figure): from the Foss Dyke (Lincolnshire), now in the British Museum; *b* a bronze statuette portraying the mounted figure popular in the eastern counties; he looks like Mars here, but may be a native war god: found at Peterborough and now in the museum there; *c* this crude carving on a slab looks, in comparison with the elegant figure in *b*, like an earthy native deity, but it may be the same one: from Nottinghamshire, now in Nottingham University Museum.

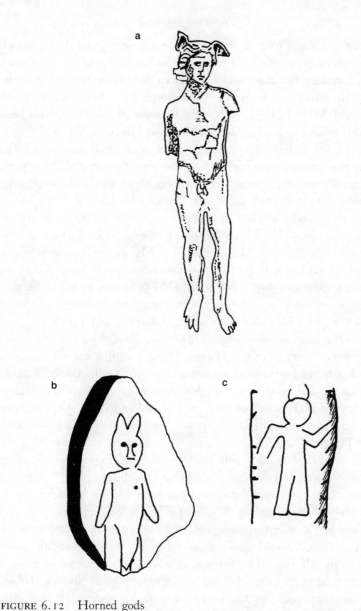

FIGURE 6.12   Horned gods

a This Romanized bronze found in Colchester and now in the British Museum is obviously Mercury with his winged helmet; but drawn crudely on stone, he could appear just another 'horned god'; carvings *b* from High Rochester (Northumberland), now in the Newcastle Antiquities Museum, and *c* from Willowburn (Cumberland), in the Carlisle Museum, are both from the Hadrian's Wall zone and could both be either local horned gods or rather dreadful representations of Mercury.

between those places with Roman settlers and those without them, though there seems to have been little difference in the favourite deities of town and countryside. But this survey has given only some indication of the range of divinities honoured in any one community. In a small fort near Dumbarton, at the furthest reach of the Romans into Scotland, have been found dedications to Jupiter, Mars, Minerva, Hercules, Victory, Diana, Apollo, Epona and the Campestres [20] The place in Britain which has yielded the record number of Roman inscriptions is Maryport, Cumberland, once the coastal fort of Alauna which was established in the early second century and contained 1000 men. They and the native community around them left dedications to Jupiter the Supreme Ruler, Vulcan, Neptune, the Virtue of the Emperor, the Victory of the Emperor, Aesculapius, Mars, the Dis Manibus (Roman deities), Setlocenia ('Goddess of Long Life'), Belatucadrus and Belenus. There are images of a spear-carrying god labelled SEG (who may be the Gallic war deity Segomo) and of the Genii Cucullati. Other figures represent Hercules, a god with radiate hair and raised arms, and a nude goddess. There are three rather menacing naked stylized females standing in a row, possibly a local version of the Matres. There is a pillar carved upon one side with a horned or crested serpent and upon the other with a human head. But the deity shown in the greatest number of reliefs is a crudely drawn horned god, nude but carrying a shield and spear. He generally has a large penis, to reinforce the general impression of *machismo*. This may be Belatucadrus, for similar images correspond to the range of the dedications to him. Such a belligerent monster, horny in both modern senses of the term, is difficult to match with a name signifying 'bright and beautiful'. But then beauty is, after all, in the eye of the beholder, and it could well be that on viewing these images we are looking at the principal god of the pre-Roman Cumbrians. Or had the soldiers made him more military and ferocious than his original form? We do not know, any more than we can tell why the garrison at Maryport seems to have been especially fond of the symbol called by Christians the St Andrews Cross, which they scratched on the breast of some of their male deities.[21] Maryport is, of course, exceptional in the range of material it has furnished, and unique in the mixture of deities commemorated. But then, on present evidence, every other community in Roman Britain seems to have had its own cocktail of worship, none reproducing precisely the same goddesses and gods as another.

There remain a few puzzles in this picture. One is that the British Celts, who apparently honoured the smith as a key figure in society, did

FIGURE 6.13   The 'Bright Beautiful One'?
Beauty in the eye of the beholder: this is almost certainly Belatucadrus, worshipped in Cumbria. From a figure scratched on a sandstone block at Maryport, now in the Senhouse Museum.

not pay more attention to the Roman smith god Vulcan and his local equivalents. The Gallic Celts did so, and the Irish literature gives an honoured place to Goibhniu, which makes the British omission the more surprising. Another oddity is that the prominence of Celtic goddesses in war, apparent both in the Irish tales and in the Roman account of Boudicca's rebellion, is not reflected in the iconography of the province. The warlike deities of Roman Britain seem mostly to have been male, while the goddesses appear to be associated more with fruitfulness, comfort and healing. Did the Romans make such a great alteration in the way in which the British Celts viewed gender roles in the divine world?

Following the pattern employed in considering the non-Roman Iron Age, we turn now to look at the sacred structures, religious professionals and festivals of Roman Britain. In sharp contrast to the small number of pre-Roman shrines identified in Britain, some 139 Romano-British temples have been recognized at the time of writing: so much more enduring are monuments built in stone. They can be divided into several different styles. Twenty of the total resemble those of Rome itself, long rectangular buildings with pillared porticoes at one end. These, naturally enough, are found near the main towns and forts where Roman influence was strongest. Some fifty-five have been described as belonging to the so-called Romano-Celtic type, found throughout the Celtic provinces of the Empire. They were round or polygonal as well as rectangular, but all had an inner precinct lying within an outer one of the same shape. The British examples are almost all south-east of a line between the Wash and the mouth of the Severn, in the most peaceful and prosperous part of the province. The same is true of the thirty-three simple round or polygonal temples, and the sixteen which are rectangular or square, with a simple entrance. The total is completed with eighteen long rectangular shrines, which are found throughout the military and civilian zones. [22]

These statistics conceal the fact that we do not actually know what most of these buildings looked like, having nothing but their foundations. In the case of the Romano-Celtic type, we think that eleven had an outer precinct wall of solid masonry. Two probably had an enclosing portico of columns instead, and the remaining forty-two cannot be reconstructed even conjecturally. The central building of such a temple, from a single ground plan, might have had a roofed portico of columns all round it, or one roof covering all, or a set of roofs, or a cloister with a central open space. [23] We do not know how interiors or exteriors were decorated. All were probably equipped with altars and cult statues, but we do not know exactly how the interior of any would have appeared. We can imagine draperies, lamps and incense-burners, but we cannot prove that any were there. Nor do we really know who worshipped in these temples, because although they were generally larger than the tiny pre-Roman shrines, most were still not big enough to admit more than a dozen people at once. Perhaps the principal ceremonies were held outside them. Are we, then, to think in terms of priests or priestesses, keeping the regular rites going on behalf of an absent community, while individuals or families dropped in for personal rites or prayers? It seems probable, but again we cannot be sure. Were the outer precincts or neighbouring street cluttered with booths from which private traders sold sacrificial animals, votive images and tablets for messages to those preparing to enter? Or were all these commodities obtainable from a temple shop? Each image seems suitable at different places, but neither can be proven. We do not know to what deity most of the recorded temples were dedicated. In fact, we cannot be absolutely sure that some of them were temples at all.

Of two major things, however, we can be certain. One is the rough chronology and distribution of temple building. During the first two centuries AD they were constructed in both town and country in Britain, and after that they continued to appear in rural districts, the towns generally seeming to be happy with the existing ones. They appeared earliest, and were always most common, in southern and eastern England, with concentrations in particularly wealthy and strongly Romanized farming regions such as the Cotswolds and the lower Severn valley, and around the Fens. None has been found in Cornwall and Devon, and few in Norfolk, east Kent or east Sussex.[24] Some of the latter communities ought to have been both Romanized enough to want them and rich enough to afford them, so there are some mysteries in their location. It is utterly unclear whether Roman Britons continued to worship in sacred groves but undoubtedly springs were still venerated and it is certain that many rituals took place outside temples, as before. This last point leads us to the second major theme of which we can be confident: that in the matter of sacred monuments the Roman period saw an enormous development of Iron Age practice. It was a development, rather than a break. Every known pre-Roman shrine in England was rebuilt as a Romano-British temple unless the settlement which it served was destroyed by conquest. A majority of the total of temples were rectangular, like the majority of the old shrines. Animal sacrifices and miniature weapons were still offered at them, as before. But the stone temples were infinitely more impressive than the wooden shrines, almost a third of them were round or polygonal instead of rectangular and the offerings were expanded to include figurines, bronze letters, tablets inscribed with prayers and curses, ceramic lamps and miniature pots.[25] In its sacred buildings as in its deities, the province was neither truly Roman nor truly British.

It is difficult to say how far this was true of religious personnel. The Druids vanish at the conquest, but whether into oblivion or by transformation into Romano-British priests, nobody can say. The latter seems the more likely fate. The Romans wiped them out only where they encouraged resistance to Imperial rule, and there seems to have been no general proscription of their order. A fourth-century scholar proudly proclaimed descent from one of them, as did some local worthies in Gaul. Yet vanish they certainly did. Women called 'druidesses' occasionally advised emperors as late as the third century, but these seem to have been Celtic soothsayers, not priestesses.[26] A real priestess, of the Roman kind, does feature in the British inscriptions, serving an eastern god, Hercules of Tyana, at Corbridge near Hadrian's Wall. Priests, both permanent and part-time, are attested in the towns and at some temples, and the huge complex around the hot spring at Bath had its own fortune-tellers.[27] It is irritating that abbreviations common in Roman inscriptions often make it difficult to determine exactly what work temple officials did. Was the 'pr. rel' who dedicated a mosaic floor at Lydney, Gloucestershire, the *praepositus religionum* (temple supervisor) or a *praefectus reliquiationis* (overseer of a naval dockyard)? Was the *interpres* at Lydney there to interpret dreams and visions, or just for foreign visitors? Or was he himself a visitor, holding the rank of *interpres* on a governor's staff?[28]

Religous impedimenta are easier to understand, because of the combination of reliefs, showing ceremonies, and artefacts. The former depict priests either throwing their robes over their heads for sacred occasions, or wearing metal crowns. Some of these crowns have been found in England, virtually all in East Anglia. Those from Cavenham Heath, Suffolk, and Hockwold-cum-Wilton in Norfolk included examples with silver plaques, others made of arched strips with a spike on top, and yet others of medallions linked with chains. Sceptres, apparently religious in function, come from Willingham Fen in Cambridgeshire and Farley Heath in Surrey. Rattles, associated with ceremonies in Roman religion (they drowned out ill-omened noises) have turned up at three sites in Norfolk and Cambridgeshire. Metal face-masks, apparently worn by priests, have been found at Bath and in East Anglia. It is possible that some of this regalia is pre-Roman. Then there are the tools of worship: axes and knives for sacrifice, and flagons and shallow bowls for cleansing and for libations. Spoons and platters indicate ritual feasts, and incense-burners and metal standards provide clues as to the appearance of ceremonies. Roman art and literature provide copious evidence of the decking of shrines with flowers, and of music to accompany rites, often with singing or chanting.[29]

It is distressing that, while having some impression of what Romano-British rituals looked like, we know less about the festivals of the province than about those of the pagan Irish. The city of Rome itself had by the time of the emperors amassed a crowded calendar of religious feasts of varying length and importance. Some were general occasions for celebration and for seasonal rites of passage, while others were observed more by particular trades or social groups.[30] But we have absolutely no idea how much of this calendar was employed in Roman Britain and to what extent the native feasts were continued. We have, indeed, only one portrait of a Romano-British festival, and that is a dubious one. It was recorded in the *Natural History* of Pliny, written in Italy while the conquest of northern Britain was in progress. He relates that for certain ceremonies the married women of the Britons would strip naked and

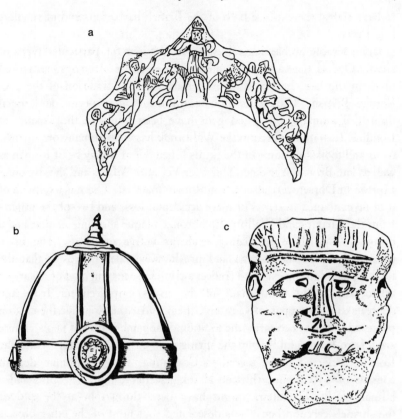

FIGURE 6.14 Priestly regalia?

a Bronze diadem from Lydney, in the museum on the site. It shows a crowned figure riding in a chariot and attended by genii and tritons. The figure itself looks like a sun god, while the presence of the tritons suggests a sea deity. It certainly does not look like an icon of Mars, yet he, identified with the British god Nodens, is often taken as the principal deity of the temple at Lydney. If this was a priestly crown, then the figure upon it may have been Mars Nodens. *b* Bronze crown with medallions showing unidentified faces. Found at Hockwold-cum-Wilton (Norfolk) and now in the British Museum. *c* Tin mask thrown into the sacred spring at Bath, now in the Roman Baths Museum; perhaps worn by a priest, perhaps a votive image.

stain their bodies black, after which they would march in procession.[31] This may be true, for it seems certain from the classical sources that Celtic warriors sometimes dyed their bodies and rushed naked into battle. But it may also be a titillating fable, brought home to Italy by somebody willing to have fun at the expense both of the British barbarians and of scholars like Pliny.

Considerable archaeological evidence survives for particular types of ritual. One is the casting of objects into water as offerings, remarked upon in the last chapter as an important regional tradition of the pre-Roman British. Thousands of coins of the Roman period and metal figures of animals, birds and gods have been found in the Thames at London. Its tributary stream the Wallbrook has yielded many ornaments, coins and tools, and some of the skulls fished out of it may be of Roman as well as late Bronze Age date. The river Ver at St Albans and the stream at Horton in Dorset were also rich in Roman material. There is too much of it to be explained in terms of mere accidental loss, and two of the objects from the Thames and Wallbrook, a bronze plaque showing an altar and a miniature sword, were plainly made as votive offerings. The main contrast between the Roman and pre-Roman water hoards is that the former, as might be expected, reflect a civilian society instead of a warrier aristocracy.[32] But then, many of the rivers employed for Iron Age deposits did not, apparently, receive them under the Romans: the custom persisted but not necessarily the location. The same is true of pools. There are no pre-Roman finds from the spring near Carrawburgh fort which the Romans believed to be sacred to Coventina. But the Roman deposit consists of 1300 coins, thirteen altars, jewellery, figurines, pins and a human skull. The altars might have been thrown in at the end of the shrine's career when it was desecrated, but most of the other objects must have been offerings. The presence of sacred waters is attested all over northern England by the word *latis*, meaning 'pool-goddess', in several Roman place names. Modern Buxton in Derbyshire as mentioned in chapter 5, was Aquae Arnemetiae, 'waters of the goddess of the grove'. Temples were sometimes built around or over ponds and springs, notable examples being at Ivy Chimneys in Essex, at Nettleton Shrub in Wiltshire, at Springhead in Kent and, of course, at Bath where the hot water, unique in Britain, satisfied physical as well as spiritual yearnings.[33]

The same devotion was displayed at those other significant waters, human-made wells. Nine of them, in Warwickshire, Hertfordshire, London, Oxford, Wiltshire, Avon, Gwent and Bedfordshire, contained human skulls. The two in London were already fleshless when deposited, but those in Hertfordshire and in Oxford were freshly severed. Those at Queen Street, London, and in Hertfordshire were put down as the well was filled in, but that in Bedfordshire was lodged in a niche as the shaft was first dug. A cistern at Caerwent, Gwent, was given two skulls and some pottery, and the skeleton of an adult human was laid over it to seal it before the wall of a house was built above. Taken together, all these heads represented both sexes with apparent impartiality. What will already be apparent is that both the initial excavation and the filling in of a well were attended by ritual, and this is borne out by other sorts of deposit. In general, pottery was put in during construction, and pottery and animals – particularly dogs, often buried in pairs – during termination. One couple was found in a well at Farnworth in Gloucestershire, two more pairs in another now under a Southwark street, and eight pairs in yet another at Staines in Surrey. At the great Roman fortress of Portchester Castle, Hampshire, a well was filled in with soil containing another pair of dogs, three skulls of sheep, thirteen of oxen and the body of an aquatic bird, a Great Northern Diver. Together these sites span the whole period of Roman occupation.[34]

In some respects, wells were akin to ritual shafts or pits, which have already been noted in pre-Roman Britain. After the conquest they seem to have become more common and widespread: eighty-one have been identified so far. Most are south of a line drawn between the Trent and the Severn, like most of the temples. The deposits are more varied than those of the pre-Roman period, including deer and pigs as well as horses, dogs and cattle, and votive metalwork, tools, oyster shells and coins as well as pottery. Indeed, the only two commodities which were deposited less often under Roman rule were ash wood and human bones. Offerings now reflected emphasis upon wealth, and less upon the natural world, but this may reflect a change of lifestyle rather than of religous intent. The objects do seem to have been less carefully placed under the Romans, as if an increase in numbers of deposits brought with it a decrease in the care taken over the ritual.[35] But some of the Roman shafts were still very elaborate. That at the temple on Jordan's Hill above Weymouth had at its bottom a stone chest, two pots and ironwork including weapons. It was then filled in with sixteen layers of ash, charcoal, and the bodies of birds, each one of the latter being placed, with a coin, between two tiles. Ravens, crows, buzzards and starlings were there: were it not for the last of these we would feel justified in saying that only species who were both predators and carrion-eaters, symbols of war and death were present. But the starlings seemed to destroy the pattern. At Wasperton, Warwickshire, a sandstone block was carved with the word *Feliciter*, 'for luck'. It was laid in a pit and upon it two sets of antlers were placed in a square, in the middle of which a fire was burned before the pit was filled. At

Bekesbourne, Kent, another pit contained pots set on a flat stone in a circle of horses' teeth.

Further examples may confirm the impression of the vast range of individual forms which the 'ritual pit' or 'shaft' could take in Roman Britain. At Ashill, Norfolk, two shafts and a pit were excavated within enclosures. The pit held a goat skull and some animal bones, and the shallower shaft an ox skull, red deer antlers and pots. The deeper one contained 100 pots, half of which were broken, pieces of antler, a boar's tusk, a bronze brooch and an iron implement. At Keston in Kent, in the first century, a shaft was dug and a dog put at its foot with three horses arranged in a triangle above. Seven more deposits of animal bones were added to the upper fill during the following decades, extending into the next century. The process may have had something to do with the establishment of a family tomb, used by owners of a neighbouring villa. In the fourth century, another shaft was sunk nearby and two dog cremations put at its bottom and covered in potsherds. We have no real idea of the precise purpose of any of these deposits, nor of the deities, if any, to whom they were offered.[36]

Boundary ditches represented a different sort of ritual pit, and at times apparently required the same rites of foundation or termination as wells. In Southwark in about AD 60, a human skull and two bowls were put in the ditch beside a Roman road. At about the same time, parts of another skull were deposited with animal bones and three broken pots in the east ditch of the fort of London. Pots and dogs were placed together in ditches inside the London city wall at Rangoon Street. Two bowls, two terracotta lamps and two cooking pots were put together in a ditch at Dipington, Kent. Genuine rubbish pits were sometimes inaugurated in the same sort of way: several at Godmanchester near Huntingdon had at least two dogs buried at the bottom of each. Sometimes hares were added. The same processes were applied to buildings in general. To put dogs, lambs, fowls, pigs, cattle, pots, horses or ornaments under the threshold or walls of new constructions was very common. Coins were placed by Roman shipwrights in the mast-steps of ships, a custom which has indeed survived to the present. The demolition of buildings was also sometimes attended by similar depositions. At Upchurch in Kent, a pottery factory was closed in the late second century, and rows of puppies in pots buried across the site.[37]

It will be obvious from all this that animal sacrifice remained as important to the religion of Roman Britain as it had been among the previous population, and that the same species – dogs, horses and cattle –

remained the favourite victims. Generally, the animal had to share the gender of the deity to whom it was offered. But also, as in the pre-Roman Iron Age, other species occurred in art as symbols of power and majesty. The most curious, and fantastic, is the ram-headed or ram-horned serpent which appears in several reliefs, and at Cirencester and in Gaul is associated with the antlered deity known around Paris as Cernunnos. Its form may have made it a symbol of potency and fertility. There are also in Britain six representations of the three-horned bull which was a popular symbol in central Gaul. Genuine species were often associated with particular deities: thus Mercury had a goat or ram (for fertility), the cock (as a herald), and the tortoise (from whose shell could be made his favourite instrument, the lyre). Virtually all the bones of sacrificed animals found at Mercury's temple at Uley, Gloucestershire, were goats, with a few cockerels. Geese were often portrayed upon statues of Mars, in a realistic tribute to these most ferocious of farmyard birds.[38] It may have been that the bodies of sacrificed animals (or what was left of them, if ritual was followed, in a Roman manner, by a feast) were always buried. Some of the other objects found in 'ritual pits' may also have played a part in ceremony. Burial may have been a way to remove them as they were now charged with potentially dangerous power, rather than as an act of worship in itself.[39] But this is only supposition, not confirmed by any literary source.

It was said earlier that human sacrifice was illegal in the Roman Empire after 196 BC. This undisputed fact may appear to conflict with the evidence of freshly severed heads being placed in wells, or the whole skeleton over the cistern at Caerwent. Perhaps it does, and there have been other finds which raise the same sinister doubts. The bodies of two babies were put into the foundations of the religious complex at Springhead. Given the high rate of infant mortality during the period, this might not appear suspicious save for the fact that they had been beheaded. At the great third-century naval fortress of Reculver in Kent, two sections were dug by archaeologists through the wall of the building, and each one struck the body of a human baby. In a settlement, this might be considered to be a way of keeping a dead child close to the family, but in a military building it looks more ominous. At the fort of Newstead, in southern Scotland, far up on the periphery of Roman rule, soldiers dug a pit and put in a human head with those of an ox and a horse.[40] None of these cases represents conclusive evidence. The heads may have been cut from people who had already died naturally, or criminals who had suffered (literally) capital punishment and were then employed ritually.

Parts of the bodies of those who had suffered execution were believed to possess magical potential into relatively modern times. The bodies and the person over the cistern at Caerwent may also have died natural deaths. But clearly some of the beliefs which had inspired people to sacrifice their fellows were still present. Even if the letter of the law was obeyed, and nobody was actually killed ritually, the presence of human remains in ceremonial deposits was still thought to be potent.

Here we touch on the large subject of burial customs. As has already been stated, neither the Celts nor the Romans held one generally accepted view of the fate of the soul after death. Roman attitudes to the dead varied. Some traditions held that they could be a menace to the living and required regular propitiation by ritual. Others stated that they needed to be comforted, or could be communed with to the profit of those still alive. Yet others proposed that they never returned to the world from which they had departed, unless there had been some tragic or evil circumstance about their deaths which might cause them to linger as ghosts.[41] There was a huge number of modes of burial within the Empire, and the already disparate and localized pattern in pre-Roman Britain was further complicated. A few generalizations can be made. Roman law dictated that, for hygienic reasons, graves and tombs should lie outside settlements, and so they usually extended along the roads leading out of a town or were placed in a selected area near a village. It seems that cremation was prodominant in the first and second centuries and inhumation in the third century. There exists no proper corpus of data regarding Romano-British burials, so comparisons must to some extent be impressionistic. But even a superficial study reveals that there were both regional and personal, as well as chronological, variations. The local traditions often continued those apparent at the end of the pre-Roman period. Thus the territory of the Durotriges, in Dorset and Somerset, contains few cremations but has a continuous history of inhumation cemeteries like those dug before the Romans arrived. The south-eastern counties, home of the Cantii and Atrebates, are remarkable for cremations with rich gravegoods both before and after the conquest. In north Essex, where the Catuvellauni had produced even wealthier cremation burials, the Romano-British raised huge round barrows with chambers in which handsome bronzes and vessels accompanied the ashes of the dead. In north Wiltshire the Roman period also saw the construction of round barrows, but with the cremations put in the centre of a circle of oak posts. And across the whole province, around towns or villas, Roman stone tombs with sarcophagi of the Mediterranean sort appeared alongside the native style of burial.[42]

One of the many things which we do not know about Romano-British funerals is what determined their form. The wishes of the deceased? Or of the family? Or of priests or priestesses? The custom of the community? Did Roman Britain have professionals who arranged burials, as in modern society? Common sense suggests that a mixture of the first four factors operated, but the evidence, which is wholly archaeological, permits of no certain answer. Once again, this literate society becomes for us, to all intents and purposes, prehistoric. Just as in every previous period, a great range of individual idiosyncrasy operated within a few widespread similarities. Even some of the latter can only be explained in terms of conjecture, or must be admitted to be mysterious. Deities are very rarely portrayed or named on tombs or gravestones, or sarcophagi. So far, Minerva has appeared three times in this context and Hercules twice, while the Dea Nutrix (the Nourishing Goddess) features at Canterbury. But the only divine figures to be found relatively often with the dead are the pipe-clay 'pseudo-Venuses', at St Albans and Carlisle, and at sites in Kent and Suffolk. If we understood what these figurines signified in any other situation, it would be easier to determine their funerary role. The idea that they were associated with women is neither proved nor disproved by these finds, for although they have not been discovered with any definitely male burials, the gender of the person accompanying them has not always been recorded or identifiable. But certain motifs are common on burial structures, such as cupids (perhaps soothing spiritual companions), axes (retaining the connotations of power and protection which presumably made them such popular images in prehistory), dolphins (perhaps indicating a voyage to the next world), poppies (symbols of sleep), stars (perhaps symbols of eternity), pine cones (associated by the Romans with mourning) and lions (possibly to indicate powerful protection, or the devouring nature of death). Within the graves, inhumed bodies are laid out with heads pointing north, north-east, east or west.

In marked contrast with the pre-Roman period, weapons were almost never buried with people, even when the dead were soldiers. Instead, the most common gravegoods were foot lamps, food vessels, keys, stones, pebbles, animals' teeth, coins and boots. The lamps may have been intended as symbolic gifts for the deceased, to assist them in finding their way to the next life, or they might actually have been left burning in the tomb or grave. The vessels may have contained food for the dead upon their journey, or as a gift for deities or spirits. The keys, perhaps, were to unlock spiritual doors, while the stones, pebbles and teeth could have been charms to protect the dead or favourite possessions of theirs during life. The coins were sometimes placed in the mouth of the corpse and sometimes beside it, one for each person, and here there is no doubt of their significance. They represented a common Roman custom whereby those who died were given their fare to pay the ferryman of the dead to row or pole them over the river Styx to their last home. The boots, stout hobnailed pairs, represented a Celtic belief, reflected in the burials of the Romano-Celtic provinces of Europe as well as Britain, that the deceased would have a long hard walk to their new home. Coins or boots were even put with cremations, in a curious blend of the symbolic and the literal. But in making this inventory, it is important to remember that most Romano-British graves held no goods at all. The large inhumation cemeteries of Somerset and Dorset have produced between them a dozen scattered cases of burials with boots: coins in the mouth have been found so far at twenty-two sites, and coins with the body at almost fifty. This apparently large total disguises the fact that they are a feature of only a minority of burials in each place. They represent twelve individuals from four cemeteries in Somerset and Dorset, and 2 per cent of the burials in the large graveyard of Roman Chichester. Lamps, though more common, were still an accessory of relatively few bodies, for example 11 per cent of those at Chichester. And there are chronological variations: coins, for instance, are very rare with first-century burials, more common in the second century, scarcer in the third, and most often found in the fourth century.[43]

Two other minority customs are worthy of extended treatment because they have appeared especially enigmatic: prone burials and decapitated bodies. All over the Roman province of Britain, the usual form of inhumation was to extend the corpse on its back. But some were put in on their sides, extended or crouched, and all over southern and eastern England a few in each district were laid prone, that is, extended and face downward. Altogether, there are a total of sixty-nine such cases from Romano-British graves, and some idea of their relative frequency may be indicated by the fact that they represented seventeen out of over 200 inhumations found in the upper Thames valley. In the Christian Middle Ages, when burial practices were much more standardized, to lay a body like this was a terrible act of malice, for it turned the face of the corpse away from the light. It was a treatment sometimes meted out to criminals and suicides. Our problem is to try to decide whether such an attitude obtained in this earlier period. It is probable that not all prone bodies were deposited for the same reason. Some are so sprawled that they appear to have been thrown into the graves by people who cared nothing for them and did not trouble about how they landed. But others were laid out carefully and deliberately. A few were placed above bodies with rich goods, in the manner of a servant or companion looking down fondly or obediently upon a superior. Others lie alone: these may have been criminals, or may have been buried by mourners who for some religious reason believed that it was to their advantage to face the earth. Decapitated bodies are a more numerous category, a total of 144 now being known. They occupy the same range, across southern and eastern England, as the prone burials (and also most of the temples and ritual pits). Some twenty-four of more than 200 Romano-British inhumations along the upper Thames had been beheaded. Again, more than one reason is probably needed to account for them. At Walkington Wold and Wor Barrow dumps of bodies were found, of which the majority were headless: these almost certainly were execution sites, beside which the victims were interred. Some of the decapitated corpses in cemeteries were also buried prone, and one might suspect these also to have been criminals, punished in death as in life. But others were laid on their backs, carefully, with rich gravegoods. Some had held high military rank. Some had the heads placed carefully between the knees, and coins were occasionally put into the mouths of these individuals. Both genders are represented, but not children. Either they had been executed and then handed over to relatives for honourable burial, or else the beheading was for religious reasons. The number concerned makes the first explanation unlikely but not impossible, given the prominence of the death penalty in Roman law. The second can only be guessed at. Was it to silence or immobilize the dead, or to set free their spirits faster, or because the head itself was used in the funeral rite? We cannot say.[44]

We should now consider some of the individual cases in which evidence for burial ritual has survived; these reinforce the impression already given of a great variety of practices. The Holborough barrow in Kent was raised over a man who seems to have been cremated in a chair with a cockerel. Five wine-jars were smashed around him before the mound was constructed. At Colchester and St Albans there were crematoria which were used regularly by townspeople. Cremation pits were used at the northern frontier fort of High Rochester, at Dartford in Kent and at the Hampshire town of Silchester. Burials were made in deep shafts at Hardham in Sussex and Bekesbourne in Kent. But at Murston and Warbank Keston in Kent and at Ewell in Surrey, the shafts were dug *near* graves, to receive layers of pottery and animal bone (heifer, sheep, deer and pig at Ewell). The Iron Age practice of burying people as satellites to an honoured body persisted in Hertfordshire. At Harpenden two cremations were put in the enclosure of a stone mausoleum, and at Welwyn three inhumations were laid in a ditch surrounding a tomb which contained a marble sarcophagus. At Springhead, Kent, a woman's dress was burned and laid beside her body. At Abingdon, Oxfordshire, an infant was burned with a dog skull and another with that of a sheep. At Winchester it was a horse's head with which a baby was interred.

Some features of individual burials strike a modern observer as sinister. A coffin containing a handful of coins was put into a cemetery at Winchester. Over it were laid the bodies of two dogs and the decapitated corpse of a young man, his head at his knees with a coin in the mouth. Was it a memorial to somebody whose body could not be recovered, and whose passage into the afterworld was assisted by offerings and three sacrifices, one human (and therefore illegal)? An inhumed body at Plaxtol in Kent was surrounded by cremations with rich goods and one vessel holding a human skull. It has a large stone on the breast: was the person a foundation burial to consecrate an elite graveyard, weighed down to stop the ghost from walking and haunting the living? At Cirencester, and at Ospringe and Lockham in Kent, rocks were piled over inhumed or cremated bodies, either to confine or to protect them. At Lockham a cremation urn was sealed with cement and at Ospringe one was packed with flints. Again, the person within was being either confined or shielded. As with beheadings and the prone corpses, we cannot tell whether love, hatred or fear inspired the funeral rites.[45]

In discussing burials, we are touching upon the sphere of 'personal religion', those relationships made by individuals with the divine which appear in the more copious Romano-British evidence but cannot in prehistory. The most striking of these consist of curses, invited from a deity to descend upon somebody who had done the worshipper wrong. They were written upon plaques: most came from Bath, where they were apparently thrown into the spring, and Uley, where they seem to have been fixed upon a wall of the temple or preserved by priests or priestesses in a room. The most common wrong which was to be redressed was theft, whether of an object or of a loved one. Punishment was generally left to the taste of the divinity concerned, though the degree requested ranged from repentance and return of the stolen goods to destruction. Sometimes

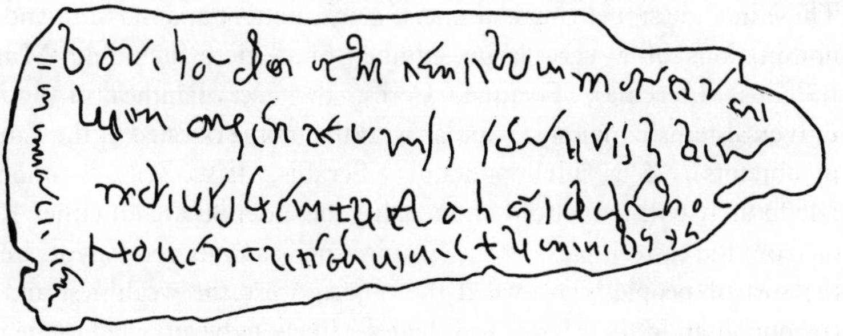

FIGURE 6.15 Curses: 'Hell hath no fury . . .'
a Lead tablet found at Uley (Gloucestershire) and now in the British Museum. The writer, Saturnina, has suffered the theft of a treasured linen cloth, and asks the god at the Uley temple to help her. But she is not sure at first of his identity: first she calls him Mars, and then Silvanus, and finally Mercury (which is correct). Whether she was made careless by her distress, or by fatigue – the temple is up a steep hill – or whether she was merely confused by the statue before her, we can never know. She may indeed have written the curse and then had difficulty in finding a shrine. *b* Tablet of lead/tin alloy, thrown into the sacred spring at Bath and now in the Roman Baths Museum. It reads: 'Basilia gives to the temple of Mars her silver ring, so long as anybody, slave or free, who knows where it is and says nothing, may be cursed in blood and eyes and have their guts eaten away . . .'

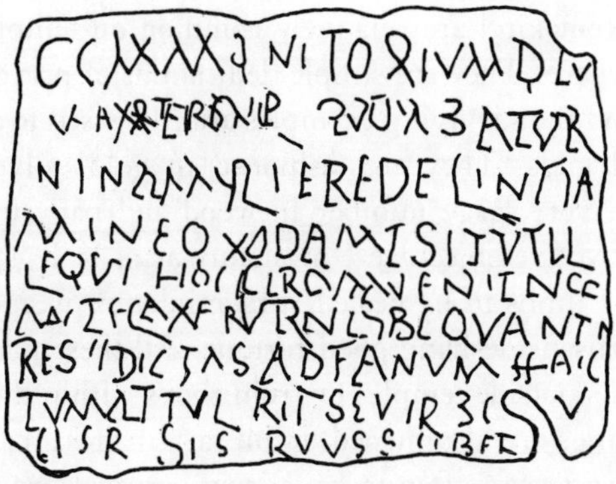

the culprit was named, sometimes clearly unknown and covered by a formula such as 'whether woman or man, slave or free'. But votive plaques of a more innocent kind are relatively common on temple sites and are also found elsewhere. They are simple dedications of prayer by a worshipper to a deity, and the surviving examples are addressed to a huge range of goddesses and gods. They are fashioned in gold, silver and bronze, and doubtless a very large number in wood and papyrus have perished. Other sorts of votive object were miniature arms or legs, from people who wished their limbs to be healed, and miniature weapons or tools from soldiers or artisans desiring good fortune. All these may well have been sold from stalls outside temples or from shops within them, as suggested earlier. But rings are also turned up on sacred sites, inscribed with dedications, and these seem often to have been personal ornaments adapted for religious purposes.[46]

Then there is the related phenomenon of personal objects and dedications inscribed with religious motifs and found upon domestic sites. These include signet rings, amulets, gems, pottery and mosaics, and carry nominations of a very large number of deities, including Minerva, Bacchus, Hercules, Fortune, Ceres, the Dea Panthea (a figure of universal female majesty, popular with the more educated of the Empire's inhabitants), Zeus Heliopolitanus, Serapis, Isis, Zeus Ammon and Medusa. It will be noticed at once that these deities are all either Roman or from the eastern parts of the Empire such as Syria and Egypt. Perhaps the sort of people who owned the objects were the wealthiest and most cosmopolitan in their tastes and the least likely to be attracted to the native deities. In fact the only one of the latter to be named in these private settings is Brigantia, the patron goddess of the north of England; and she is a special case, for she was greatly promoted (perhaps even invented) by the imperial government in the early third century in an attempt to focus the communal loyalties of the inhabitants of the northern military zone. However, a large number of anonymous deities appear on pottery and other personal possessions. A smith god who appears upon some pots may be Vulcan or some Celtic deity. Some of the figures are very standardized: the same image of an armed woman is identified in some settings as Minerva, but in others as the Dea Panthea, Victory or Brigantia.

With many of these items there arises the question, in most cases insoluble, of whether the image of a deity was an object of personal devotion or just a decoration. A host of associated problems arise from the same sort of material. The mosaic factories at Cirencester, among the most important in the province, used images of Orpheus and Venus as their trade marks. So a purchaser need have had no personal attachment to these divinities when ordering such a floor to be laid. The frequency with which hunting and gladiatorial scenes appear upon Romano-British mosaics may reflect an interest in death and resurrection, or just a pleasure in these most exciting forms of entertainment. Scenes upon pottery may reflect religious beliefs or illustrate myths. Is one upon a sherd from Colchester, showing men in animal skins and antlers within a woodland setting, portraying a ritual or an episode from a story? Another enigmatic sherd was found at Horsey Toll, Cambridgeshire, and manufactured in a pottery in the Nene valley. It shows a man ejaculating while running towards a naked woman who is holding a huge phallus in one hand and pointing towards her genitals with the other. Was this illustration a charm to promote fertility or just a piece of coarse humour? Phalluses appear as often upon Romano-British sites as upon those of the Neolithic. Fashioned in stone or upon pottery, they sometimes bear wings; those upon a sherd of a vessel made at Colchester have legs as well. Phallic amulets have been found in Shropshire, and a child's necklace dug up at Catterick in Yorkshire had six phalluses suspended from it. They were carved upon the bridge abutment, bath-house and wall of the headquarters at the fort of Chesters upon Hadrian's Wall. They appear upon the town wall of Lincoln and the fort wall at Maryport. Clearly, in many contexts

FIGURE 6.16   Universal symbols
A stone head, shaped like a phallus and carved with three circles: found at Eype, Dorset and now in the Dorset County Museum, it is one of the largest phallic objects to survive from Roman Britain. They seem to have been made to confer strength as much as fertility.

they represented not so much fertility as virility, strength, protection and power. They gave buildings a reinforced ability to stand.[47]

One service which Romano-British holy places did not apparently provide for visitors was that of oracles. But a 'haruspex' made divinations at Bath and individuals did receive, and record, visions. Throughout the Empire, it was believed that deities did occasionally appear or speak invisibly to humans in the course of their daily lives; but it was also agreed that most divine apparitions occurred to people in their dreams, and Artemidorus of Daldis published a five-book guide to their significance. The section upon erotic encounters is particularly extensive. Thus, to dream of Artemis naked meant disaster, and while a view of Aphrodite topless was fine a full frontal was propitious only for a prostitute. Sex with Aphrodite was auspicious if you enjoyed it, but invariably a bad sign if with goddesses regarded as chaste.[48] In Britain two inscriptions have survived, at Bath and at Hadrian's Wall fort of Carvoran, by individuals who believed that they had received personal visions. The Carvoran one was set up by an officer, M. Caecilius Donatianus, who had been addressed by the goddess Virgo Caecilius ('the heavenly virgin'). He believed her to be either the same being as, or allied or related to, the Anatolian Great Mother (Cybele), Ceres, the goddess of Syria and (loyally) the current empress Julia Domna. Irritatingly, he did not record what she had said.[49]

Thus it may be seen that Romano-British religion provided lavishly for both the group and the individual. It included a literally limitless choice of deities, some of whom could be identified with others, according to personal taste. A variety of forms of temple and worship, and indeed of attitudes to the divine, complemented this tremendous range of potential protectors. It was a system well suited to an empire which had bound so many local cults and traditions within a powerful military and bureaucratic system. Whether the native peoples of north-western Europe had enjoyed an equal freedom of religious manoeuvre is unknown. The pre-Roman British and Irish Celts might have felt able to honour the tutelary goddesses and patron gods of other districts and tribes, and to identify them with one another, or they might not. But the imperial system appears to have fitted neatly over the plethora of British deities, without any sign of strain or conflict.

The range of choice of holy places was not, of course, limited to temples. In a later period the Christian monk Gildas could write sneeringly of the Romano-British that they 'heaped divine honours' on 'mountains, hills and rivers'.[50] The rivers (and pools) have been considered, and it seems likely that many wild places or natural features near settlements were regarded as sacred and served as settings for communal or personal rites. And as the history of the province wore on into the third and fourth centuries, another kind of holy place became popular in southern England. This was a temple or complex of buildings set in a lonely part of the countryside, often on a steep hill or beside springs, and intended as a destination for pilgrims. Some seem to have been dedicated to a principal deity but to have permitted or provided for the veneration of others. A few of these structures were based around temples founded in the earlier years of the province, but all were either developed or built for the first time in the second half of the imperial Roman age. Most of those known were constructed in the modern counties of Somerset, Wiltshire, Avon and Gloucestershire, around which they were spaced with apparent care. Seven sites lie around the circumference of a great battered ellipse, broken open to the south-west side by the Bristol channel. A brief descriptive tour of them, made (in a very un-Roman fashion) anti-clockwise, may indicate something of their nature. We start at Brean Down, a square fourth-century temple in the Romano-Celtic style, built on the crest of a peninsula jutting into the sea below the bay which now contains Weston-super-Mare. It was probably cut off on the landward side by marshes, so that access would have required a ferry journey as well as a steep climb. Beside the temple was a smaller building in which antlers were stored. They were clearly cult objects here as in the Neolithic and early Bronze Age, but their precise significance is as opaque as in those earlier periods. To the south-east is Brent Knoll, a tall isolated hill then begirt by water, where finds indicate the possible presence of another shrine. But the nearest certain site is due east at Pagan's Hill, on a promontory overlooking the river Chew where a Romano-British temple was constructed around AD 300. It was levelled too effectively to permit the excavators to find cult objects, but the latter occur thickly at the next place in the sequence, Lamyatt Beacon. This was a temple with aisles and alcoves, built at the end of the third century on a high ridge overlooking the Brue valley. It had a large cult statue of Mars, but also statuettes of Hercules, Mercury and Minerva, as well as the brooches and antlers already noted at Brean Down. Not so far away in Wiltshire was Cold Kitchen Hill, near Brixton Deverill. Excavations of the temple there have produced pots, coins, beads, antlers, model axes and spears, and brooches showing an armed horseman. The last two commodities indicate that Mars was probably, once more, the principal deity. Northwards in a valley near Nettleton Shrub, Wiltshire, was a

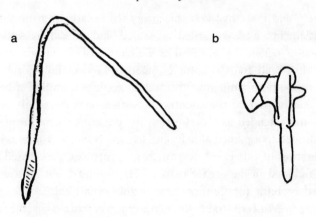

FIGURE 6.17   Votive objects, I
a Miniature bronze spear, dedicated – presumably by a soldier asking for success – at Woodeaton (Oxfordshire), and now in the Ashmolean Museum. It may have been bent deliberately, to 'kill' it and send it to the spirit world. *b* Miniature axe, found at Kirmingham (Humberside). Axes were potent religious symbols from the Neolithic if not before, and specimens or copies of them are found dedicated on all sorts of ritual monument from every period of ancient British paganism.

large third-century complex of buildings around some springs. They contained a statue of Diana, and dedications to Silvanus and to Mercury and Rosmerta, but the principal deity seems to have been Apollo 'the hound lord'. People made the journey there to be healed of ills, and one of the buildings was probably a dormitory for them. Westwards across the Cotswolds was the religious centre at Uley, mentioned above, which stood on the crest of the scarp overlooking the Vale of Berkeley. There a second-century temple was rebuilt and extended in the fourth century to provide the centre of pilgrimage in honour of Mercury at which suppliants left their requests upon votive tablets.[51] And across the Severn, in a remote part of the forest of Dean, was Lydney.

This site deserves an extended treatment, partly because of its fame and importance and partly because it illustrates some of the difficulties of interpretation attendant upon Romano-British archaeology. The Roman buildings there are set (like so many of these rural holy places) on the crest of a very steep ridge commanding a fine view, in this case of the Severn estuary. They seem to belong to the late third century and consist of a temple, a set of baths, a large rectangular structure and a long range running up to the baths. The purposes of both the last two edifices are unknown. The big rectangular building has been called a guest house, in which pilgrims could lodge, simply because we do not know what else it could have been. The long one has been described as intended for 'sacred sleep', being a place to which worshippers could retire for uninterrupted and solitary rest, in the course of which visions might be granted in dreams. This identification rests solely upon the fact that similar buildings exist beside temples in Asia Minor and Greece, and in fact the purpose of those structures is itself a matter of guesswork. It has been suggested that the baths may have been used for ritual purification as well as for refreshment after the journey thither. This is, again, no more than an intelligent supposition. The principal deity has been assumed to have been Mars Nodens, to whom two votive plaques were dedicated there. He was more than a local god, for his name appears also upon the bases of two statuettes found near Lancaster, but nothing more is known of him. Attempts by some scholars to identify him with the Irish god Nuadha are based upon nothing more than the similarity of the names. But was he the only deity, or even the main deity, of Lydney? Also discovered there were a bronze relief of a sea god, one of a sun god in a chariot, a statuette of a female figure with a horn of plenty, and a dedication to the Roman woodland god Silvanus. Any of these might have possessed more importance than Nodens, whom the chance survival of evidence may have inflated in our eyes. The temple interior was divided into cubicles or chapels, perhaps for private worship, perhaps for different deities or perhaps merely for insulation. A single find of a miniature votive arm has produced a general opinion that the complex was devoted to healing, although this may have been only an aspect of its services. Several

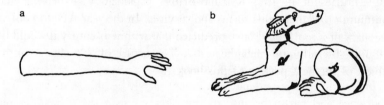

FIGURE 6.18   Votive objects, 2
a Votive bronze arm, found on the temple site at Lydney (Gloucestershire): left by a person who wanted their own arm to be healed. *b* The Lydney Hound, a bronze figurine found on the same site as the arm and now in the adjoining museum. Dogs featured very prominently in the cult at Lydney, but we can only guess at the part they played.

figurines of dogs, one a truly superb work of art, have inspired the notion that these animals were part of the cult of Nodens and were kept on the site. Another foreign parallel, with the temple of the physician god Aesculapius at Epidauros, has engendered the further suggestion that the animals licked the affected part of the sick to heal them, as at the Greek shrine. This may well be true, but they may equally have been Otherworld creatures, spiritual beings associated with the place, rather than flesh and blood. Among the few things that we can say with certainty about Lydney are that it was well endowed and much visited. Its handsome mosaic floors testify to its wealth, while the number of pins found there indicate the former presence of many dedicatory plaques once fixed to its walls. This only makes more poignant the fact that we can reconstruct with confidence so little of its active life.[52]

This west country tour will have indicated some of the forms taken by the isolated late imperial rural temples and shrines . Other examples of temples such as those at Brean Down, Pagan's Hill and Cold Kitchen Hill are found within the ramparts of pre-Roman hill forts such as Maiden Castle in Dorset and South Cadbury in Somerset. The great Iron Age ramparts must have been crumbled and overgrown when they were built, but the high lonely situation perfectly suited the fashion for these holy places. More examples of complex sites such as Lydney and Nettleton Shrub are Frilford in Oxfordshire (which included an amphitheatre and a cemetery), Springhead in Kent and Gosbecks Farm near Colchester. The great site at Chedworth in Gloucestershire, long presumed to be a villa, may be another such.[53]

Implicit in this account of the fashion for remote pilgrimage shrines is a theme which has run quietly through the whole chapter: that during the last centuries of its life, Romano-British paganism was thriving and continuing to elaborate its forms and services. In the year AD 300 only a visionary or a fool would have predicted that within a century it would be in ruins, literally and metaphorically. The nature of that change is the subject of the next portion of this book.

7

The Clash of Faiths (AD c.300–c.1000)

Those familiar with British pre-history, or who have followed the chapters of this book, will recognize that at various times in the millennia before the Christian era an old religion or set of religions may have been replaced. The process could in each case have been violent or peaceful. The evidence of the spade suggests that the centuries 3200–2500 BC and 1600–800 BC may represent such periods of transition, the latter having a particularly strong claim. But this is no more than conjecture: had the Romans not been a literate civilization then we would consider that their invasion probably brought new faiths to Britain rather than allowing new and old to flourish within a different sort of culture. But even the data yielded by archaeology would lead us to suppose that between AD 300 and AD 1200 the British Isles were taken over by a different religion which gradually removed all competitors. The crucial addition of literary sources enables us to learn its name, Christianity, and to chart in varying detail its progress and vicissitudes. They confirm that the greatest alteration in the religious history of Europe (whatever happened before history began) was the replacement of a very heterogeneous polytheism with a single faith acknowledging one deity and relatively uniform in its theology, architecture, organization and ritual. They also establish that the crucial century in the story of this change was the fourth, even if the process was not completed until the fourteenth (when Lithuania became the last part of the continent to convert). The history of the Christianization of the British Isles would fill (and has filled) a large book in itself. Here we are concerned with the interlocking phenomenon of the decline and disappearance of the other religions.

First, it is worthwhile to make some basic points about the contrasts between late Roman paganism and Christianity, and about the reason for the success of the latter. It owed its triumph to the fact that it was adopted by the rulers of the Roman Empire, by far the most powerful, admired and respected state in Europe. This remained true even after its western provinces had fallen to Germanic invaders during the fifth century, for those newcomers acquired the Christian faith along with most other aspects of a civilization which to them symbolized strength, self-confidence and prestige. After the fourth century, for a European ruler to remain pagan was to cut his or her territory off from the main network of states which contained the greatest centres of power, wealth and culture. It was this fact which turned the new religion into an irresistible force, and so the conversion of the Roman emperors was the crucial element in its progress. Indeed, it completely reversed its fortunes, because in the first decade of the fourth century it had suffered the most intense persecution it had ever known. Rulers anxious to bring greater unity and stability to an empire recovering from decades of invasion and civil war were more ready than ever before to identify Christians as subverters of the political and religious order. The history of Christianity in the fourth century is so remarkable that it could readily be called miraculous, consisting of a series of near-incredible strokes of luck – or acts of providence.

The first came in 312, at the end of the great persecution, when the young emperor Constantine won the battle of the Milvian Bridge and seized Rome. He had apparently seen the shape of a cross in the sky beforehand, and been told by Christians that it was a sign that he would conquer by means of that faith. There followed an amazingly fortunate victory, and Constantine was persuaded. He went on to defeat his remaining rivals in turn and to become ruler of the whole Empire, establishing the Christian Church as its most favoured religion and leaving three healthy sons to carry on the work. This work was not halted until 361, when the last of Constantine's family, Julian, turned out to be a pagan by conviction and set about restoring the old cults. But fortune acted again: within two years he was killed in an otherwise insignificant skirmish, when on campaign against the Persians. He left no son, nor even a respected pagan general capable of succeeding him. His army chose a Christian, and so the emperors remained, once more, until 391, when the western provinces were seized by a usurper, Eugenius. He had ruled only four years when the Christian emperor of the east, Theodosius the Great, joined battle with him by the river Frigidus. Eugenius erected two statues of gods to give power to his army, but was defeated and executed. After that the emperors were always Christian. The main charge against Christianity had been that by insulting the deities it would bring disaster to those who adopted it. Constantine proved that, on the contrary, its god consistently brought victory when pitted against others. And the pattern held thereafter, for providence seemed to ensure that it was the pagan emperors who brought catastrophe upon themselves.

How did the newly dominant religion differ from the pagan cults as a moral and social force? With respect to this question popular prejudice has undergone something of a shift during the last fifty years. In the first half of this century there was still a widespread notion that the tenets of the Gospels must have exercised some beneficial effect upon a cruel, tyrannical and debauched Empire. This view was fostered by novelists and by flim-makers rather than by scholars, who had long recognized that the early Christians were more interested in getting people into heaven than in improving this world, and accordingly took most of the features of the late Roman Empire which are repulsive to modern taste, such as slavery, torture and a harsh penal code, in their stride. As for political behaviour, the new religion had been adopted by emperors because it appeared to increase chances of success in ruthless and bloody competiion. Its god was a god of battle and of victory. Having said that, it did have certain attractions for private persons. It sidestepped the social hierarchy rather than attacking it, offering a sense of communal solidarity and individual moral worth in a world of increasingly rigid social boundaries. Unlike the pagan 'mystery religions' and confraternities, it admitted all ranks of society and both sexes. Whereas pagan philanthropists gave to the whole local community or to institutions, Christians provided charity to the poor. And the new faith offered an absolutely guaranteed, and attractive, afterlife.[1] This much can be said, then, in reply to the traditional view of Christianity's effect upon the Roman world. But in very recent years, as the Christian faith continues to lose its grip upon the popular imagination and the national culture, an opposite ideology has been articulated. It belongs to that radical section of contemporary thought which produced 'alternative archaeology' and sustains belief in the golden age of the Neolithic Mother Goddess, and rests upon the same instincts as those visions: that the ancient world embodied many of the ideals of these modern writers and that a series of evil occurrences drew Western civilization away from them. The case is, again, thoroughly unacademic and embodied in works of fiction, tracts and radical periodicals rather than scholarly books. But its main tenets are clear: that the emergence of Christianity as the dominant faith produced a deterioration in the position of women in society, a loss of respect for the natural environment, the destruction of many beautiful buildings and works of art and literature, a much more repressive attitude to human sexuality and a general narrowing and policing of intellectual horizons. This series of proposals is worth addressing if we are to gain some sense of the qualitative change produced by the Christian conversion, and they will be tackled in the order stated above.

Was the early Christian Church anti-feminist? At first sight, the answer seems resoundingly positive, for unlike the pagan cults it had no female deity and no priestesses. Yet this stark contrast is in need of some further consideration. The Church soon sprouted a plethora of women saints, led by Mary the Queen of Heaven herself, to provide divine female patrons for those who wanted them. Communities of nuns offered women a place within the ecclesiastical structure. And the contrast is further lessened by the fact that women were decidedly underprivileged in the format of Roman paganism. There seem to have been far fewer priestesses than priests, and like the Christian nuns the pagan holy women were usually expected to be chaste. It does not seem that a Roman priestess ever wielded such influence over emperors as certain nuns did over some sixteenth- and seventeenth-century Spanish monarchs. But all this is beside the major point, that Christianity appears to have been the cult in the pagan Roman Empire which most notably attracted the enthusiastic support of women. At least half of the total number of martyrs made during the episodes of persecution by pagans were female, and a clear majority of the most celebrated were girls. There are no surviving membership lists for the early Christian communities, but a single remarkable statistic was provided when the local police seized a Christian church at Cirta, North Africa, in 303. The congregation had left some of their clothing there, and the haul consisted of sixteen male tunics and eighty-two female tunics. Pagan critics regularly mocked Christianity as an 'irrational' religion to which female minds were particularly susceptible. Among the fourth-century aristocracy of the city of Rome itself, it was quite common to find Christian wives of pagan husbands. To comprehend, in part, the attraction it is necessary to remember how much Roman society placed women in general, and unmarried or widowed women in particular, at a disadvantage. The Christians, by contrast, stressed the equality of congregations before Christ and encouraged single women to remain unattached, not because it kept them independent but because it preserved their chastity.[2]

Much modern popular feminist writing, though, has tended to eulogize not the pagan Romans (who are quite correctly regarded as patriarchal) but the pagan Celts. This has been possible largely because we know so much less about the latter that, in this context as in many others, they are easily subsumed into fantasy. Indeed, since it is now believed that all early Celtic literature was not only written down but composed centuries after the coming of Christianity, we strictly speaking know nothing about the gender roles of the pagan Celts. But both the fiction and the law codes of early medieval Ireland are so unlike those of other Christian lands that they must reflect native traditions about social roles even if they tell us little about the context of pagan religion. The laws permitted either partner to initiate divorce proceedings, as at Rome, and, like the Roman codes, allowed married women control of their own property.[3] The tales have several very strong female characters, including queens, prophetesses, enchantresses and warrior women. Romano-British history furnishes us with two genuinely powerful female rulers, Boudicca and Cartimandua. But all this information must be kept in perspective. The law codes show that women were still very definitely regarded as the second sex. Husbands were allowed concubines, but wives were expected to have only one man. As for the literature, the Greek myths remind us that a society which was very clearly dominated by men could compose and enjoy tales which included female personalities in strong roles. The warrior women in the Irish stories, like the Amazons of whom the Greeks wrote, do not usually appear in the society in which the other characters move, but in a hazily located land across the sea. On the whole, the female characters of the Irish myths and legends employ the same weapons – seduction and sorcery – as those of the medieval romances, and are as strongly disliked by the narrators for doing so. The world of those stories is very clearly one in which men predominate, although women at times disrupt their affairs. The greatest of all the epics, the *Tain Bo Cuailnge*, is sprinkled with misogynist comments and its most powerful female character, the magnificent Queen Medb, is not the heroine but the scheming villainess, pitted against a male hero. As suggested in an earlier chapter, the pagan Irish do not seem to have had priestesses or a system of royal succession which allowed queens to inherit. Nor is there any hint in the literature that the position of women in society had undergone any alteration during the period of the conversion to Christianity. In Britain Cartimandua and Boudicca commanded by virtue of their place in a royal family, rather than by any special privilege granted to women. Boudicca's husband, the King of the Iceni, faced death leaving no son and two daughters; fearing that the latter would not be strong enough to hold the realm, he made the Roman emperor joint heir in order to win his protection. Instead, the Romans seized the tribal territory and its people rallied to Boudicca, who was both willing and able to lead a ferocious counter-attack. It was her husband's death and an emergency which had flung her into prominence. In Ireland the Cáir Adomnain (Adomnán's Law) has sometimes been taken as a Christian measure to limit the public role of women. Made in 697, it forbade women to attend armies upon campaign, and this is occasionally interpreted as signifying the end of the Celtic tradition of female warriors. But the existence of that tradition has already been questioned, and the directive concerned did not state that women fought: it could equally (and more probably) have been referring to camp followers. Certainly the intention of the churchmen concerned, as was made plain by the later history of the law, was to render warfare at once less attractive, by depriving male fighters of female companions, and less dreadful, by subtracting women from the victims and booty of battle. In the same spirit the prohibition was extended in 803 to include clerics, who might have inspired and comforted armies. Its object was not patriarchy, but peace. Thus it cannot be supposed that the conversion of the non-Romanized Celts was a blow to women. In fact the seventh-century Irish *Life of Brighid* makes the point that the Christian faith could enable them to escape the tyranny of husbands and fathers. The position of women certainly deteriorated during the Middle Ages, but this change in society is too late to be attributed to the conversion.

Did the early Christian Church encourage a more destructive attitude to the natural environment? Again, the evidence at first sight seems to support the proposition. Pagans all over Europe venerated certain groves of trees as sacred. The Romans believed that all natural things were associated with spirits which had to be respected, while the Irish Celts believed that every district was under the protection of a goddess, whose custody of the land had to be honoured. Christians, on the other hand, taught that the whole natural world had been given into the dominion of humans, and cut down the old sacred groves. But such a contrast will not stand up to further analysis. The followers of Christ may have felled the groves, but they sanctified many springs in the name of their own faith and they stopped the slaughter of huge numbers of animals in the course of rituals. More important, the peoples of Europe and the Mediterranean lands have shown the same disposition to destroy or manipulate the natural world since the Stone Age. Comments upon the damage done in the British Mesolithic, Neolithic and Bronze Age have been made in previous chapters; the Iron Age Celts in what became England may have had their holy stands of trees, but this did not stop them from clearing virtually all the large areas of forest spared by their predecessors, especially in the midlands.[4] Under the pagan Roman Empire, the remaining woods were stripped from much of the North African coast, producing an ecological catastrophe when most of the ploughed-up soil was washed into the Mediterranean. It seems to have been in the same period that the lion was exterminated in Europe, the elephant and the hippopotamus in North Africa and the bear in England. Christianity was absolutely irrelevant to this process.

Did the Church destroy beautiful works of architecture, art and literature? Here the indictment is much more easily sustained, though qualifications still have to be made. It is beyond doubt that the triumphant Christians immolated an enormous quantity of sculpture, painting, mosaic and metalwork which portrayed pagan deities. The loss of this material must be accounted a disaster to the human race. Historians (and modern pagans) must regret the parallel destruction of manuscripts containing pagan liturgies, hymns and prayers, although it is not certain that these would have been very numerous, as most cults were defined by ceremonies, not texts. But the Church did preserve the great majority of the celebrated works of pagan literature. In Ireland its members created a literate culture which drew on pre-Christian traditions. The Christian Empire did try to save the temples, especially in towns, and from 399 a series of laws enjoined their preservation and conversion to other uses. In practice local zealots often ignored this legislation but there are also many cases of obedience to it. It should be added, too, that there is not one single recorded case, throughout Europe, of the early or medieval Church demolishing a prehistoric megalithic monument, though this is probably an indication of the extent to which these structures had ceased to represent the foci of living faiths. Enough local superstition still clung to them to warrant the Christianization of a few of them with the erection of carved crosses or the building of churches nearby, but the contrast with the Church's hostility to holy places still in use by pagans is striking. And to hold the Christians entirely responsible for our loss of the works of art which they did destroy is ahistorical. So little remains of the Christian churches, sculptures, metalwork, paintings, mosaics and literature of late antiquity and the early Middle Ages that it is all too clear that time would have spared only a fraction of those works which Christian followers removed.

Did the early Church have a repressive attitude towards human sexuality? Here the answer is resoundingly affirmative, but the context is important. It needs to be stressed that late pagan antiquity was slightly less tolerant in these matters than most societies in modern Europe and America. Inhabitants of the Roman Empire had a multiplicity of attitudes to this issue, as to most others, but the combination of law codes, official letters and literature suggests powerfully that there were certain common assumptions. Heterosexual intercourse was regarded as a good thing, but only inside marriage. Prostitution flourished on an enormous scale, as in Victorian England, as a safety valve – for men – against the deficiencies of that institution. Opinion was divided over the question of whether the active partner in a homosexual act should be condemned, but united to revile the passive partners and any lesbians: in sexual matters of any kind the admired individual was the man on top. Priestesses, as already noted, were expected to be chaste. Anybody wishing to participate in a religious ceremony or to consult an oracle was expected to abstain from sexual intercourse for a short period of days beforehand as part of the process of purification. There were a few temples in the Greek parts of the Empire which kept prostitutes, but no recorded religious rite within the Imperial domains involved sex. When the government condemned the mystery religion of Dionysus at Rome for being 'orgiastic' (in English translation) they produced no firm evidence to prove the charge. All that seems certain about these devotees is that they started hostile rumours because they became hysterical, drunken or flamboyantly noisy at their ceremonies. The fact that certain emperors were accused of a range of sexual vices demonstrates not that they committed them but that hostile writers could presume upon a general public disgust with these practices and use them in vilification. The Germanic invaders of the Empire proved to be even less tolerant, and in their first law codes they prescribed savage penalties for adultery and homosexuality.[5]

But what of the Celts? Here again, our relative lack of knowledge has allowed the modern imagination, especially in fictional work such as that of Marion Zimmer Bradley, to flourish. It must be stressed, again, that the Irish law codes and literature show a society in which marriage was as admired an institution as in the Roman Empire. Here, however, the safety valve was not prostitution but the right of husbands to take concubines. There is certainly no evidence to connect Celtic rituals with sexuality. Nobody suggests that the king's sacred marriage with the tutelary goddess involved an act of intercourse with a human woman, though Gerald of Wales (as already mentioned) came up with the story, unlikely in its context, that bestiality was incorporated. When Sir James Frazer ransacked the folklore collections of Europe for traces of fertility rites, the most erotic he could find were Ukrainian and German customs whereby young married couples rolled over the fields to quicken them. He assumed that in pre-Christian times they had made love literally and not symbolically, but this is unprovable. Across the whole ancient world there were cults which celebrated human fertility, but they did not do so by sexual behaviour. The great goddesses Cybele, Diana of Ephesus, Isis and Vesta were servied by celibate priests or priestesses, offering up their sexuality to increase the power of their deity. At the festival of the Liberalia in March, a giant phallus was pulled around the central Italian countryside in a cart and then crowned with a wreath. But the individual who crowned it had to be the most virtuous married woman of the community.[6] A horrifying example of what, it seems, could happen to people who flouted the sexual conventions of a prehistoric British community has been uncovered at Garton Slack in Yorkshire. There, in the Iron Age, a woman aged about thirty and a man about ten years younger were taken down into a deep pit. They were pinned to the ground side by side with stakes driven through their arms, and buried alive. The woman had been pregnant.[7] And yet, even by the standards of Celtic, Germanic or Roman morals, the early Christians were dramatically puritanical. Alone of all the known religions of ancient Europe, they condemned sex altogether and taught that virginity was the only truly virtuous state. Filled with a sense of the approaching end of the world, they saw only evil in intercourse under any circumstances.[8] Even after centuries had passed and the church was prepared to concede some dignity to the institution of marriage, it still preached that celibacy was more godly.

Finally, did the Church enforce a narrowing of intellectual horizons? The answer, from a subjective modern standpoint, must be that it did, because of its insistence that there was only one religious doctrine as well as only one deity. The vigorous and wide-ranging speculative debate of pagan antiquity came to an end, and the best minds of the Empire were turned instead to defining the details of Christian belief. The result, inevitably, was that the victory of the Church was followed at once by schism as the churchmen disagreed, and Christians expended as much energy in struggling with each other as in combating paganism. And as paganism faded, heretical Christian movements continued to emerge. Moreover, the insistence upon a single omnipotent god made belief in the power of magic a heresy in itself, since all events depended upon the will of the deity and not upon those of humans or spirits. The pagan Romans, like most ancient peoples and modern tribal societies, prescribed the death penalty for those who killed or who harmed property by witchcraft: in a system which believes in magic and has capital punishment for normal murder or arson, there is no other logical situation. It was pagan writers like Lucan who produced the enduring European literary stereotype of the destructive witch as an ugly old woman. But the first Christian emperors went much further, to decree the execution of all who worked magic, even to those who merely wore amulets.[9] The pagan Roman world could not condemn heresy, nor produce witch-hunts: Christian Europe did both, on a huge scale.

Yet, again, qualifications and additions have to be made to these statements. The pagan Roman Empire, as mentioned earlier, executed hundreds of Christians for refusing to endorse the validity of its system of religion. There is no doubt from the sources that it did so in appalling ways, including burning alive, drowning and throwing them to hungry beasts; young girls were sent to brothels. All this was judicial atrocity, and in addition pagan mobs murdered some of the followers of Christ without any official sanction.[10] By contrast, once in power the Christians tended to attack deities but spare humans: they destroyed images and wrecked holy places while leaving the worshippers alone. There is no recorded case of an execution of a person for following the older religions in the first two centuries of the Christian Roman Empire. Nor is there a certain one of the death of any at the hands of a Christian mob. The philosopher Hypatia, torn apart by a crowd at Alexandria in 415, is the best apparent example, but it is not clear that she suffered for her religion or that her murderers were all Christians.[11] Nor were heretics put to death, for the victorious sections of the early Church were only concerned to deprive them of places of worship, not of life. The exception was Priscillian, beheaded in late fourth-century Spain, and he died at the hands of an insecure and short-lived regime whose actions were condemned by its successors. After him there were no more executions for unorthodox Christian doctrines in western Europe until the eleventh century, when the great medieval burnings began. Furthermore, the ferocious new laws against magic were in practice a means for rulers to control rather than to annihilate astrology, necromancy and other occult disciplines. Constantius, the emperor who decreed them, was celebrated for his own obsession with portents and spells. The prosecution of magic under the Christian Empire and the monarchies which succeeded it remained very much what it had been in pagan times. In both eras it was a means of getting rid of political rivals, while at a popular level the occasional individual seems to have been executed or murdered for alleged destructive witchcraft. The concept of a satanic conspiracy to destroy Christendom, resulting in scores of thousands of executions, did not appear until the fifteenth century. Indeed, in those parts of western Europe which were the home of, or taken over by, Germanic tribes, it seems that the Church ended a tradition of hunting and killing witches. The earliest law codes issued by the northern invaders of the Roman Empire specify penalties for women who were believed to go abroad at night and destroy men by magic. Then these clauses are revoked, often explicitly at the insistence of churchmen. The Lombard code of 643 may serve as an example: 'Let nobody presume to kill a foreign serving maid or female slave as a witch, for it is not possible, nor ought to be believed by Christian minds.' In 789 Charlemagne imposed Christianity upon the people of Saxony, and proclaimed to them: 'If anyone, deceived by the Devil, shall believe, as is customery among pagans, that any man or woman is a night-witch, and eats men, and on that account burn that person to death . . . he shall be executed.'[12] Thus it might be argued that the spread of Christianity initially resulted in an improvement in the treatment of both religious dissenters and alleged witches. Certainly the early Church cannot be held responsible for the mass burnings of heretics which commenced seven centuries after its installation in power, or the great witch hunt which began eleven centuries later. During that long interval, Christendom itself changed.

It is time now to trace the story of the end of Celtic and Romano-British paganism in the British Isles, in so far as it can be traced at all. The legal background to it is complex, as the following sequence of dates will indicate. From 312 to 331 all religions were tolerated, though Christianity alone received official favour. In 331 the lands and treasuries of temples began to be confiscated and in 337 pagan sacrifices were banned. A few pagan holy centres were closed down before 357, when a universal closure was ordered. But in 361 paganism was restored by Julian, and although the emperors were Christian again from 363 they introduced a general toleration of faiths. There was some official discrimination against paganism, and some seizure of temple property, but in 391–4 the western half of the Empire was once again under the control of pagans. It was only in 394, when Theodosius took it over, that a complete closure of temples and abolition of sacrifices was decreed, and in the next decade Britain slipped out of Imperial control. Thus the prohibition of pagan worship was a slow and fitful process which only became complete at the very end of the province's history. Furthermore, it is an important question, and one difficult to answer, whether the imperial decrees against the old religions were generally enforced.

Evidence from elsewhere in the Roman world suggests that the time and the rigour of their enactment varied greatly between districts. Early fifth-century Athens, a principal city of Roman Greece and a short sail from the imperial seat at Constantinople, was full of distinguished citizens who were openly pagan. The great statue of Athene stood in the Parthenon until 487. In the sixth century the emperors based at Constantinople still had to purge pagans from their own court and administration, and a scatter of tombs in the eastern provinces still carried traditional invocations. The impression is that all over the Roman world between the mid-fourth and mid-sixth centuries, paganism was in peaceful, gradual and erratic decline. There were few dramatic incidents in the process, and it comes to an end imperceptibly in the sixth century when the last of the old religions apparently disappear. The fundamental reason why this extinction was so quiet and so protracted was that Roman paganism was not a fighting faith. It had no ideology of conversion or resistance and no tradition of martyrdom, and was bound up with concepts of civic authority, public ceremonial, service to the state and communal pride which the Christians could easily hijack. And such an immense range of cults could not easily make any common cause against attack, so they were picked off piecemeal or simply collapsed one by one for lack of funds. When Julian tried to rebuild paganism as a religion capable of meeting the Christian challenge, he could do so only by imitating the concepts and the structure of the Church. His early death prevents any assessment of how far his dream was practicable. Certainly he wrote bitter complaints about the apathy he encountered in the pursuit of it. This does not mean that paganism 'died naturally' in the Roman world: rather, it was not able to resist Christian pressure when the emperors were themselves Christian and prepared to outlaw the older cults.[13]

There are absolutely no literary sources which deal directly with the end of Romano-British paganism, and the archaeological evidence is beset with difficulties. One hinges upon the fact that the province's monuments are dated by coins bearing the heads of emperors and found in the successive levels of occupation. The regimes which succeeded Roman rule after the 400s did not mint any, and so chronology suddenly falls back once again upon Carbon 14 or upon the artefacts in various levels of a site. Whereas coins can date a site to a decade or even a year, in their absence we can get no closer than the century. Another problem is that the foundations of Christian churches and of pagan temples can look very similar, and that the followers of the old religions and the new could be buried in an identical fashion. Yet another is that in late fourth-century

Britain, beset by attacks from beyond the frontiers and by economic decline, both public and private buildings of all kinds fell into decay. With baths, villas and town halls crumbling for lack of funds, it is not surprising that temples did likewise, whatever changes in religion were occurring.

All these difficulties must be borne in mind while considering the following evidence from the west country, the area with the best supply of material. Up until the middle of the fourth century most of the temples here continued to flourish, and so did all manner of pagan burial practices. There are few exceptions, such as Nettleton Shrub where the religious complex was replaced with a cross-shaped building, probably a church. Then, in the 360s, Britain was overwhelmed by invasions and had to be reconquered by an Imperial army. The rural temples at Brean Down and Lamyatt Beacon apparently went out of business, but so did the probable church at Nettleton Shrub, being replaced by a farm with a pagan shrine attached. Destruction and decay in the region's towns are suggested by two inscriptions. One is at Cirencester, where the local Roman governor in the late fourth century restored the column carrying a statue of Jupiter. The other is at Bath, where an altar was raised by a centurion who rebuilt 'a holy place wrecked by insolent hands'. But the dating of both is very imprecise, the damage mentioned at Bath may have been inflicted by either plunderers or Christians, and the 'holy place' may not have been at Bath itself. The rural cult centres at Uley and Lydney survived the 360s intact and Pagan's Hill, though damaged, remained in use. At the end of that decade a new temple was built within the decayed ramparts of the huge Iron Age hill fort of Maiden Castle in Dorset. The discovery here of the base of a cult statue of Diana, a plaque dedicated to Minerva and votive objects suggests that it was another centre for pilgrimage at which more than one deity was honoured, along the lines of Lamyatt Beacon, Nettleton and Lydney. At Uley pagan worship certainly lasted until the 380s, when the buildings were demolished, the big statue of Mercury broken and the votive objects thrown out. A new, smaller building was erected on the site and by the fifth century this had been expanded and contained stone altars. The lack of any votive material strongly suggests that it was a Christian church. In the late fourth century small structures were built upon the ruins of the temples at Brean Down, Pagan's Hill and Lamyatt Beacon, and replaced the little shrine at South Cadbury. Again, they yielded no trace of pagan worship and were either Christian holy places or farms. Before 400 evidence of paganism in the homestead at Nettleton gives out and a cemetery was dug there which seems to have been Christian. It is quite impossible to say at present when use of the big temple at Bath ceased, although again it appears to have been by the end of the fourth century. But Lydney, and the relatively new centre at Maiden Castle, remained in business until the very end of Roman rule, and the cults there were only abandoned at some time in the fifth century.[14]

In no other region is it yet possible to compare the fate of a group of religious sites as readily as in the west country. But the overall pattern is reproduced elsewhere in the province: the old religions hold up well until the mid-fourth century, go into decline after 360 and vanish somewhere in the mysterious period when imperial rule was replaced by a group of petty kingdoms. The west does seem to have been a little unusual in the relatively high number of temples which may have been reconstructed as Christian churches or monasteries. Generally, and especially in the towns, the shrines of the new religion were built away from those of the old. This was the rule throughout the Empire, the Christians usually believing that the temples were haunted by demons which had been worshipped there. As in the west country, most of the temples fell into decay rather than suffering destruction. Having said that, there are a number of cases where pagan buildings and religious objects came to a violent end. Uley, noted above, was one: another was at the fort beside modern Caernarfon, where the shrine of Mithras was burned out and then razed. A well at Southwark contained several broken statues of gods and Genii, with charred building debris. At Lower Slaughter in Gloucestershire, three altars, three headless statues, three stone votives, some reliefs and some stone rubble were dumped in the well of a farm. Many damaged bronze figures have been found in the Thames at London Bridge. They were accompanied by the head of a giant bronze statue of the deified emperor Hadrian, which had been hacked from its shoulders. Limbs torn from other statues have been dug out of the wells of Roman London. It is as if the people who disposed of these images so detested them that after desecration they had to be buried or drowned rather than melted down, so that their metal could not be reused.[15] But we cannot recover the circumstances, or fix the dates, of these acts of destruction.

Nor can we do the same for the sole apparent case of the opposite phenomenon, of Christian objects converted for the use of pagans. This consists of the thirty-two spoons found near Thetford in 1979 engraved with the name of the god Faunus, each time followed by a different epithet. They also bear Christian symbols and have the form of the spoons commonly used in the fourth century for Christian baptism. Whether they were used by apostates, or by pagans who had bought up a stock of baptismal spoons from a silversmith, we cannot say.[16] Certainly there are many proven cases in the fourth-century Empire of individuals who honoured Christ and his divine father together with other deities. One of them cast his votive tablet into the sacred spring of Sulis Bath, cheerfully identifying himself as a Christian while he made his prayer.[17] Such eclecticism renders still more difficult the problem mentioned above, of identifying the adherents of the old and new faiths from their burials. Most early Christians were buried without gravegoods and laid out with heads to the west and feet to the east. But then so were many pagans, and although it remains to be shown that Christ's followers used any other orientation for bodies, they certainly deposited goods at times. Some of the richest treasures to survive from the early medieval kingdom of the Franks were placed in royal tombs in the great churches of Cologne and St Denis. A woman at York was buried with her ornaments and jars and a bronze plaque carrying the characteristic Christian message 'Hail sister, may you live in God'.[18]

The final end of public pagan worship in the former province is utterly impossible to date or to locate, but the only two contemporary sources for the history of sub-Roman Britain suggest that it occurred in the course of the fifth century. One is the *Life of St Germanus*, written somewhere between 480 and 494, which describes a visit by a Gallic bishop to the island in 429. A large part of his mission was to preach and to convert, and the text makes it absolutely plain that his efforts were directed not at paganism but at heresy. He was fighting the Christian doctrine of Pelagianism, winning back those who had been convinced by it and preventing any further defections from orthodoxy. He was also concerned to encourage the Romanized British in their resistance to barbarian attacks from modern Scotland and Germany. Nowhere is it suggested that he attached any importance to quelling the old religions. Yet it is also noteworthy that when wishing to say mass upon military campaign, he had to construct a makeshift building because of the lack of churches in the countryside. The very faint impression given by the *Life* of a Christian faith strong in the towns but weak outside them, confident of eventual victory over paganism without having mopped it all up in rural areas, is amply borne out by the early fifth-century sources in Italy and Gaul.[19] The other sub-Roman British text to survive is *The Ruin of Britain* by Gildas, which was written either at the end of the fifth century or (much more probably) in the early or middle part of the sixth. His principal task was to castigate the British rulers, and the society, of his time for a range of sins. It is striking that he did not include paganism among them. He speaks sneeringly of its former hold upon the British, and describes the crumbling statues of gods and goddesses still visible among the remains of deserted Roman towns.[20] But his strictures in this regard are always applied to the past, and the text gives an inescapable impression of being composed at a time when Christianity was wholly triumphant among the inhabitants of the former Roman province. The last traces of the older cults, already badly damaged by the end of Imperial rule, expired certainly within the next century and a half, and probably a much shorter period than that. They were destroyed not by the decrees of emperors, but within the almost totally obscure little Celtic states which formed in the void left by the withdrawal of the legions.

In the same period Christianity leaped the former frontier, to claim the Celts who had never been brought under Roman rule. This process is the more remarkable in that it was not propelled by the power of Imperial Rome, nor by any desire of the peoples concerned for closer links with a 'civilized' world which at that moment was in decline. It succeeded apparently because of the sheer power of the message being preached, to which the existing religions had no effective answer. But we know almost nothing about what actually occurred. The only surviving sources from the period of the conversion are two works of St Patrick, the *Confession* and *Letter to Coroticus*, which cast only a very oblique light upon the missionary effort. Otherwise, we have some annals and lives of saints composed by churchmen one or two centuries later. They tell us little or nothing about the establishment of the new faith, being principally intended to entertain readers while schooling them in Christian living, and to account for the origins of particular cults and institutions within the Church. Very often their writers seem to have had no real facts at their disposal.[21] As a result only the following can be said about the end of Irish paganism. According to the Chronicle of Prosper of Aquitaine, there were already some Christians in Ireland in 431, though they may have been British traders or slaves rather than natives. The writings of Patrick, produced at some time in the second half of that century, show that although the missionary effort was by then making headway, it still had a formidable task. They also portray it as inspired by clergy, like himself, from sub-Roman Britain. Patrick spoke of suffering from threats, but encountering no actual violence and making 'countless numbers' of converts and gaining grants of land for churches from many kings. During the sixth century, Irish paganism seems to have collapsed. The last king to celebrate a *feis*, the symbolic marriage to a tutelary goddess, was Diarmait Mac Cerbaill at Tara in 560. Diarmait himself had such a bad reputation in Irish Christian legend, as an enemy of saints and patron of Druids, that it seems very likely that he still adhered to the old beliefs. On the other hand, his memory was revered by the very important monastery of Clonmacnoise, so that he could not have been hostile to Christianity in general and perhaps changed his own religion during his reign. Two of his sons bore unmistakably Christian names. His death in 565 removed the last figure in Irish history (or semi-history) who might have professed the pagan Celtic religions.

From this tiny quantity of information, it can be suggested that the conversion of Ireland was a notably peaceful affair. Christian Irish tradition never claimed that a single saint was put to death in the course of the missionary effort, in notable contrast both to the number of martyrs made in northern Europe and to the number of Irish kings who were killed during power struggles during the sixth and seventh centuries. The early medieval Irish law codes and penitentials prescribed no savage penalties for paganism. The former degraded Druids socially to the status of freemen, and later ordered penance for taking an oath before a heathen priest. Church canons which seem to be of the sixth century portray an Irish Christian community existing peacefully if priggishly alongside the unconverted. Such a transitional period is also suggested by the tale *Betha Beraigh*, in which a king decided to give land neither to his own chief Druid nor to St Berach, for fear that one would curse him if he gratified the other. Certainly, the great weakness of Irish paganism was that its central figure was the sacred king of each district. Once he converted, it automatically fell to pieces within his realm. And clearly the lure of the Christian message proved irresistible to one after another.[22].

In Britain north of the former province, the old faiths survived longer. There is no evidence of a missionary effort from the Romanized area into the Highlands, athough archaeology has testified to the development of a Christian culture among the tribes just north of the frontier who had been in direct contact with the Romans. It is found in Galloway during the fifth century and along both sides of the Forth by the sixth. Its progress was slow and again low-key, leaving no memory of heroic saints or of confrontations. Further north, Christianization began only towards the end of the sixth century, propelled by an energetic set of missionaries from Ireland who used the bridgehead provided by an Irish kingdom in Argyll. By the time of Columba's death in 597, Christianity was established in parts of the western Highlands and Isles, and during the next hundred years it spread over most of the remainder of Scotland. It encountered a rougher reception here than in Ireland: Donnán of Eigg founded several churches in the Hebrides, but was slaughtered on the island from which he took his name, along with an entire monastic community, in 617. The conversion of this area, and of the far north, seems to have been effected only at the end of the seventh century. The tribes of Ross, Sutherland and the neighbouring islands appear to have been the last people in the British Isles to adhere to the old religions.[23]

One of the most striking features of the sub-Roman period is that even while Christianity was gaining ground in the north and west of the archipelago, it was losing its first foothold. This was because, during the fifth and sixth centuries, more and more of the former province was conquered by pagan Germanic tribes, Angles, Saxons and Jutes, crossing the North Sea. As the British churches resolutely refused to have anything to do with these barbarians, every district occupied by them was effectively removed from allegiance to Christ and a new set of other beliefs imposed instead. By the last decade of the sixth century, the area given over to this imported paganism consisted of virtually everywhere east of the Pennines, the Severn, and Someset: about two thirds of modern England. This religion, or these religions, must now be admitted to consideration along with the prehistoric faiths of the British Isles. The task is no easier than that of reconstructing the beliefs of the pre-Roman Celts, and considerably less easy than a consideration of Romano-British cults. The early English peoples were illiterate until their conversion to Christianity, and the literature which they left in the first centuries after that event is far smaller in quantity than that of the Irish in the same period. Their archaeological remains are no more scrutable to us than those of any other pre-literate culture of these islands. The names and attributes of their deities are very similar to those of other German and Scandinavian tribes, some of whom play a role in an extensive collection of tales surviving from the High Middle Ages, especially in Iceland. But virtually all of these are the works of sophisticated and creative authors living after the coming of the Christian faith to their peoples. They can be used only with great caution to reconstruct the original beliefs of the society in which they were written, let alone, by analogy, those of the Anglo-Saxons.

One refreshing aspect of the task is that at least the early English have been much less susceptible to the sort of modern fantasies imposed upon the pre-Christian Celts and the megalith builders. This is partly because of the starker and more gloomy attitude towards nature and the supernatural embodied in Anglo-Saxon literature, the work of a warrior society entering a hostile land filled with crumbling towns and villas. The authors of poems such as *The Ruin* and *The Wanderer* were people who had been through a very different sort of experience from those who composed the Celtic tales. Furthermore, the Anglo-Saxon works are much more overtly Christian. The net result of all this, plus the paucity of evidence, is that Anglo-Saxon paganism has attracted relatively little interest from either academic or amateur, from either orthodox or 'alternative' scholars. Among modern pagans it has none of the frisson of mystery and excitement attached to the word 'Celtic'.

So let us take a look at all that can be known about Anglo-Saxon paganism. The pioneering studies of Brian Branston have been greatly improved on in the last decade by Gale Owen, and recent years have seen a lot of work upon burial customs. Here the same sequence of topics will be followed as was employed when dealing with the pre-Roman, and the Romanized, Celts. First, what deities did the early English recognize? Both place names and genealogies indicate that the most important was the god Woden. The former commemorate him in Kent, Essex, Hampshire, Wiltshire, Somerset, Staffordshire, Bedfordshire and Derbyshire. Sometimes they occur in clusters, indicating local centres of especial enthusiasm for his worship: the most important is around Wiltshire's Vale of Pewsey. As for genealogy, six of the eight Anglo-Saxon royal houses trace their descent from him, and as that of the South Saxons is missing, only one (of the East Saxons) definitely does not. The fourth day of the English week was named after him. A tenth-century homily establishes him as the dominant character among the deities, a cunning deceiver venerated by humans upon hills and at crossroads. The *Nine Herbs Charm* calls him an enchanter. This personality makes him the exact equivalent of the German Wotan and the Norse Odin. But a similar character must have been shared by many of the Celtic gods of Gaul, or they would not have been identified so readily with Mercury, the travelling trickster worshipped by the Romans. And Woden is also the exact equivalent of the Celtic Lugh. The homily mentioned above makes a comparison between Mercury and Woden, and the Roman god presided over the same weekday. After this paramount deity, the most popular was Thunor. Although a smaller number of places are named after him, they are found in Essex, Sussex, Wiltshire, Somerset, Hampshire, Kent, Surrey and Hertfordshire and are more common in the first five counties than those associated with any other divine being. His character as a god of the sky and thunder is suggested by his identification with Roman Jupiter, a comparison made by the same homily, and reflected in the fact that in

FIGURE 7.1   Horned god or warrior in horned helmet?
The makers of this gilded buckle, from a cemetery at Finglesham (Kent), left no
decisive evidence. Now in the Institute of Archaeology, Oxford.

Anglo-Saxon and Roman calendars they preside over the fifth day of the
week. In this and in their personality they fulfil much the same functions
as the Scandinavian Thor, the German Donner ('Thunder') and the
Rhenish Celtic god Taranis ('the Thunderer'). The hammer and the
swastika both seem to be Thunor's symbols, and to denote thunderbolts.
Miniatures of the former have been found in seventh-century English
graves at Gilston and Kingston in Kent, while the latter sign is very
common on cremation urns. It must be noted that the graves concerned

were female, indicating that Thunor had a protective role for people in general.

After these two great figures comes a string of others. There was Tiw, who was almost certainly a war god. This is suggested by his patronage of the third day of the English week, given by the Romans to Mars, and by the appearance of his rune upon weapons dug up in Kent, specifically swords from Faversham and Gilston and spears from Holborough. His name occurs only four times in those of places, but these are widely scattered, in Surrey, Hampshire, Worcestershire and Warwickshire. Friday takes its name from Frigg or Friga, who, because she was associated with the day given by Romans to Venus, ought to have been a goddess of love or festivity. No place names can definitely be linked with her, although three in Hampshire and two in Yorkshire are possibly derivations.

These figures conclude the lists of deities associated with weekdays and places, but other sources supply the names of a few more. A poem, *The Dream of the Rood*, and a seventh-century hymn by Caedmon, both compare Christ to the god Frey. In the *Dream*, he is 'the Frey of mankind'. In the Norse literature Frey was a handsome young deity, and

FIGURE 7.2 Cinerary urn
This urn, from Sancton (Yorkshire) bears two runes linked with gods: on the right-hand side is the T for the war deity Tiw, and there are three specimens of the swastika, often associated with lightning and so with the storm god Thunor.

it may be that his good looks and pleasant reputation made him a flattering parallel for the Christian saviour. Or it may be that the Anglo-Saxon god had associations of self-sacrifice or of a comforting role towards humans which made the comparison yet more appropriate. The East Saxon kings traced their descent, uniquely, not from Woden but from a god called Seaxnet, known in German Saxony as Saxnot. He may have been a tribal patron. We know that the rulers of Wessex and Kent did not originally claim Woden for an ancestor, but copied their genealogies from that of Northumbria. Indeed, all the others may have done likewise. A runic poem mentions Ing, whom the Icelanders identified with Frey, while the biographer of Alfred the Great, Asser, speaks of the god Geat. Finally, the historian Bede states that the Anglo-Saxon names for March and April were taken from those of two goddesses, Hreda and Eostre (before the English adopted the Roman names used ever since). The latter also provided the enduring English name for the Christian feast of Easter.[24]

At first sight, then, it may appear that the Germanic and Norse peoples had a few widely venerated deities instead of the many local cults of the Celts, Romans, Greeks and Near Eastern peoples. This may just be possible, but it is far more likely to be a trick of evidence. Our sources for the religious pluralism of the Celts consist of the Irish Dinnshenchas and the icons and inscriptions provided by the Roman occupation of Gaul and Britain. Strip these away and we are left with the literature of the early medieval period, which gives an impression of a pantheon of deities commanding widespread respect. The use of names of places and festivals reinforce this picture, because it is necessarily selective. Without the Dinnshenchas we would not know that many of the place names of Gaelic Ireland derived from tutelary goddesses. Lacking such a source, we tend to assume that any Anglo-Saxon personal name connected to an English settlement is that of a human founder, unless it happens to be that of a deity mentioned in the few literary sources. But it may have been, in an unknown number of cases, that of a divine protector. The twelfth- and thirteenth-century Scandinavian literature, especially that by the accomplished and sophisticated Icelander, Snorri Sturluson, is likely to give an even more partial and distorted picture of the Germanic paganism than the Irish epic tales do of the old religions of their land. When naming their days, the Christianized English took the Roman week and substituted the names of those of the deities which seemed to correspond to the characters of the gods and goddesses concerned. Sunday and Monday they simply adopted directly, and (interestingly) they also took Saturday because they seem to have had no equivalent to the god of the countryside and old age, Saturn.

There is no evidence to indicate that the Anglo-Saxon regarded Woden, Thunor, Tiw and the others as a group or family in the way they were portrayed by Snorri. There is, on the contrary, firm evidence from the Roman and Greek sources, and slight evidence from the Irish sources, that writers would impose such a structure upon a range of disparate figures. Traces in the early English literature of shadowy divinities such as Geat, Eostre, Hreda and Seaxnet, who are not found in the medieval stories, indicate that Anglo-Saxon paganism may have been as rich and diverse as that of the southern and western European peoples.

This chain of reasoning is connected to an associated problem: that the contrast between Celt and German is made far too often and too sharply by scholars. Writers of books on 'the gods of the Celts' have included the Rhineland thunder-god Taranis, and looked hard for parallels to him further west. Few or none of them notice that he is the same personality as the Anglo-Saxon Thunor, across the river. Scholars of German and Norse mythology identify the Scandinavian Odin, the German Wotan and the Anglo-Saxon Woden as the same figure. Scholars of Celtic mythology have decided that the names Lugh, Lud, Lug and Lleu, from Ireland to the Alps, denote the same god. But few or none notice that in many respects they are probably *all* the same individual or divine stereotype, the multi-talented, creative trickster and enchanter. Such a figure might appeal to the most mobile social groups – traders, poets or mercenaries. In terms of artefacts, the pre-Roman people of northern Europe display a patchwork of local styles within a framework of general similarity, and the later Imperial frontier has absolutely no relevance to the picture. The case seems to have been similar with respect to religion. There was certainly a linguistic division, between the Celtic and Germanic tongues. But there is no reason to suppose that it fell perfectly along the boundary of the Empire. In terms of religion as in all other matters save the politics of states, one should think of a spectrum shading gradually across the continent and its offshore islands. In Britain the contrast seems rather abrupt, partly because of the difference already mentioned in the sources for Irish and Anglo-Saxon beliefs, and partly because history had shifted these two widely spaced parts of the spectrum next to each other. As it is, we lack too much information from too many different places to determine the degree of similarity or dissonance between the pre-Roman cults of the British Isles and those that arrived with the English settlers. One contrast alone can be suggested at this point. Running through early Anglo-Saxon literature is an overwhelming sense of an all-powerful destiny ('Wyrd') which shapes the whole world, and is greater than deities themselves. This is utterly lacking in the stories and poems of the Irish and Welsh: as noted above, the English had come from a different sort of land and been through a different set of experiences. But then, as will be shown later, it may not be a pagan concept.

Now to temples, religious officials and festivals. Very little is known about the holy places of the Anglo-Saxons. Traces of them in place names are scattered across the map. 'Ealh', meaning 'temple', is only found twice, in Kent, but 'hearh', hilltop sanctuary, occurs across the midlands and south-east and 'weoh', or 'sacred space' is common throughout the whole great area settled by the pagan English – with one curious exception, which is that there are no recognizable names echoing pre-Christian holy places north of the Humber. Perhaps the peoples up there used words which we do not recognize, or else chose to alter the place names after conversion to Christianity. Some of these sites in the south are still quite impressive locations: the 'Gumeninga Hearh', hilltop sanctuary of the Gumenings, still rises sharply from the lower Thames valley with the modern name of Harrow-on-the-Hill. In addition there are examples of 'legh' or 'leah', a cleared space, being linked with the names of Woden and Thunor. There arises a strong probability that, like most northern Europeans, the early English often employed hills or groves as sacred places without need of buildings. But 'ealh' does mean a structure, and Bede spoke of temples having existed in Northumbria, Kent and East Anglia. Yet only one possible example of such a building has been located and excavated, at Yeavering in Northumberland, which was a seat of the seventh-century Northumbrian monarchs. It was wooden, rectangular and large, measuring 17 feet across and 35 feet long. It had a roof, and a fenced enclosure around the entrance which contained posts, perhaps for images or trophies. No domestic rubbish was found within or around it, but a large pit dug inside was filled with animal bones, especially ox skulls. The ground to one side was strewn with more animal bones, a massive post had stood near one corner, and an inhumation cemetery was sited nearby. The whole structure had been burned down, but whether by Christians, or in war, none can say.

Nothing like it has been found on any other pagan English site. Indeed, no other possible Anglo-Saxon holy place has yielded any evidence of ritual activity, with the probable exception of another 'hearh', Harrow in Sussex, where a dump of over 1000 ox skulls argues for something more than just a slaughterhouse. The explanation presumably lies in the same two factors which account for the paucity of known Iron Age shrines: that the people did not require formal religious buildings and that the latter are hard to distinguish from other timber structures. An alternative suggestion might be that the early English temples are buried underneath parish churches. There is, after all, a much-quoted letter from Pope Gregory the Great to Abbot Mellitus, in June 607, asking him to tell his missionaries in England to convert the pagan buildings for Christian use instead of destroying them. But so far no excavations beneath existing or former Saxon churches have uncovered any traces of pre-Christian activity by the same culture. It may be that our sample is as yet too small, or that the churchmen on the spot preferred to ignore the Pope and continue to observe Gregory's own previous instructions to raze the temples to the ground. This is precisely what Bede records as having happened in Northumbria. Certainly more ecclesiastical archaeology is needed to resolve the issue.[25]

In its material, shape and deposits, the Yeavering temple is very similar to those of the British Iron Age, and what is known of the early English religious officials is also strongly reminiscent of those who appear in the Celtic sources. Again, there is no trace of priestesses, and abundant evidence for priests. Bede repeatedly mentions them, and credits the Northumbrians with having a high priest, just as Irish kings had a Chief Druid. One of the principal functions of the Celtic religious officials was to divine the future, and in the poem *Beowulf* the 'wise men' of a kingdom feature as 'examining the omens'. The Anglo-Saxons likewise had the concept of ritual prohibitions which the Irish called *geisa*: for example, the high priest of the Northumbrians could not carry arms or ride a male horse. The fact that this taboo was attached to a priest and not a king might be thought to indicate that the English lacked the Irish concept of sacred monarchy. But that is not so: the Anglo-Saxon sources make it clear that kings were the focal point of tribal life, and responsible not merely for success in war but for good harvests. If the weather turned bad or an epidemic struck, it was the ruler, not the priest, who was liable to be in trouble. But this concept, as noted before, is found throughout the ancient world. What is missing in early English kingship is the Irish concept of the *feis*, the sacred marriage of the successful monarch to the land. But, as has been pointed out, there is no trace of this among the British Celts either. The main distinction between the Celtic and Germanic priesthoods seems to be that the former comprised a learned class, responsible for the nurturing of tribal traditions, to an extent that the latter did not.[26]

A greater contrast appears to be evident between the festivals of the two groups of peoples. Those of the pagan English are known almost entirely from the book written by the eighth-century scholar Bede, about the workings of the calendar. His references to pre-Christian practice, though invaluable, are slight and probably incomplete. He states unequivocally that the greatest sacred occasion was the winter solstice, which marked the beginning of the year and was known as the Modranicht, the 'Mother Night'. He also records that in February the people offered cakes to their deities, that September was Halegmonath, 'Holy Month', and so presumably had ceremonies, and that November was Blod-Monath, 'Blood Month', when cattle were slaughtered before the winter set in, and some used in sacrifices. He adds that the feast of the goddess Eostre, after whom the month later called April was named, was the great spring festival.[27] All this suggests a calendar very different from the neat Irish system of quarter days, which began the year on 1 November and was apparently indifferent to the solstices. It may be that the cakes offered in February might have been at a time close to the Irish feast of Imbolc, and that the cattle slaughter took place near the Irish Samhain. But overall, the contrasts are striking. We are still left to wonder about two major points. One is that not all the Celtic peoples may have used all or some of the Irish calendar, and the feasts of Britain and Gaul may have borne a greater similarity to those of the Anglo-Saxons. The other is that according to Bede the early English attached no importance to Midsummer, the feast counterpoised to their great Mondranicht which in historical times was celebrated by all peoples of northern Europe including Germans, Slavs and Celts. The feast of Eostre was probably their equivalent of the tremendous rejoicing at the return of greenery, known across the whole Continent and British Isles and held variously on May Day or St George's Day since records begin. But in addition, the Gallic tribes, as shown earlier, and the Goths at the far end of Europe[28] had certain rituals to correspond to phases of the moon, as the Anglo-Saxons may also have done. Of the appearance of English pagan festivals we have an indication in the celebrated letter of Gregory to Mellitus, copied by Bede. The Pope had been told that they built shelters of branches around their temples and sacrificed oxen.

What of metaphysical beliefs, religious images and ceremonies? Of the first, little can be said save that Christian Anglo-Saxons had a stoical and slightly oppressive sense of the workings of Wyrd, mentioned above. In Bede's *Ecclesiastical History* there is a famous passage in which the high priest of Northumbria describes the pagan English view of life and death as being like the experience of a sparrow who flies out of a freezing night into a warm hall full of feasting and merriment, and then out into the night again. It is a marvellous image, and may well be a record of

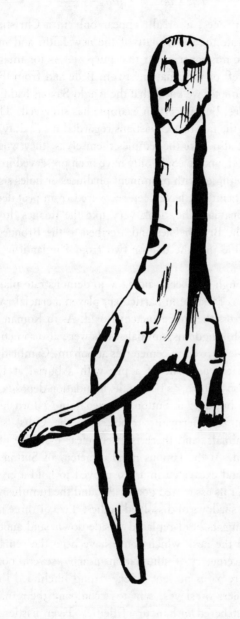

FIGURE 7.3   What did Anglo-Saxon gods look like?
No certain images of Anglo-Saxon deities are known, but this one is from a very
similar culture and probably gives a good impression: carved from an oak branch
and preserved in a bog at Broddenbjerg (Denmark), it is now in the National
Museum of Antiquities in Copenhagen.

genuine belief. But it does, after all, appear only in a Christian work intended to demonstrate the superiority of the new faith, and may have been concocted by the missionaries for that purpose. As for imagery, we are almost totally bereft of information. From Bede and from the letters of Gregory which he quotes we know that the Anglo-Saxons had figures of deities in their temples, but no certain example has survived. This must be ascribed in part to the fact that Christians regarded it as a duty to make bonfires of them; but also, like the temples themselves, they would have been fashioned of wood, and so could only have been preserved in bogs. A few examples, crude effigies with prominent phalluses or holes signifying vulvae or detachable genitalia, have been recovered from peat deposits in Germany and Scandinavia. They look very like the images dug out of similar locations in the British Isles and ascribed to the Bronze or Iron Ages: it is just possible that the one or two from England are Anglo-Saxon.

Of ceremonies enough has been said now to demonstrate plainly that animal sacrifice, and ox sacrifice in particular, played a crucial role. This was, after all, true across the entire ancient world. As in Roman Britain, so in the early English kingdoms, animal skulls were also sometimes put in human graves: those of oxen in cemeteries at Soham, Cambridgeshire, and Caister-by-Norwich, and one of a pig with a burial at Frilford, Oxfordshire. They also feature, as before, as foundation deposits, such as the ox's head under a building at Sutton Courtenay in Oxfordshire. The Romans insisted that the Germanic tribes, like the Celts, sacrificed humans as well as animals, and there is fairly clear evidence of this in Anglo-Saxon England. At the famous royal cemetery of Sutton Hoo in Suffolk, an oval mound excavated in 1989 proved to hold a cremation, later robbed of most of its associated goods. Around the tumulus were ten graves containing the shadows of dissolved bodies. Two or three had been decapitated, one having its head replaced upside down, and another had matter pulled around the neck which could have been the remains of a strangling rope. In a cemetery of inhumations nearby, several bodies had been beheaded. The remains present a very strong likelihood that these were burials of retainers or slaves, sent to accompany their masters or mistresses, or else butchered in honour of deities. Even nastier was the evidence at the grave of a nobleman found at Sewerby on the Yorkshire Wolds. A woman, perhaps a maidservant, had apparently been thrown in alive on top of the corpse and its goods, pinned down and then buried under piles of rocks.[29]

It is, indeed, funeral customs which have provided the most copious evidence of pagan English beliefs. The literature, such as *Beowulf*, *The Seafarer* and *The Fortunes of Men*, suggests that cremation was the principal mode, and on the whole archaeology bears this out. But this statement conceals an immense range of variation. The only valid generalization is that the early English liked to bury people in the earth, and often with goods. Cremation was preferred amongst the Angles of the north and inhumation among the Saxons of the south, but both modes were found virtually everywhere. The co-existed in the same cemetery, perhaps representing family traditions. Of the burial grounds so far located in East Anglia, twenty-four held mostly cremations, thirty-four mostly inhumations, seventeen seem equally mixed and thirty-seven remain so far unexcavated. The two modes of burial were given to both wealthy and ordinary individuals, although in some East Anglian cemeteries the rich tended to be inhumed and the lower orders cremated. Cremation was to some extent standardized, burned remains being placed in urns which varied in size according to the age and status of the deceased. But they had a highly complex iconography of decoration, and the variety of good placed with the remains varied greatly even within the same county. Indeed, only about half of the known cremations were accompanied by goods at all.

Inhumation was also distinguished by a fairly standard practice, the corpse being laid out fully dressed, with all ornaments of the living. Children were often placed crouching, but adult bodies were virtually all extended upon their backs, and all had their heads pointing within an arc from north-west to south. Almost all the men were accompanied by belts and knives, and some by tools, swords, shields or spears. So far a total of 5476 Anglo-Saxon inhumations have been recorded by excavators, and the features stated above are widespread enough to support the idea that it was deemed essential for bodies to be properly dressed and equipped in order to fare well in the next world. Sometimes vessels for food or drink were placed with them. Children were often given weapons or jewellery too old for them, either because it was assumed that they would continue to grow in the afterlife or else to equip spiritual guardians for them.[30] Just as in the Romano-British period, some of the bodies were decapitated, prone or held down with boulders. Fifty of the headless bodies were found dumped at once in a mass grave near Thetford, Norfolk; this presumably represents the site of a massacre, heads having been taken as trophies. Those recently located at Sutton Hoo may, it has been suggested, have been sacrificed. That leaves a total of twenty-nine found scattered around the various cemeteries, and a figure that small (out of 5416 inhumations, excluding the Thetford and Sutton Hoo sites) suggests victims of a battle, execution or, again, sacrifice. A total of thirty-eight prone bodies had been found by 1981, to which may now be added several of those in the satellite graves around the mounds at Sutton Hoo. Some of the thirty-eight were found laid across the burials of wealthy individuals, and one (at Spong Hill, Norfolk) was placed beside a wooden burial chamber of a noble and then covered in heavy stones. This pattern suggests strongly that the prone position was used by the Anglo-Saxons to confine the spirit of a dead person, either by ensuring that it remained and guarded the spot or to prevent it from seeking vengeance upon the burial party. The former seems more likely, and the evidence adds force (though not proof) to the suggestion that the prone burials of Roman Britain represented the same idea.[31]

By 1964 about 1150 early English cemeteries were known, and since then about thirty-five more have been identified (the uncertainty of number derives from the difficulty of telling whether two neighbouring burial grounds were originally a single large one). They vary tremendously in size, but most are small, consisting of only a few individuals. On the other hand, although less than fifty held more than 100 graves each, some of these were really gigantic. Some 2000 cremations and fifty-eight inhumations have been discovered at Spong Hill in Norfolk, while almost 2000 burials are recorded at Lovedon Hill in Lincolnshire, 800 at Mucking in Essex, and 600 at another Lincolnshire site, Elsham.[32] The fact that these places are all in eastern seaboard counties almost certainly reflects the density of English settlement there, but also, perhaps, local custom. An opposite extreme of tradition is suggested by the evidence from Bernicia, the kingdom north of the river Tees which became part of Northumbria in the seventh century. Its people shunned the habit of cremation burials so popular with their fellow Angles, and indeed they buried very few of their number at all. Whether they exposed the bodies, or burned them and scattered the remains, or dropped ashes or bones into water, we cannot say. What is especially striking about this pattern is that it may have been copied from the native British, for there are very few graves in the region from the Bronze and Iron Ages and the sub-Roman period, despite dense settlement. Thus a local funerary tradition may have survived a millennium and a half, if not longer, and taken the arrival of the Germanic invaders in its stride.[33] It is also arguable that the early English adopted the notion of raising burial mounds from their encounters with the prehistoric examples visible in the British landscape. All the known fifth-century English graves are flat, but round or oval tumuli appear over some of the sixth century and occur more frequently on sites from the early part of the seventh. They remained the preserve of a few, and not necessarily of all those who were apparently the most important: out of the 2058 graves recorded at Spong Hill, just four were covered by mounds. At places in Derbyshire, the Yorkshire Wolds and Wiltshire, the newcomers saved themselves labour by inserting their dead into Neolithic, Bronze Age, Iron Age or Romano-British round barrows. A total of seventy-one were put into a large late Neolithic or early Bronze Age specimen at Uncleby in the Wolds. But it should be added that some of the mounds raised by the English themselves covered some of the most richly provided burials. Whether the notion of tumulus building was in fact gained from the natives is not a soluble question, because round or oval burial mounds were constructed at places in Scandinavia and Germany during the same period. Anglo-Saxon culture was notably eclectic: the finds from the single large cemetery at Spong Hill showed traces of influence from Norway, Denmark, Sweden and Germany. Nor can we say whether or not the huge number of flat graves had any markers, for wooden memorials may have rotted away.[34]

The most celebrated Anglo-Saxon barrows of all are those which cover the most famous sort of early English funeral deposit, the ship burials of the Suffolk coast. Ships feature as receptacles for bodies in several literary sources for German and Scandinavian society: in *Beowulf*, in Viking sagas and in an Arab traveller's account of the Swedish settlers in Russia. The prominence of vessels in the rock art of the Scandinavian Bronze Age was noted in an earlier chapter, and the beliefs which inspired these pictures may have carried over into the period represented by the literature. But three riders should be added to that statement. The first is that the written sources do not make the theological significance of the ships much clearer than the carvings do. At times they seem to be transports to the next life: at others only rather glamorous and convenient burial chambers. Second, the rite itself varied. The stories sometimes show ships being set adrift with the body and sometimes burned, at sea or upon land. Those in Suffolk were buried. The third point is that the use of vessels for funerary purposes in England is confined to two cemeteries in one district of one county. It may have been brought there, like some of the styles of artefact in those cemeteries, from Sweden.

Of the two sites, the most famous is Sutton Hoo, because of the wonderful treasure discovered there in 1938. It was piled inside a clinker-built ship 90 feet long beneath an oval mound, and probably accompanied a body which had completely vanished because of the acidic soil. All circumstances combine to date the deposit to the 620s or 630s, and the most likely person to have occupied the grave would have been Raedwald, king of the East Angles. The ship when in use could have seated about forty oarsmen, and some clue to its symbolic significance may be provided by the presence among its cargo of a purse which contained thirty-seven coins and three pieces of gold of equivalent size. These could have represented the payment for a complete crew of ghostly rowers, and two small ingots in the same bag might have been the wages of the steersman. But renewed excavation at Sutton Hoo since 1983 has revealed this burial to represent only one of a number of modes present at a very complex site. Six of the eighteen round barrows there have now been opened, and none has revealed another interment in a ship. In one a vessel up to 65 feet long had been placed *over* a wooden burial chamber; in another a cremation was left in a bronze bowl; in another more burned remains were put in an oak tray; and in another an infant with a tiny sword and spear lay within an oak coffin. Around all these tombs, presumably the resting place of a royal family, were single flat graves in which bodies had been placed in all postures and without goods. Almost half showed signs of violence, and the impression of sacrificial victims afforded by these remains was rendered a virtual certainty by the discovery of the satellite burials around another cremation, described earlier. Fresh excavations have also turned up important new evidence in the other cemetery, a few miles away at Snape. This is of similar date, though it may have been commenced earlier, near the end of the sixth century, and have fallen out of use as the site at Sutton Hoo was opened. One ship burial in a 50-foot vessel was found there during the last century, along with cremations under some of the other mounds and in flat graves. Another body has now been uncovered in a vessel, although this is a mere dinghy, and a score of other inhumations have been found. What is impressive about these latter discoveries is the sheer range of burial practice which they reveal. Corpses were laid in coffins or wooden chambers, upon biers and among pieces of charred timber, and in many different postures.[35]

It is obvious from all this that the early English had as many different traditions of burial as the people of the Iron Age or of Roman Britain. Indeed, customs seem to have become more varied as time went on, even within the same community, until they were at their most heterogeneous upon the eve of the arrival of Christianity. People who attached great importance to attiring bodies for the next world and laying them out with great care shared graveyards with those who burned their dead to ashes.

Members of the same dynasty, or at least the same court, followed utterly divergent practices. The great question is whether these differences were due to religious belief, social rank or mere personal whim. J. D. Richards, on the strength of his study of cinerary urns, tends to the view that issues of rank and prestige were more significant. The excavator of Sutton Hoo, Martin Carver, favours a mixture of social and spiritual factors but stresses the former, while William Filmer Sankey, who is working at Snape, and Rosemary Cramp, an expert upon Northumbria, prefer the idea that religious beliefs were by far the most important determinants of practice.[36] It can be said, therefore, that upon present evidence the problem is not soluble. But there is plenty to suggest that the early English might have been almost as richly varied in their cults and their metaphysical ideas as the pagan Romans.

This is all that is at present known about the religions of the Anglo-Saxon invaders. They proved to be short-lived phenomena, whatever important traces they may have left in archaeology, in the names of places and (perhaps) in culture. By the middle of the sixth century, only about a hundred years after the immigration had become significant and while it was still in progress, the new kingdoms were almost surrounded by Christians. To the north and west were the native British and Irish, while to the south and east the Franks, who had overrun Gaul, had accepted the new faith. It seems probable that only the haughty refusal of the British Church to preach to the newcomers allowed English paganism to survive as long as it did. In 597 Pope Gregory the Great broke with previous practice and decided to send an official mission from Rome to bring Christianity to a group of northern barbarians. On an impulse he chose the English, and despatched a group of preachers to Kent, where the presence of a Frankish wife to the king meant that they had a small foothold. The monarch concerned, Ethelbert, swiftly accepted their faith and used his tremendous authority, as the strongest Anglo-Saxon monarch of the time, to diffuse it. The King of Essex was his nephew, the King of Northumbria his son-in-law and the future King of East Anglia his fosterling. All accepted the missionaries from Rome, while Irish monks from St Columba's churches came down into the north to second their efforts. The Franks sent over more Christian evangelists. As a result of all this pressure, the English accepted the faith of Christ in the equivalent of just one long lifetime: about eighty-seven years after Ethelbert welcomed Gregory's priests, the last pagan district, the Isle of Wight, was won over. The process is much better documented than the conversion of the Celtic peoples by virtue of two very good sources, Bede's *Ecclesiastical*

History and the Anglo-Saxon Chronicle. Just as in Ireland, there seems to have been very little bitterness between the old and new faiths, despite the destruction of the holy places and images of the former. There are no certain cases of Christians being martyred, although the medieval legend of St Sidwell, said to have been killed by farmers in Devon, may be based upon fact. The only well-attested case of a pagan put to death by Christian zealots is that of a priest in Sussex. As in Ireland, the political power and sacred status of English kings meant that the missionary effort was largely directed at them. When a king converted, his people either had to follow his example or kill him. Occasionally this latter course did occur, as in the case of Eorpwold of the East Angles, and the people of Essex returned to the old rites for a while after their first adoption of Christianity was followed by an epidemic. Sometimes Christian monarchs were succeeded on the throne by pagan relatives who ejected the missionaries, while Raedwald of East Anglia was noted not only for permitting both religions to co-exist but for worshipping with both. If the great ship burial at Sutton Hoo was indeed his, then they would explain the presence of a set of Christian baptismal spoons in an ostentatious pagan monument. There is certainly no sign of any sort of military crusade mounted by Christianized monarchs against their neighbours, or vice versa: rather, the religious question was subject – rather haphazardly – to the fortunes of war, and war was endemic in the seventh-century British Isles. The greatest enemy of the Christians was Penda, ruler of Mercia, because he killed no less than five neighbouring kings who had accepted the new faith. But the religion of his victims was more or less irrelevant to Penda, who saw them as political rivals, and his staunchest ally was the Christian Celtic king, Cadwallon. Overall, although the progress of the faith of Christ was uneven it was still rapid and the conversion of the English was completed before that of the northern British Celts. The fact that Christianity was professed by the wealthier and more respected realms of Europe must have counted in bringing about the persuasion of the Anglo-Saxons to its ways. But, as in Ireland and Scotland, one feels that it also must have provided a power of argument and a confidence and unity of belief which the tribal cults could not match.

By the end of the seventh century, British Christianity was almost secure – but not completely. Only about a hundred years after the end of the process of conversion, its offshore monasteries came under attack from new pagan adventurers, the Vikings of Scandinavia. During the next 300 years the whole of the British Isles had to reckon with these people, and they settled thickly in all three of the later realms of England,

FIGURE 7.4   Vikings and Christianity
From its style of decoration, this cross at Middleton (Yorkshire) seems to have
been the work of Vikings: as so often in the art of these people, a Christian
monument is decorated with somewhat un-Christian motifs. Is this heavily
armed warrior a representation of a living man? Or of a character from a story?
Or of a god? Or is it a picture of somebody laid out in a grave, with his goods?

Scotland and Ireland. But their impact upon religion was slight, for they tended to accept Christianity within a few decades at most of their permanent establishment in most areas. Nor did they drive out the churchmen from much of the land they conquered, which greatly assisted the speed of conversion and limited the extent of apostasy among the existing populations. As a consequence, little need be said here about their beliefs, which seem to have been almost identical to those held by the Anglo-Saxons: their known deities were certainly the same.

Furthermore, the surviving evidence for Viking paganism in the British Isles is as limited as that for any of the pre-Christian cults. Carved stones in northern England and the Isle of Man bear scenes from Viking mythology, including a few involving pagan deities. But the episodes seem in most cases to have been chosen to harmonize with Christian teaching: thus the dragon is the symbol of evil in both cultures, the treacherous god Loki could be equated with Satan and the Viking legend of the destruction of the old deities at Ragnarok might be held to represent the end of a world succeeded by the Christian one. Most, if not all, of these stones are themselves crosses. Only at Sockburn, in County Durham, are there scenes which have no obvious Biblical correspondences. One scene portrays the god Tyr having his hand bitten off by the wolf Fenris, and another could display a Valkyrie welcoming a dead warrior to the hall of slain heroes, Valhalla. But these images are themselves set in a church, and may be no more than echoes of a lost past. Temples or sanctuaries have not yet been identified on any Viking site in the archipelago. The hammer, symbol of the thunder-god Thor (counterpart to the English Thunor), has been found on silver amulets dug up near Goldsborough, Yorkshire, and on tenth-century coins minted by the Viking kingdom of York. That we know the names and personalities of some Viking deities is due to tales about them recorded, and in most or every case reworked, by Christian authors. As in the cases of the Welsh, Irish and Anglo-Saxon texts, the fact that they tell us very little about the content of the old religion may have been due to ignorance rather than to distaste. The Viking literature shares with these other bodies of work an additional characteristic, that scholars during the 1980s have become even more sceptical of its value for the study of pre-Christian customs. For example, the hitherto notorious rite of the 'Blood Eagle', the killing of a defeated warrior by pulling up his ribs and lungs through his back, has been shown to be almost certainly a Christian myth resulting from the misunderstanding of some older verse.[37]

As in earlier ages, our principal evidence derives from archaeology.

On the river Hull, at Skerne, a ritual deposit has been found of a sort very familiar from Iron Age and Romano-British contexts but so far missing from those of the Anglo-Saxons. Beneath a jetty or bridge abutment were lodged cattle, horses, dogs, an adze, a spoon and a sword which from its style dates the whole assemblage to the ninth or tenth century. By 1965 a total of thirty-four other swords from the Viking period had been found in English rivers, and the relative absence of other kinds of hardware suggests that these had been offerings and not accidental losses. Much more numerous are burials, which are found throughout the far north of Scotland and its islands, and in Man. Virtually all are inhumations and some are richly furnished, the men with weapons and tools and the women with jewellery. Several were in, under or beside boats, but as in the Anglo-Saxon cases the significance of these is not clear. Horses and dogs were sometimes interred with the humans, whole or burned to fragments. Women occasionally accompanied wealthy male corpses, and at Ballateare, on the Isle of Man, there is little doubt that one was sacrificed for the purpose, for her skull was sheared off at the back by a sword or axe blow. Comparable cases in Scandinavian graves indicated that the rite, though not routine, was widespread.[38]

By the early eleventh century the kingdoms of Scandinavia themselves had all accepted Christianity, and the last possible threat to the paramountcy of that religion in the British Isles was removed. But how complete was its control? Did the old cults live on in a new guise? Or survive in secret? And to what extent were they revived, at any time up to the present moment? These questions must be the subject of the next and final chapter.

Legacy of Shadows

In the search for 'pagan survivals' the historian encounters three enormous problems. The first is that Christianity incorporated many elements of ancient paganism. All that its founder had supplied was a code of ethics and (arguably) a cult of his own figure as a saviour and redeemer, set within a Jewish theological and ritual structure. In order to make the transition from Judaism to the Gentile world, the new religion had to take on many of the trappings and some of the thoughts of the older cults. Patristic scholars today still dispute the extent to which Hellenistic philosophy (especially that of the Stoics) influenced the Church Fathers even as early as St Paul and St John the Apostle. The 'basilican' shape of the first stone churches, and the use of candles, incense, wreaths and garlands, altars, formal liturgies, clerical hymns, vestments, choral music and sermons were all borrowed from paganism. Some of the iconography of Christian saints bore a striking resemblance to images of the former deities. Images of the Virgin drew upon some of the attributes of the chaste goddesses Artemis and Diana. There are a few notable examples of direct continuity. Some of the Black Madonnas of Italy and Sicily occupy churches upon the sites of notable temples to Ceres and Cybele, goddesses of fertility, and their cults are associated with the growth and the harvesting of crops. Their colour may be intended to increase their identification with the soil. The famous Virgin of Chartres Cathedral in France is a figure taken from a fourth-century pagan altar. Most remarkable is the case of the Madonna and Child at Enna in Sicily, which were actually statues of Ceres and her daughter Proserpina, housed in a church built upon the former temple of the goddess. They were only removed to a museum during the nineteenth century, upon the orders of Pope Pius IX.[1] During the sixth century it became more common all over the former Roman world to transform pagan buildings into churches. At Rome itself, those of Santa Maria on the Capitol and Santa Maria Maggiore stand upon the platforms of great temples to Juno, and there are also Santa Maria Sopra Minerva and the present day Pantheon, the most wonderful surviving monument constructed by the emperor Hadrian. And the bishop, presiding over most of the world's Christians with what was originally the nickname of Pope ('Daddy'), bears the formal title of Pontifex Maximus, supreme priest of the pagan city of Rome.

In the British Isles examples of such direct transference are easy to find. St Brighid, as said, was alsmost certainly a goddess; and there is St Gobnet, whose name is suspiciously similar to that of the smith god Goibhniu. The suspicion seemed to be confirmed when his early medieval shrine at Ballyvourney, in County Cork, was excavated in the 1950s. It turned out to be built over a great pre-Christian industrial site, consisting of at least 137 forges.[2] The cases of the re-use of pagan holy structures as churches, cited earlier, are paralleled in Britain by the apparent Christianization of temples such as Nettleton Shrub and Uley, as mentioned in the previous chapter. There are in addition famous instances of the placing of medieval churches next to, or within, prehistoric monuments – as if to remove the risk that the latter might be rival foci of devotion. The two most notable are probably that of Rudston on the Yorkshire Wolds, with Britain's tallest standing stone in its yard, and the ruined one at Knowlton in Dorset, placed in the middle specimen of a row of three henges.

It is also well known that many Christian festivals were fixed, by Church Councils, upon dates already associated with major pagan celebrations. The Scriptures themselves specify no calendar of ritual and so this, like much else, was developed in part from the models of the older religions. The Nativity of Christ was fixed to replace the Imperial feast of the Birthday of the Unconquered Sun, thereby linking its celebration to all the different pre-Christian commemorations of the mystery of the winter solstice. The decision to do so was taken in the fourth century, but two centuries elapsed before it was accepted by all the various churches. The approximate timing of Easter was indicated in the New Testament by the fact that the arrest, execution and resurrection of Christ followed the Hebrew spring festival of the Passover. But when a formal decision was taken to determine its date, in the fourth century, it was set according to the solar and lunar calendars: the first full moon after the vernal equinox. Nearly 400 more years were to pass before the whole Christian world was reckoning the equinox at the same date and the feast at the same phase of the moon. Over the same period, several major ancient festivals were Christianized by being awarded to particular patrons: thus, Samhain's importance was recognized by its transformation into All Saints' Day and Midsummer Day became the feast of St John the Baptist.

Having said all this, it is important not to take too far the process of identification of the old religions with the new one. There is a powerful tendency, which began with Protestant reformers, was continued by nineteenth-century anti-clericalists and is preserved by many modern writers, to assume that medieval Christianity was simply paganism given a thin layer of Scripture. Two swift case-studies may give some idea of its dangers. One concerns the cult of Michael the Archangel, the glamorous, bewinged, spear-bearing, dragon-slaying, shining saint especially associated with the tops of hills and crags. He is regularly taken as a Christianization of a solar deity, and his symbol of the spear has caused him to be identified in particular with the Celtic god Lugh. But a careful study of the development of his cult[3] shows that it arose in fifth-century Italy and spread to France and England during the seventh century. There was nothing particularly 'Celtic' about it, and it came latest to Ireland where the memory of Lugh ought to have been strongest. His earliest churches tended not to be built over the remains of solar shrines: rather, he was a saint of high and wild places which, with the growth of the habit of prigrimages during the Middle Ages, made splendid goals for the faithful. He was a product of the development of Christianity itself rather than an importation into it. Then there is the question of the genuine ancient Gaelic feast of Imbolc, which according to many modern writers was transformed into the Christian one of Candlemas, the Purification of the Blessed Virgin Mary. Some recent authors have linked Candlemas in addition with the Roman Lupercalia, or suggested that Imbolc was a 'fire feast', and that its flames were perpetuated in those of the Christian candles. A few contemporary 'witches' have asserted that behind the festival of the Purification lay a pre-Christian celebration of the recovery of 'the Goddess' from giving birth to the 'new year's Sun God'.[4] There is absolutely no evidence for this last idea, which is purely and simply a paganization of Christianity, but the relationship between Imbolc and Candlemas is more subtle and deserves extended discussion. The Purification had to be celebrated by Christians because it commemorated one of the most important episodes in the early life of Jesus, his presentation at the Temple and his recognition as the Messiah by Simeon and Anna. Once Christmas was fixed upon 25 December, the Purification had to occur upon 2 February, being the time appointed for this ceremony, according to Hebrew law, after a birth. Its especial association with candles, evident during the course of the early Middle Ages, was suggested by Simeon's words, read out at the service, that the child would be 'a light to lighten the Gentiles'. All this was determined by churchmen sitting in councils around the Mediterranean and representing lands very far from the Gaelic area in which Imbolc was known. Nor is there any evidence that ceremonies involving fire were employed in the Gaelic feast, which was Christianized in its own right, very appropriately, as the holy day of that great saint of the Gaels, Brighid. So Imbolc and Candlemas were separate in their origins and observation. *But* in some Gaelic or semi-Gaelic districts, notably northern Scotland, the great Christian feast came to replace that of St Brighid in the popular imagination as the quarter day which marked the beginning of spring.[5]

There are two contradictory impulses at work in the common modern tendency to see paganism everywhere in medieval Christianity. One, referred to above, is to debunk the Christian faith (or particular versions of it). The other, which first appeared in the eighteenth century and is very marked at the present, is that of people who are emerging from Christianity and wish to take with them what they like about that religion while jettisoning the rest. A classic example of this latter process is the belief in the former existence of a 'Celtic Christianity', which combined the best features of both old and new religions and tolerated both, until it was wiped out and replaced by metropolitan, 'Catholic' Christianity during the Middle Ages. According to this view, the Culdees, a monastic movement within the Gaelic world during the eighth and ninth centuries, were the inheritors of the former wisdom of the Druids. In recent times a feminist angle has been given to the story by citing the case of Irish priests active in the sixth century who allowed women to assist in the administration of the Eucharist. From this example it has been argued that the 'Celtic Church' was also more admirable in its treatment of women than later Christianity. This is all part of the 'pseudo-Celtism' discussed in chapter 5, one of its most succinct and influential exponents of late being the earth mystic John Michell.[6] No careful scholar has ever propounded it and nor do the more responsible modern 'popular' writers on the ancient Celts like Caitlín Matthews. During the sixth and seventh centuries the churches of the British Isles differed from the others in western Europe in the way in which they calculated the date of Easter and administered the tonsure, and in other relatively trivial ways. They also permitted priests to marry, in common with many other early medieval Christian groups (and those of the Greek world never abandoned this practice). But in no way did they preserve more pagan observations than other followers of Christ. During the seventh and eighth centuries they brought their ritual practices into conformity with those of Rome, and after 750 the Céli Dé or Culdees arose. These were the exact opposite of recipients of pre-Christian wisdom, being an ascetic movement of monks, 'the vassals of God', who condemned the laxity of many existing religious houses and demanded a stricter and yet more puritanical devotion.[7] As for the Irish priests who were assisted by women, they were not in the least representative of their homeland, but were a pair of itinerant eccentrics loose in Brittany, and their practices were unorthodox in a number of different ways.[8] In recent years Kathleen Hughes has led religious historians in questioning any concept of 'Celtic Christianity', arguing convincingly that the differences between the churches of Wales and Ireland in particular were at least as important as their similarities.

In this context it must be stressed that the cases of real or apparent continuity from paganism to Christianity, cited above, are exceptional. We saw in the previous chapter that the overwhelming majority of temples and shrines seem not to have been re-used, and that virtually all images of former deities were destroyed if they fell into the hands of Christians. Nor are some of the exceptions as convincing as they might first appear. The henge at Knowlton may merely have represented a ready-made shelter and churchyard for the medieval people who constructed the church inside. The standing stone at Rudston may just have been a well-known local landmark, and the place of parish worship built beside it accordingly. Most early medieval religious buildings in the British Isles, as asserted before, seem to stand or have stood upon formerly unused ground. It is better to say, not that the Christian Church took the older religions into itself, but that it provided a parallel service to them. It had the rite of initiation, dependence upon a saviour figure and assurance of personal salvation characteristic of the mystery religions. Like the old faiths, it gave victory in battle and its holy men and women were reputed to work miracles. It included a cult of the bones of its martyrs which continued the reverence paid to pieces of consecrated human skeleton, and the sense of their magical power, evident at times since the Neolithic. Like the faiths which it replaced, it provided centres of pilgrimage and healing, at which votive objects were offered. Its central rite was sacrifice, but this now took the form of a symbolic offering up of the saviour figure who had obviated the need for further loss of life by giving himself. Its saints acted as local guardians, personal protectors and patrons of particular activities, just like the former deities.

And just like them, they had their cult statues. In place of Lares, Penates, Genii and Junos, there were now ministering angels. There was no longer need to sacrifice to the *numen* of rulers, but they were still accorded semi-divine status. They were, like priests, anointed with holy oil. The Roman emperors were portrayed with haloes like Christ and the saints (and pagan solar deities), while monarchs of the Celtic and Germanic states asserted and won the privilege of being the only laity to be interred inside churches along with clerics. The new religious calendar was fundamentally Hebrew, not that of the classical pagans, with a service every seven days instead of a succession of seasonal feasts. But the latter soon appeared, and the greatest provided a means of marking the progress from the plunge into midwinter, through the lean times until spring and through this to midsummer, with a series of blessings and liturgies. As already noted, it incorporated several older festivals, but it was not dependent upon them. Lughnasadh was given only the feast of St Peter in chains, while the allocation of SS Philip and James to Beltine, or May Day, hardly did justice to its non-Christian importance: in the new calendar it was overshadowed upon either side by Easter and by Ascension Day and Pentecost, which had no direct pre-Christian ancestors. Great saints like the Apostles Peter, James, Andrew and Paul were given feast days which had formerly no religious significance in the northern European world. A large part of the reason for Christianity's victory in places such as Ireland, where it depended solely upon its own merits, is surely that it offered everthing already given by the old cults, and added a confident promise of eternal bliss. When looking for 'pagan survivals' in the medieval Church, it is not enough for historians to detect parallels, relics or imitations of paganism. It is necessary to demonstrate that certain things, although now existing within a Christian structure, kept alive a memory of, and reverence for, the old deities. Otherwise they were part of Christianity.

The second besetting problem of the subject consists of the relationship between religion and magic. Historians, theologians and anthropologists seem to be in general agreement upon the distinction between the two. Religion consists of an offering up of prayers, gifts and honour to divine beings who operate quite independently of the human race and are infinitely more powerful than it. Those actions may be aimed at obtaining favour or merely at maintaining the existing order, but whatever the inspiration of the worshipper, the decision as to whether or not any response will be made lies entirely with the deity or deities concerned. Magic, by contrast, consists of a control worked by humans over nature by use of spiritual forces, so that the end result is expected to lie within the will of the person or persons working the spell or the ritual. In theory anybody ought to be able to carry out either, but in practice most societies have produced specialist practitioners in both. The folklore collections made within Europe during the past two centuries have revealed the two phenomena operating at different levels. For many a nineteenth-century villager, church-going was an activity designed to ensure that the worshipper secured a better life after death and that the whole community, whether conceived of as the village, the district or the state, was protected from harm. The same person would often employ a magical remedy for matters apparently too trivial for the concern of Almighty God: to heal illness in a human or in animals, to trace stolen or lost property, to increase the yield of a particular plot of land, to gain a compatible marital partner or to ward off malice. In other words, magic did a lot of the work later taken over by pharmaceutical medicine, fertilizers, insurance schemes and advertisement columns. Those practising it were generally devout Christians and saw charms and rituals in the same functional sense as these modern commodities and services. Such magic had, in the eyes of its practitioners or purchasers, nothing to do with the great contest between God and Satan: it was concerned with the morally neutral forces of nature, which could be turned to good or bad effect just like the physical natural world.[9]

The two spheres, of course, generally overlapped and sometimes combined. Strictly speaking, religion can do all the work of magic, and the fact that humans have sought the latter in addition has been the result of modesty (not wishing to trouble deities), frustration (the deity has not responded), double insurance, pride and curiosity (the desire to work spiritual power directly) and considerations of convenience and expense. In many tribal societies the priest and the sorcerer have been the same individual, and the distinction between the two roles, if one can be drawn, lies in whether the benefit is being sought for many or for a single person. But in historic European societies the difference has been fairly clear, and they have shared with most of humanity, up to the last 200 years, a chronic fear of the use of magic by private individuals for destructive purposes. In the intensely localized, competitive society of the early Irish literature, it generally features as another weapon in the feuding between kingdoms. In the Greek, Roman and Old Norse texts, destructive sorcery is more often the work of specialists within a community, for the exercise of personal vindictiveness, for the extortion of gifts or respect, or for hire to others. These sources make clear something that is obvious also in the

large number of modern studies of communities in Africa and Asia: that
the alleged worker of bad magic is usually a woman or an old person, and
most often both. There is nothing mystical in this, for in all these human
structures of power, spells are thought to be the natural recourse of those
who lack physical strength. The young and strong strike blows, while the
old and feeble have to employ curses. All the literary sources for
European paganism also make plain that magic of any kind was not
connected with the worship of deities. Whether courtly or rural, learned
or traditional, benign or malignant, it was an art or science, not part of a
religion. The distinction in pre-Christian society between a priestess or
priest and a sorcerer or witch was usually plain.[10] The former were
essential to the well-being of a community, the latter potentially useful but
also menacing. As noted earlier, the sort of women who were accused of
bad witchcraft in Elizabethan England are already found as fully formed
literary stereotypes in the satires of Lucan and Grettir's Saga.

Christian teaching attempted, as was also noted earlier, to blur the
difference between paganism and magic by declaring that the latter could
only be worked by employing demons whom the older religions had
revered. It held that true benefits could only be gained by prayer,
attributed to its own saints powers of magic superior to those of any other
humans, and recorded great catalogues of miracles to prove both points.
It was also Christian orthodoxy that any attempt to divine the future was
an interference with the will of God and so an insult to the Almighty. But
while the new faith was apparently very successful in providing
alternative and parallel functions to the former cults, it was much less
effective in preventing recourse to magic, at all levels of society. After all,
it was a religion, and no more able to satisfy the impulses which drove
people to use spells than any other. Moreover, the theological issues were
by no means clearly defined. Any Christian could take the point that
worshipping a different deity, or the Devil, was a grievous sin. But was
astrology truly so, if it only aimed at the intepretation of God's wishes, as
did theologians? Where did the borders lie between chemistry, alchemy
and sorcery? Or between using herbs for their physical properties and for
their occult significance? In an age of such imperfect science, in which
cause and effect were so little understood, who could distinguish a magical
process from a medical, or a botanical, or a chemical one? Was it wrong to
enslave a demon and force it to work for a good cause? So the Church in
many ways lost the battle with magic in the course of the Middle Ages. Its
councils continued from time to time to forbid lists of occult practices, but
failed to root them out, even from its own clergy. During the later

medieval period there seems to have been a marked increase in the production of magical texts, while astrology came to be sponsored by most royal courts. Near the end of the fifteenth century the Florentine Platonists gave a respectable philosophical and theological basis to the study and employment of spiritual powers by devout Christians. Medieval European sorcery took many forms and drew upon many authorities, notably Greek, Arabic and Hebrew, but the resulting *mélanges* were distinctively the products of the Christendom of the time.[11] As for the village folk magic, this was to survive intact until the disappearance of traditional village life in most parts of Europe within living memory.

Thus, magic of any kind cannot, strictly speaking, be described as 'paganism'. It was separate from the worship of the old deities, could flourish within a Christian culture and was a constant factor before and after the Christian conversion. But there remains a considerable semantic problem, that of formerly religious practices which had been converted into magic. One case of this is animal sacrifice. As late as the nineteenth century, farmers in Cornwall, Wales and many parts of Scotland were recorded as slaughtering one member of a herd of cattle to protect the rest from sickness.[12] There was no longer any sense that the animals concerned were being offered to a deity, and the rite of sacrifice had become occasional. It was simply felt that the voluntary production of a victim would ward off misfortune, as if by a law of nature. The same is true of the use of animals as foundation deposits. A goat's skull was found underneath a late Saxon hut at Chichester, and four horses' skulls beneath the doorway of a fourteenth-century house in the now abandoned village of Thuxton in Norfolk. The Romano-British rite of termination was echoed when a boundary ditch was filled in during the twelfth century, with the skulls of a dog and a stag at the bottom. Ralph Merrifield, who has done so much to document magical practices uncovered by archaeology, has counted five cases in which pots were placed in the walls of buildings under construction, spanning the thirteenth to the seventeenth centuries and ranging in character from a farmhouse to Chichester Cathedral. Pots and horses' skulls were put under the floorboards of many churches and houses until the nineteenth century, but from the Tudor period at the latest, the reason was given that they improved the acoustics of the building above. More traditional was the reason given for the custom of walling up dead cats or chickens or animal bones, which persisted until far into the reign of Victoria: it was held, in some indefinable fashion, to give strength and good fortune to the structure.[13]

All these activities were, unmistakably, 'relics of paganism'. They can also be described as 'pagan survivals', in the sense that they had survived from paganism. But paganism had not survived with them, for they were the work of Christians who had detached them from any previous religious context.

A parallel problem concerns the fate of those natural features, such as groves, wells and rivers, which had been sacred to the old religions. It has been said earlier that an unknown number of holy wells were apparently Christianized by re-dedication to a saint. But the custom of casting votive offerings into water was turned into magic. Many medieval pilgrims' badges have been found in English rivers and streams, especially near towns. Over 250 were found in the bed of the Thames at London, beneath what had apparently been a ferry crossing.[14] The people who threw them in were not pagans but Christians who had been devout enough to journey to the shrines of their faith. And yet, on homecoming, they had committed the symbols of their pilgrim status to the water, in a gesture long pre-dating Christianity. They can only have believed that they would benefit by doing so. The tradition of the wishing-well, a combination of sacrifice and natural place designed to bring good fortune to the giver, has been the last incarnation of the water hoards of prehistory. The fate of holy trees was rather different, partly because those of the former cults could easily be felled or left to die off naturally. There exists now no place in the British Isles which can conclusively be identified as the exact site of a pagan sacred wood or single tree. But in early medieval Ireland there still existed giant specimens which were such a focus of local pride and affection that they fulfilled some of the role (if they were not the same trees) as the former holy timber. One was at Tortan in County Meath, revered by the southern Ui Niall, while another was cut down by the King of Tara in 982 to humiliate the Dal Cais ruler in whose territory it stood.[15] They had kept their place in the sentiments of the tribes even while apparently losing all direct religious connotations. The 'gospel oaks' remembered in several English place names, prominent landmarks under which open-air sermons were preached, may represent a Christianization of the association between trees and sanctity. The arcane properties granted to several species in folklore and books of spells, notably to ash, birch, rowan and elder, may be an echo of their status in pre-Christian worship, or may have been part of a magical tradition independent of the old cults.

The distinction between pagan religion and magic is all the more important in that we know a great deal about Anglo-Saxon magic and herb lore and so have a lot of material to underpin the contrast.[16] In fact, one of the ironies of nineteenth-century racial and cultural stereotypes is that we possess far more arcane texts from the supposedly prosaic early English than from the supposedly imaginative and mystical Celts who were their contemporaries. On the other hand, it does perhaps say something about the differences between the two groups of peoples that the Welsh and Irish tended to write tales involving enchantments and the Angles and Saxons tended to write manuals instructing the reader in how to work them. Whether the substance of English and Celtic magic differed very much seems doubtful when the two sets of sources are compared. Both cultures, for example, possessed a rudimentary system of symbolic writing at the time of Christianization, the Irish ogham and the Germanic runes. Both used it for inscriptions and for spells and divinations. The technique of the latter, described in the Irish story *Tochmarc Etain* and by the Roman historian Tacitus when writing of the Germanic tribes, is identical: to cut wands of wood, carve the script on them and then cast them to form what pattern they wished.[17] It seems plain from the Anglo-Saxon magical texts that they were not linked to the veneration of the old deities but were, like occult lore in general, capable of employment by practitioners of any faith. But again there is an ambivalence attached to certain cases. What of the charm contained in an English text composed between 950 and 1050, which bids the reader make farmland fruitful by cutting turves in a particular manner and asking the 'Mother of Earth' to become bountiful.[18] Is this a reference to an actual former goddess? Or is it a philosophical abstraction? Or is it the work of somebody learned in the Greek texts, from which they had gained Hesiod's myth of the female earth, Gaia, with whom the male sky mated? If a real goddess was involved, was the person performing the charm expected to believe in her? Or had she simply become part of a line of doggerel? Next, let us consider the Tolvan Stone and Men-an-Tol in Cornwall, prehistoric megaliths with holes through them. In recent centuries, it was a local custom for parents to pass sick children through the apertures in the belief that they would thereby be healed. Was this a lingering memory of the actual purpose for which the stones were raised? Or did the country people invent stories and customs about these monuments, millennia after their original significance had been completely forgotten? The latter does seem more likely, not just because of the huge span of time involved, but because the Tolvan may not have possessed its hole (or so large a hole) when first erected, and the Men-an-Tol is most probably part of a dismembered Neolithic tomb. So while both these examples could, with different degrees of likelihood, be described as possible 'relics of paganism', no positive assertion should be based upon either. To repeat: no act of magic, however frowned upon by the Church, can be used to prove the continued existence of the old religions of the British Isles unless there is firm evidence that it involved a belief in those religions.

The third great problem facing historians arises from the fact that the medieval world incorporated into its culture the art and letters of pagan antiquity, with tremendous admiration and enthusiasm. The Christian love affair with the classical ancient world grew more intense as the Middle Ages wore on, making the physical and literary images of Greece and Rome an inseparable part of so-called western civilization. It is obvious that when a modern writer compares somebody to Mars or Jove or Hercules, this is not a declaration of pagan Roman beliefs, and that when a modern plutocrat decorates a garden with statues of deities or nymphs, these are not objects of worship. Likewise, we know that Botticelli, Titian, Velázquez and Lord Leighton were all Christians even though they painted images of Venus. The faith of Michelangelo and Bernini is not in doubt, although one sculpted Bacchus and the other Apollo. It is considerably less widely appreciated that medieval Celtic writers drew upon their past in precisely the same way. When the Earl of Argyll marched off to war in 1513, his bard could still compose a poem comparing him to Lugh.[19] The most Christian of Anglo-Saxon literature is peppered with pagan references and comparisons. In *The Dream of the Rood*, as mentioned earlier, Christ is compared to Frey. Moreover, the Crucifixion, which is the main subject of the poem, does not sound very much like the episode recorded in the Bible. The 'young hero' mounts 'the marvellous tree'. He recounts how 'the warriors left me standing laced with blood; I was wounded to death with darts'. It has often been suggested that this scene was inspired not by the story of Christ's death but by that of the Norse and Germanic god Balder. But Balder was shot with a single arrow, fired by a fellow god, not wounded to death upon a tree, with many darts. Is this perhaps instead a memory of human sacrifice as practised by the pagan Germanic tribes? Or a piece of pure imagination? Other pieces of early English writing show more straightforward transpositions. Royal land grants dated 872, 901 and 977 describe the Christian god as a thunder deity, like the old Thunor. The famous *Nine Herbs Charm* claims that the herbs concerned were created by Christ while hanging on the cross. But it goes on to describe how Woden killed an adder with rune magic. In the poem *Judith*, heaven and hell are conflated with the Norse and Germanic equivalents, Valhöle and Niflhel. In *Beowulf*, the monster Grendel is made to be a son of Cain. The genealogies of the royal houses were extended beyond Woden and Seaxnet to include the Old Testament patriarchs from Adam to a son of Noah. In both art and literature, the figure of Satan was readily identified with the villain of the Norse gods, Loki. Upon the seventh-century Franks Casket were carved the German myth of Wayland and the Adoration of the Magi, the second subject being labelled because it was less familiar to the initial owners.[20] That such references vanish from English works during the eleventh century is due not to greater Christianization but to the Norman Conquest, which wrenched the country away from the northern cultural world. All the items cited above were Christian.

One of the great difficulties involved in separating out the elements of early medieval civilization in the British Isles is that it mixed Christianity with not only north European but Graeco-Roman cultures. The latter could be as potent and novel a force in some places as the Scriptures and the writings of the Church Fathers, and all our literary records of the early Irish, Welsh and Anglo-Saxons are filtered through both. This, it now seems to be generally accepted among scholars that the figures of the Three Norns or Wyrd Sisters in Norse and Germanic mythology are borrowed from those of the Three Fates in Greek mythology, and had no native equivalents. It is very likely that when writing of the Tuatha de Danaan, the Irish were not recording something in which their ancestors actually believed but fitting old deities into a structure inspired by the Greek pantheon. The Norse myths, culminating in the superb prose of Snorri Sturluson, were certainly subjected to the same process. It is not at all clear whether the Anglo-Saxon preoccupation with an all-encompassing destiny, 'Wyrd', was actually part of a pagan world picture or the result of the writings of the late Roman Christian Boethius. The latter propounded a philosophy identical with the concept of 'Wyrd' which was very influential in early medieval Europe and made a great impact in England. A classic case of this sort of dilemma is represented by the Icelandic poem *Havamal*, in which the god Odin sacrifices himself to himself and so gains arcane wisdom. It is one of the most haunting passages in Norse literature, in which modern readers can feel close at last to the inner world of northern European paganism. Or can they? Can it be that the entire episode is the Crucifixion translated into Scandinavian myth? Christ and Odin are both hanged upon a tree (the latter being the common medieval term for a scaffold, applied very often to the cross). Both are pierced by spears, thirst, cry out and are resurrected with infinitely greater glory

(Odin after nine days, Christ after three). All this is surely too much to be coincidental, and although present-day scholars are divided over whether it is a Christian poem or not, it seems beyond question that its form was heavily influenced by Christianity. So, after all, it seems to tell us little about the nature of the older religions of Scandinavia.[21] All this presents the searcher for pagan survivals with two further restrictions. First, that the reappearance of a pagan image in a Christian concept only demonstrates the survival of paganism itself if it can be shown to have a religious purpose, and is not being used as an analogy or for its aesthetic value. A statue of a Madonna which was fashioned in the manner of a pagan goddess was not, thereby, a pagan image. Second, that our notion of the pre-Christian cults themselves is severely affected by the transmission of evidence for them through a double filter of Christianity and Graeco-Roman classicism. With all these reservations in mind, we can now ask for how long the pagan religions of the British Isles managed to survive the adoption of Christianity by their rulers.

The most important single source of evidence for this consists of law codes and legal orders issued by rulers, Church councils and bishops. In the seventh century, during which the conversion took place, it is not surprising to find signs of continued vitality in the old religions. The last surviving code for the kingdom of Kent, issued near the very end of the century and almost sixty years after the old cults had been proscribed, still forbids sacrifices to pagan deities. So does the 'Penitential of Theodore', written at about the same time. On the other hand, the laws of Ine of Wessex, composed around 700 and some half a century after the conversion of his predecessors, make no reference at all to non-Christian practices. We lack evidence to show whether this was because the Christianization of the west country was, untypically, complete by that date or because Ine (though himself by all accounts very devout) felt constrained to tolerate the older faiths. If the latter were the case, then the collapse of the old religions came soon after, for the eighth-century evidence for their continuation is very weak. Bede's Penitential, drawn up in Northumbria in the 730s, does not mention them. They do feature in the Canons of Egbert, Archbishop of York, which were composed around 740. But the practices described really rank as magic or superstition rather than full-blown religion; people are not supposed to use sorcerers to exorcise their houses or to trace criminals, nor to employ spells of purification, nor to treat springs as holy. The Synod of 786–7 only prohibited magic and the old custom of using self-inflicted scars as symbols of courage and identity. During the next century both pagan religion and magic seem to have vanished from these sources.[22] It seems reasonable to surmise from them what is also indicated by the *History* of Bede: that the pre-Christian religions of the English were defunct by the 730s, leaving behind a residue of superstitions and folk practices, customs which continued to figure as matters of concern in Wessex during the following two centuries. At the end of the ninth, the laws of Alfred the Great forbid the use of the names of former deities in oaths. In the 990s a letter directed to the Bishop of Sherborne shows the church struggling to reach a compromise with customs of which it disapproved but which were not sufficiently serious in its eyes to be forbidden. The West Saxons had maintained a tradition of holding wakes for the dead, with feasting, songs and laughter around the corpse. It was decided that if the clergy were invited to attend these, they should not partake of the feast themselves and should discourage the merriment.[23]

Further north, however, the reintroduction of paganism by the Vikings posed a much graver problem. The ecclesiastical response is contained in the large body of directives composed between 1000 and 1002 by Wulfstan, Archbishop of York. His office made him responsible for the whole northern province of the Church, where the Danish newcomers had settled most thickly and where the last pagan king had reigned as late as the 980s. Against the practices imported or revived by this influx, Wulfstan issued canons in his own right and composed legal codes for monarchs.[24] These were detailed, specific and apparently comprehensive. They forbade necromancy, auguries, incantations and any other kind of magic. They outlawed the use of pagan songs and games upon Christian feast days, and prohibited the worship of non-Christian deities and the veneration of the sun, moon, fire and water. Wulfstan mentions sacrifices and images, and although he does not speak about temple buildings he repeatedly condemns the existence of sanctuaries around wells, springs, rocks and trees, especially the elder. All this does draw quite a good picture of a flourishing paganism in the north at the opening of the eleventh century. Yet it seems to have succumbed very swiftly to the campaign of repression. In the early 1020s, the powerful new monarch of England and Denmark, Canute, adopted Wulfstan's prohibitions in a code issued for his whole English realm. Heavy fines were prescribed to enforce it and they appear to have met with little resistance, for after this non-Christian practices once again vanish from the sources.

What remain, during the High Middle Ages, are the steady and unavailing campaign against magic, and occasional complaints by churchmen about aspects of what may be termed folk traditions. Between 1238 and 1295 a Bishop of Worcester, one of Wells, one of Exeter, one of Winchester and one of Hereford all issued orders against the veneration of springs or wells and (much more rarely) trees. This was not a sustained programme of repression by 'the Church' so much as a series of initiatives by unusually stringent prelates against practices which the local people, and indeed, most churchmen, would probably have considered to be Christian. In some cases it was only a specific case which was in question, where popular devotion was thought to have gone too far. Likewise, in the same period – a notable one for self-conscious reform and improvement by ecclesiastics – a Bishop of Worcester forbade the crowning of mock-kings at popular revels.[25] Once the great age of episcopal house-cleaning was over, so were such directives. How effective they were can be judged from the steady growth in the cult of wells (to judge by the number of chapels built over them), and the large number of Tudor references to 'kings', 'queens', 'lords' and 'princes' at local feasts and games. All this evidence, from the Conversion to the Reformation, is taken from the English sources, which are by far the most abundant. But the law codes and ecclesiastical decrees and penitentials of Wales, Ireland and Scotland do not show any greater concern with the problem of surviving paganism during the Middle Ages. In fact they display less.[26]

We are left with a few cases of actual, or apparent, worship of non-Christian deities.[27] But all are isolated incidents and none can positively be described as a 'survival'. At Bexley in Kent, in 1313, one Stephen Le Pope made wood and stone images of gods in his garden and worshipped them. Upon the same night on which he commenced these devotions, he murdered his maidservant. He seems to have been deranged. At Inverkeithing in Fife, during 1282, the priest led the small girls of his parish around a crude human image, carrying a phallus on a pole; he also forced some of his congregation to strip and to whip each other. His career was cut short when he was killed by a parent of one of the girls. Like Le Pope, he seems to have been mentally disturbed. Members of a society conditioned to fear idolatry and sexuality would be very likely to express unbalance of the mind by obsession with both. The events at Frithelstock Priory, in Devon, were of a different kind. There in 1351 the monks erected a chapel in a wood nearby, where they installed an altar, a rack of candles and an image which the Bishop of Exeter described as being of 'proud and disobedient Eve or of unchaste Diana' rather than of the Virgin Mary. To this they attracted the local people, and made money out of them by reading their futures according to the casting of lots. The racket was broken up by the bishop, who had the chapel and its contents destroyed. The only other evidence we have that bears on the case is that the priory already had a bad reputation: in 1340 its sub-prior had to do penance for laziness and sexual misconduct. What is missing is any indication of the viewpoint of the monks themselves. It would be very interesting to know whether they were conducting a self-conscious parody of the Christian religion, or whether they were so ignorant and undisciplined that they genuinely did not realize that they were acting outside it. Whatever the truth of the matter, there is nothing in the story to indicate that they were acting in accordance with a local pre-Christian cult. Rather, like the individuals at Bexley and Inverkeithing, they were deviants from medieval Christianity. It is probable that the destruction of records has removed evidence for other cases such as these, and for other ecclesiastical initiatives against popular customs. But the survival of episcopal and conciliar documents from the High Middle Ages, and of records of church courts from the later Middle Ages, provide a sufficiently good sample for us to be sure that the overall picture is not distorted.

This means one of two things. Either the old religions were effectively dead by the mid-eleventh century, despite the fresh injection of pagan cults by the Vikings; or the Christian establishment chose to call off the attack upon them around that time, and contented itself for the next half a millennium with sniping away at trivialities such as the occasional well or tree. The second option may sound very unlikely, yet such was the implication of a theory which was stated confidently by many writers until the 1960s and found its way into some of the most widely used academic textbooks. This held that the bulk of the population of Europe remained pagan, under a Christian ruling class, until the fifteenth century. Then, according to this thesis, the Chruch launched a full-scale attack upon the old faith, accusing it of being demonic witchcraft, and the result was the Great Witch Hunt of the next 300 years in which paganism was finally destroyed. The idea that the people who were tried for witchcraft in early modern Europe were actually devotees of a pre-Christian religion has a long pedigree. It was apparently first propounded in 1828 by Karl Ernst Jarcke, a professor of criminal law at the University of Berlin. It was heard again in 1839, from the director of the archives of Baden, Franz Josef Mone, who was probably influenced by Jarcke, and it was further developed by one of the most popular French scholars of the age, Jules Michelet. The latter devoted a book to the subject, re-creating the rites of the medieval witches with tremendous flights of imagination and describing them with all the sympathy due from a modern liberal to an oppressed class and culture. It was, of course, a bestseller. None of these authors was a good historian, even by the standards of the time: the first two belonged to different professions, while Michelet's success was due to the power of his prose and his fiery appeals to national pride. None carried out any systematic research. But the wide readership of Michelet's *La Sorcière* ensured a proportionate currency in the last century for the notion that the witches of Christian Europe were practitioners of an older religion.

This idea was almost certainly exploited in the 1890s by an American called Charles Godfrey Leland. A wonderful swashbuckling character, he operated as a lawyer and as a soldier of fortune, and lived with native Americans and European gypsies: his profession is best described, with admiration, as that of adventurer. In 1899 he published what he stated to be the gospel of the medieval witch cult, presented to him by one Maddelena, a member of a hereditary group of witches in Tuscany. The portrait of that cult contained within this work is essentially that of Michelet, emphasizing the role of its members as agents of social justice, deploying spells and poisons against corrupt and oppressive members of the ruling classes. This radicalism happened, of course, to mirror Leland's own political beliefs. The name of the goddess worshipped by the witches is also that given in Michelet: Herodias (the significance of which will be discussed later), rendered in Leland's *Vangelo* (the name which he gave to his 'gospel') into Italian as Aradia. Leland's text also has the Frenchman's picture of the 'religion' as one conducted principally by priestesses. Now, since its publication, no historian or folklorist or (indeed) modern witch has uncovered any trace of the sort of hereditary cult in Tuscany which Leland claimed to exist. And experts in medieval Italian literature have found no similarities in it to his so-called *Vangelo*, which he claimed to be fourteenth-century. It reads, in fact, like an unmistakably nineteenth-century work. It does at least seem to be an original composition, so that Leland cannot be accused of plagiarism. He can, however, very easily be accused of forgery. To suggest that he was duped in turn, by the mysterious 'Maddelena' and her pals, is to do him an injustice: a man of Leland's energy, enterprise, fluency and barefaced cheek was quite capable of producing such a work upon his own. It has never been taken seriously by any conscientious scholar of the Middle Ages.[28]

But for most of the twentieth century, the work of all these writers upon this subject was eclipsed by that of a British academic, Margaret

Alice Murray. All who met her in the course of her prodigiously long life seem to have agreed upon the power of her personality, which was by turns a delight and a terror to her colleagues. She was physically tiny, which proved a blessing for scholarship: she was turned away from her chosen profession, nursing, because she was deemed to be too small for it. Instead, she became an Egyptologist, and was indeed the first woman to make a mark in this discipline. Her industry was as remarkable as her energy, for she produced over eighty books and articles upon the ancient Near East, and we shall always be indebted to her for their careful cataloguing of data. According to other experts in the field, her ability to interpret evidence was more dubious, for she had a tendency to draw hasty conclusions and make unsupported assertions. It was this formidable combination of scholarly strengths and weaknesses which she brought to bear, in the 1910s, upon the question of the Great Witch Hunt. Her approach was to document the long-established theory that it represented the extermination of European paganism, using records of the early modern witch trials. The result, published in 1921, was *The Witch Cult in Western Europe*. This book deserves our respect in that it was the first attempt to study the Great Witch Hunt dispassionately, as an aspect of social history, and employing a fairly large quantity of material contemporary with the events described. But both her sources and her treatment of them were seriously defective. The former consisted of a few well-known works by Continental demonologists, a few tracts printed in England and quite a number of published records of Scottish witch trials. The much greater amount of unpublished evidence was absolutely ignored. She began with the premiss that the trials were of a genuine religion, and reconstructed it from the confessions of the accused and the writings of their persecutors. She was fairly objective in her sympathies, so that when her material specified that witches indulged in orgiastic sexual behaviour, human sacrifice and cannibalism, she set this down as the truth. But she did suggest that in its joyous nature, the witch religion had some superiority to Christianity. And her treatment of her sources was the utter reverse of impartial. She ignored or misquoted evidence which indicated that the actions attributed to the alleged witches were physically impossible. Or she rationalized it, by suggesting that an illusion of flying was created by drugs and that accounts by women of the coldness of the Devil's penis were produced by penetration of them with an artificial phallus as part of a fertility rite.

Furthermore, she pruned and rearranged her evidence ruthlessly to support her assertion that the 'religion' concerned was standard throughout Europe. Thus she mangled data continually to fit her assertion that all witches operated in covens of thirteen, though it is obvious even from the limited data which she scanned that most of the accused were solitary individuals. Her portrayal of the festivals of the cult was of the same nature. It commenced with the bald assertion that the most important were May Eve and Hallowe'en, with two lesser ones at Candlemas and Lammas. Thse were, of course, simply the quarter days of the Gaelic year, and her scheme rests upon the confession of a single Scottish 'witch', Isobel Smyth, at Forfar in 1661. She found a lot of evidence that persons accused in Scotland, and in one case in Lancashire, had specified Hallowe'en as a time for their activities, doubtless drawing upon the arcane reputation of the old feast of Samhain. She also found a single Scottish trial at which Lammas was mentioned, though that just happened to be the major holiday during the time in which the people concerned were accused of having operated. And that was all her evidence; but it was sufficient for her to speak about the quarter days as the main celebrations of the witch cult of 'western Europe'. At Candlemas, she suggested, a wheel-like dance of torch-bearers had been performed. She did not provide a reference for this notion and it seems to have been her own invention. To the great festivals she gave the name 'Sabbaths', a term used to describe meetings of witches by the early modern demonologists (because the same writers held the Jewish faith to be the antithesis of Christianity, an explanation which is patent in their work but which Dr Murray brushed away with a simple denial). She also spoke of gatherings for purposes of business instead of religion, which she termed 'esbats'. This expression actually occurs only in a single source, used by a French intellectual who did not himself give it this meaning. But Dr Murray was happy to declare it to be another general rule of her 'cult'. She did note that both in Britain and on the Continent alleged witches stated that they revelled upon a variety of Christian and traditional holidays. But, having set her system in place, she was able to dismiss these as aberrations.[29]

This method of operation was buttressed by an apparently wilful ignorance of context and an obstinate refusal to ask any awkward questions – even very obvious ones. Dr Murray's ignorance of ancient paganism in Western Europe prevented her from realizing that the rituals imputed to early modern witches were not antique rites but parodies of contemporary Christian ceremonies and social mores. Her failure to study Continental sources obviated the need to wonder why the Great Witch Hunt was confined to certain places and certain times, and why the 'witch cult' failed to persist in areas in which it was never persecuted. But, even her limited information and sphere of interest should have driven her to ask why it was that, out of a genuine popular religion, it was almost always just the female devotees who were arrested. Or why the Devil at the covens, whom she insisted was a mortal man in disguise, was *never once* apprehended. She had constructed her image of medieval paganism. It had ancient Gaelic festivals, and a congregational structure found in the pages of sixteenth-century demonologists. It worshipped the Horned God – Dr Murray's paganization of the Christian Satan who featured in the early modern accusations and confessions – and also the Goddess – whom she took from high medieval records of magical practices. And she was convinced that she was correct.

It may well be wondered how her book ever managed to convince anybody who knew anything about the reality of the Great Witch Hunt. But there was nobody around in 1921 who did, no systematic local study having been made. Dr Murray's thesis seemed, at the least, an argument worth making and after its publication by Oxford University Press it took its place on the shelves of most university and public libraries. There it found a very wide readership. From the start it had critics, notably G. L. Burr, who pointed out some of the weaknesses in its methodology.[30] In 1929 L'Estrange Ewen published the first in his series of calendars of English records of witch trials which appeared over the next ten years and were to prove the utter falsity of the Murray portrait, for England at least.[31] But both Burr and Ewen were read mainly by specialists in the subject, whereas the fame of *The Witch Cult in Western Europe* continued to bring it to the favourable attention of academics as well as the general public during these succeeding decades. Its argument was repeated as fact in many of the standard textbooks of early modern history up to the mid-1960s, including those of Sir George Clark and Christopher Hill. From 1929 to 1968 Dr Murray supplied the section upon witchcraft in the *Encyclopaedia Britannica*, and summarized her book there as if it were universally accepted and unquestionably correct. In fact it had the curious status of an orthodoxy which was believed by everybody except those who happened to be experts in the subject.

And what of Margaret Murray herself in these later years? She coped with her critics by the simple device of ceasing to read any reviews of her work. Her response to Ewen was to attack his publication in general terms and with brutal rudeness, while failing to discuss the details of them. And she continued to develop her own theory. In 1933 she brought out *The God of the Witches*, which restated the main points of *The Witch*

Cult with a few additions and changes of tone. One new element was to trace the previous history of the Horned God by declaring any horned human or animal deities in the ancient Near East or Europe to be forms of the same entity. Another, taken from the very influential scholar Sir James Frazer, consisted of the notion that in antiquity kings were sacrificed after reigning for a set number of years. As part of her campaign to convince readers that paganism flourished into the High Middle Ages, she suggested that the only high medieval king to die violently and mysteriously, William Rufus, was such a sacrificial victim. She also proposed that Thomas à Becket died in place of a monarch. When she wished to make large-scale and dubious assertions, she would state confidently that they were generally accepted among anthropologists. This was an effective tactic because very few historians of early modern Europe had read any anthropology at that time. But then Dr Murray did not seem to have read any either, except Frazer. Another feature of *The God of the Witches* was an increase in Dr Murray's tacit sympathy with her witch cult, to which she now gave the evocative name of the Old Religion, copied from Leland. She still accepted that it included sacrifice and cannibalism, but insisted that this was part of a degeneration brought about by Christian persecution.[32]

Dr Murray returned to the subject once more in the 1950s. The time was opportune, for not only had her existing two books inspired an increasing number of imitations[33] but the repeal of the Witchcraft Act in 1951 drew further public attention to the question. So in 1952 *The God of the Witches* was republished, and two years later she brought out *The Divine King in England*. This extended her theory concerning William Rufus and Becket to make every violent royal death and almost every execution of a failed politician in England until 1600 a sacrifice under the laws of the Old Religion. What the book did prove, beyond any reasonable scholarly doubt, was that Dr Murray knew nothing about the political history of medieval and early modern England. As before, logical weaknesses did not worry her any more than the contexts of her evidence. She did not trouble to ask, for example, how royal and noble participation in the cult of the Divine King came to an end with the Tudor dynasty, or why no churchmen (including those hostile to the monarchs and politicians concerned) should ever have tumbled to what was going on. No reputable historian ever accepted the argument of *The Divine King*, but *The Witch Cult* was still taken seriously by some ten years later, and in 1962 (the year before Margaret Murray's death), Oxford University Press brought that book out in the first of a series of paperback editions, and so made it available to a wider public than ever before.

The credibility of 'the Murray thesis' only really collapsed in academe during the 1970s, when it was at last systematically attacked by the authors of works which had a very large readership. Two in particular, Keith Thomas in 1971 and Norman Cohn in 1975 exposed her misrepresentation of evidence.[34] During the past two decades a score of detailed local studies of the Great Witch Hunt, spanning Europe, have demonstrated beyond a shadow of a doubt that its victims were not practitioners of an Old Religion.[35] Most were solitary individuals with a bad reputation among their neighbours. When local panics occurred and mass arrests were made, those who confessed to working in groups were providing stock replies designed to satisfy their interrogators. The Great Hunt was produced by a combination of four factors. One was the age-old, pre-Christian popular fear of destructive witchcraft. Another was a new belief among intellectuals in a satanic crusade to subvert Christendom. A third was a long-term rise in population and price levels, making the populace more vulnerable to natural disasters and more prone to terror of witches. And the fourth – and the most important – was the struggle between Reformation and Counter-Reformation which produced a tendency among magistrates and churchmen to believe that they were witnessing a final war between God and the Devil, taking many forms. None of this had anything to do with paganism. Nor did it have much to do with traditional folk magic, for although local healers and workers of good spells were sometimes accused of satanic witchcraft, they seem to have represented only a minority of those arrested. Indeed, in some countries (such as France) they helped to detect destructive witches.[36] The vast majority of the 40,000 or so people who perished during the Great Witch Hunt[37] were distinguished only by the fact that they had made enemies. A neat piece of symmetry was achieved in the 1980s when another strong-minded female academic, Christina Larner, re-examined the Scottish sources upon which Dr Murray had so heavily depended, and augmented them with much unpublished material. In this manner she provided, at last, a true picture of the Witch Hunt in that country.[38]

In recent years, also, studies of witchcraft beliefs in existing tribal societies have permitted us some first-hand experience of the tensions and thought processes which helped to produce the European hunt. E. E. Evans-Pritchard undertook the first such project, his famous report upon the Azande appearing in 1937, but for our purposes the most important was probably the research of J. R. Crawford among the Shona of what was then Rhodesia.[39] What was especially interesting about this was that it provided superb evidence of the ways in which people could be persuaded to accuse themselves of witchcraft: one of Dr Murray's principal arguments for the existence of a genuine witch religion was that individuals would (very occasionally) surrender themselves and confess to all the rites imputed to witches. Among the Shona in the 1950s and 1960s were found women who freely admitted to going abroad at night and to destroying other humans by magic. When cross-examined rigorously by sceptical British authorities, they were proved to have dreamed these things (having become obsessed with them because of the suspicions of their neighbours) and become persuaded that what they imagined in their sleep was occurring in reality. This vivid set of anthropological insights brings home the true tragedy of the Great Witch Hunt in Europe. Its victims' crimes had no existence outside the imagination. Unlike medieval or early modern heretics they had no organization and no literature of their own. Unlike those, also, they had no territorial bases and no option of escaping execution by recanting their beliefs. Their offences were illusory, their punishments very real.

What urgently requires further investigation is that world of dreams and fantasies which, in the early modern period, could have such dreadful consequences. We have as yet only fragmentary evidence, requiring augmentation, of a vivid medieval realm of the imagination which extended across the whole of Europe and through most of the period. One aspect of it was the Wild Hunt, a belief held by many people between the ninth and fourteenth centuries that during their sleep their spirits were snatched away to ride in a ghostly cavalcade, led by a figure who was sometimes male but usually female. The tradition is best recorded in the German lands, where the phantom leader was variously known as Perchta, Berhta, Berta, Holt, Holle, Hulda, Foste, Selga, Selda, Herne, Herla, Berchtold and Berhtolt. In Italy and France people also believed in the nocturnal cavalcade, but here it was composed of a benevolent troupe of ghostly females who gave good fortune wherever they wandered. Some people believed that the shining woman who led the troupe was served by devotees at banquets.[40] Churchmen gave this presiding figure two different names. One was Diana, perhaps because a phantom female rider could best be equated with the Roman goddess of the hunt; or perhaps because Diana of Ephesus was the only pagan deity named in the New Testament. The other was Herodias, after the most wicked woman who features in that Testament. Around 900 the Church issued the famous *Canon Episcopi*, which claimed that literal belief in such nocturnal experiences, to which women were said to be especially prone, was folly because they were illusions inspired by demons.[41] The *Canon*, re-enacted at various times until the Council of Treves in 1310, gave the legendary leader of these processions both the names stated above. Both in turn made an impression upon the more careless modern studies of medieval witchcraft. Margaret Murray made Diana the goddess of her putative cult, although, drawing more upon the very different early modern records, she concluded that the Horned God had become much more important. Michelet took the name Herodias for the deity of his presumed witch religion, and so Leland's goddess, as described, became 'Aradia'. Sustained and thorough research is needed into these images of the early medieval world and into the processes which threw them up so vividly into the minds of sleepers.

Now that the principal argument for the existence of a surviving medieval pagan religion has been demolished, it is time to take a fresh look at various motifs in art and literature which have often been taken as further evidence of enduring paganism. In the arts there are three figures above all which have excited interest: the Wild Man, the Sheela-na-Gig and the Green Man. The first is most swiftly dealt with. It was a male, entirely covered in hair, inhabiting the wilderness and living like a wild animal or very primitive hominid. Occasionally it featured in groups or with a female and young of its kind. It is found in both literary texts and in paintings or engravings. The appearances in literature make the task of tracing its genesis, evolution and significance relatively easy.[42] Its origins appear in the writings of Herodotus, the Greek of the fifth century BC, who made a catalogue of the beastly habits of certain remote tribes in order to assist the definition of civilized society by way of contrast. Later Greek authors, and Romans such as the elder Pliny, extended his list. The conversion of the Roman world to Christianity meshed this tradition with a new one, the turning of some former deities into demons. In this case the hairy, club-carrying woodland spirits such as satyrs, which the pagan ancient world regarded as essentially amoral, became devils in the writings of St Jerome, and monsters in those of St Isidore of Seville. But it was only with the flowering of high medieval culture in the twelfth

FIGURE 8.1   The Wild Man
a In repose, from a French drawing of *c.* 1500, in Bibliothèque National, MS Fr. 2374, f. 3ᵛ; *b* in action, from a German engraving by Master ES, *c.* 1460, in the Ashmolean Museum, PA 1306.

century that these ancient models were merged into a single stereotype. It appeared with particular regularity between 1300 and 1550, and especially in the Germanic lands, which had the greatest tracts of forest. The medieval Wild Man was a godless and repulsive savage like the distant barbarians of classical geographers. But he lurked in the woods of Europe like the satyrs. His function in the medieval imagination was to be a bogey in a world obsessed with religious and social order, an awful warning of the consequences of a lack of either. He only began to disappear with the coming of a mood of greater confidence and expansion in the sixteenth century, as his image was slowly transformed into that of the noble savage. Thus, although he was based on ancient models, he was essentially a figure of the Christian Middle Ages.

The other two forms belong to the world of architecture, appearing as sculptures carved upon medieval buildings. They have no appearances in drawings, paintings or woodcuts and no contemporary literature refers to them. Thus they are much more enigmatic. The Sheela-na-Gig is a naked female figure, squatting facing the viewer with legs spread open to reveal the vulva, often exaggerated in size. Most are very ugly by the standards of both modern and medieval taste, being bald, plump and leering. The Green Man is a human head, almost always male, with foliage entwined about it and often sprouting from the mouth and nostrils too. Sheelas are found upon churches and (in Ireland) castles or other secular buildings, commonly upon the exterior walls but also in a variety of other situations. The classic locus for Green Men is roof bosses, although they are found in different contexts. In a very influential article which appeared in 1939, Lady Raglan proposed that the Green Man (a name which she herself gave to the carvings) was an equivalent of a character who danced, covered in foliage, in May Day processions. The purpose of that figure was itself not very clear, but folklorists were then inclined to view it as a representation of a spirit of fertility. This identification seemed to indicate that the images carved in the churches were of pre-Christian origin and related directly to pagan beliefs. Margaret Murray's theory of an Old Religion existing through the Middle Ages seemed to provide a context for this. During the 1950s imaginative writers such as T. C. Lethbridge proposed that Sheela-na-Gigs were also images from a fertility cult and furnished further proof of the vitality of medieval paganism. In 1975 Ronald Sheridan and Anne Ross stated roundly that 'medieval grotesque art stems directly from earlier pagan beliefs, [and] that the representations are pagan deities dear to the people which the Church was unable to eradicate and therefore allowed to subsist side-by-side with the objects of

Christian orthodoxy'. They went on to accuse academic scholars of 'almost a conspiracy of silence' over the subject.[43]

In fact academics were not conspiring but neglecting. No proper research had been carried out into these images and in default of it they were not prepared to rush into judgements as those two writers did. And that situation was about to end. In 1977 Jørgen Andersen published the first systematic study of the Sheela-na-Gig. He proved a number of important things. First, that it was a wholly medieval phenomenon, appearing in the late eleventh century, becoming common in the twelfth and continuing in Ireland with increasing rarity until the last were fashioned in the sixteenth century; second, that although Sheelas were found across England and Ireland, the earliest specimens seemed to exist in south-western France; and third, that they were apparently much more popular in Ireland than in Britain, as well as lasting longest there. It was only there, too, that they were fashioned upon secular buildings such as castles and mills as well as upon churches, although they occurred first upon the latter. The term used for them by scholars was simply the common Irish Gaelic expression for an immodest woman. In 1986 Anthony Weir and James Jerman greatly extended Dr Andersen's achievement. They revealed that Sheelas had spread out from Aquitaine around 1050, reaching Poitou and then (around 1070) northern Spain, before crossing to England in the next century. The earliest which can be dated there, in Herefordshire, were certainly brought over as part of a French school of carving patronized by Oliver de Merlimont. They seem to have got to Ireland slightly later. They travelled with two other motifs, the beaked head and the biting horse's head, and were part of the great high medieval architectural style known as Romanesque. What distinguished the motifs of the British Isles from those of the Continent was that males displaying their genitals are more common in France and Spain than women, while in the islands that situation is reversed. Even so, these two authors found an impressive number of Sheelas on the European mainland: France and Ireland both have about seventy surviving and Spain and England about forty each. There appear to be no images like them in Celtic or Romano-Celtic art. Elsewhere in the Roman Empire there did exist splay-legged female figures displaying their bellies and vulvas; these are found especially in Egypt. But they are generally modelled in clay and never carved upon buildings, were often half-clothed, and lacked the ugliness of the western Sheelas. This, and their distant geographical location, argues against their use as a source of inspiration for the latter.

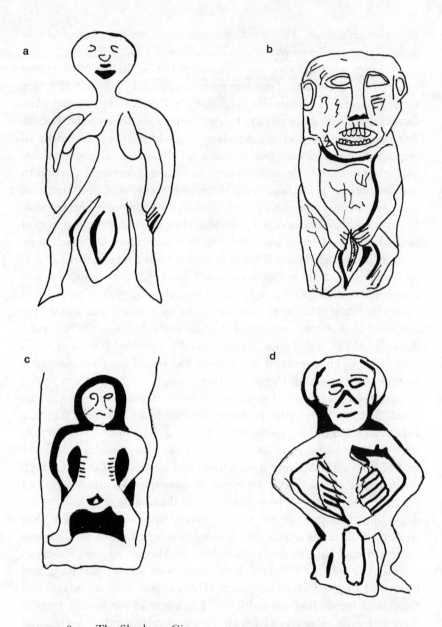

FIGURE 8.2   The Sheela-na-Gig

a On the outside wall of the church at Oaksey (Wiltshire), with the largest vulva on a surviving Sheela; *b* from Killua in Westmeath, now in the British Museum; *c* from Blackhall Castle (Co. Dublin); *d* from Easthorpe church (Essex), now in the Colchester Museum.

So Drs Weir and Jarman looked for the significance of the Sheelas within the general context of Romanesque art. It is plain that the purpose of this art was generally to teach the viewers Christian dogma and morality, with a heavy emphasis upon the perils of sin. The carvers usually represented the human body as ugly, deformed, twisted and base (unless it happened to be that of a saint), thus emphasizing the lack of spirituality and decorum associated with the flesh. Hence the very common Romanesque motif of the contorted acrobat, often displaying his anus or genitals. The architectural context of English Sheelas frequently seems to be part of this pattern. At Studland in Dorset, for example, one appears upon a corbel in a sequence which also includes phallic males, coupling pairs, mouth-pullers, tongue-pokers and beard-pullers. Hence,

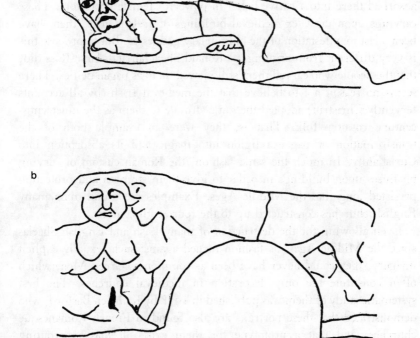

FIGURE 8.3   The excited male in English medieval church art
a Crawling along the east end of the church at Abson (Avon); *b* advancing on a Sheela-na-Gig above a window at Whittlesford (Cambridgeshire).

argued the two writers, it would make perfect sense to interpret the grotesque, repulsive Sheela as a representation of the hideous nature of female lust. They suggested that the predominance of males displaying genitalia on the Continent may have been due to the greater concern there with the sin of male masturbation.

All this is very convincing, but as the two historians themselves point out, it fails to explain the presence of some of the later Irish Sheelas upon structures such as castles. Here it is necessary to look again at the examples quoted by Jørgen Andersen of several nineteenth-century antiquarians who were told by local Irish people that Sheelas were intended to ward off evil. He added the testimony of a German traveller in Ireland during the 1840s, who heard that a man afflicted with bad luck could have the curse averted by persuading a loose woman to expose herself to him.[44] One senses here a very different tradition from that of Romanesque, and it seems wise to suggest that the device of the Sheela, which arrived in Ireland as part of a Christian campaign against sin, was absorbed there into a native belief in powerful female protectors. These carvings upon the later medieval buildings of Ireland may, then, have been a last manifestation of the old tutelary goddesses. But to propose this is very different from arguing, as Ronald Sheridan and Anne Ross did, that the people who carved them still viewed them as pagan deities. There seems no reason not to believe that the medieval Irish (by all accounts fervently Christian) adopted the same attitude to them as the nineteenth-century country folk. That is, they were an example both of the transformation of pagan religion into magic and its absorption into Christianity. In much the same fashion, the Roman custom of carving phalluses upon buildings in order to give them strength and protection persisted long into the Middle Ages. Examples are found upon many English churches constructed up to the fourteenth century.[45]

Even allowing for the destruction of many Irish and English Sheelas since the Middle Ages, as fashion turned against such sexually explicit imagery, they could never have been as common as Green Men, which often constitute the only decoration in medieval churches. The first systematic study of them was published in 1978 by Kathleen Basford, who demonstrated that these portraits are also found in French Romanesque churches, and that a prototype for them exists in masks sprouting vegetation which come from Roman sites in the Rhineland and at Rome itself. She added that the examples of these images in churches were from the beginning more demonic and menacing than those of the ancient Romans. In the thirteenth century the faces became more human,

FIGURE 8.4   The Green Man: deity, demon or metaphor?
a From a roof boss in the Lady Chapel of Ely Cathedral; *b* from a roof boss in
the Black Prince's Chantry, Canterbury Cathedral (unusual, in that the face
appears benign); *c* from a roof boss in the cloisters of Norwich Cathedral;
d from a roof boss at Sampford Courtenay parish church (Devon).

although still usually anguished or evil. But in the late Middle Ages,
when (like Wild Men but unlike Sheelas) they were much more abundant
than before, they reverted to being devilish again. She concluded that
they were surely representations of lost souls or wicked spirits, rather than
symbols of spring and of rebirth. It may be relevant that to some
medieval Christian authors, leaves were associated with sins of the flesh.[46]
Lady Raglan's original comparison with the foliage-covered figure who
danced in May Day processions was shattered in 1979 by Roy Judge, who

proved that this folk ritual had itself only appeared in the late eighteenth century.[47]

None of these images could have been a beloved pagan deity, placed in churches by popular demand. The context of this idea was destroyed with the collapse of the Murray thesis, but like that thesis it could hardly have been argued at all by anybody with a real knowledge of the Middle Ages. No churchman across the entire span of the period described them as such. St Bernard, in a passage most accessibly printed by Sheridan and Ross,[48] did inveigh against the burgeoning fashion for Romanesque sculpture at the beginning of the twelfth century: but his invective does not in fact prove the point suggested by these authors, for he condemned the images as grotesque, silly and expensive, not as pagan. There is abundant evidence, mostly from the fourteenth and fifteenth centuries, for the sort of people who paid the masons and commissioned the carvings. Occasionally the whole parish did so, but much more often those responsible were churchmen (above all bishops and abbots), landowners and wealthy merchants.[49] The central point of *The Witch Cult in Western Europe* was that ordinary people remained adherents of the 'Old Religion' while the ruling class was Christian. And it was that class which determined how churches were decorated. The Wild Man, Sheela-na-Gig and Green Man were all products of that tremendous upswelling of medieval culture which has commonly been called the Twelfth-Century Renaissance. And like the more famous later Renaissance it was a Christian movement, even though it drew upon ancient ideas and images.

Before disposing of the visual arts, one further representation needs to be considered. It occurs mostly in medieval rolls and carved ivories and shows a female figure suckling animals, with the name Terra, signifying (in Latin) the earth. There never was any popular Roman goddess with that name. Instead, medieval thinkers used the idea of Mother Earth just as Greek philosophers had used that of Gaia (from which Terra was almost certainly derived): as an abstraction, not as a being to be worshipped. As such, she could fit very easily into Christian discourse.

We now turn to forms of architecture which have been taken as 'pagan survivals', or to the sole one of these to have been identified in the British Isles. This is the maze, or labyrinth, which modern 'earth mystics' have celebrated as a very ancient structure which played a part in pre-Christian rites and which continued to be fashioned in the Middle Ages, perhaps as part of the continuation of those rites.[50] In dealing with this theory we are once again hampered by a lack of scholarly research. The best study of the subject is now old and was never more than a pioneering work.[51] What can be said with certainty is that the rectangular labyrinth first appears upon coins minted in Crete between 500 and 430 BC. It became the symbol of the island in that period, joined after 200 BC by the circular labyrinth. It may have been suggested by the ruins of the vast and complex Bronze Age palace at Knossos, and was certainly associated by the time of the coins with the myth of the hero Theseus who slew the half-human Minotaur within such a Cretan maze. Its only other certain appearance before the Christian era is upon an Etruscan vase from Tragliatella in Italy, which probably dates from somewhere in the same period as the coins. Here, however, the reference is not to Theseus but to the city of Troy (the name of which is scratched inside), and it is connected with horsemen, who are portrayed beside it. Roman literature makes the combination understandable: it consists of a game of skill for riders, who took their mounts around a labyrinthine pattern. This game was traditionally said to have been devised by the Trojans. The Cretan image spread to the coinage of states in nearby Asia Minor, and labyrinths of both shapes became a favourite motif of Roman art, often explicitly associated with the Theseus myth. They also appear in the pavements of a few eighth- to tenth-century Christian churches, again with references to Theseus and the Minotaur. These pavement mazes became common in French and Italian churches and cathedrals of the twelfth and thirteenth centuries, the fashion for them being part of Romanesque decoration. What is uncertain about these, as about Sheelas and Green Men, is their significance. During the nineteenth century it was suggested that people had to crawl through them as acts of penance, or that they symbolized the journey of the soul to heaven, or that they enabled the faithful to make token pilgrimages, by treading their winding ways with prayer. No real evidence exists to support or refute any of these theories.

There is no maze recorded in the British Isles which can certainly be said to have been in existence before the Romans arrived. We have already considered the putative one on Glastonbury Tor. Two carved upon the wall of Rocky Valley near Tintagel, Cornwall, have been called Bronze Age but may in fact be from any century up to the last one. Roman mosaic labyrinths have been found at Caerleon in Gwent and Harpham in Humberside, and high medieval examples survive carved upon the stonework or laid in the floors of six churches, in Essex, Cornwall, Cambridgeshire, Leicestershire, Humberside and Bristol, and in Ely Cathedral. All these may be regarded as outliers of the Continental traditions described above, but England has in addition a form of its own, the labyrinth cut in turf. These are recorded from Kent to Cumberland, but they are or were concentrated in Yorkshire and the east midlands, where four still exist. All which can be dated were made in the period 1500–1800, when they were carved by local landowners or by villagers acting upon their own initiative. Their purpose at that time was for sport, as every extant source makes clear: they are relics of 'Merrie England'.[52] The association with games is reinforced by the fact that their names commonly incorporated those of Troy and Julian (for example Troy Town and Julian's Bower). One of the most often quoted Latin texts of the Middle Ages and early modern period was Virgil's *Aeneid*. It includes a passage in which Trojan youths perform the trick mentioned above, of threading their way through a labyrinth on horseback. The relationship of the English turf mazes to this story seems to be virtually proved by the fact that the leader of the youths concerned was called Julus. Statements by modern writers of 'earth mysteries' texts, that these Tudor and Stuart structures might have been re-cuttings of older monuments, are at present utterly unsupported by evidence. Nor can we establish any date for the remaining labyrinths in the British Isles which do not fall into the previous categories, such as those chalked upon the walls of a quarry in Surrey, that formed of pebbles on one of the Isles of Scilly and that carved upon a stone in the Wicklow Mountains and now in the National Museum of Ireland. None of them has at present any obvious connection to the subject of this book.

So we come to motifs and characters which appear in the medieval literature of these islands. Most of those drawn from pagan antiquity, as said above, may be considered part of the general cultural heritage of European civilization and have no relevance to the question of surviving religions. But there are a few which, for differing reasons, are of special interest. One is the Holy Grail, which features in high medieval romances as the cup which was used at the Last Supper, the chalice of the first Christian communion. In these stories, it is often accompanied by the lance which pierced the side of Christ upon the cross. Both were held to exist within an enchanted Christian Otherworld, and to be made visible to mortals only under special circumstances, for example after the display of extraordinary merit. Until the late nineteenth century all this was presumed to be part, indeed the finest distillation, of the imagination of medieval Christendom. But between 1860 and 1920 a number of writers competed with each other to claim an origin for the concept in non-Christian sources. Alfred Nutt and A. C. L. Brown claimed that it descended from Celtic religion, the Grail from the cauldron of the Daghda and the lance from the spear of Lugh. Jesse Weston, a pupil of

Dr Nutt, and W. A. Nitze preferred the belief that it was a memory of a pagan Roman mystery tradition, while Paul Hagen suggested that it embodied mystical philosophies brought from the Orient. All except the last of these proposals have relevance to the preoccupations of this chapter. The problem with the 'Celtic' explanation is that the objects do not match. Spear and lance may be good counterparts, but the Grail, usually a goblet or platter carried by a single maiden, does not correspond very well to the huge inexhaustible cauldron filled with food which was kept by the Daghda. The 'Roman' explanation has the greater problem that, like an Indian magician's rope, it floats upon empty air. There is absolutely no equivalent to the Holy Grail and lance in classical art or literature, and the proponents of the mystery religion thesis were arguing purely from what they felt to be likely, given an utter lack of evidence, employing abstracted themes of death and resurrection and of presumed male and female symbolism.

On the other hand, none of the authors who proposed a Christian origin for these motifs came any closer to substantiating their arguments. Writing in the same years as the proponents of the theories listed above, Richard Heinzel, Wolfgang Golther, W. W. Newell and Rose Peebles all tried to reassert the idea that the Grail legend was wholly part of the Christian tradition. They failed either to trace its evolution from earlier writings of that faith, or to explain why it suddenly became immensely popular in the short period from 1170 to 1200. The plain fact is that although the authors of the earliest known examples of the Grail legend did refer to previous authorities, none of the latter has survived. Given the medieval tendency to forgery, fabrication and citation of fictional predecessors, we cannot be sure that they ever existed. But scholarly interest in the matter was satisfied by the publication in 1917 of Lizette Andrews Fisher's splendid study. This did account for the timing of the legend by documenting the tremendous new emphasis upon the doctrine of transubstantiation in late twelfth-century western Christendom. As the greatest of all communion chalices, the Grail was the literary embodiment of this preoccupation, and the accompanying stress upon the power of the Holy Blood also directed attention to the lance which had shed it. Thus the stories woven around both can most convincingly be seen as part of high medieval Christian culture, whether or not the Celtic theme of the nourishing and inspiring cauldron played any role in it. That idea remains a remote possibility, but the Fisher thesis stands up without it.[53] The concept of the Holy Grail has recently been the subject of reinterpretations by modern pagans which make beautiful and evocative reading but add nothing to our knowledge of its history.[54] It can safely be left out of any consideration of the ancient religions of these islands.

A quite different problem of possible pagan survivals in literature concerns certain high medieval Welsh poems which have been taken at times for evidence of pre-Christian Celtic beliefs. The most heavily used (or abused) of these are among the fifty-eight contained in a manuscript compiled around 1275 and known as *Canu Taliesin*, the Book (more properly the Song) of Taliesin. During the eighteenth-century revival of interest in Welsh culture, and passion for things 'Druidic', these suffered especially badly from the 'pseudo-Celticists'. Between 1784 and 1838 Edward Williams, Owen Pughe, the Revd Edward Davies and the Hon. Algernon Herbert all mistranslated them to suit their own theories of 'primitive religion'. Williams and Pughe went further by adding texts of their own composition. Those of the former did exceptional damage because they were innocently printed by Lady Charlotte Guest in 1849 as part of her edition of medieval Welsh tales translated into English, already mentioned: *The Mabinogion*. There they were read and believed by an enormous number of people, including Robert Graves who reinterpreted them in *The White Goddess* and so built a fantasy upon a forgery. The error of Lady Charlotte was especially unfortunate in that during the same year in which *The Mabinogion* appeared, Thomas Stephens published the first critical analysis of the *Canu* and suggested that some of its contents were twelfth-century instead of all dating from the dawn of Welsh letters as had been assumed. In 1858 D. W. Nash proposed that they might all be high medieval and in 1868 William F. Skene produced the first accurate edition and translation. During the 1940s Sir Ifor Williams subjected the *Canu* to further analysis and demonstrated that the poems are of various different ages and traditions. Twelve out of the fifty-eight he considered to belong to the sixth century and the original Taliesin, while all the so-called mystical poems seemed to be considerably later. In 1960 he published the definitive edition of the *Canu*, but like the patriot he was, he did so only in Welsh and so failed to put his achievement at the disposal of English readers. All that subsequent scholarship has done to alter his judgements is to suggest that even the so-called original poems may be no earlier than the ninth century and that Taliesin himself may never have existed.[55] Meanwhile, non-academic writers upon 'the Celtic mysteries' continue to interpret the 'mystical' poems of the volume as fragments of very ancient religious experience, with the same gusto as their spiritual predecessors two centuries before.[56]

So what are these poems? The most famous is probably *Golychaf Wledic*

Pendevic Gúlat Ri ('I Shall Praise the Sovereign'), known popularly in modern times as *Preiddeu Annwfn*, the Spoils of Annwn. It boasts of the worthiness of the narrator, extols Christianity but sneers at monks and refers to, rather than describes, seven journeys to, or attacks upon, fortresses which seem to exist in a magical Otherworld. Then there is *Kat Godeu* ('The Battle of Godeu'), which opens with the narrator describing how he has lived many lives and taken many forms. It goes on to speak of a real battle, but this turns into a contest between different species of tree and shrub. The boast of having known many things and taken many shapes is also made at the end of *Torrit Anuyndaúl* ('It Broke Out Vehemently'), which extols a fiery deity and mentions many legendary steeds. It is also the main subject matter of *Bard Yman* ('A Bard is Here'), in which the narrator identifies himself as Taliesin. *Gúaút Lud Y Maúr* ('The Praise of Great Lud') is a poem of prophecy, telling of devastation and glory and the blessing of the land by the eating of the Speckled Cow. Another prophetic composition is *Daronwy*, in which feature a magic wand and two iron-winged ladies. *Kadeir Teyrnon* ('The Chair of the Leader') mentions three mysterious fortresses and The Giant Wall. All these poems are in the same obscure, allusive style and slide from fact to fantasy in the same way; most contain passages of great beauty. Nobody in the modern world can prove what any of them means, which is (of course) the source of their attraction for theorists and also the reason why the pseudo-Celticists had to ignore or invent whole passages in order to impose their interpretations. The poems are mysterious in two senses. First, they deal in prophecy, fantastic imagery and supernatural themes. Second, they constantly refer to places, characters and incidents without explanation or identification, on the assumption that their audience is well acquainted with them. In some cases the modern reader actually can be, such as those of Arthur and characters from the Triads and from the eleventh-century compilation known as 'the branches of the Mabinogi'. Wherever identifiable, the allusions are almost all drawn from Welsh literature composed between 900 and 1080. There are also a few Biblical references: *Daronwy* appears to speak of the Five Monarchies foretold in the Book of Daniel, and much of the tone and imagery of this poem, and some others, may be influenced by the Book of Revelation. But a great many of the allusions are to previous works which vanished long ago. This is the principal reason why we cannot understand these compositions.

But in another sense their context would appear to be perfectly plain. In the type of Welsh which they use, the known subjects to which they refer and the tone which they adopt, they belong almost beyond question to one distinctive period in the history of Welsh letters. This is the age of the Gogynfeirdd, or 'fairly early poets', which lasted from about 1080 to about 1350.[57] It commenced as a large-scale, self-conscious national revival in response to the Norman invasions, and was the work of a closely knit literary class, the bards, who took great pride in their superiority over ordinary poets. The symbol of this was the chair in which they were installed when they were recognized as masters. They placed heavy emphasis upon the powers of inspiration on which they drew, crediting themselves with the ability to divine the future and to infuse patrons with the capacity for heroic achievements. Thoroughly and devoutly Christian, they drew upon a wide variety of literary sources, including Irish, Greek and Roman texts or tales, and the Scriptures. But most of all they harked back to the Welsh writers of the early Middle Ages, although they had difficulty in understanding them. Modern textual analysis has revealed that the Welsh authors of the thirteenth century had already ceased fully to comprehend the language in which ninth-century texts were composed;[58] and those of the ninth century had only the haziest idea of the history and culture of their people a couple of hundred years before.[59]

For the purposes of this book, what is fascinating about the Gogynfeirdd is that they seem actually to have created a new mythology, instead of merely working with characters from pagan legend. They did this by elevating human or semi-human characters to the status of deities. There are three examples of this process: Ceridwen, Gwyn ap Nudd and Arianrhod. Ceridwen, Kerritwen, Cyridwen or Cyrridwen first appears in the tale *Hanes Taliesin* which, although only extant in a sixteenth-century text, would appear from its language to have been composed in the ninth century.[60] She features as a mother skilled in sorcery who brews a cauldron intended to confer the gift of inspiration upon her son. Accidentally, the magic of it passes into her servant Taliesin, whom she then pursues through a series of changes of shape and finally swallows, only to give birth to him afresh as a marvellously gifted child. The elements of this story – the marvellous child, the person who is swallowed and then reborn, the accidental tasting of a dish which confers great gifts – are found in others all over Europe and Asia: there is nothing especially Welsh about any of them. Ceridwen does not appear in any other early literature, and her name suggests that she was created for this tale alone: it means 'crooked woman', which would suit well the personality of a witch or a sorceress. But her function as the creatrix of a cauldron which conferred inspiration very much appealed to the Gogynfeirdd, who prized this quality above all, and they turned her into a sort of Muse. Cynddelw Brydydd Mawr (d. 1200) could write 'How mysterious are the ways of Ceridwen.' Llywarch ap Llywelyn (d. 1220) asked 'for inspiration from the cauldron of Ceridwen' and hailed her as 'the ruler of Bardism'. The poem *Kadair Kerritwen* ('The Chair of Ceridwen'), in *Canu Taliesin*, speaks of her chair, her cauldron and her laws. *Deus Ren Rimawy Awen* ('God Supreme be Mine the Evening Prayer'), from the Black Book of Carmarthen, calls her 'the goddess of various seeds, the various seeds of poetic harmony, the exalted words of the master bard'. The modern 'pseudo-Celticists' further inflated her status to that of a pre-Christian deity, which she fairly clearly was not.

Gwyn ap Nudd appears in *Culhwch and Olwen*, which is apparently tenth-century, as a warrior of King Arthur. The poem *Taru Trin Anuidin Blaut* ('A Bull Of Battle Was He'), from the Black Book, is probably twelfth-century, and refers to him as a great fighter. But in the Life of St Collen, which is a text composed in either that or (more probably) the next century, he has become divine ruler of an underworld entered through Glastonbury Tor. And by the early fourteenth century he has grown into the pre-eminent spirit of darkness, enchantment and deception. As such he features in two of the poems of Dafydd ap Gwilym. In *Y Dyllvan* ('The Owl'), that bird is his favourite and he sports in marshes, while *Y Niwl* ('The Mist') is conjured up by him. Arianrhod appears in *Math, Son of Mathonwy*, which took its present form in the late eleventh century, as a powerful, beautiful and selfish queen or noblewoman capable of working unbreakable curses. Her talent for enchantment was later inflated, so that in *Kadair Kerritwen* she is both 'the greatest disgrace of the Britons' and 'of splendid appearance, dawn of serenity', capable of casting a rainbow about a court to protect it. One of the constellations of the sky became named 'Castle of Arianrhod' after her residence in *Math*. She had grown into one of the great sorceresses of medieval legend, an equivalent to Morgana le Fay and Melusine in the English and French literature. Along with her, Ceridwen and Gwyn, the high medieval Welsh writings contain mention of one more character invested with apparent supernatural qualities, the mysterious Hu. He does not seem to appear at all before the age of the Gogynfeirdd, to some of whom he was a patron of Britain. In *Canu Taliesin's Echyris Ynys Guaut Hu Ynys* ('Disturbed is the Isle with the Praise of Hu'), he is 'the severe ruler'. Cynddelw identified him with Jesus, and they may, indeed, have been the same, the name deriving from 'Jesu'. Sion Kent (d. 1420), referring to the 'men of Hu' as making 'false and vile predictions', may have been speaking either of the Welsh or of clerics.

The Gogynfeirdd inherited one very important supernatural concept intact: that of Annwn or the Otherworld. It is the almost precise equivalent of the enchanted realm of the Irish tales, being located beneath the earth and in contact with the mortal realm through concealed doors. The difference is only that in the Welsh literature its threatening aspects are stressed more than its delights: it performs the same function in the stories as the magical forests of the French, English and German romances. From the tale of Pwyll, which took its final form in the late eleventh century, to the poems of Dafydd ap Gwilym 300 years later, its brooding presence remains constant. With it, this brief consideration of the work of the high medieval bards may be concluded.[61] Their texts call for much more research, of the same fine quality as that recently carried out upon earlier Welsh literature. But on present evidence it still seems reasonable to suggest that they can be credited with protraying divine or semi-divine beings who were unknown to their Christian predecessors. As it does not seem that they had access to any more texts or traditions than those older writers, it is proposed here that they invented these beings themselves: in which case, the supernatural figures of the Gogynfeirdd are of no interest to the student of pre-Christian beliefs.

From all the above, it may be concluded that the official conversion of the British Isles to Christianity left no surviving pre-Christian religions, either in remote areas or as 'underground' movements. In that sense the victory of the new faith was born relatively swift and absolute. But, as has always been recognized, paganism did bequeath an enormous legacy of superstitions, literary and artistic images and folk rituals to the culture of later ages. We now need to look in detail at these folk rituals, and to ask a question which reverses the sequence considered in the earlier part of this chapter: how far can we reconstruct the rites and ideologies of ancient religions by studying the ceremonies and beliefs embodied in the folklore of Christian Europe? Here at once we encounter three interrelated problems: the lack of sustained co-operation between historians and folklorists, the nature of the evidence and the lack of caution with which this question has been approached by earlier scholars. The first of these is in part a reflection of the tendency of academic historians – until the last twenty years – to devalue the consideration of social topics in general, and that of popular belief in particular. Although the balance has been redressed by an enormous quantity of recent research, a great deal more is needed, together with rigorous examination of the ideas already propounded. Folklorists, for their part, have too often been enthusiastic amateurs with very little sense of the difficulties inherent in the material with which they are working. They have very commonly tended to view popular culture as a static and timeless entity, have made insufficient effort to relate customs to changing contexts and have interpreted data in accordance with prevailing theories and attitudes which are not tested by any demonstrable facts. These criticisms, of course, do not do justice to some practitioners of the subject, notably to Kathleen Briggs and some of her pupils and to the authors of texts within the Folkore Society's Mistletoe Series. But interaction between the two disciplines remains limited, and the study of folklore is still not entirely respectable within universities, where it tends to feature as a rather eccentric interest of individual members of history or English departments.

The problems presented by the data have already been suggested in chapter 5. The main one is that the vast majority of popular beliefs and practices were recorded for the first time only after 1750, so that we have little idea of their actual antiquity. Even for those that can be documented back to the Middle Ages, their significance is frequently difficult to demonstrate. Like the Romans at the Lupercalia, communities have often engaged in activities which had become meaningless to the performers by the time that they emerged into history. Recent work has tended to stress the eclectic, inventive and reactive nature of popular culture and the unreliability of oral tradition.[62] Discussion earlier in this book of the Rillaton legend and early Welsh and Irish literature has indicated some of the traps set in this field for the unwary. In traditional cultures the notion of time is generally very hazy and can mislead a careless researcher. In 1565 the villagers of Mere in Wiltshire instituted an arrangement whereby a Cuckoo King presided over the annual parish feast, with a Prince to assist him who became the next year's 'monarch'. This lapsed in 1573 and was revived in 1576. In 1577 it was described as performed according to 'old custom'. Thus twelve years and nine performances could be sufficient to give a ritual the reputation of antiquity in Elizabethan England.[63] Many of the 'ancient' practices and pieces of lore recorded by nineteenth-century scholars may have been comparatively recent inventions.

As for careless and over-schematic interpretations, the most damaging and the most magnificent were made by the person whom many consider to have been the British founder of the science of anthropology, Sir James Frazer. This shy and gentle Scot was in a very literal sense one of the most academic of writers, for he spent almost his whole professional career in the vicinity of his rooms at Trinity College, Cambridge. From the libraries and bookshops of that university and of London, he obtained huge numbers of ancient, medieval and early modern texts, of contemporary collections of European folklore, and of reports upon tribal peoples in the non-European world which was being explored and conquered in his lifetime. All this information he pressed into the service of a passionate personal quest: to demonstrate that Christianity rested upon the same principles as other early and primitive religions, and that therefore it deserved to be treated with the same objectivity, and ultimately with the same contempt. The results were the three successive multi-volume editions of *The Golden Bough*, published between 1890 and 1915, followed by the single-volume digest of 1922.[64] The centre-point of these was the theory that behind the myth of the Crucifixion and Resurrection lay a universal ancient tradition of a sacred king who reigned over his people for a set term and was then sacrificed for the good of the realm, to be replaced by another as part of a rite of renewal. But along with this he either produced or popularized several other concepts within the study of pre- or non-Christian beliefs, such as taboo, the scapegoat, the sequence of old European fire festivals, and the impression that the whole concern of ancient paganism was with fertility. The book, in all its various forms, remains a marvellous compendium of human ritual activity. Some of its author's ideas, such as those regarding taboo and the scapegoat, still stand up relatively well today. Others were only a more sophisticated version of orthodoxies of his own day, such as his Corn Mother who is an incarnation of the prehistoric Great Goddess. He cannot reasonably be blamed for working with them. Nor can he be held responsible for the further development of his ideas by later writers. It was Robert Graves, not Frazer, who turned the Corn Maiden and Mother into the Triple Goddess, and published Sir James's theory concerning the Crucifixion in a very crude form in his novel *King Jesus*. It was some modern pagans who imposed upon his set of 'fire festivals' a schematization which ignored the facts in a way of which Frazer was never guilty.

But it must be added that *The Golden Bough* itself had very serious flaws. At this distance in time, and in view of its fame, it is important to note that it was *never* accepted by most historians and theologians, the specialists in its field. As soon as the first edition appeared its weaknesses were demonstrated, effectively, by colleagues such as Andrew Lang. Frazer, as has already been stated, had piled together material from all over the world and all ages, ignoring contexts and discrepancies alike. It was also striking that he had not been able to produce a single actual example of a monarch being slain and replaced in the way in which he held to be universal. Frazer's response to his critics was to republish the whole work with even more data, including, at last, one account of sacred kingship of the sort which he had postulated, from a tribe in the Sudan. But this was not, and is not, enough to support his theory, and his further accumulation of evidence was unavailing when he treated it all in the same unsatisfactory manner as before. To an extent Sir James admitted defeat when, in his third edition, he called off the attack upon Christianity which had inspired the whole work. But he left all his other stereotypes standing.

So, if *The Golden Bough* did not convince fellow scholars in the author's field, how did it become a classic? The answer is that it appealed to two other groups. One consisted of the practitioners of the new science with which his name is now especially associated: anthropology, the study of those whom he termed 'savages'. But the anthropologists swiftly adopted three rules above all which Frazer always broke: meticulous personal fieldwork; due regard to the context of each observation; and the avoidance of a patronizing and omniscient attitude towards tribal peoples. No professional anthropologist now accepts most of Frazer's arguments, or his approach. But he made an enduring impact also upon another group, which consisted quite simply of the general public. To anybody not expert in the field concerned, *The Golden Bough* could appear convincing as well as entertaining. Margaret Murray and Robert Graves have been mentioned as devotees, and reflections of Frazer's portrait of ancient paganism can be found in a plethora of works of fiction and amateur folklore published up to the present day.

What, then, can be done to answer the original question, of the detection of pre-Christian belief and ceremony in later popular culture? A few customs can confidently be traced in this way. One, the kindling of sacred bonfires and the driving of livestock between or around them, was dealt with in chapter 5 on the Celts. Another, the rolling of a burning wheel downhill to symbolize the motion of the sun, was recorded in fourth-century Gaul, the charred pieces being placed in a temple to Apollo. Wheels (usually blazing) featured in midsummer eve celebrations all over Europe in the nineteenth century.[65] The one which right up to the 1950s was pushed down Mam Tor by the villagers of Leudon, Devon, was probably the last appearance in Britain of the symbol which had been carved and forged since the early Bronze Age. Yet another tradition was mentioned in the famous letter from Gregory to Mellitus: the decking of Anglo-Saxon temples with garlands and making of bowers around them. This is also known from descriptions of Greek and Roman festivals, and was continued in the decoration of churches with greenery so evident in the late medieval and early modern churchwardens' accounts. The seasonal choices there are quite clear: holly and ivy at Christmas, birch at Midsummer, flowers at various spring and early summer feasts. The stringing of leaves and blooms all over Europe on May Morning or St George's Day reflects the same custom, although there is no proof as yet that the maypole was not a medieval invention. Across the northern part of the Continent there was also a tradition of dances or plays which involved the stylized killing and resurrection of one of the participants. Although Sir James Frazer was wrong in declaring confidently that these commemorated the actual killing of a ruler, they do seem to have embodied a very widespread prehistoric concern with the theme of death and rebirth and its enactment in ritual.

The British equivalents of this drama are the northern Sword Dance and the southern Mummers' Play, and the latter shows especially well how much of an accretion of characters and ideas folk rituals can be.[66] Performances of such a play have now been recorded from 824 different English communities, but the earliest definite one dates from the 1730s. The characters and topical references of the known texts are taken from a period spanning the years 1600–1815, and the basic cast seem to be derivatives of *The Seven Champions of Christendom*, published in 1596. A few ingredients existed in a civic pageant staged in London in the 1550s, but beyond that the various sources for entertainments of all kinds (which are quite copious back to the fourteenth century) contain no trace of this sort of play. But the centrepiece of the action, a combat between champions in which one is killed and then revived, is an enactment of a theme so common and widespread that it must be archaic. And the Mummers include a genuinely ancient character, known usually as Beelzebub but sometimes as Humping Jack or Happy Jack. He takes very little part in the action and his main function is to introduce himself and his equipment, which consists of a club and a pan. What we have here is, apparently, that deity known in Ireland as the Daghda and in Gaul as Sucellus, who was always represented carrying this weapon and a vessel. His image is also carved upon the west wall of the medieval church at Copgrove in Yorkshire. But, as mentioned in previous chapters, there is no indication that this god was, or these gods were, popular in Britain. It would be fascinating to know by what route of tale-telling or of artistic transmission such a personality came to feature so prominently in southern England.

Two other enduring characters of folk ritual were condemned in one version of the penitential attributed to Theodore, Archbishop of Canterbury, and composed at some time around the year 700: 'To those who go about at the Kalends of January garbed as a stag or an old woman, taking the form of beasts, clad in the skins of beasts and assuming the heads of beasts; who transform themselves into animals, three years penance, for the thing is devilish.' St Aldhelm, who died in 685, also expressed horror at the wearing of animal costumes (especially of stags) by revellers. Both the disguises mentioned in the penitential were also the target of Continental churchmen, a cryptic example being in the *Vita Sancti Eligii*, which proclaims 'Let nobody on the Kalends of January make abominable and ridiculous things – old women, or stags, or games'.[67] All these complaints were unavailing. Animal masks continued to take many ritual forms up till the modern period. There was the hobby horse, so popular in Tudor entertainments. There were the horses' skulls or images carried around York, Derbyshire and Lancashire up to the present century, and which still feature in midwinter customs in Kent and Glamorgan. And there are the stags' antlers borne in the Horn Dance, performed to this day at Abbots Bromley in Staffordshire and once, also, a midwinter rite. As for the 'old woman', a man dressed as one was still an essential part of the cast of many Mummers' Plays, May Games, morris dances and the Horn Dance in the early modern and modern periods. Like Beelzebub, 'she' had no necessary part in the action and generally just looked on, but was for some forgotten reason considered to be a necessary component of the custom. Perhaps 'she' was once a patronal goddess, as the animal costumes may have represented deities or spirits. But it must also be borne in mind that in the classical ancient world, to don masks or the clothing of the opposite sex was a sign of festival, of the relaxation of normal rules and boundaries and of merrymaking.[68] The stag and the hag may have been symbols of revelry rather than incarnations of the divine, although both were certainly features of pagan celebration.

Other aspects of the defunct religions were absorbed into folk customs. A major one was sacrifice, which, as shown above, became part of the world of superstition and magic. It also got incorporated into Christian rites in certain remote areas: oxen were killed in honour of St Benyo at Clynnog Fawr in Gwynedd until 1589 and to St Maelrubha in Wester Ross until 1678. Both traditions then encountered reforming churchmen and were suppressed, having survived centuries of other Christian masters who apparently regarded the practice as acceptable.[69] But the concept of sacrifice was also embodied in popular ritual. One of the most blatant translations of an offering to a pagan deity persisted on the Isle of Lewis in the Outer Hebrides until the mid-seventeenth century. At Hallowe'en fishermen would go down to the shore, kneel at the edge of the waves and repeat the Christian Paternoster. One of them then waded in up to his waist, poured out a bowl of ale and asked a mysterious being called Shoney (Johnny) for a good catch over the next year. Then they went to St Malvey's chapel and sat in silence for a while before making merry in the fields for the rest of the night.[70] Folk traditions also reveal something of an apparent progressive debasement in people's minds of the Celtic tutelary goddesses. In the early medieval Irish Metrical Dinnshenchas they are still regarded as benevolent and protective, figures upon whom local loyalty was focused. The Scottish chiefly family of MacDougall of Dunollie possessed until modern times a belief that it had a divine female patron which even washed its linen. But the folklore collections made in Celtic lands during the past two centuries show landscapes populated with horrific female spectres who prey upon humans or who are harbingers of death. Like the tutelary goddesses they are especially associated with hills and bodies of water, but their aspect is far more that of the terrifying female deities of war. The Irish *ban-sidhe* and *lian-sidhe*, the Welsh *cyhiraeth* and *gwrach y rhibyn* and the Highland Scottish *glaistig*, *bean-nighe*, *vow*, *cannachan* and *muireartach* are all of this kind.[71] Northern English traditions of monsters such as Jenny Greenteeth and Peg Powler, who live in rivers and drown small children, are ghastly reincarnations of figures such as Verbeia and Coventina. They are all a vivid demonstration of the truth that deposed deities can very effectively be transformed into demons.

This concludes what can briefly be said, at present, about the fate of the pre-Christian faiths of these islands. But it has been claimed by several recent writers that those faiths survived in secret until the present century, when changing attitudes enabled them to re-emerge. Certainly a system of religion calling itself paganism has become one of the fastest-growing (perhaps the fastest-growing) in Britain today. Its adherents are numbered at the least in thousands and at the most in tens of thousands, and regard themselves as having a direct relationship with the cults which preceded Christianity. Their publications are now numerous enough for the (literally) uninitiated to form a good impression of their beliefs and practices.[72] Virtually all are products of that particular section of the movement called Wicca, but this does seem to be the original and by far the most influential part of the modern faith. In view of the claims of some of its members it would appear to be a worthwhile exercise to conclude this book with an overview of what is known of the inception of modern British paganism and of how it compares with that of the ancient world.

The public history of Wicca begins with the repeal of the Witchcraft Act of 1736, legally known as 9 Geo II, cap. 5. This was not the survivor of the murderous statutes of the early modern period but their very antithesis, a heavy-handed piece of Enlightenment rationalism. Its fundamental principle was that witchcraft and magic did not exist, and that belief in them was part of a childish and more barbaric age. It therefore forbade anybody to accuse another person of practising either, and prescribed a maximum of a year's imprisonment for anyone who *claimed* to practise either. Henceforth people were in no danger of being hauled into court because their enemies suspected them of witchcraft, and in theory nobody could suffer for engaging in it in private. But any self-styled witch, magician or fortune-teller who advertised her or his craft was vulnerable to prosecution. How severely the Act was enforced against such people may be doubted. Village 'cunning men' and 'wise women' are recorded as operating freely in many places during the nineteenth century. The *Conjuror's Magazine*, which commenced publication in 1791, was the first of a string of periodicals in which individuals and groups advertised themselves openly as workers of magic and divination. But until its last decade, the Act did result in a steady trickle of suits, mostly lodged by dissatisfied customers. In June 1951 it was replaced by 14 Geo VI, cap. 33, the Fraudulent Mediums Act, which reduced the scope and penalty of the law to a maximum fine of £50 for those who set out deliberately to deceive clients who sought magical or spiritual remedies. The record of the debates upon the alteration, printed in *Hansard*, made it plain that the step was taken in order to grant toleration to the spiritualist churches. It was supported by MPs of all parties and several religions, as a further move towards full liberty of belief, and opposed by none.

The measure created greater public interest in the whole subject of witchcraft and magic. Margaret Murray, as we have seen, took advantage of this with one fresh publication and one reprint, and in 1954 she contributed an approving preface to a book called *Witchcraft Today*, by Gerald Broisseau Gardner. The reason for her approval was quite obvious: the work claimed to furnish further proof of her theory about the survival of the Old Religion by stating that it had not been destroyed during the Great Witch Hunt but had gone into hiding and persisted there in secret until the present day, when it at last felt able to declare its continued existence. The author was a man of seventy years, who had spent most of his life outside England as a colonial civil servant. During that service he became involved with a range of occult practices, including native Malay rituals and spiritualist mediums, and after his retirement to England in 1936 he made contact with groups who worked with magic. One was a Rosicrucian organization, another the Ordo Templi Orientis which was led by the famous (or notorious) ceremonial magician Aleister Crowley. In 1941 Dr[73] Gardner published a novel, *A Goddess Arrives*, set in archaic Cyprus and extolling the glories of ancient paganism and of Woman. Another novel followed in 1949, *High Magic's Aid*, in which the view of history and the set of rituals portrayed in *Witchcraft Today* and his unpublished Book of Shadows appear fully fledged. Thus it would appear that he adopted his system of religion in the 1940s. That he did not do so in isolation is indicated by very slight evidence of a group of people who met in the New Forest around 1940 and styled themselves witches, with whom he was in contact.[74] In the 1970s an individual styling himself 'Lugh' contributed five pieces to the periodicals *The Wiccan* and *The Cauldron*, claiming that this 'coven' was one of several founded by George Pickingill of Canewdon in Essex, one of the last of the old-fashioned village 'cunning men'. 'Lugh' made the further claim that Pickingill, who died in 1909, was a hereditary witch and had made his occult knowledge available to the founders of the celebrated nineteenth-century association of magicians, The Hermetic Order of the Golden Dawn.[75] If any evidence to support these assertions had been produced, then a significant contribution to the history of religion would have been made. But it never was, and in default of it a problem remains, which is that George Pickingill's name was made familiar to the general public by means of his prominence in Eric Maple's bestseller, *The Dark World of Witches*, which appeared in 1962. This book established him as one of the best known of the old-style village magicians. Mr Maple himself was not aware that he was anything more, and others (including myself) who have talked to people who remembered Pickingill have found no indications that he claimed a pedigree, founded covens, dealt in high ritual magic or mixed with the London occultists. Unless the proof in question can be furnished, it must be suspected that 'Lugh' was attempting to invent a past for his own faith. In its absence, the only solid evidence for the origins of Wicca consists of the works of Gerald Gardner himself.

These amply bear out the statements of his friends, that he was a person of great charm and of insight into human nature. Another claim by those who admired him, that he was greatly learned, can only be admitted with some reservations. His writings show a considerable knowledge of what had been printed about witchcraft and magic during his lifetime, but a very hazy grasp of history and a lack of any sustained research into older texts. His view of early thirteenth-century England, laid out in *High Magic's Aid*, was apparently based upon a cross between *The Witch Cult in Western Europe* and *Ivanhoe*, and represents a vision of the past even more wildly inaccurate than either. It has Margaret Murray's view of the persecution of paganism as witchcraft, but shows it in full progress some 400 years too early, at a time when Dr Murray herself recognized that there was no sign of witch-hunting. It has Sir Walter Scott's (erroneous) idea that England around 1200 was still bitterly divided between Norman and Saxon, and the language, descriptions and characterization also sound remarkably like Scott's. Garner's exposition of the traditional rituals of the witch religion and of its history, revealed in this book and in his later works, seems to have drawn upon two very different sources. One, unsurprisingly, consisted of the magical practices of the Ordo Templi Orientis and of the Golden Dawn, from which this order was descended. Most of these were put together, in turn, by G. S. L. Mathers, who drew upon the teachings of 'Eliphas Levi' (mentioned earlier), upon medieval grimoires (handbooks of magic) which Mathers published and which Gardner also used directly (as he said in *High Magic's Aid*), upon Masonic practice and upon Mather's own imagination. For higher authority Mathers and his associates appealed to a mysterious and probably non-existent German branch of the original Rosicrucian Order (which was itself probably nothing more than a legend). Interestingly, none of them in either public or private writings, ever buttressed their claims by reference to George Pickingill and the illustrious descent claimed for him by 'Lugh'. From these rituals came the bound and blindfolded initiation; the symbolic scourging; the ceremonial focus of a circle containing an altar; the use of pentagrams and triangles; the invocation and banishment of spirits; the appeal to the guardians of the four cardinal points of the compass; the use of incense and water; the notion that divine forces are drawn into one or more of the celebrants; and the impedimenta of a sword and two knives, one black- and one white-handled.[76]

Gardner's second source, from which he drew the context of these rites, appears to have been the work of those modern authors who had proclaimed the continued existence of ancient paganism as a witch cult through the Middle Ages. From Margaret Murray he adopted the term the 'Old Religion', the Horned God and the Goddess, the organization of covens, the idea that this religion had essentially been concerned with fertility, and the celebration of the four Gaelic quarter days as festivals. From Leland he took the idea that witches carried out their rituals naked, and arguably the idea that the cult had survived in secret. From English folk customs were drawn the term for marriage within this faith, 'handfasting', and certain rites such as the leaping of fires. As the key text of the ceremonies, Gardner and his group(s) presented the 'Book of Shadows', which remained unpublished in his lifetime but has appeared in various forms since.[77] This he is said to have claimed to be sixteenth-century, whereas in fact it is recognizably a mid-twentieth-century compilation drawing upon a remarkable range of sources, including the grimoires, Leland, Crowley and a poem by Rudyard Kipling(!). The beings invoked include Hebrew demons from the medieval texts translated by Mathers, Egyptian deities from translated hieroglyphic inscriptions employed by the Golden Dawn, a few Graeco-Roman goddesses and gods, figures from Celtic mythology and medieval romance, and Leland's Aradia. Some of the Gardnerian practices may well have been original. For example, there seems to be no previous appearance of the five fold kiss upon initiation, though it may have existed among the rituals of Crowley's Ordo. And to the quarter days identified as major witch festivals by Margaret Murray, Gerald Gardner and his companions added the solstices and the equinoxes. They deserve credit for launching what is probably the most eclectic religion in the history of the world.

This religion proved to be a tremendous success, especially among people who were not already conversant with the sources from which it had been drawn.[78] It was apparently an immeasurably ancient system of native wisdom and worship. It gave equal emphasis to both genders, as deities, officiators and participants. It provided a context for the working of practical magic. It afforded a close relationship with the natural world and with the rhythm of the year. It joyously celebrated the pleasure principle and personal freedom. It provided the gratification of being initiated into a mystery cult meeting in private, and of ascending its grades through a process of training and experience. Yet it was also very inclusive, all members of a coven participating significantly in rituals. And because its instruments were very portable, its units were small and it required no special buildings, it could be taken up with ease and rapidity. Thus *Witchcraft Today* (and its sequel, *The Meaning of Witchcraft*) sold very well, and during the 1950s and 1960s covens on the Gardnerian model sprang up all over Britain and beyond, especially in the United States. After the death of Gardner himself in 1964, figures with a yet greater talent for publicity and education appeared within the tradition which he had founded. Some claimed to represent entirely independent covens, now likewise emerging from the secrecy into which they had been driven long ago, but even some of their admirers seem to recognize that this was most unlikely. The main development of the tradition itself in these two decades resulted from the impact of Robert Graves's *The White Goddess*, so that the female deity of the religion became the triple one, Maiden, Mother and Crone, of Graves's imaginary ancient world.[79]

How did the 'Wicca'[80] which was developed in these years actually compare with the paganism of antiquity? One fundamental difference is that it deliberately blurs the distinction between religion and magic, and that most of its practices are drawn from the latter. The vital significance of the consecrated circle, in the modern cult as in the medieval sorcery from which it is derived, is that spirits or forces are raised and gathered within it and the humans concerned work with them. It would have been inconceivable to any ancient European pagan of whose thought we have evidence, that the purpose of religious ritual was to 'raise' a deity and 'work' with her or him. No ancient goddess or god worth the name could be summoned by worshippers, to a particular place, and there employed. The modern emphasis is upon a series of techniques which confer benefit upon the celebrants or their objectives, the ancient one upon a set of ceremonies intended to give pleasure to, and therefore to earn reward from, divine beings. That is why the rites of the present-day witches or pagans are apparently totally lacking in the universal ancient principle of sacrifice. By assuming that witchcraft and paganism were formerly the same phenomenon, they are mixing two utterly different archaic concepts and placing themselves in a certain amount of difficulty. The advantage of the label 'witch' is that it has all the exciting connotations of a figure who flouts the conventions of normal society and is possessed of powers unavailable to it, at once feared and persecuted. It is a marvellous rallying-point for a counter-culture, and also one of the few images of independent female power in early modern European civilization. The disadvantage is that by identifying themselves with a very old stereotype of menace, derived from the pre-Christian world itself, modern pagans have drawn upon themselves a great deal of unnecessary suspicion, vituperation and victimization which they are perpetually struggling to assuage.

Another notable distinction between the 'Old Religion' and the old religions lies in the two presiding divine figures of the former, goddess and god. From the beginning Wiccans recognized that the ancient world worshipped an enormous number of deities of both genders. They incorporated a selection within their rituals, but made it plain that these were not individual beings but different names, and aspects, of the great couple. This is a vision very remote from the genuine polytheism of antiquity. Initiates of the 'mystery religions' regarded their presiding deities as the mightiest of all, and sometimes identified them with others of mighty reputation: but they did not thereby declare that these major figures were the only gods or goddesses. A few Neo-Platonist philosophers taught that all deities were manifestations of a single divine spirit, but this is a rather different concept from the 'duotheism' of today's pagans. That is part of a more general characteristic of their faith, summed up by two of their most prolific authors as 'the creative polarity of complementary opposites', such as 'male/female, light/dark, fertilising/formative, intelligence/intuition', or 'cyclical and linear, synthesizing and analytical, monolithic and mobile'.[81] This sort of dualism is not rooted in European antiquity: if it derives from any old tradition it is from that strain of Near Eastern thought found in Zoroastrianism, Manichaeanism and Christianity. In view of this it is ironically appropriate that another characteristic of the writings of contemporary British pagans consists of an intense and consistent hostility to the Christian Church. The follies and deficiences of this institution are regularly held up to ridicule and abuse. Such bitterness may be therapeutic for those who have recently rejected Christianity, and is natural in view of the conviction of modern pagans that the Church was directly responsible for the Great Witch Hunt with whose victims they identify. But anyone who is indifferent to the faith of Christ is likely to find the barrage of vilification tedious. It may also be wondered whether such a sustained attack upon what is still the most powerful religion in Britain does not provoke a proportionate dislike, and increase the tendency of people to mistake modern paganism or witchcraft for satanism and to harass its adherents. But then the positions of paganism and Christianity in England today are precisely the reverse of those found in antiquity: it is the former which is the brash newcomer religion, meeting in private and making ferocious public attacks upon the old, respectable, dominant faith which is built into the institutions of government. Like early Christianity, also, it is accused by some enemies of nefarious practices of which it is innocent, and has a problem of public relations. Pagans in the Roman Empire did, of course, write against the followers of Christ as well. But their complaints, which are preserved in the works of Julian, Porphyry, Minucius Felix, Tertullian, Tatius and the younger Pliny, were not the same as those voiced by people who call themselves pagans today. They condemned Christians for indulging in horrific rites (a slander), for treason, blasphemy and irreverence, and for provoking deities who might punish the whole community. They spoke, inevitably, as part of an establishment.

There are other differences between old and new. No known cult in the ancient world was carried on by devotees who all worshipped regularly in the nude like the witches portrayed by Leland and inspired by Gardner (although many present-day pagans prefer to have robed ceremonies). The enormous difference in the societies concerned has produced proportional changes of preoccupation: the concern of the archaic religions with glorifying rulership and war is understandably missing from the modern one. The anxiety to produce food and wealth has been replaced by an equally powerful one to preserve the natural environment which that process of production has now largely destroyed. And no known pre-Christian people celebrated all the eight festivals of the calendar adopted by Wicca. Around the four genuine Gaelic quarter days are now ranged the Midwinter and September feasts of the Anglo-Saxons, the Midsummer celebrations so prominent in folklore and (for symmetry) the vernal equinox, which does not seem to have been commemorated by any ancient northern Europeans. Nor do most members of the present cults have permanent temples or other sacred spaces, as the all-important circles can be created and removed at will, a concept familiar in magic but alien to the old religions. All told, the paganism of today has virtually nothing in common with that of the past except the name, which is itself of Christian coinage.[82] But if Wicca and its successors are viewed as a form of ritual magic, then they have a distinguished and very long pedigree, stretching back through the Ordo Templi Orientis and the Golden Dawn to Levi, the New Templars, the Rosicrucians and the Freemasons, and so beyond these to the early modern and medieval texts which derived by many stages from those of Hellenistic Egypt.

During the 1970s and 1980s, modern paganism became yet more eclectic. It did not expand and enrich its repertoire by a closer study of the past, but spread sideways to combine with other modern traditions.[83] From the 'earth mysteries' it took the idea of leys and of earth energies. From the upsurge of Celtic 'revivalism' came the teachings of *Barddas* (yet again), the retranslation of Margaret Murray's four 'witch festivals' into their Gaelic names, and a greater prominence for such figures as Ceridwen and Arianrhod. From native American traditions appeared totemic animals, spirit-quests, medicine wheels, sweat lodges and shamanic visions. From the religions of the east (mostly strains of modern Hinduism) came meditative techniques, mandalas, chakras and the Third Eye. The writings of the psychologist Carl Jung proved immensely influential, frequently being treated as a discovery of objective truth about the past rather than accurately as unproven hypotheses. His concepts of synchronicity, archetypes, the shadow and the collective unconscious were especially useful in imposing modern concepts upon old sources. People persuaded by them no longer had to accept the actual context and apparent message of the latter: they could claim that, like a psychologist treating a patient, they were probing through to realities of which the people leaving the evidence had themselves been unaware. All these importations, imposed to differing degrees and indifferent proportions upon the original Wicca, resulted in a more extensive and diverse religion, or interlocked series of cults. In the same period Wiccan groups gave an enhanced importance to differing elements within the original cult, such as Celtic, or Saxon, or Norse, and increased the diversity of practice contained within the modern label of 'pagan'. But the greatest influence of all was exerted by radical feminism. In the early decades of Wicca the Horned God was more or less the equal of the Goddess, but by the 1980s he had generally become the junior partner, her 'son and consort'. A heavy new emphasis had also been made upon an association, proposed by Gardner at the beginning, between the witches' female deity, the prehistoric Earth Mother and the belief in prehistoric matriarchies.

The latter has an interesting history. The idea that all human society was once led by women was made popular in some radical circles during the 1960s by the books of Elizabeth Gould Davis, Helen Diner and Robert Graves, and received a further impetus from those of Phyllis Chester and Evelyn Read in the first half of the next decade. All ultimately depended for their factual material upon *Das Mutterrecht* ('Matriarchy') by a retired Swiss judge, Johann Jakob Bachofen, which appeared in 1861. Bachofen drew his data from Greek sources, notably Herodotus, and advanced a theory, which they supported fairly well, that in some ancient societies women had occupied a more powerful position than they possessed in the Graeco-Roman world and in subsequent European and Near Eastern history. From this he went on, with less justification, to argue that all human societies had passed through an age in which women ruled. The only real development in this idea over the next 120 years was that whereas Bachofen has proposed that this theoretical matriarchy had been a disaster for everybody, Helen Diner suggested that it had been good for women and her successors proclaimed that it had been marvellous for humanity and for the planet as well. Meanwhile, the same questioning impulse of the 1960s, which produced both contemporary feminism and the demolition of the academic orthodoxy concerning the Mother Goddess, led scholars to re-examine the sources upon which Bachofen had depended. They now had at their disposal a great deal more information about the societies upon which the Greeks had written, and about the motivation of authors such as Herodotus, than had been available in 1861. The cumulative effect of all this material was to destroy any convincing argument for the existence of matriarchal, matrilinear or matrifocal peoples in the ancient Mediterranean world or Near East.[84] The collapse in the 1980s of that concerning the Picts (described in an earlier chapter) completed the process for the whole of Europe, As was also remarked earlier, the question of gender relations in prehistoric societies is wide open and probably insoluble. But the combination of Bachofen's myth with modern paganism proved extremely potent. By the late 1970s it had become part of the creed of both radical feminists and much Wiccan and Wicca-derived religion that witchcraft, goddess-worship and women's rights were intermingled. Both could portray the Old Religion as goddess-centred, and the Great Witch Hunt as a deliberate attack upon feminism as well as on paganism. This ideology provided a further excellent reason for modern pagans to ignore those pre-Christian religions of which we have real evidence, as 'patriarchal', and to concoct beliefs and rituals conceived to approximate better to a faith set in a prehistoric fairyland. It also equipped many of them with an intense moral fervour and a martyrology, which are the characteristics of a tough and durable faith and which, to the sorrow of the emperor Julian, the cults of his Empire did not possess. It remains to be seen whether it has given even greater potential to modern paganism, or whether the latter has become increasingly associated with a counter-culture.

It may be observed that the 'earth mysteries', the 'Celtic mysteries' and Wicca have during the past twenty years all become movements which build, like medieval scholasticism, upon closed systems of belief. Up to about the 1970s, the bibliographies appended to their books contained works by 'establishment' scholars as well as by people of their own persuasion. After then, all have tended to read only one another and to write only for one another. All have almost totally ignored the tremendous outpouring of new academic publications relevant to their interests. In the case of Wicca, its initiates have paid no attention to the important recent work upon either ancient paganism or the Great Witch Hunt. Two of them took some fleeting notice of Norman Cohn's attack upon the Murray thesis, but only to dismiss it with a few general and quite inadequate remarks, ignoring the vast bulk of a detailed, meticulous and formidable book.[85] By the 1980s, 'craft lore', sometimes called 'oral tradition', was deemed by some Wiccan writers as important as historical sources.[86] This did not appear to be a conscious process of censorship so much as a genuine loss of contact with thought worlds other than their own.[87] But at the same time, more in America than in its homeland, modern paganism was developing a parallel tendency which a historian can only applaud. By trial and error some groups were discovering that brand new rituals worked as well as those prescribed in supposedly (if dubiously) old Books of Shadows. Others were conscientious enough to examine the ancient sources which were claimed to support key works such as *The White Goddess* and found that they did not in fact do so. The result was a growing admission that modern paganism might well be a recent creation which draws upon ancient images but employs them in a new way and for modern needs. One might add here that this view does fit very well into one genuine Graeco-Roman tradition, that anybody could make up their own religion provided it did not harm others. 'Gareth Knight' (a splendidly romantic pseudonym) of Arkana Paperbacks proclaimed elegantly that 'the esoteric students of the present and future will be ones who take what they can find, in eclectic freedom, for the immediate purpose in hand'.[88] Still more delightful is the candour of Margot Adler: 'The most authentic and hallowed Wiccan tradition – stealing from any source that didn't run away too fast.'[89] But all this does leave somebody with a genuine love of and interest in the peoples of the ancient world, prepared to accept them upon their own terms and for their own sake, feeling acutely sad and lonely.

What, then, after so many pages, can be said about the pagan religions of the ancient British Isles? First, that we know very little about them. An immense quality of recent work has served to show that most of what we had formerly believed that we knew is either wrong or unprovable. In fact, the only groups about which we can speak with any confidence are those of Roman Britain, some aspects of which remain a mystery and which may obscure, rather than reveal, the nature of the native cults. Second, that part of our uncertainty derives from our discovery of a tremendous diversity of ritual practice and architecture, over both space and time, which may reflect an equal diversity of belief and which almost defies generalization. The peoples of our remote past have emerged as more creative, more dynamic, more fascinating and more baffling. Third, that the old religions of these islands perished a very long time ago, and absolutely. They fell before Christianity both because of tricks of fortune and because they were not well equipped to resist the new faith, but they left an enormous and varied cultural legacy. And partly because of our ignorance of them and partly because of our different needs and circumstances, they are lost to us for ever.

16 October 2010
5 January 2015
4 February 2019 – Kempton Pierce

Notes

CHAPTER I   THE MYSTERIES BEGIN

1 Peter Ucko, 'Ethnography and Archaeological Explanations of Funerary Remains', *World Archaeology* 1969, 1, 262–77; Alexandra Tuckwell, 'Patterns of Burial Orientation in the Round Barrows of East Yorkshire', *London University Institute of Archaeology Bulletin* 1975, 12, 95–123; John Wymer, *The Palaeolithic Age*, London, 1982, pp. 165–8, 250–3; Desmond Collins, *Palaeolithic Europe*, London, 1986, p. 283.

2 A. P. Currant, R. M. Jacobi and C. B. Stringer, 'Excavations at Gough's Cave, Somerset 1986–7', *Antiquity* 1989, 63, pp. 131–6.

3 Michael A. Jochim, 'Palaeolithic Cave Art in Ecological Perspective', in Geof Bailey (ed.), *Hunter–Gatherer Economy in Prehistory*, Cambridge, 1983, ch. 19.

4 J. G. Lalanne, 'Découverte d'un bas-relief à representation humaine dans les fouillages de Laussel', *L'Anthropologie* 1911, 22, pp. 257–60; J. G. Lalanne and Jean Bouysonnie, 'Le Gisement palaeolithique de Laussel', *L'Anthropologie* 1941–6, 50, pp. 1–163; Andre Leroi-Gourhan, *Treasures of Prehistoric Art*, New York, n.d., p. 47; S. Giedion, *The Eternal Present*, vol. 1: *The Beginnings of Art*, Princeton, n.d., p. 470; Alexander Marshack, *The Roots of Civilisation*, New York, 1972, p. 335; Franz Hančar, 'Zum Problem Venusstatuetten in Eurasiastischen Jungpaläeolithikum', *Prähistorische Zeitschrift* 1939–40, 30–1 (1–2), pp. 85–156; Alfred Salomny, *Jahrbuch fur Prähistorische und Ethnographische Kunst*, Leipzig, 1931, pp. 1–6; Chester S. Chard, *Northeast Asia in Prehistory*, Madison, 1974, pp. 20–6; Collins, *Palaeolithic Europe*, pp. 271–81; Clive Gamble, 'Interaction and Alliance in Palaeolithic Society', *Man* 1982, n.s., 17, 92–107; Margaret Ehrenburg, *Women in Prehistory*, London, 1989, pp. 66–76.

5 Peter Ucko, *Anthropomorphic Figurines of Predynastic Egypt and Neolithic Crete*, London, 1968, p. 411.

6 Gamble, 'Interaction and Alliance in Palaeolithic Society'.
7 Peter Ucko and Andrée Rosenfeld, *Palaeolithic Cave Art*, London, 1967; John E. Pfeiffer, *The Creative Explosion*, New York, 1982; Paul G. Bahn and Jean Vertut, *Images of the Ice Age*, Leicester, 1989; N. K. Sandars, *Prehistoric Art in Europe*, Harmondsworth, 1985; Pamela Russell, 'Who and Why in Palaeolithic Art', *Oxford Journal of Archaeology* 1989, 8, 237–50.
8 Steven J. Mithen, 'To Hunt or to Paint: Animals and Art in the Upper Palaeolithic', *Man* 1988, 23, 671–95.
9 Ucko and Rosenfeld, *Palaeolithic Cave Art*, pp. 45–9, 97; Giedion, *The Beginnings of Art*, pp. 477–81; Leroi-Gourhan, *Treasures of Prehistoric Art*, p. 347; Susanne de Saint-Mathurin and Dorothy Garrod, 'La Frise sculptée de l'abri de Roc aux Sorciers', *L'Anthropologie* 1951, 55, pp. 413–25; Abbé Henri Breuil, *Four Hundred Centuries of Cave Art*, [Montignac, 1952], pp. 152–70, 334–5; Collins, *Palaeolithic Europe*, pp. 271–81; Pfeiffer, *The Creative Explosion*, p. 107.
10 John B. Campbell, *The Upper Palaeolithic of Britain*, Oxford, 1977; R. Charles, 'Incised Ivory Fragments and Other Late Palaeolithic Finds from Gough's Cave', *Proceedings of the University of Bristol Spelaeological Society* 1989, 18 (3), pp. 400–8.
11 Pfeiffer, *The Creative Explosion*, pp. 47, 61, 64; Paul Ashbee, *The Ancient British*, Norwich, 1978, pp. 53–4.
12 Susan Palmer, *Mesolithic Cultures of Britain*, London, 1977; I. G. Simmons, G. W. Dimbleby and Caroline Grigson, 'The Mesolithic', in I. G. Simmons and M. J. Tooley (eds), *The Environment in British Prehistory*, London, 1981, ch. 3; Pfeiffer, *The Creative Explosion*, pp. 149–52.
13 George Lambrick, *The Rollright Stones*, London, 1988, p. 111.
14 Lance Vatcher and Faith Vatcher, 'Excavation of Three Post-Holes in Stonehenge Car Park', *Wiltshire Archaeological and Natural History Magazine* 1973, 68, pp. 57–63; Royal Commission on Historical Monuments (England), *Stonehenge and its Environs*, Edinburgh, 1979, p. 33. I am grateful to Michael Green of English Heritage for drawing my attention to these features and to Julian Richards of the Wessex Archaeological Trust and Richard Harrison of the Bristol University Department of Archaeology for supplying further information.

CHAPTER 2   THE TIME OF THE TOMBS

1 J. P. Mallory, *In Search of the Indo-Europeans*, London, 1989, p. 168.
2 Paul Ashbee, 'A Reconsideration of the British Neolithic', *Antiquity* 1982, 56, pp. 134–8; Ian Kinnes, 'Circumstance not Context: The Neolithic of Scotland as Seen from the Outside', *Proceedings of the Society of Antiquaries of Scotland* 1985, 115, pp. 19–21; Richard Bradley, *The Social Foundations of*

Prehistoric Britain, London, 1984, pp. 7–13; Anna Ritchie, 'The First Settlers', in Colin Renfrew (ed.), *The Prehistory of Orkney*, Edinburgh, 1985, pp. 36–53; Timothy Darvill, *Prehistoric Britain*, London, 1987, pp. 48–50; H. N. Savory, 'The Neolithic in Wales', in J. A. Taylor (ed.), *Culture and Environment in Prehistoric Wales*, British Archaeological Reports, British Series, 76 (1980), pp. 207–14.

3 Rodney Castleden, *The Stonehenge People*, London, 1987, pp. 30–7, 67–123; Darvill, *Prehistoric Britain*, pp. 70–4; Bradley, *The Social Foundations of Prehistoric Britain*, p. 13; Aubrey Burl, *Prehistoric Avebury*, New Haven, 1979, pp. 81–3; A. G. Smith, 'The Neolithic', in I. G. Simmons and M. J. Tooley (eds), *The Environment in British Prehistory*, London, 1981, pp. 144–69; Göran Burenhult, 'The Archaeology of Carrowmore', in *The Archaeology of Carrowmore*, Stockholm, 1984, p. 139; Philip Dixon, 'The Neolithic Settlements on Crickley Hill', in Colin Burgess et al. (eds), *Enclosures and Defences in the Neolithic of Western Europe*, British Archaeological Reports, International Series, 403 (1988), ch. 4; Roger Mercer, *Hambledon Hill*, Edinburgh, 1980 and 'Excavations of Carn Brea', *Cornish Archaeology 1981*, 20, pp. 1–204; Margaret Ehrenburg, *Women in Prehistory*, London, 1989, ch. 3.

4 Burenhult, *The Archaeology of Carrowmore*; Colin Renfrew (ed.), *The Megalithic Monuments of Western Europe*, London, 1981; Grahame Clark, 'The Economic Context of Dolmens and Passage Graves in Sweden', in Vladimir Markotic (ed.), *Ancient Europe and the Mediterranean*, London, 1977, pp. 35–49.

5 Ashbee, *The Ancient British*, pp. 84–9; Savory, 'The Neolithic in Wales', pp. 216–17, and 'The Role of Iberian Communal Tombs in Mediterranean and Atlantic Prehistory', in Markotic, *Ancient Europe and the Mediterranean*, pp. 161–80; Robert Chapman, 'The Emergence of Formal Disposal Areas and the "Probelm" of Megalithic Tombs in Prehistoric Europe', in Robert Chapman, Ian Kinnes and Klaus Randsborg (eds), *The Archaeology of Death*, Cambridge, 1981, pp. 71–81; Bradley, *The Social Foundations of Prehistoric Britain*, pp. 14–16; Ian Hodder, 'Burials, Houses, Women and Men in the European Neolithic', in David Miller and Christopher Tilley (eds), *Ideology, Power and Prehistory*, Cambridge, 1984, pp. 52–65; Richard Bradley and Robert Chapman, 'Passage Graves in the European Neolithic – A Theory of Converging Evolution', in Burenhult, *The Archaeology of Carrowmore*, pp. 348–56.

6 Sean ÓNualláin, 'Irish Portal Tombs', *Journal of the Royal Society of Antiquaries of Ireland 1983*, 113; Peter Harbison, *Pre-Christian Ireland*, London, 1988, pp. 42–56; Michael J. O'Kelly, *Early Ireland*, Cambridge, 1989, pp. 87–97.

7 George Lambrick, *The Rollright Stones*, London, 1988, pp. 115–16;

Timothy Darvill, *The Megalithic Chambered Tombs of the Cotswold–Severn Region*, London, 1982 and *Prehistoric Britain*, pp. 63–8; Savory, 'The Neolithic in Wales', pp. 217–22; C. T. Barker, 'The Long Mounds of the Avebury Region', *Wiltshire Archaeological and Natural History Society Magazine* 1984, 79; Audrey Henshall, 'The Chambered Cairns', in Renfrew, *The Prehistory of Orkney*, pp. 83–117; Kinnes, 'Circumstances not Context', pp. 31–9; Niall M. Sharples, 'Individual and Community: The Changing Role of Megaliths in the Orcadian Neolithic', *Proceedings of the Prehistoric Society* 1985, 51, pp. 59–74; Aubrey Burl, *The Stonehenge People*, London, 1987, pp. 5–20; Ian Hodder and Paul Shant, 'The Haddenham Long Barrow', *Antiquity* 1988, 62, pp. 349–53; Philip Harding and Christopher Gingell, 'The Excavation of Two Long Barrows', *Wiltshire Archaeological and Natural History Magazine* 1986, 80, pp. 7–22.

8 A. E. P. Collins, 'Excavation of a Double-horned Cairn at Audleystown', *Ulster Journal of Archaeology* 1954. 17, pp. 7–56 and 'Further Work at Audleystown Long Cairn', *Ulster Journal of Archaeology* 1959, 22, pp. 47–70; H. O'N. Hencken, 'A Long Cairn at Creevykeel', *Journal of the Royal Society of Antiquaries of Ireland* 1939, 69, pp. 53–98; R. De Valera, 'The Court Cairns of Ireland', *Proceedings of the Royal Irish Academy* 1960, 60C, pp. 9–140; Michael J. O'Kelly, *Early Ireland*, pp. 87–97; Sean ÓNuallain, 'The Central Court-Tombs of the North-west of Ireland', *Journal of the Royal Society of Antiquaries of Ireland* 1976, 106, pp. 92–117; D. M. Waterman, 'The Excavation of a Court Cairn at Tully', *Ulster Journal of Archaeology* 1978, 41, pp. 3–14; Burenhult, *The Archaeology of Carrowmore*; Harbison, *Pre-Christian Ireland*, pp. 47–65.

9 J. X. W. P. Corcoran, 'The Excavation of Three Chambered Cairns at Loch Calder, Caithness', *Proceedings of the Society of Antiquaries of Scotland* 1967, 97, pp. 1–75; Niall Sharples, 'The Excavation of a Chambered Cairn, the Ord North', *Proceedings of the Society of Antiquaries of Scotland* 1981, 111, pp. 21–62.

10 J. T. Chesterman, 'Burial Rites in a Cotswold Long Barrow', *Man* 1977, n.s., 12, pp. 22–32; Savory, 'The Neolithic in Wales', pp. 219–20; W. J. Britnell and H. N. Savory (eds), *Gwernvale and Penywyrlod*, Cambrian Archaeological Monographs, 2 (1984); Julian Thomas, 'The Social Significance of Cotswold–Severn Burial Practices', *Man* 1988, n.s., 23, pp. 534–56; Julian Thomas and Alasdair Whittle, 'Anatomy of a Tomb – West Kennet Revisited', *Oxford Journal of Archaeology* 1986, 5, pp. 129–56; Darvill, *Megalithic Chambered Tombs*; Michael Shanks and Christopher Tilley, 'Ideology, Symbolic Power and Ritual Communication', in Ian Hodder (ed.), *Symbolic and Structural Archaeology*, Cambridge, 1982, pp. 135–41; Alan Savile et al., 'Radiocarbon Dates from the Chambered Tomb at Hazleton', *Antiquity* 1987, 61, pp. 108–19.

11 Shanks and Tilley, 'Ideology, Symbolic Power and Ritual Communication'; I. J. Thorpe, 'Ritual, Power and Ideology: A Reconstruction of Earlier Neolithic Rituals in Wessex', in Richard Bradley and Julie Gardiner (eds), *Neolithic Studies*, British Archaeological Reports, British Series, 113 (1984), pp. 42–55; Burl, *The Stonehenge People*, pp. 22–9; Harding and Gingell, 'The Excavation of Two Long Barrows'; Stephen Pierpoint, *Social Patterns in Yorkshire Prehistory*, British Archaeological Reports, British Series, 74 (1980), p. 214; B. E. Vyner, 'The Excavation of a Neolithic Cairn at Street House, Loftus, Cleveland', *Proceedings of the Prehistoric Society* 1984, 50, pp. 151–95; Stuart Piggott, 'Excavation of the Dalladies Long Barrow, Fettercairn, Kincardineshire, *Proceedings of the Society of Antiquaries of Scotland* 1972, 104, pp. 23–47; Royal Commission on Historical Monuments (England), *Stonehenge and its Environs*, Edinburgh, 1979; Kinnes, 'Circumstance not Context', p. 139; Paul Shand and Ian Hodder, 'Haddenham', *Current Archaeology* 1990, 118, pp. 339–42.

12 Shanks and Tilley, 'Ideology, Symbolic Power and Ritual Communication'.

13 Aubrey Burl, *Rites of the Gods*, London, 1981, chs 3, 4 and 'By the Light of the Cinerary Moon', in C. L. N. Ruggles and A. W. R. Whittle (eds), *Astronomy and Society in Britain during the Period 4000–1500 BC*, British Archaeological Reports, British Series, 88 (1981), pp. 248–56; David Fraser, *Land and Society in Neolithic Orkney*, British Archaeological Reports, British Series, 117 (1983), p. 365; Timothy Darvill, *Prehistoric Gloucestershire*, Gloucester, 1987, p. 51; O'Kelly, *Early Ireland*, p. 87.

14 Glyn Daniel, *The Megalith Builders of Western Europe*, London, 1958.

15 Michael Dames, *The Silbury Treasure*, London, 1976, p. 51.

16 Ruth Whitehouse, 'Megaliths of the Central Mediterranean', and David Trump. 'Megalithic Architecture in Malta', in Renfrew, *The Megalithic Monuments of Western Europe*, chs 4, 5.

17 For a summary, see Mallory, *In Search of the Indo-Europeans*, pp. 184, 234–43. As this present book went to press, Professor Gimbutas's new book, *The Language of the Goddess*, became available (London, Thames and Hudson, 1990). Its many illustrations make it another wonderful gift to artists: that apart, it is a personal dream-world infused with the author's political preoccupations. It makes a wholly arbitrary and selective interpretation of the prehistoric symbols which it reproduces, and tacks on to this an interpretation of the historic Great Witch Hunt which is based not even upon dubious scholarship but upon assertions of modern pagans made without research. Overall, the book is an extended and very beautiful radical feminist tract.

18 Pronounced 'Chahtal Hyooyook'.

19 Riane Eisler, *The Chalice and the Blade*, San Francisco, 1987.

20 Ian Hodder, 'Contextual Archaeology: An Interpretation of Çatal Hüyük and a Discussion of the Origins of Agriculture', *London University Institute of Archaeology Bulletin* 1987, 24, pp. 43–56.

21 B. Coles and J. Coles, *Sweet Track to Glastonbury*, London, 1986, p. 81.

22 R. Rainbird Clarke, *Grimes Graves*, London, 1966, pp. 22–3.

23 M. Avery, 'The Neolithic Causewayed Enclosure, Abingdon', and R. Kenward, 'A Neolithic Burial Enclosure at New Wintles Farm', in H. J. Case and A. W. R. Whittle (eds), *Settlement Patterns in the Oxford Region*, Council for British Archaeology Research Reports, 44 (1982), chs 1, 2; Reay Robertson-Mackay, 'The Neolithic Causewayed Enclosure at Staines', *Proceedings of the Prehistoric Society* 1987, 53, pp. 23–128; Burl, *Prehistoric Avebury*, pp. 104–9; Bradley, *The Social Foundations of Prehistoric Britain*, pp. 27–37; Sharples, 'Individual and Community'; Alasdair Whittle, 'Earlier Neolithic Enclosures in North-west Europe', *Proceedings of the Prehistoric Society* 1977, 43, 329–48; Mercer, *Hambledon Hill*; Peter Drewett, 'The Excavation of a Neolithic Causewayed Enclosure on Offham Hill, East Sussex', *Proceedings of the Prehistoric Society* 1977, 43, pp. 201–41; John Hedges and David Buckley, 'Excavations at a Neolithic Causewayed Enclosure, Orsett, Essex', *Proceedings of the Prehistoric Society* 1978, 44, pp. 219–308; Helen M. Bamford, *Briar Hill Excavation*, Northampton, 1985; Darvill, *Prehistoric Britain*, pp. 57–63 and *Prehistoric Gloucestershire*, pp. 40–2; Thorpe, 'Ritual, Power and Ideology', pp. 47–9, 114–29; Burgess et al., *Enclosures and Defences*; Alasdair Whittle, 'A Pre-enclosure Burial at Windmill Hill', *Oxford Journal of Archaeology* 1990, 9, pp. 25–8; J. G. Evans, 'The Landscape Setting of Causewayed Camps' and Christopher Evans, 'Acts of Enclosure', in John Barrett and I. A. Kinnes (eds), *The Archaeology of Context in the Neolithic and Bronze Age*, Sheffield, 1988, pp. 73–95.

24 Darvill, *Prehistoric Britain*, pp. 75–6; Lambrick, *The Rollright Stones*, pp. 119–21; Burl, *Prehistoric Avebury*, p. 112; Bradley, *The Social Foundations of Prehistoric Britain*, pp. 35–7; Castleden, *The Stonehenge People*, pp. 24–6.

CHAPTER 3   THE COMING OF THE CIRCLES

1 Michael J. O'Kelly, *Newgrange*, London, 1982; Michael Herity, *Irish Passage Graves*, Dublin, 1974; Aubrey Burl, *Rites of the Gods*, London, 1981, pp. 80–90; Muiris O'Sullivan, 'The Art of the Passage Tomb at Knockroe', *Journal of the Royal Society of Antiquaries of Ireland* 1987, 117, pp. 84–95; George Eogan, *Knowth and the Passage Tombs of Ireland*, London, 1986; Peter Harbison, *Pre-Christian Ireland*, London, 1988, pp. 56–82; Martin Brennan, *The Stars and the Stones*, London, 1983.

2 Niall M. Sharples, 'Excavations at Pierowall Quarry', *Proceedings of the Society of Antiquaries of Scotland* 1984, 114, pp. 75–125 and 'Individual and

Community: The Changing Role of Megaliths in the Orcadian Neolithic', *Proceedings of the Prehistoric Society* 1985, 51, pp. 59–74; P. J. Ashmore, 'Neolithic Carvings in Maes Howe', *Proceedings of the Society of Antiquaries of Scotland* 1986, 116, pp. 57–62; Burl, *Rites of the Gods*, pp. 74, 113–18; David Fraser, *Land and Society in Neolithic Orkney*, British Archaeological Reports, British Series, 117 (1983), pp. 401, 426–35; Audrey Henshall, 'The Chambered Cairns', in Colin Renfrew (ed.), *The Prehistory of Orkney*, Edinburgh, 1985, pp. 83–117; Colin C. Richards, 'Altered Images: A Re-examination of Neolithic Mortuary Practices in Orkney' and John Barber, 'Isbister, Quanterness and the Point of Cott', in John Barrett and I. A. Kinnes (eds), *The Archaeology of Context in the Neolithic and Bronze Age*, Sheffield, 1988, pp. 42–62.

3 Timothy Darvill, *Prehistoric Britain*, London, 1987, p. 85; Paul Ashbee, 'A Reconsideration of the British Neolithic', *Antiquity* 1982, 56, pp. 134–8; Sean o'Nualláin and Paul Walsh, 'A Reconsideration of the Tramore Passage-Tombs', *Proceedings of the Prehistoric Society* 1986, 52, pp. 25–9; Harbison, *Pre-Christian Ireland*, p. 100; Michael J. O'Kelly, 'A Wedge-shaped Gallery Grave at Island, Co. Cork', *Journal of the Royal Society of Antiquaries of Ireland* 1958, 88, pp. 1–23; and *Early Ireland*, Cambridge, 1989, pp. 115–21; A. Cremmin-Madden, 'The Beaker Wedge Tomb at Moytirra, Co. Sligo', *Journal of the Royal Society of Antiquaries of Ireland* 1969, 99, pp. 151–9; Michael J. O'Kelly, 'A Wedge-Shaped Gallery Grave at Baurndomeeny, Co. Tipperary', *Journal of the Cork Historical and Archaeological Society* 1960, 65, pp. 85–115.

4 Richard Bradley, 'Studying Monuments', and I. J. Thorpe and Colin C. Richards, 'The Decline of Ritual Authority and the Introduction of Beakers into Britain', in Richard Bradley and Julie Gardiner (eds), *Neolithic Studies*, British Archaeological Reports, British Series, 133 (1984), chs 5, 6; Richard Bradley et al., 'Sample Excavation of the Dorset Cursus', *Proceedings of the Dorset Natural History and Archaeological Society* 1984, 106, pp. 128–32; Julie Gardiner, 'Intra-Site Patterning in the Flint Assemblage from the Dorset Cursus', *Proceedings of the Dorset Natural History and Archaeological Society* 1985, 107, pp. 87–93; C. J. Bailey, 'Fieldwork in the Upper Valley of the South Winterbourne', *Proceedings of the Dorset Natural History and Archaeological Society* 1984, 106, pp. 134–7; Richard Bradley and Richard Chambers, 'A New Study of the Cursus Complex at Dorchester on Thames', *Oxford Journal of Archaeology* 1988, 7, pp. 271–90; Francis Pryor, 'Personalities of Britain: Two Examples of Long-Term Regional Contact', *Scottish Archaeological Review* 1984, 3, pp. 8–15; John Hedges and David Buckley, *Springfield Cursus and the Cursus Problem*, Chelmsford, 1981.

5 T. Clare, 'Towards a Reappraisal of Henge Monuments', *Proceedings of the Prehistoric Society* 1987, 53, pp. 457–77; Hedges and Buckley, *Springfield Cursus*; Bradley and Chambers, 'The Cursus Complex at Dorchester on

Thames'; H. J. Case, 'The Linear Ditches and Southern Enclosure, North Stoke', in H. J. Case and A. W. R. Whittle (eds), *Settlement Patterns in the Oxford Region*, Council for British Archaeology Research Reports, 44 (1982), pp. 60–70.

6 Peter Drewett, 'The Excavation of a Neolithic Causewayed Enclosure on Offham Hill, East Sussex', *Proceedings of the Prehistoric Society* 1986, 52, pp. 25–9; Richard Bradley and Roy Entwhistle, 'Thickthorn Down Long Barrow – a New Assessment', *Proceedings of the Dorset Natural History and Archaeological Society* 1985, 107, pp. 174–6; Sharples, 'Individual and Community'; Bailey, 'The Upper Valley of the South Winterbourne'.

7 I. J. Thorpe, 'Ritual, Power and Ideology: A Reconstruction of Earlier Neolithic Rituals in Wessex', in Bradley and Gardiner, *Neolithic Studies*, p. 54; Richard Bradley, *The Social Foundations of Prehistoric Britain*, London, 1984, pp. 32–7.

8 Argued well by Burl in *Rites of the Gods*, pp. 54, 57, though by 1987 he seemed to have added the views of the authors cited in note 7.

9 T. Clare, 'Towards a Reappraisal of Henge Monuments', *Proceedings of the Prehistoric Society* 1986, 1987, 52–3, pp. 281–316, 457–77; A. F. Harding, *Henge Monuments and Related Sites of Great Britain*, British Archaeological Reports, British Series, 175 (1987); O'Kelly, *Early Ireland*, pp. 132–6.

10 Personal communication from David Urie.

11 Burl, *Rites of the Gods*, pp. 118–23; Darvill, *Prehistoric Britain*, p. 88 and *Prehistoric Gloucestershire*, Gloucester, 1987, p. 89; A. M. ApSimon et al., 'Gorsey Bigbury', *Proceedings of the University of Bristol Spelaeological Society* 1976, 14 (2), pp. 153–83; Margaret E. C. Stewart et al., 'The Excavation of a Henge, Stone Circles and Metal Working Area at Moncreiffe, Perthshire', *Proceedings of the Society of Antiquaries of Scotland* 1985, 115, pp. 125–50.

12 Aubrey Burl, *The Stone Circles of the British Isles*, New Haven, 1976, taking into account an extra three on Bodmin Moor recorded in a forthcoming survey by Peter Rose.

13 George Lambrick, *The Rollright Stones*, London, 1988, pp. 121–3.

14 Burl, *The Stone Circles of the British Isles*.

15 Aubrey Burl, 'Coves: Structural Enigmas of the Neolithic', *Wiltshire Archaeological and Natural History Magazine* 1988, 82, pp. 1–18.

16 Richard Bradley, 'Studying Monuments', in Bradley and Gardiner, *Neolithic Studies*, pp. 62–4.

17 Aubrey Burl, *Prehistoric Avebury*, New Haven, 1979, pp. 112–30, 165; Michael Dames, *The Silbury Treasure*, London, 1976; Bradley, *The Social Foundations of Prehistoric Britain*, p. 43.

18 Burl, *Prehistoric Avebury*, pp. 67–8, 143–93.

19 Euan W. MacKie, 'Wise Men in Antiquity', in C. L. N. Ruggles and A. W. R. Whittle (eds), *Astronomy and Society in Britain During the Period 4000–1500 BC*, British Archaeological Reports, British Series, 88 (1981),

pp. 113–49; G. J. Wainwright, *Mount Pleasant*, London, 1979, and *The Henge Monuments*, London, 1989, pp. 126–33.

20 Burl, *The Stonehenge People*, chs 3–5, used somewhat selectively.

21 Stephen Pierpoint, *Social Patterns in Yorkshire Prehistory*, British Archaeological Reports, British Series, 74 (1980); J. Mortimer, *Forty Years' Researches in British and Saxon Burial Mounds of East Yorkshire*, London, 1905, pp. 23–42.

22 Ian Kinnes, *Round Barrows and Ring-ditches in the British Neolithic*, British Museum Occasional Papers, 7 (1979) and 'Circumstance not Context: The Neolithic of Scotland as Seen from the Outside', *Proceedings of the Society of Antiquaries of Scotland* 1985, 115, pp. 41–4; Burl, *Prehistoric Avebury*, pp. 120–2 and *The Stonehenge People*, pp. 47–8; Richard Bradley et al., 'The Neolithic Sequence in Cranborne Chase' and 'The Neolithic Sequences in the Upper Thames Valley', in Bradley and Gardiner, *Neolithic Studies*, chs 7, 8.

23 Rodney Castleden, *The Stonehenge People*, London, 1987, pp. 67–88; Darvill, *Prehistoric Britain*, pp. 82–6; Bradley, *The Social Foundations of Prehistoric Britain*, pp. 48, 61–5; Thorpe and Richards, 'Decline of Ritual Authority', and Rosamund Cleal, 'The Late Neolithic in Eastern England', in Bradley and Gardiner, *Neolithic Studies*, chs 6, 10; H. N. Savory, 'The Neolithic in Wales', in J. A. Taylor (ed.), *Culture and Environment in Prehistoric Wales*, British Archaeological Reports, British Series, 76 (1980), pp. 222–7.

24 Burl, *Prehistoric Avebury*, pp. 112, 123; Julian Thomas, 'The Social Significance of Cotswold–Severn Burial Practices', *Man* 1988, n.s., 23, p. 556; Alasdair Whittle, 'Contexts, Activities, Events – Aspects of Neolithic and Copper Age Enclosures in Western and Central Europe', in Colin Burgess et al. (eds), *Enclosures and Defences in the Neolithic of Western Europe*, British Archaeological Reports, International Series, 403 (1988), pp. 1–19; Grahame Soffe and Tom Clare, 'New Evidence of Ritual Monuments at Long Meg and Her Daughters, Cumbria', *Antiquity* 1988, 62, pp. 552–7.

25 Sharples, 'Individual and Community'; Kinnes, 'Circumstance not Context', pp. 41–4; Burl, *Rites of the Gods*, pp. 177–9; Savory, 'The Neolithic in Wales', p. 225; Henshall, 'The Chambered Cairns'; Sandra Øvrevik, 'The Second Millennium BC and After', in Renfrew, *The Prehistory of Orkney*, pp. 131–6; Timothy Darvill, *The Megalithic Chambered Tombs of the Cotswold–Severn Region*, London, 1982, p. 26.

26 Bradley, *The Social Foundations of Prehistoric Britain*, pp. 32–7; Kinnes, 'Circumstance not Context', p. 44.

27 Thomas, 'Cotswold–Severn Burial Practices', p. 556.

28 Julian Thomas and Alasdair Whittle, 'Anatomy of a Tomb – West Kennet

Revisited', *Oxford Journal of Archaeology* 1986, 5, pp. 155–6, proposed in
addition to the two theories cited earlier in this chapter.

CHAPTER 4   INTO THE DARKNESS

1 Richard J. Harrison, *The Beaker Folk*, London, 1980; Alasdair W. R.
Whittle, 'Two Neolithics?', *Current Archaeology 1980*, 6, *pp. 329–34, 371–3*;
Colin C. Richards, *'The Decline of Ritual Authority and the Introduction of
Beakers into Britain'*, in Richard Bradley and Julie Gardiner (eds), *Neolithic
Studies*, British Archaeological Reports, British Series, 133 (1984), ch. 6;
Aubrey Burl, *The Stonehenge People*, London, 1987, ch. 6; Timothy Darvill,
Prehistoric Britain, London, 1987, p. 89. Claims made by Dr Burl for the
Stonehenge area will be better judged when the Wessex Archaeological Trust
completes its current project. Preliminary indications are that it is unlikely to
favour his view: see Julian Richards, review of Burl, *The Stonehenge People*
and Rodney Castleden, *The Stonehenge People*, London, 1987, *Antiquity*
1987, 61, 502–3.
2 Aubrey Burl, *Prehistoric Avebury*, New Haven, 1979, pp. 186–98, 226,
233; Caroline Malone, *Avebury*, London, 1989.
3 Burl, *The Stonehenge People*, chs 5–6, used cautiously.
4 G. J. Wainwright, *Mount Pleasant*, London, 1979; Richard Bradley,
'Maumbury Rings', *Archaeologia* 1975, 105, pp. 1–98; Richard Bradley
and Julian Thomas, 'Some New Information on the Henge Monument at
Maumbury Rings', *Proceedings of the Dorset Natural History and Archaeological
Society* 1984, 106, pp. 132–4.
5 Richard Bradley et al., 'The Neolithic Sequence in the Upper Thames
Valley', and Rosamund Cleal, 'The Later Neolithic in Eastern England', in
Bradley and Gardiner, *Neolithic Studies*, pp. 131, 135–8; Colin Burgess,
'The Bronze Age in Wales', in J. A. Taylor, *Culture and Environment in
Prehistoric Wales*, British Archaeological Reports, British Series, 76 (1980),
p. 254; Timothy Darvill, *Prehistoric Gloucestershire*, Gloucester, 1987, p. 88;
Richard Bradley, *The Social Foundations of Prehistoric Britain*, London,
1984, p. 79; Margaret E. C. Stewart et al., 'The Excavation of a Henge,
Stone Circles and Metal Working Area at Moncreiff, Perthshire',
Proceedings of the Society of Antiquaries of Scotland 1985, 115, pp. 125–50;
Aubrey Burl, *The Stone Circles of the British Isles*, New Haven, 1976 and
Rites of the Gods, London, 1981, p. 59; Peter Harbison, *Pre-Christian
Ireland*, London, 1988, pp. 87–93; Roger Mercer, 'The Excavation of a
Late Neolithic Henge-type Enclosure at Balfarg', *Proceedings of the Society of
Antiquaries of Scotland* 1981, 111, pp. 63–171.
6 Darvill, *Prehistoric Britain*, pp. 90–1; Burl, *Rites of the Gods*, pp. 131–41;
D. N. Riley, 'Radley 15, A Late Beaker Ring Ditch', in H. J. Case and

A. W. R. Whittle (eds), *Settlement Patterns in the Oxford Region*, Council for British Archaeology Research Reports, 44 (1982), pp. 76–80.

7 Burl, *Rites of the Gods*, p. 137; Harbison, *Pre-Christian Ireland*, pp. 87–92.

8 Heather M. Tinsley, 'The Bronze Age', in I. G. Simmons and M. J. Tooley (eds), *The Environment in British Prehistory*, London, 1981, pp. 239–47; Ann Lynch, *Man and Environment in S. W. Ireland*, British Archaeological Reports, British Series, 85 (1981), pp. 121–2.

9 Alexandra Tuckwell, 'Patterns of Burial Orientation in the Round Barrows of East Yorkshire', *London University Institute of Archaeology Bulletin* 1975, 12, pp. 95–123; Andrew Lawson, 'The Bronze Age in East Anglia', in C. Barringer (ed.), *Aspects of East Anglian Prehistory*, Norwich, 1984, pp. 146–7.

10 Burl, *The Stone Circles of the British Isles*, pp. 106–22, 213–24; Aileen Fox, *South West England 3500 BC–AD 600*, Newton Abbot, 1973, pp. 68–78; Lynch, *Man and Environment in S.W. Ireland*; Michael J. O'Kelly, 'A Wedge-shaped Gallery Grave at Island, Co. Cork', *Journal of the Royal Society of Antiquaries of Ireland* 1958, 88, pp. 1–12; plus a lot of walking.

11 Burl, *The Stone Circles of the British Isles*, pp. 115–22, 167–90, 254–72 and *Rites of the Gods*, pp. 179–85; R. A. S. Macalister et al., 'On a Bronze Age Interment with Associated Standing Stone and Earth Ring near Naas', *Proceedings of the Royal Irish Academy* 1913, 30, pp. 351–60; S. P. O'Riordan, 'Excavations of some Earthworks in the Curragh', *Proceedings of the Royal Irish Academy* 1950, 53, 254–8.

12 Frances Lynch, 'Bronze Age Monuments in Wales', in Taylor, *Culture and Environment in Prehistoric Wales*, pp. 233–9.

13 Tuckwell, 'Patterns of Burial Orientation'.

14 Trevor Watkins et al., 'The Excavation of an Early Bronze Age Cemetery at Barns Farm, Dalgety, Fife', *Proceedings of the Society of Antiquaries of Scotland* 1982, 112, 48–141.

15 Sir Cyril Fox, 'Two Bronze Age Cairns in South Wales', *Archaeologia* 1938, 87, pp. 129–80.

16 Christopher Chippindale, *Stonehenge Complete*, London, 1983; Michael W. Pitts, 'On the Road to Stonehenge', *Proceedings of the Prehistoric Society* 1982, 48, pp. 75–132. When the Wessex Archaeological Trust publishes its current survey, we shall at least be acquainted with what we do not know about Stonehenge.

17 Several details taken from Burl, *The Stonehenge People*, ch. 9. His is by far the finest modern account, although many of its assumptions outrun the available evidence.

18 Bradley, *The Social Foundations of Prehistoric Britain*, p. 89.

19 Burl, *Prehistoric Avebury*, pp. 243–4.

20 Wainwright, *Mount Pleasant*.

21 John Barrett and Richard Bradley, 'The Ploughshare and the Sword' and

'Later Bronze Age Settlement in South Wessex and Cranborne Chase', in John Barrett and Richard Bradley (eds), *Settlement and Society in the British Later Bronze Age*, British Archaeological Reports, British Series, 83 (1980), chs 1, 9.

22 J. P. Mallory, *In Search of the Indo-Europeans*, London, 1989, ch. 5.

23 Sinclair Hood, *The Minoans*, London, 1971; G. Cadogan, *Palaces of Minoan Crete*, London, 1976; Margaret Ehrenburg, *Women in Prehistory*, London, 1989, pp. 109–18.

24 Peter Gelling and Hilda Ellis Davidson, *The Chariot of the Sun*, London, 1969.

25 See Geoffrey Ashe, *The Glastonbury Tor Maze*, Glastonbury, 1979, for a sympathetic account.

26 Burl, *The Stonehenge People*, ch. 10.

27 Burl, *Rites of the Gods*, pp. 150–4 and *Prehistoric Avebury*, pp. 207–8.

28 Burl, *Rites of the Gods*, p. 152.

29 Ibid., pp. 160–4.

30 Aubrey Burl, 'By the Light of the Cinerary Moon', and I. J. Thorpe, 'Ethnoastronomy: Its Patterns and Archaeological Implications', in C. L. N. Ruggles and A. W. R. Whittle (eds), *Astronomy and Society in Britain During the Period 4000–1500 BC*, British Archaeological Reports, British Series, 88 (1981), pp. 243, 276–85.

31 John Barnatt and Gordon Moir, 'Stone Circles and Megalithic Mathematics', *Proceedings of the Prehistory Society 1984*, 50, pp 197–216; Douglas C. Heggie, *Megalithic Science*, London, 1981; J. D. Patrick and C. S. Wallace, 'Stone Circle Geometries', in Douglas C. Heggie (ed.), *Archaeoastronomy in the Old World*, Cambridge, 1982, pp. 231–63; Gordon Moir, 'Some Archaeological and Astronomical Objections to Scientific Astronomy in British Prehistory', in Ruggles and Whittle, *Astronomy and Society*, p. 223.

32 Burl, *The Stone Circles of the British Isles* and *Prehistoric Avebury*, pp. 117, 124.

33 Moir, 'Stone Circles'; Graham Ritchie, 'Ritual Monuments', in Renfrew, *The Prehistory of Orkney*, pp. 126–7; Clive Ruggles, 'A Critical Examination of the Megalithic Lunar Observatories', in Ruggles and Whittle, *Astronomy and Society*, ch. 6; D. C. Heggie, 'Megalithic Astronomy: Highlights and Problems', and Clive Ruggles, 'Megalithic Astronomical Sightlines', in Heggie, *Archaeoastronomy in the Old World*, pp. 1–24, 83–105.

34 Euan MacKie, 'Wise Men in Antiquity?' and Jon Patrick, 'A Reassessment of the Solstitial Observatories at Kintraw and Ballochroy', in Ruggles and Whittle, *Astronomy and Society*, pp. 115–16 and ch. 5; T. McCreery, A. J. Hastie and T. Moulds, 'Observations at Kintraw', in Heggie, *Archaeoastronomy in the Old World*, pp. 183–9.

35 A. S. Thom, J. M. D. Ker and T. R. Burrows, 'The Bush Barrow Gold Lozenge', *Antiquity 1988*, 62, pp. 108–19.

36 Burl, *Prehistoric Avebury*, p. 215 and *The Stonehenge People*, pp. 73–6; Castleden, *The Stonehenge People*, p. 152; Chippindale, *Stonehenge Complete*, p. 233; R. J. C. Atkinson, 'Aspects of the Archaeoastronomy of Stonehenge', in Heggie, *Archaeoastronomy in the Old World*, pp. 107–15.

37 Richard Bradley and Richard Chambers, 'A New Study of the Cursus Complex at Dorchester on Thames', *Oxford Journal of Archaeology* 1988, 7, pp. 27–90; Aubrey Burl, 'Science or Symbolism: Problems of Archaeo-astronomy', *Antiquity* 1980, 54, pp. 191–200; Burl, 'By the Light of the Cinerary Moon'; Aubrey Burl, 'Pi in the Sky', in Heggie, *Archaeoastronomy in the Old World*, pp. 150–66.

38 Castleden, *The Stonehenge People* ,p. 154; A. Lynch, 'Astronomy and Stone Alignments in S.W. Ireland', in Heggie, *Archaeoastronomy in the Old World*, pp. 205–13.

39 Burl, 'Pi in the Sky', pp. 150–5.

40 Paul Devereux and Ian Thomson, *The Ley Hunter's Companion*, London, 1979, p. 41.

41 Ibid., p. 38; Michael Dames, *The Silbury Treasure*, London, 1976, p. 66; John Michell, *The View Over Atlantis*, revised edition, London, 1975, p. 129.

42 Nigel Pennick and Paul Devereux, *Lines on the Landscape*, London, 1989, p. 14.

43 Michael Dames, *The Avebury Cycle*, London, 1977, p. 89.

44 John Michell, *The New View Over Atlantis*, London, 1983, p. 97.

45 E.g. Dames, *The Avebury Cycle*, pp. 28–9.

46 Pennick and Devereux, *Lines on the Landscape*, ch. 1.

47 Guy Underwood, *The Pattern of the Past*, London, 1969; Tom Graves, *Dowsing Techniques and Applications*, London, 1976 and *Needles of Stone Revisited*, Glastonbury, 1986; Sig Lonegren, *Spiritual Dowsing*, Glastonbury, 1986. The last of these summarizes the attitude of those who believe in 'dowsable leys' with the greatest clarity and warmth of spirit.

48 John Michell, *The Old Stones of Lands End*, Bristol, 1974.

49 Pennick and Devereux, *Lines on the Landscape*, p. 13.

50 Michell, *The View Over Atlantis*, p. 38.

51 Ibid., pp. 27, 29.

52 Michell, *The New View Over Atlantis*, p. 169.

53 Michell, *The Old Stones of Lands End*; John Barnatt, *Prehistoric Cornwall: The Ceremonial Monuments*, Wellingborough, 1982, pp. 113–18.

54 Lonegren, *Spiritual Dowsing*, pp. 43–52, puts it with most charm.

55 Devereux and Thompson, *The Ley Hunter's Companion*, pp. 47–8.

56 Ian Cooke, *Mermaid to Merrymaid*, Penzance, 1987.

57 Richard N. Bailey, Eric Cambridge and Dennis H. Briggs, *Dowsing in Church Archaeology*, Wimborne, 1988; Philip Rahtz, review of Bailey, Cambridge and Briggs, *Dowsing in Church Archaeology*, Antiquity 1988, 62, pp. 808–9.

58 Dames, *The Avebury Cycle*.

59 Burl, *The Stonehenge People*, pp. 218–20; Lynch, *Man and Environment in S.W. Ireland*, ch. 6.

60 Sandra Øvrevik, 'The Second Millennium BC and After', in Renfrew, *The Prehistory of Orkney*, pp. 131–6; Maxwell Dacre and Ann Ellison, 'A Bronze Age Urn Cemetery at Kimpton, Hampshire', *Proceedings of the Prehistoric Society* 1981, 47, pp. 147–203; A. F. Taylor and P. J. Woodward, 'A Bronze Age Barrow Cemetery', *Archaeological Journal* 1985, 142, pp. 73–149; Carol S. M. Allen et al., 'Bronze Age Cremation Cemeteries in the East Midlands', *Proceedings of the Prehistoric Society* 1987, 53, pp. 187–221; Anne Ellison, 'Deverel–Rimbury Urn Cemeteries', and T. G. Manby, 'Bronze Age in Eastern Yorkshire', in Barrett and Bradley, *Settlement and Society*, chs 6, 15; Harbison, *Pre-Christian Ireland*, pp. 103–4, 149; Michael J. O'Kelly, *Early Ireland*, Cambridge, 1989, pp. 210–14. A possible exception to the lack of monuments is Flag Fen, for which see chapter 5.

61 M. J. Rowlands, 'Kinship, Alliance and Exchange in the European Bronze Age', Nicholas Johnson, 'Later Bronze Age Settlements in the South-West' and John Barrett and Richard Bradley, 'The Later Bronze Age in the Thames Valley', in Barrett and Bradley, *Settlement and Society*, chs 2, 8, 12.

62 Mary Braithwaite, 'Ritual and Prestige in the Prehistory of Wessex', in David Miller and Christopher Tilley (eds), *Ideology, Power and Prehistory*, Cambridge, 1989, ch. 7.

63 Bradley, *The Social Foundations of Prehistoric Britain*, pp. 91–114.

64 Heather M. Tinsley, 'The Bronze Age', in Simmons and Tooley, *The Environment in British Prehistory*, pp. 211–47; D. A. Spratt (ed.), *Prehistoric and Roman Archaeology of North-east Yorkshire*, British Archaeological Reports, British Series, 104 (1982), pp. 120, 160–5; Darvill, *Prehistoric Gloucestershire*, pp. 121–3; Lynch, *Man and Environment in S.W. Ireland*, pp. 123–4; Andrew Lawson, 'The Bronze Age in East Anglia with Particular Reference to Norfolk', in Barringer, *Aspects of East Anglian Prehistory*, pp. 141–2.

65 An exception being Colin Burgess, 'The Bronze Age in Wales', in Taylor, *Culture and Environment in Prehistoric Wales*, p. 266.

66 Paul Ashbee, *The Ancient British*, Norwich, 1978, pp. 184–98; Burl, *Rites of the Gods*, pp. 210–33.

67 Burl, *Prehistoric Avebury*, pp. 243–4; Bradley, *The Social Foundations of Prehistoric Britain*, pp. 106–7; Wainwright, *Mount Pleasant*; Stewart et al., 'The Excavation of a Henge'; Richard Bradley, 'From Ritual to Romance: Ceremonial Centres and Hill Forts', in Graeme Guilbert (ed.), *Hill-Fort Studies*, Leicester, 1981.

68 Lesley Adkins and Roy A. Adkins, 'Neolithic Hand Axes from Roman Sites in Britain', *Oxford Journal of Archaeology* 1985, 4, pp. 69–75; Robin Turner

and J. J. Wymer, 'An Assemblage of Palaeolithic Hand Axes from the Roman Religious Complex at Ivy Chimneys', *Antiquaries Journal* 1987, 67, pp. 43–60; Ralph Merrifield, *The Archaeology of Religion and Magic*, London, 1987, pp. 10–11.

69 A. F. Harding, *Henge Monuments and Related Sites of Great Britain*, British Archaeological Reports, British Series, 175 (1987), p. 52; Dames, *The Silbury Treasure*, pp. 14–15.

70 Burl, *Rites of the Gods*, pp. 13–14, seems to be the most recent example.

71 Leslie V. Grinsell, *Folklore of Prehistoric Sites in Britain*, Newton Abbot, 1976, p. 91.

CHAPTER 5   THE PEOPLE OF THE MIST

1 Timothy Darvill, *Prehistoric Britain*, London, 1987, p. 158; Timothy Champion, 'The Myth of Iron Age Invasions in Ireland', in B. G. S. Scott (ed.), *Studies of Early Ireland*, Belfast, 1985, pp. 39–44.

2 What follows is based mainly upon the principal writings of the people named in the discussion. For a short, lively summary see Stuart Piggott, *The Druids*, London, 1968, ch. 4, and Prys Morgan, 'From a Death to a View', in Eric Hobsbawm and Terence Ranger (eds), *The Invention of Tradition*, Cambridge, 1983, ch. 3.

3 Lewis Spence, *The Magic Arts in Celtic Britain*, London, 1945; also *The Mysteries of Britain*, London, n.d., *The History of Atlantis*, London, 1930 and *Encyclopaedia of Occultism*, New York, 1974 (reprint).

4 Caitlín Matthews, *The Elements of the Celtic Tradition*, Shaftesbury, 1989, sums up her work. She and John Matthews have advertised a book entitled *Taliesin: The Shamanic Mysteries of Britain*, to be published by the Aquarian Press in 1991.

5 Martin Seymour-Smith, *Robert Graves*, London, 1983. The whole of this book needs to be read in order to understand Graves's attitude to facts.

6 G. A. Wait, *Ritual and Religion in Iron Age Britain*, British Archaeological Reports, British Series, 149 (1985), pp. 191–3; J. J. Tierney, 'The Celtic Ethnography of Poseidonios', *Proceedings of the Royal Irish Academy* 1959–60, 60, pp. 189–275; Daphne Nash, 'Reconstructing Poseidonios's Celtic Ethnography: Some Considerations', *Britannia* 1976, 7, pp. 111–26.

7 Kenneth Hurlstone Jackson, *The Oldest Irish Tradition*, Cambridge, 1964.

8 Brynley F. Roberts (ed.), *Early Welsh Poetry: Studies in the Book of Aneirin*, Aberystwyth, 1988; J. Rowland, *The Welsh Saga Englynion*, London, 1990; Lesley Alcock, 'Gwŷr y Gogledd: An Archaeological Appraisal', *Archaeologia Cambrensis* 1983, 132, pp. 1–18.

9 Kenneth Hurlstone Jackson, *The International Popular Tale and Early Welsh Tradition*, Cardiff, 1961.

10 Liam Breatnach, 'Canon Law and Secular Law in Early Ireland', *Peritia* 1984, 3, pp. 439–59; Kim McCone, 'Dubthach Maccu Lugair and a Matter of Life and Death', *Peritia* 1986, 5, pp. 1–35; Donnchadh ÓCorráin, Liam Breatnach and Aidan Breen, 'The Laws of the Irish', *Peritia* 1981, 3, pp. 382–438; Patrick Wormald, 'Celtic and Anglo-Saxon Kingship: Some Further Thoughts', in Paul E. Szarmach (ed.), *Sources of Anglo-Saxon Culture*, Kalamazoo, 1986, pp. 154–6; Michael J. O'Kelly, *Early Ireland*, Cambridge, 1989, pp. 254–5; J. P. Mallory, 'The Sword of the Ulster Cycle', in Scott, *Studies on Early Ireland*, pp. 99–114; Bernard Wailes, *The Irish Royal Sites in History and Archaeology*, Cambridge Medieval Celtic Studies, 3 (1982); David Greene, 'The Chariot as Described in Irish Literature', in Charles Thomas (ed.), *The Iron Age in the Irish Sea Province*, Council for British Archaeology Research Reports, 9 (1972), pp. 59–73; Stuart Piggott, *The Earliest Wheeled Transport*, London, 1983, pp. 235–8.
11 Nicholas B. Aitchison, 'The Ulster Cycle: Heroic Image and Historical Reality', *Journal of Medieval History* 1987, 13, pp. 87–116; T. C. Champion, 'Written Sources and the Study of the European Iron Age', in T. C. Champion and J. V. S. Megaw (eds), *Settlement and Society: Aspects of West European Prehistory in the First Millennium BC*, Leicester, 1985, pp. 9–22; Kim McCone, *Pagan Past and Christian Present in Early Irish Literature*, Maynooth Monographs, 3 (1990).
12 Alfred P. Smith, *Warlords and Holy Men*, London, 1984, pp. 57–72.
13 Wait, *Ritual and Religion in Iron Age Britain*, pp. 217–24. Much of the detail of what follows is based on Proinsias MacCana, *Celtic Mythology*, London, 1983.
14 MacCana, *Celtic Mythology* pp. 28–67.
15 Wait, *Ritual and Religion in Iron Age Britain*, p. 219; MacCana, *Celtic Mythology*, pp. 64, 85–6; Dio Cassius, *Roman History*, 62, 6–7. As with the work of Aubrey Burl, so with that of Proinsias MacCana, I use material recorded in it without necessarily drawing the same conclusions.
16 MacCana, *Celtic Mythology*, pp. 34–5, 85, 90–1, 95; John O'Donovan and Whitley Stokes (eds), *Sanas Chormaic*, Dublin, 1868, pp. 4, 23, 63; Francis John Byrne, *Irish Kings and High Kings*, London, 1973, p. 144; McCone, *Pagan Past and Christian Present*, pp. 162–3.
17 Wait, *Ritual and Religion in Iron Age Britain*, pp. 220–1; Miranda Green, *The Gods of the Celts*, Gloucester, 1986, p. 37.
18 Wait, *Ritual and Religion in Iron Age Britain*, p. 219; MacCana, *Celtic Mythology*, pp. 42, 69–73; Maire MacNeill, *The Festival of Lughnasa*, Oxford, 1962, chs 4–18.
19 Wait, *Ritual and Religion in Iron Age Britain*, p. 195; MacCana, *Celtic Mythology*, pp. 29–31.
20 O'Donovan and Stokes, *Sanas Chormaic*, p. 54.

21 Aubrey Burl, *Rites of the Gods*, London, 1981, pp. 213, 226–7 and sources cited there.

22 O'Kelly, *Early Ireland*, pp. 289–95.

23 Peter Harbison, *Pre-Christian Ireland*, London, 1988, p. 158; O'Kelly, *Early Ireland*, p. 284; Paul Ashbee, *The Ancient British*, Norwich, 1978, p. 229; John Waddell, 'From Kermaria to Turoe?', in Scott, *Studies on Early Ireland*, pp. 21–8.

24 Isabel Henderson, *The Picts*, London, 1967, p. 67.

25 J. H. Bettey, 'The Cerne Abbas Giant: The Documentary Evidence', *Antiquity*, 1981, 55, pp. 118–21.

26 R. D. Van Arsdell, *Celtic Coinage of Britain*, London, 1989.

27 Wait, *Ritual and Religion in Iron Age Britain*, pp. 154–77.

28 Ibid., p. 155; Burl, *Rites of the Gods*, p. 225.

29 A. Lane-Davies, *Holy Wells of Cornwall*, Truro, 1970, P. Logan, *The Holy Wells of Ireland*, Gerrards Cross, 1980; J. Meyrick, *A Pilgrim's Guide to the Holy Wells of Cornwall*, London, 1982; M. Quiller-Couch and L. Quiller-Couch, *Ancient and Holy Wells of Cornwall*, London 1894; P. O. Leggat and D. V. Leggat, *The Healing Wells*, Redruth, 1987; Francis Jones, *The Holy Wells of Wales*, Cardiff, 1954.

30 Harbison, *Pre-Christian Ireland*, pp. 155–92; J. P. Mallory, *Navan Fort*, Belfast, 1985; Wailes, *The Irish Royal Sites* and 'Dun Ailinne', in D. W. Harding (ed.), *Hillforts, Later Prehistoric Earthworks in Britain and Ireland*, London, 1976, pp. 319–38.

31 Charles Thomas, 'Souterrains in the Sea Province: A Note', in Thomas, *The Iron Age in the Irish Sea Province*, pp. 75–8; Ian Cooke, *Mermaid to Merrymaid*, Penzance, 1987, pp. 115–18; Burl, *Rites of the Gods*, pp. 215–16; Richard Warner, 'Irish Souterrains: Later Iron Age Refuges', *Archaeologia Atlantica* 1980, 3, pp. 81–100; Lloyd Laing and Jennifer Laing, *Celtic Britain and Ireland, AD 200–800*, Dublin, 1990, pp. 127–31.

32 Wait, *Ritual and Religion in Iron Age Britain*, pp. 200–3, 231; Henderson, *The Picts*, p. 67; P. W. Joyce, *Ancient Ireland*, Dublin, 1920, i.233–6; Pliny The Elder, *Natural History*, xvi.95; Piggott, *The Druids*.

33 Strabo, *Geographia*, 4.4.6; Pomponius Mela, *De Chorographia*, III.5.6.48.

34 Wait, *Ritual and Religion in Iron Age Britain*, pp. 228, 265–8; D. A. Binchy, 'The Fair of Tailtu and the Feast of Tara', *Eriu* 1958, 18, pp. 113–36; Byrne, *Irish Kings and High Kings*, pp. 7–26; Giraldus Cambrensis, *Topographia Hiberniae*, III.xxv.

35 Wormald, 'Celtic and Anglo-Saxon Kingship', p. 159; Byrne, *Irish Kings and High Kings*, pp. 20–1.

36 Wormald, 'Celtic and Anglo-Saxon Kingship', p. 160.

37 Marie-Louise Sjoestedt, *Gods and Heroes of the Celts*, London, 1949, p. 36; Wait, *Ritual and Religion in Iron Age Britain*, p. 222.

38 Thomas Kinsella (ed.), *The Tain*, 1970, p. 27.

39 Myles Dillon (ed.), *The Cycles of the Kings*, London 1946, p. 31.

40 MacNeill, *The Festival of Lughnasa*, p. 3.

41 Jeffrey Gantz, *Early Irish Myths and Sagas*, London, 1983, *passim*; T. G. E. Powell, *The Celts*, London, 1963, p. 152; MacCana, *Celtic Mythology*, pp. 126–8; Dillon (ed.), *Cycles of the Kings*, p. 28; Wait, *Ritual and Religion in Iron Age Britain*, pp. 228–9; Lady Gregory (ed.), *Gods and Fighting Men*, London, 1905, pp. 165–8.

42 Jeffrey Gantz (ed.), *The Mabinogion*, London, 1976, pp. 61–3, 130–3; Geoffrey Ashe, *The Landscape of King Arthur*, Exeter, 1987, p. 169.

43 Wait, *Ritual and Religion in Iron Age Britain*, p. 201; T. D. Kendrick, *The Druids*, London, 1927, pp. 117–18.

44 Pliny, *Natural History*, xvi.95.

45 All the above details are taken from Binchy, 'The Fair of Tailtu and the Feast of Tara', pp. 123–4, 128–31.

46 MacNeill, *The Festival of Lughnasa*, ch. 14.

47 E. C. Cawte, *Ritual Animal Disguise*, Ipswich, 1978, pp. 157–63.

48 MacNeill, *The Festival of Lughnasa*.

49 Swift overall views can be obtained from William Grant Stewart, *The Popular Superstitions and Festive Amusements of the Highlanders of Scotland*, second edition, London, 1851; Kevin Danaher, *The Year in Ireland*, Cork, 1972; T. Gwynn Jones, *Welsh Folklore and Folk Custom*, Cambridge, 1979.

50 Wait, *Ritual and Religion in Iron Age Britain*, pp. 205, 226.

51 Kendrick, *The Druids*, p. 110.

52 Richard Bradley, 'The Interpretation of Later Bronze Age Metalwork from British Rivers', *International Journal of Nautical Archaeology* 1979, 8, pp. 3–6; Ralph Merrifield, *The Archaeology of Religion and Magic*, London, 1987, p. 24; Margaret Ehrenburg, 'The Occurrence of Bronze Age Metalwork in the Thames: An Investigation', *Transactions of the London and Middlesex Archaeological Society* 1980, 31, pp. 1–15; Green, *The Gods of the Celts*, pp. 138–48; Burl, *The Rites of the Gods*, pp. 207–8; Francis Pryor, 'Flag Fen', *Current Archaeology* 1990, 119, pp. 386–90; Wait, *Ritual and Religion in Iron Age Britain*, pp. 15–50; Sir Cyril Fox, *A Find of the Early Iron Age from Llyn Cerrig Bach*, Cardiff, 1946; Andrew Fitzpatrick, 'The Deposition of La Tene Metalwork', in Barry Cunliffe and David Miles (eds), *Aspects of the Iron Age in Central Southern Britain*, Oxford, 1984, pp. 178–90.

53 Richard Bradley, 'The Destruction of Wealth in Later Prehistory', *Man* 1982, ns., 17, pp. 108–22; Barry Cunliffe, *Iron Age Communities in Britain*, second edition, London, 1978, p. 313; Ehrenburg, 'Bronze Age Metalwork in the Thames'; Richard Bradley and Ken Gordon, 'Human Skulls from the River Thames: Their Dating and Significance', *Antiquity* 1988, 62, pp. 503–9; John Barrett and Richard Bradley, 'The Later Bronze Age in the Thames Valley', in John Barrett and Richard Bradley (eds), *Settlement and Society in*

the British Later Bronze Age, British Archaeological Reports, British Series, 83 (1980), pp. 260–5.

54 Richard Bradley, *The Social Foundations of Prehistoric Britain*, London, 1984, pp. 120–6.

55 Wait, *Ritual and Religion in Iron Age Britain*, p. 207.

56 Green, *The Gods of the Celts*, pp. 146–8.

57 Wait, *Ritual and Religion in Iron Age Britain*, pp. 51–82; Anne Ross, *Pagan Celtic Britain*, London, 1968, ch. 5.

58 Graham Webster, *The British Celts and their Gods under Rome*, London, 1986, pp. 70–1.

59 Wait, *Ritual and Religion in Iron Age Britain*, pp. 126–52.

60 Anna Ritchie, 'Orkney in the Pictish Kingdom', in Colin Renfrew (ed.), *The Prehistory of Orkney*, Edinburgh, 1985, p. 189; Henderson, *The Picts*, p. 141.

61 Wait, *Ritual and Religion in Iron Age Britain*, p. 153.

62 Ibid., pp. 206–7.

63 Powell, *The Celts*, p. 152.

64 Merrifield, *The Archaeology of Religion and Magic*, p. 150; Green, *The Gods of the Celts*, p. 128; J. A. J. Gowlett, R. E. M. Hedges and I. E. Law, 'Radiocarbon Accelerator Dating of Lindow Man', *Antiquity* 1989, 63, pp. 71–9.

65 G. C. Dunning, 'Salmonsbury', in Harding, *Hillforts*, pp. 116–17.

66 Darvill, *Prehistoric Britain*, p. 159; Burl, *The Rites of the Gods*, pp. 215–16; Wait, *Ritual and Religion in Iron Age Britain*, pp. 83–8, 120.

67 O'Kelly, *Early Ireland*, ch. 12.

68 P. J. Ashmore, 'Low Cairns, Long Cists and Symbol Stones', *Proceedings of the Society of Antiquaries of Scotland* 1978–9, 110, pp. 346–55; Ritchie, 'Orkney in the Pictish Kingdom', pp. 189–91.

69 Wait, *Ritual and Religion in Iron Age Britain*, pp. 83–110; Barry Cunliffe, *Danebury*, London, 1983, pp. 160–5.

70 Rachel Bromwich (ed.), *Trioedd Ynys Prydein*, Cardiff, 1978, p. 89.

71 Darvill, *Prehistoric Britain*, p. 158; Rowan Whimster, *Burial Practices in Iron Age Britain*, British Archaeological Reports, British Series, 90 (1981).

72 Darvill, *Prehistoric Britain*, p. 158; Whimster, *Burial Practices in Iron Age Britain*; Cunliffe, *Iron Age Communities in Britain*, pp. 316–17; Green, *The Gods of the Celts*, pp. 129–30; E. W. Black, 'Romano-British Burial Customs and Religious Beliefs in South-east England', *Archaeological Journal* 1986, 143, pp. 203–4; Merrifield, *The Archaeology of Religion and Magic*, pp. 65–6.

CHAPTER 6   THE IMPERIAL SYNTHESIS

1 H. J. Rose, *Ancient Roman Religion*, London, 1948, pp. 11–12; Valerie J. Hutchinson, 'The Cult of Bacchus in Roman Britain', and G. Lloyd-

Morgan, 'Roman Venus', in Martin Henig and Anthony King (eds), *Pagan Gods and Shrines of the Roman Empire*, Oxford, 1986, pp. 135–46, 179–88.

2 Joan P. Alcock, 'The Concept of Genius in Roman Britain', in Henig and King, *Pagan Gods and Shrines*, pp. 113–34; Rose, *Ancient Roman Religion*, pp. 23–7, 38–40.

3 Martin Henig, *Religion in Roman Britain*, pp. 28, 200–3; Rose, *Ancient Roman Religion*, pp. 18, 25, 41.

4 Martin Henig, 'Some Personal Interpretations of Deity in Roman Britain', in Henig and King, *Pagan Gods and Shrines*, pp. 159–70; Rose, *Ancient Roman Religion*, pp. 13–16; Robin Lane Fox, *Pagans and Christians*, London, 1986, pp. 64–101; Thomas Wiedemann, 'Polytheism, Monotheism and Religious Co-existence: Paganism and Christianity in the Roman Empire', in I. Hamnett (ed.), *Religious Pluralism and Unbelief*, London, 1990.

5 Henig, *Religion in Roman Britain*, pp. 32–3; Fox, *Pagans and Christians*, pp. 69–72.

6 Henig, *Religion in Roman Britain*, pp. 32–3, 66, 85 and ch. 5; Fox, *Pagans and Christians*, pp. 27–101; Rose, *Ancient Roman Religion*, pp. 17, 27.

7 Miranda Green, *The Religions of Civilian Roman Britain*, British Archaeological Reports, British Series 24 (1976), pp. 67–78; Joan Alcock, review of Green, *The Religions of Civilian Roman Britain*, *Britannia* 1978, 9, pp. 501–2; Henig, *Religion in Roman Britain*, chs 4, 5 and 'Art and Cult in the Temples of Roman Britain', in Warwick Rodwell (ed.), *Temples, Churches and Religion: Recent Research in Roman Britain*, British Archaeological Reports, British Series, 77 (1980), p. 110.

8 Henig, *Religion in Roman Britain*, p. 59; Graham Webster, *The British Celts and their Gods under Rome*, p. 54.

9 Miranda Green, *The Gods of the Celts*, Gloucester, 1986, ch. 2 reaches opposite conclusions from the same material.

10 G. A. Wait, *Ritual and Religion in Iron Age Britain*, British Archaeological Reports, British Series, 149 (1985), p. 195–6.

11 Green, *The Gods of the Celts*, pp. 95–7, 103–7; R. G. Collingwood and R. P. Wright (eds), *The Roman Inscriptions of Britain*, vol. 1, Oxford, 1965; Webster, *The British Celts*, pp. 59–60; Eric Birley, 'The Deities of Roman Britain', *Aufsteig und Niedergang der Romanischen Welt*, II. 18. 1, pp. 3–112.

12 Webster, *The British Celts*, pp. 73–9; Anne Ellison, 'Natives, Romans and Christians on West Hill, Uley', in Rodwell, *Temples, Churches and Religion*, p. 327.

13 Green, *The Gods of the Celts*, ch. 3; Webster, *The British Celts*, pp. 63–6; Collingwood and Wright, *The Roman Inscriptions of Britain*; Henig, *Religion in Roman Britain*, pp. 48–9; Sylvia Barnard, 'The Matres of Roman Britain', *Archaeological Journal* 1985, 142, pp. 237–45.

14 Green, *The Religions of Civilian Roman Britain*, p. 27 and *The Gods of the Celts*, pp. 85–91; Webster, *The British Celts*, pp. 66–70.

15 Isabel Henderson, *The Picts*, London, 1967, p. 67; Green, *The Religions of Civilian Roman Britain*, p. 115 and *The Gods of the Celts*, pp. 92, 195–8; MacCana, *Celtic Mythology*, p. 144.

16 Webster, *The British Celts*, pp. 73–9; Henig, *Religion in Roman Britain*, pp. 47–8; Green, *The Gods of the Celts*, pp. 103–9; Lindsay Allason-Jones and Bruce McKay, *Coventina's Well*, Chesters, 1985.

17 Webster, The British Celts, pp. 72–3.

18 Green, *The Religions of Civilian Roman Britain*, p. 72 and *The Gods of the Celts*, pp. 85–91; L. J. F. Keppie, 'Roman Inscriptions from Scotland', *Proceedings of the Society of Antiquaries of Scotland* 1983, 113, pp. 391–404.

19 Green, *The Gods of the Celts*, pp. 103–9, 196–8.

20 Henig, *Religion in Roman Britain*, p. 89.

21 J. B. Bailey, 'Catalogue of Roman Inscribed and Sculptured Stones . . . Discovered in and near the Roman Fort at Maryport', *Transactions of the Cumberland and Westmorland Antiquarian and Archaeological Society* 1915, n.s., 15, pp. 135–73; G. R. Stephens, 'An Altar to Vulcan from Maryport', *Transactions of the Cumberland and Westmorland Antiquarian and Archaeological Society* 1988, 88, pp. 29–31.

22 M. J. T. Lewis, *Temples in Roman Britain*, Cambridge, 1966; D. R. Wilson, 'Romano-British Temple Architecture: How Much Do We Actually Know?', and Warwick Rodwell, 'Temples in Roman Britain: A Revised Gazetteer', in Rodwell, *Temples, Churches and Religion*, chs 1, 18.

23 Wilson, 'Romano-British Temple Architecture'.

24 Lewis, *Temples in Roman Britain*, pp. 49–56; Rodwell, 'Temples in Roman Britain'.

25 G. A. Wait, *Ritual and Religion in Iron Age Britain*, British Archaeological Reports, British Series, 149 (1985), pp. 178–86.

26 Henig, *Religion in Roman Britain*, p. 37; T. D. Kendrick, *The Druids*, London, 1927, pp. 94–8.

27 Henig, *Religion in Roman Britain*, pp. 135–6.

28 R. E. M. Wheeler and T. V. Wheeler, *Excavation of the Prehistoric, Roman and Post-Roman Sites in Lydney Park*, Oxford (Society of Antiquaries), 1932, pp. 103–4.

29 Henig, *Religion in Roman Britain*, pp. 130–42; Green, *The Gods of the Celts*, pp. 23–4.

30 H. H. Scullard, *Festivals and Ceremonies of the Roman Republic*, London, 1981.

31 Pliny, *Natural History*, xxii.2.

32 Ralph Merrifield, *The Archaeology of Religion and Magic*, London, 1987, pp. 26–9. Sadly, one of the most spectacular sites at which such deposits have been claimed must now be removed from the record: the cavern of Wookey

Hole in Somerset. Finds of skulls and other human bones in the River Axe, which flows through the cave, coupled with local traditions about a sorceress who dwelt there, gave rise to some understandably romantic speculations. But recent investigations have shown that the skeletal remains were almost certainly washed out of a Romano-British cemetery in the fourth chamber: C. J. Hawkes et al., 'Romano-British Cemetery in the Fourth Chamber of Wookey Hole Cave', *Proceedings of the University of Bristol Spelaeological Society* 1978, 15, pp. 23–52.

33 Webster, *The British Celts*, pp. 78–9; Green, *The Gods of the Celts*, pp. 148–64; Allason-Jones and McKay, *Coventina's Well*.

34 Merrifield, *The Archaeology of Religion and Magic*, pp. 45–8.

35 Wait, *Ritual and Religion in Iron Age Britain*, pp. 61–82.

36 Merrifield, *The Archaeology of Religion and Magic*, pp. 36, 42–4; Green, *The Gods of the Celts*, pp. 135, 172–3.

37 Merrifield, *The Archaeology of Religion and Magic*, pp. 32, 49–54; Green, *The Gods of the Celts*, pp. 172–3, 176–8.

38 Proinsias MacCana, *Celtic Mythology*, London, 1983, pp. 44–7; Green, *The Gods of the Celts*, pp. 169–95; Henig, *Religion in Roman Britain*, p. 131 and 'Religion in Roman Britain', in Malcolm Todd (ed.), *Research on Roman Britain: 1960–89*, Britannia Monograph Series, 11 (1989), p. 224.

39 Merrifield, *The Archaeology of Religion and Magic*, p. 44.

40 Green, *The Gods of the Celts*, p. 131; Merrifield, *The Archaeology of Religion and Magic*, p. 51.

41 Henig, *Religion in Roman Britain*, p. 30; Fox, *Pagans and Christians*, pp. 102–67.

42 Roger Leach, 'Religion and Burials in South Somerset and North Dorset', in Rodwell, *Temples, Churches and Religion*, pp. 337–52; Bruce N. Eagles, 'Pagan Anglo-Saxon Burials at West Overton', *Wiltshire Archaeological and Natural History Society Magazine* 1986, 80, pp. 103–20; E. W. Black, 'Romano-British Burial Customs and Religious Beliefs in South-east England', *Archaeological Journal* 1986, 143; Martin Millet, 'An Early Roman Burial Tradition in Central Southern England', *Oxford Journal of Archaeology* 1987, 6, pp. 63–8.

43 Leach, 'Religion and Burials'; Joan Alcock, 'Classical Religious Belief and Burial Practice in Roman Britain', *Archaeological Journal* 1980, 137; Black, 'Romano-British Burial Customs', pp. 220–5; Webster, *The British Celts*, p. 125.

44 M. Harman, T. I. Molleson and J. L. Price, 'Burials, Bodies and Beheadings in Romano-British and Anglo-Saxon cemeteries', *Bulletin of the British Museum of Natural History (Geology)* 1981, 35, pp. 145–88; Black, 'Romano-British Burial Customs', p. 225; Merrifield, *The Archaeology of Religion and Magic*, pp. 71–5.

45 Black, 'Romano-British Burial Customs', pp. 204–11, 225–7; Alcock,

'Classical Religious Belief', pp. 56–62; Merrifield, *The Archaeology of Religion and Magic*, pp. 71–6.

46 Henig, *Religion in Roman Britain*, pp. 152–3.

47 Ibid., pp. 154–5, 178–9; Webster, *The British Celts*, pp. 43–51, 83–99; Anthony Weir and James Jerman, *Images of Lust*, London, 1986, pp. 145–6.

48 Fox, *Pagans and Christians*, pp. 102–67; Henig, 'Religion in Roman Britain', p. 223.

49 Henig, *Religion in Roman Britain*, pp. 154–5.

50 Gildas, *De Excidio* iv.3.

51 W. J. Wedlake, *Excavation of the Shrine of Apollo at Nettleton, Wiltshire*, London, 1982; Ellison, 'Natives, Romans and Christians', pp. 310–27; Leach, 'Religions and Burials', pp. 332–5.

52 The basic report is Wheeler and Wheeler, *Sites in Lydney Park*. For an example of what a modern historian can make of it, see Green, *The Gods of the Celts*, pp. 159–61.

53 R. Hingley, 'Location, Function and Status: A Romano-British Religious Complex', *Oxford Journal of Archaeology* 1985, 4, pp. 201–12.

CHAPTER 7   THE CLASH OF FAITHS

1 Robin Lane Fox, *Pagans and Christians*, pp. 265–335. Much of what follows is based upon this deservedly celebrated book, which summarizes what is known so far and adds a great deal more.

2 Ibid., pp. 306–11.

3 Donnchadh ÓCorráin, 'Marriage in Early Ireland', in Art Cosgrove (ed.), *Marriage in Ireland*, London, 1985, ch. 1; Liam Breatnach, 'Canon Law and Secular Law in Early Ireland', *Peritia* 1984, 3, pp. 439–59; Donnchadh O'Corráin, Liam Breatnach and Aidan Breen, 'The Laws of the Irish', *Peritia* 1984, 3, pp. 382–438.

4 Judith Turner, 'The Iron Age', in I. G. Simmons and M. J. Tooley (eds), *The Environment in British Prehistory*, London, 1981, pp. 264–7.

5 Most of this is in Fox, *Pagans and Christians*, pp. 336–51.

6 Martin Henig, *Religion in Roman Britain*, London, 1984, pp. 30, 167.

7 Aubrey Burl, *Rites of the Gods*, London, 1981, p. 215.

8 Fox, *Pagans and Christians*, pp. 351–74.

9 Richard Kieckhefer, *Magic in the Middle Ages*, Cambridge, 1989, pp. 36–42.

10 Fox, *Pagans and Christians*, pp. 419–92; Thomas Wiedemann, 'Polytheism, Monotheism and Religious Co-existence: Paganism and Christianity in the Roman Empire', in I. Hamnett (ed.), *Religious Pluralism and Unbelief*, London, 1990.

11 Mary R. Lefkowitz, *Women in Greek Myth*, London, 1986, pp. 107–9.

12 Kieckhefer, *Magic in the Middle Ages*, pp. 29–42, 186–93; Norman Cohn, *Europe's Inner Demons*, Brighton, 1975, pp. 206–10.

13 This picture has been put together over the last 50 years, by the work of A. D. Nock, J. Ferguson, T. Lindsay, D. N. Robinson, A. Frantz, W. D. Simpson, C. Boissier, P. Labriole, A. Alfoldi, H. Bloch, A. H. M. Jones, P. Brown, S. Dill, W. Kaegl, J. F. Matthews, J. A. McGeachy, P. Petit, A. Cameron and A. Toynbee.

14 Philip Rahtz and Lorna Watts, 'The End of Roman Temples in the West of Britain', in P. J. Casey (ed.), *The End of Roman Britain*, British Archaeological Reports, British Series 71 (1979), pp. 183–201, and sources cited there. I do not find it easy to accept the suggestion of these two authors that Uley, Brean Down and Lamyatts Beacon might have been reconsecrated to new pagan cults at the end of the fourth century. The complete absence of votives argues against it.

15 Lloyd Laing, 'Segontium and the Post-Roman Occupation of Wales', in Lloyd Laing (ed), *Studies in Celtic Survival*, British Archaeological Reports, British Series, 37 (1977), pp. 57–8; Ralph Merrifield, *The Archaeology of Religion and Magic*, London, 1987, pp. 96–101.

16 Dorothy Watts, 'The Thetford Treasure: A Reappraisal', *Antiquaries Journal* 1988, 68.

17 Defixio, Roman Baths Museum.

18 Roger Leach, 'Religion and Burials in South Somerset and North Dorset', in Warwick Rodwell (ed.), *Temples, Churches and Religion: Recent Research in Roman Britain*, British Archaeological Reports, British Series, 77 (1980), pp. 337–52; Philip Rahtz, 'Grave Orientation', *Archaeological Journal* 1978, 135, pp. 1–14; E. W. Black, 'Romano-British Burial Customs and Religious Beliefs in South-east England', *Archaeological Journal* 1986, 143, pp. 212–20; Edward James, 'Burial and Status in the Early Medieval West', *Transactions of the Royal Historical Society* 1989, fifth series, 39, p. 26; Lindsay Allason-Jones, *Women in Roman Britain*, London, 1989, pp. 162–3.

19 E. A. Thompson, *Saint Germanus of Auxerre and the End of Roman Britain*, Woodbridge, 1984, pp. 15–19. I cannot find Professor Thompson's evidence quite sufficient to support his suggestion 'that towards the middle of the fifth century Britain was still an overwhelmingly pagan country'. With perfect logic, he argues from different sections of the *Life* both that Germanus's debate with the Pelagians took place in a state ruled by pagans and that the army which he led to victory over the barbarians (belonging to that or a neighbouring state) was already Christian. This situation, although possible, seems a little unlikely, and makes me wonder whether both he and I are not taking somewhat too literally a text which may be incapable of providing more than a very limited and confused picture of events.

20 *De Excidio*, iv.2–3.

21 Kathleen Hughes, *Early Christian Ireland: Introduction to the Sources*, London, 1972.

22 Maire de Paor and Liam de Paor, *Early Christian Ireland*, London, 1958, pp. 27–48; Francis John Byrne, *Irish Kings and High Kings*, London, 1973, pp. 90–105; Clare E. Stancliffe, 'Kings and Conversion', *Frühmittelalterliche Studien* 1980, 14, pp. 59–94; Kathleen Hughes, *The Church in Early Irish Society*, London, 1966, pp. 39–64.

23 Alfred Smyth, *Warlords and Holy Men*, London, 1984, pp. 27–8, 34–5, 84–115.

24 Brian Branston, *The Lost Gods of England*, London, 1957, pp. 29–30 and chs 6–10; Gale R. Owen, *Rites and Religions of the Anglo-Saxons*, Newton Abbot, 1981, pp. 24–37; Hermann Moisl, 'Anglo-Saxon Royal Genealogies and Germanic Oral Tradition', *Journal of Medieval History* 1981, 7, p. 235.

25 Branston, *The Lost Gods of England*, pp. 30–3, 45; Owen, *Rites and Religions of the Anglo-Saxons*, pp. 41–5; Stancliffe, 'Kings and Conversion', p. 60.

26 Owen, *Rites and Religions of the Anglo-Saxons*, pp. 50–61; Patrick Wormald, 'Celtic and Anglo-Saxon Kingship: Some Further Thoughts', in Paul E. Szarmach (ed.), *Sources of Anglo-Saxon Culture*, Kalamazoo, 1986, pp. 154–66.

27 Bede, *Works*, ed. Rev J. A. Giles, Oxford, 1843, book 4, pp. 178–9.

28 Herwig Wolfram, *History of the Goths*, Berkeley, 1988, pp. 106–11.

29 Owen, *Rites and Religions of the Anglo-Saxons*, pp. 45–7; 'Sutton Hoo', *Current Archaeology* 1990, 118, pp. 353–8.

30 Owen, *Rites and Religions of the Anglo-Saxons*, pp. 61–95; Bruce N. Eagles, 'Pagan Anglo-Saxon Burials at West Overton', *Wiltshire Archaeological and Natural History Society Magazine* 1986, 80, pp. 103–20; M. Faull, 'British Survival in Anglo-Saxon Northumbria', in Laing, *Studies in Celtic Survival*, pp. 5–8; Martin Carver, 'Kingship and Material Culture in Early Anglo-Saxon East Anglia', in Stephen Bassett (ed.), *The Origins of Anglo-Saxon Kingdoms*, Leicester, 1989, pp. 147–52; J. D. Richards, 'Style and Symbol: Explaining Variability in Anglo-Saxon Cremation Burials', in Stephen D. Driscoll and Margaret R. Nieke (eds), *Politics and Power in Early Medieval Britain and Ireland*, Edinburgh, 1988, pp. 145–61; J. D. Richards, *The Significance of Form and Decoration of Anglo-Saxon Cremation Urns*, British Archaeological Reports, British Series, 166 (1987).

31 M. Harman, T. I. Molleson and J. L. Price, 'Burials, Bodies and Beheadings in Romano-British and Anglo-Saxon Cemeteries', *Bulletin of the British Museum of Natural History (Geology)*, 1981, 35, pp. 145–88; Owen, 'Sutton Hoo' and *Rites and Religions of the Anglo-Saxons*, ch. 3.

32 Catherine Hills, 'The Archaeology of Anglo-Saxon England in the Pagan Period: A Review', *Anglo-Saxon England* 1979, 8, pp. 318–26; Carver, 'Kingship and Material Culture'.

33 Rosemary Cramp, 'Northumbria: The Archaeological Evidence', in Driscoll and Nieke, *Politics and Power in Early Medieval Britain and Ireland*, pp. 72–3.

34 Owen, *Rites and Religions of the Anglo-Saxons*, pp. 67–79; Eagles, 'Pagan Anglo-Saxon Burials'; Carver, 'Kingship and Material Culture'.

35 Owen, *Rites and Religions of the Anglo-Saxons*, ch. 4; Carver, 'Kingship and Material Culture'; 'Sutton Hoo'; William Filmer Sankey, 'Snape', *Current Archaeology* 1990, 118, pp. 348–52.

36 Cramp, 'Northumbria', p. 71; Richards, 'Style and Symbol'; Carver, 'Kingship and Material Culture'; Sankey, 'Snape', p. 358.

37 Branston, *The Lost Gods of England*, pp. 148–60; Owen, *Rites and Religions of the Anglo-Saxons*, pp. 27, 170–6; Roberta Frank, 'Viking Atrocity and Skaldic Verse: The Rite of the Blood Eagle', *English Historical Review* 1984, 99, pp. 332–43; Richard N. Bailey, *Viking Age Sculpture in Northern England*, London, 1980, ch. 6.

38 Merrifield, *The Archaeology of Religion and Magic*, pp. 107–8; Barbara E. Crawford, *Scandinavian Scotland*, Leicester, 1987, pp. 116–69; Peter Foote and David M. Wilson, *The Viking Achievement*, London, 1970, pp. 410–14.

CHAPTER 8   LEGACY OF SHADOWS

1 Leonard W. Moss and Stephen C. Cappannari, 'In Quest of the Black Virgin', in James J. Preston (ed.), *Mother Worship*, Chapel Hill, 1982, pp. 53–74.

2 Francis John Byrne, *Irish Kings and High Kings*, London, 1973, p. 144; Michael J. O'Kelly, 'St Gobnet's House, Ballyvourney', *Journal of the Cork Historical and Archaeological Society* 1952, 57, pp. 18–40.

3 Nicholas Orme, 'St Michael and his Mount', *Journal of the Royal Institution of Cornwall* 1986–7, n.s., 10, pp. 32–4.

4 For different treatments of these themes, see Margaret Alice Murray, *The Witch Cult in Western Europe*, Oxford, 1921, p. 13; Stewart Farrar, *What Witches Do*, London, 1971, p. 93; Caitlín Matthews, *The Elements of the Celtic Tradition*, Shaftesbury, 1989, p. 83.

5 See the testimony of Isobel Smyth in Murray, *The Witch Cult in Western Europe*, p. 110.

6 E.g. John Michell, *The View Over Atlantis*, revised edition, London, 1975, pp. 144–5.

7 For an easy summary, see Kathleen Hughes, *The Church in Early Irish Society*, London, 1966.

8 First cited as significant in Rose Jeffries Peebles, *The Legend of Longinus*, Bryn Mawr, 1911, pp. 209–10.

9 For the English evidence, see the accumulated data in the successive volumes of *Folk-lore*, of the 'County Folklore' series published by the Folk-Lore Society, and of the 'Folklore of the British Isles Series' published by Batsford.

10 Richard Kieckhefer, *Magic in the Middle Ages*, Cambridge, 1989, ch. 3; Norman Cohn, *Europe's Inner Demons*, Brighton, 1975, ch. 11.

11 Kieckhefer, *Magic in the Middle Ages*.

12 Lewis Spence, *The Magic Arts in Celtic Britain*, London, 1945, pp. 44–9.

13 Ralph Merrifield, *The Archaeology of Religion and Magic*, London, 1987, pp. 118–26.

14 Ibid., p. 108.

15 *Metrical Dinnshenchas*, iv.240; *Annals of Innisfallen*, year 982.

16 British Library, Harleian MS 585; T. O. Cockayne, *Leechdoms, Wortcunning and Starcraft of Early England*, 3 vols, Rolls Series, London, 1864–6; G. Storms, *Anglo-Saxon Magic*, The Hague, 1948; J. H. G. Grattan and C. Singer, *Anglo-Saxon Magic and Medicine*, Oxford 1952; W. Bonser, *The Medical Background of Anglo-Saxon England*, London, 1963; N. F. Barley, 'Anglo-Saxon Magico-Medicine', *Journal of the Anthropological Society of Oxford* 1972, 3, pp. 67–77.

17 For runes, see R. W. Elliott, *Runes: An Introduction*, Manchester, 1959; R.I. Page, *An Introduction to English Runes*, London, 1973.

18 Printed in Brian Branston, *The Lost Gods of England*, London, 1957, pp. 38–40.

19 Printed most accessibly in Kenneth Hurlstone Jackson, *A Celtic Miscellany*, London, 1951, pp. 263–4.

20 For many such examples, see William A. Chaney, 'Paganism to Christianity in Anglo-Saxon England', *Harvard Theological Review* 1960, 53, pp. 198–208.

21 E. O. G. Turville-Petre, *Myth and Religion of the North*, London, 1964, pp. 42–50; E. G. Stanley, *The Search for Anglo-Saxon Paganism*, Cambridge, 1975, pp. 83–96, 94–122; Chaney, 'Paganism to Christianity', p. 203.

22 Henry Gee and William John Hardy, *Documents Illustrative of English Church History*, London, 1896, pp. 41–2; John Johnson (ed.), *A Collection of the Laws and Canons of the Church of England*, Oxford, 1850, vol. 1, p. 219; Arthur West Haddan and William Stubbs (eds), *Councils and Ecclesiastical Documents Relating to Great Britain and Ireland*, Oxford, 1871, vol. 3, p. 189; Commissioners of Public Works, *Ancient Laws and Institutes of England*, London, 1840, *passim*.

23 D. Whitelock, M. Brett and C. N. L. Brooke (eds), *Councils and Synods, with other Documents Relating to the English Church*, Oxford 1981, vol. 1, p. 218; Commissioners of Public Works, *Ancient Laws and Institutes*, p. 25.

24 Whitelock et al., *Councils and Synods*, vol. 1, pp. 304–5, 309, 319, 409, 461–3, 489; Commissioners of Public Works, *Ancient Laws and Institutes*, *passim*.

25 F. M. Powicke and C. R. Cheney (eds), *Councils and Synods*, Oxford, 1964, pp. 265, 303, 622, 722, 1044.

26 Ludwig Bieler (ed.), *The Irish Penitentials*, Dublin, 1963; Haddan and Stubbs, *Councils and Ecclesiastical Documents*, vol. 1.

27 W. H. Mandy, 'An Incident at Bexley', *Woolwich and District Antiquarian Society Annual Report and Transactions* 1920–5, 23, pp. 25–37; Jeffrey Burton Russell, *Witchcraft in the Middle Ages*, Ithaca, 1972, p. 164; R. P. Chope, 'Frithelstock Priory', *Report and Transactions of the Devonshire Association* 1928, 61, pp. 175–6.

28 Cohn, *Europe's Inner Demons*, pp. 102–3; Jules Michelet, *La Sorcière*, Paris, 1862; Charles Godfrey Leland, *Aradia, or the Gospel of the Witches*, London, 1899.

29 Murray, *The Witch Cult in Western Europe*, esp. pp. 97–123. The biographical details are from Margaret Alice Murray, *My First Hundred Years*, London, 1963 and *Dictionary of National Biography* (1961–70), pp. 777–9.

30 In *The American Historical Review* 1921–2, 27, pp. 780–3 and 1934–5, 40, pp. 491–2.

31 C. H. L'Estrange Ewen, *Witch Hunting and Witch Trials*, London, 1929, *Witchcraft and Demonianism*, London, 1933, *Witchcraft in the Star Chamber*, London, 1938, *Witchcraft in the Norfolk Circuit*, Paignton, 1939.

32 Details of her own attitude to magic are supplied by *Dictionary of National Biography* (1961–70), pp. 777–9 and Murray, *My First Hundred Years*, pp. 175–83.

33 Two in 1947 alone: A. Runeberg, *Witches, Demons and Fertility Magic*, Helsingfors, 1947; R. T. Davies, *Four Centuries of Witch Beliefs*, London, 1947.

34 Keith Thomas, *Religion and the Decline of Magic*, London, 1971, pp. 514–19; Cohn, *Europe's Inner Demons*, pp. 102–25.

35 Philip Tyler, 'The Church Courts at York and Witchcraft Prosecutions', *Northern History* 1969, 4; Antero Heikkinen, *Paholaisen Liitolaiset*, Helsinki, 1969; Alan Macfarlane, *Witchcraft in Tudor and Stuart England*, London, 1970; Bengt Ankarloo, *Trolldomsprocesserna i Sverige*, Stockholm, 1971; Bente G. Alver, *Heksetro og Troldom*, Oslo, 1971; H. C. E. Midelfort, *Witch-hunting in Southwestern Germany*, London, 1972; E. William Monter, *Witchcraft in France and Switzerland*, London, 1976; Russell Zguta, 'Witchcraft Trials in Seventeenth Century Russia', *American Historical Review* 1977, 82; Gerhard Schormann, *Hexenprozesse in Nordwestdeutschland*, Hildesheim, 1977 and *Hexenprozesse in Deutschland*, Göttingen, 1981; R. Muchembled, *Sorcières du Cambresis*, Paris, 1977 and *La Sorcière au Village*, Paris, 1979; A. Soman, 'Les Procès de Sorcellière au Parlement de Paris', *Annales* 1977, 32; M. S. Dupont-Bouchat, W. Frijhoff and R. Muchembled, *Prophètes et Sorciers dans le Pays-Bas*, Paris, 1978; J. W. Evans, *The Making of the Habsburg Monarchy*, London, 1979, ch. 11; Gustav Henningsen, *The Witches' Advocate*, London, 1980; Christina Larner, *Enemies of God: The Witch Hunt in Scotland*, London, 1981 and

Witchcraft and Religion, London, 1984; Robin Briggs, *Communities of Belief*, London, 1989, chs 1–3; Ruth Martin, *Witchcraft and the Inquisition in Venice*, London, 1989.

36 See in particular Briggs, *Communities of Belief*, ch. 1.

37 This figure is my own, based upon the cumulative import of all the works cited in note 35. Before the 1970s, and this detailed local case-work, scholars guessed that the total of executions stood at about a million. Cecil Williamson, the owner of a 'Museum of Witchcraft', arbitrarily decided upon the figure of nine million in 1951. This inflated estimate was copied by the writer Gerald Gardner, and duly adopted by modern paganism as part of its faith, being quoted by radical feminists such as Andrea Dworkin and radical socialists such as Ken Livingstone. In 1987 Brian Levack, surveying the accumulated data, reckoned the true figure at about 60,000 (Brian Levack, *The Witch Hunt in Early Modern Europe*, London, 1987, ch. 1). From the material which has come in since, and a reluctance to accept Professor Levack's estimates for Switzerland and Eastern Europe (where many local totals are still guesses), I would take the risk of arguing for this lower one.

38 Larner, *Enemies of God*, *Witchcraft and Religion*.

39 J. R. Crawford, *Witchcraft and Sorcery in Rhodesia*, London, 1967. The significance of this study was first pointed out by Cohn, *Europe's Inner Demons*, pp. 219–23.

40 Russell, *Witchcraft in the Middle Ages*, chs 3–4; Cohn, *Europe's Inner Demons*, ch. 11.

41 Discussed in Midelfort, *Witch-hunting in Southwestern Germany*, ch. 1.

42 Richard Bernheimer, *Wild Men in the Middle Ages*, Cambridge, Mass., 1952; Timothy Husband, *The Wild Man*, New York, 1980.

43 Ronald Sheridan and Anne Ross, *Grotesques and Gargoyles*, Newton Abbot, 1975, p. 8.

44 Jørgen Andersen, *The Witch on the Wall*, London, 1977, ch. 1.

45 Anthony Weir and James Jerman, *Images of Lust*, London, 1986, p. 147.

46 Ibid., pp. 106–8, 148; Kathleen Basford, *The Green Man*, Ipswich, 1978.

47 Roy Judge, *The Jack-in-the-Green*, Ipswich, 1979.

48 Sheridan and Ross, *Grotesques and Gargoyles*, p. 16.

49 E.g. J. H. Bettey and C. W. G. Taylor, *Sacred and Satiric: Medieval Stone Carvings in the West Country*, Bristol, 1982, pp. 6–10.

50 E.g. Janet Bord, *Mazes and Labyrinths of the World*, London, 1976.

51 W. H. Matthews, *Mazes and Labyrinths: A General Account of their History and Development*, London, 1922.

52 Ibid., chs 8–10.

53 Lizette Andrews Fisher, *The Mystic Vision in the Grail Legend and in the Divine Comedy*, New York, 1917, summarizes the earlier debates. Material has been added here from Alfred Nutt, *Studies on the Legend of the Holy Grail*,

Folklore Society, 1888; Peebles, *The Legend of Longinus*; Jessie L. Weston, *From Ritual to Romance*, New York, 1957 (reprint).

54 John Matthews, *At the Table of the Grail*, London, 1984; Prudence Jones, *The Path to the Centre*, Wiccan Publications 4, 1988.

55 William F. Skene (ed.), *The Four Ancient Books of Wales*, Edinburgh, 1868, reviews all previous work in his preface. Sir Ifor Williams, *Lectures on Early Welsh Poetry*, Dublin, 1944, contains the crucial essays by that scholar, and the latest thought is well represented by David Dumville, 'Early Welsh Poetry: Problems of Historicity', in Brynley F. Roberts (Ed.), *Early Welsh Poetry: Studies in the Book of Aneirin*, Aberystwyth, 1988, pp. 1–16.

56 E.g. John Matthews and Caitlín Matthews, *Taliesin: The Shamanic Mysteries of Britain*, Wellingborough, 1991.

57 For a quick summary, see Ceri W. Lewis, 'The Court Poets', in A. O. H. Jarman and Gwilym Rees Hughes (eds), *A Guide to Welsh Literature*, vol. 1, Swansea, 1976, ch. 6.

58 Kathryn A. Klar, 'What Are the Gwarchanau?', in Roberts, *Early Welsh Poetry*, pp. 97–137.

59 David Dumville, 'Sub-Roman Britain: History and Legend', *History* 1977, 62, pp. 173–92.

60 Williams, *Lectures on Early Welsh Poetry*, ch. 4.

61 Skene's 1868 edition remains the best comprehensive text and translation of the Books of Taliesin, Aneirin, Carmarthen and Hergest (and is still not very good). Definitive individual editions are *Canu Taliesin*, ed. Ifor Williams, Cardiff, 1960; *Canu Aneirin*, ed. Ifor Williams, Cardiff, 1938; *Canu Llywarch Hen*, ed. Ifor Williams, Cardiff, 1935; *Trioedd Ynys Prydein*, ed. Rachel Bromwich, Cardiff, 1978; *Pedeir Keine Y Mabinogi*, ed. Ifor Williams, Cardiff, 1930.

62 E.g. Peter Burke, *Popular Culture in Early Modern Europe*, London, 1978; Barry Reay (ed.), *Popular Culture in Seventeenth Century England*, London, 1985; Eric Hobsbawm, 'Inventing Traditions', in Eric Hobsbawm and Terence Ranger (eds), *The Invention of Tradition*, Cambridge, 1983, pp. 1–14.

63 T. Baker, 'The Churchwarden's Accounts of Mere', *Wiltshire Archaeological and Natural History Society Magazine* 1908, 35, pp. 37–55.

64 For this and what follows, see Robert Ackerman, *J. G. Frazer: His Life and Work*, Cambridge, 1907.

65 Sir James Frazer, *The Golden Bough*, abridged edition, London, 1922, pp. 622–3; Miranda Green, *The Gods of the Celts*, Gloucester, 1986, pp. 164–5.

66 R. J. E. Tiddy, *The Mummers' Play*, Folcroft, 1923; E. K. Chambers, *The English Folk-Play*, New York, 1964 (reprint); E. C. Cawte, Alex Helm and N. Peacock, *English Ritual Drama: A Geographical Index*, London, 1967; A. E. Green, 'Popular Drama and the Mummers' Play', in David Bradby, Louis James and Bernard Sharratt (eds), *Performance and Politics in Popular*

Drama, Cambridge, 1980; Georgina Smith, 'Chapbooks and Traditional Plays', *Folklore* 1981, 92, pp. 208–17; Thomas Pettitt, 'Early English Traditional Drama', *Research Opportunities in Renaissance Drama* 1982, 25, pp. 1–30; Craig Fees, 'Mummers and Momoeri: A Response', *Folklore* 1989, 100 pp. 240–7; Alan Brody, *The English Mummers and their Plays*, Philadelphia, 1969.

67 E. K. Chambers, *The Medieval Stage*, Oxford, 1963 (reprint), vol. 2, p. 302; S. Addy, 'Guising and Mumming in Derbyshire', *Journal of the Derbyshire Archaeological and Natural History Society* 1907, 29, pp. 37–42; E. C. Cawte, *Ritual Animal Disguise*, Ipswich, 1978. The famous passage from the Penitential is printed in Commissioners of Public Works, *Ancient Laws and Institutes*, vol. 2, p. 293.

68 E. K. Chambers, *The Medieval Stage*, vol. 2, pp. 235–40.

69 Public Record Office, SP 12/224/74; Spence, *The Magic Arts*, p. 49; Ruth Morris and Frank Morris, *Scottish Healing Wells*, Sandy, 1982, p. 190.

70 M. Martin, *A Description of the Western Isles of Scotland*, London, 1700, pp. 28–9.

71 Spence, *The Magic Arts*, pp. 85–92.

72 Gerald Gardner, *High Magic's Aid*, London, 1949, *Witchcraft Today*, London, 1954, *The Practice of Witchcraft*, London, 1959; Stewart Farrar, *What Witches Do*, London, 1971; Janet Farrar and Stewart Farrar, *The Witches' Way*, London, 1984, *The Witches' Goddess*, London, 1987, *The Life and Times of a Modern Witch*, London, 1988, *The Witches' God*, London, 1989; Patricia Crowther and Arnold Crowther, *The Witches Speak*, Douglas, 1965; Vivianne Crowley, *Wicca: The Old Religion in the New Age*, Wellingborough, 1989; Doreen Valiente, *Where Witchcraft Lives*, London, 1962, *Witchcraft for Tomorrow*, London, 1978, *An ABC of Witchcraft Past and Present*, London, 1984 (reprint), *The Rebirth of Witchcraft*, London, 1989; Margot Adler, *Drawing Down the Moon*, second edition, Boston, 1986; Caitlín Matthews and John Matthews, *The Western Way*, London, 1985.

73 So he styled himself, although neither of the universities from which he claimed degrees has any record of such an award. Friends of his have described his academic title as 'honorary', which in this case seems to mean self-awarded: Valiente, *The Rebirth of Witchcraft*, ch. 3.

74 Francis King, *Ritual Magic in England*, pp. 176–80; Valiente, *An ABC of Witchcraft*, pp. 154–7, *The Rebirth of Witchcraft*, ch. 3; Farrar and Farrar, *The Witches' Way*, appendix A.

75 'Lugh', *Old George Pickingill*, London, 1982; Valiente, *The Rebirth of Witchcraft*, ch. 12.

76 King, *Ritual Magic in England*; Ellic Howe, *The Magicians of the Golden Dawn*, London, 1972; Israel Regardie, *The Golden Dawn*, 4 vols, London, 1937–40.

77 E.g. Farrar, *What Witches Do*; Farrar and Farrar, *The Witches' Way*; Valiente, *Witchcraft for Tomorrow*, *The Rebirth of Witchcraft*.

78 For an ungracious reaction from one versed in ritual magic, see King, *Ritual Magic in England*, pp. 175–81. For a gentler but still critical one, see Stewart Farrar's introduction to the 1974 reprint of Leland's *Aradia*.

79 Gardner, *Witchcraft Today*, *The Practice of Witchcraft*; Valiente, *Where Witchcraft Lives*; Crowther and Crowther, *The Witches Speak*; Farrar, *What Witches Do*; Adler, *Drawing Down the Moon*, pp. 41–93.

80 An Anglo-Saxon word meaning 'knowledge'. It appears in Gardner, *The Practice of Witchcraft*, as the formal name for his cult.

81 Farrar and Farrar, *The Witches' Goddess*, pp. 11, 18.

82 It was long thought that 'paganus' meant 'countryman', as Christianity was initially an urban religion. But Robin Lane Fox, *Pagans and Christians*, London, 1986, pp. 30–1, argues convincingly that it is at least as likely to have meant a civilian, one not enrolled in the army of God.

83 Valiente, *Witchcraft for Tommorow*, *An ABC of Witchcraft*, *The Rebirth of Witchcraft*; Matthews and Matthews, *The Western Way*; Farrar and Farrar, *The Witches' Way*, *The Witches' Goddess*, *The Life and Times of a Modern Witch*, *The Witches' God*; Crowley, *Wicca*; Starhawk, *The Spiral Dance*, San Francisco, 1979; Prudence Jones and Caitlín Matthews, *Voices from the Circle*, Wellingborough, 1990.

84 Mary R. Lefkowitz, *Women in Greek Myth*, London, 1986; William Blake Tyrrell, *Amazons: A Study in Athenian Mythmaking*, Baltimore, 1984; Edith Hall, *Inventing the Barbarian*, Oxford, 1989; Simon Pembroke, 'Women in Charge: The Function of Alternatives in Early Greek Tradition and the Ancient Idea of Matriarchy', *Journal of the Warburg and Courtauld Institutes* 1967, 30, pp. 1–35.

85 These are Adler, *Drawing Down the Moon*, pp. 49–52 and Crowley, *Wicca*, p. 47.

86 E.g. in the section on Arianrhod in Farrar and Farrar, *The Witches' Goddess*.

87 I have personally found modern pagans to be highly intelligent and eager for information, and merely utterly unaware of developments in history and archaeology. When I discussed the latest work on the Great Witch Hunt with an editor of *The Wiccan*, she immediately asked me to write a short summary of it, with bibliography, for her periodical. It appeared in the issue of Imbolc 1990.

88 Matthews and Matthews, *The Western Way*, p. xii.

89 Adler, *Drawing Down the Moon*, p. 93. To an outsider such as myself, this is by far the finest book yet written about modern paganism, although Jones and Matthews, *Voices from the Circle* is a better and more recent survey of the British cults.

Additional Source Material

The following is a list of works not referred to specifically in the notes.

Geoffrey Ashe (ed.), *The Quest for Arthur's Britain*, London, 1968.

Paul Ashbee, 'Mesolithic Megaliths', *Cornish Archaeology* 21, 1982, pp. 3–22.

G. Barker and D. Webley, 'Causewayed Camps and Early Neolithic Economies in Central Southern England', *Proceedings of the Prehistoric Society* 44, 1978, pp. 161–86.

Owen Bedwin, 'Excavations at the Neolithic Enclosure at Bury Hill', *Proceedings of the Prehistoric Society* 47, 1981.

Raymond Buckland, *Buckland's Complete Book of Witchcraft*, St Paul, Minn., 1988.

D. G. Buckley et al., 'Excavation of a Possible Neolithic Long Barrow or Mortuary Enclosure at Rivenhall', *Proceedings of the Prehistoric Society* 54, 1988, pp. 77–91.

James P. Carley, *Glastonbury Abbey*, Woodbridge, 1989.

Jill Cook, 'Marked Human Bones from Gough's Cave, Somerset', *Proceedings of the University of Bristol Spelaeological Society* 17, 1986, pp. 275–85.

H. P. R. Finberg, *West Country Historical Studies*, Newton Abbot, 1969.

Andrew Fleming, 'The Myth of the Mother Goddess', *World Archaeology* 1, 1969, pp. 247–61.

Christopher Gingell, 'Twelve Wiltshire Round Barrows', *Wiltshire Archaeological and Natural History Magazine* 80, 1988, pp. 19–76.

A. Gransden, 'The Growth of the Glastonbury Traditions and Legends in the Twelfth Century', *Journal of Ecclesiastical History* 27, 1976, pp. 337–58.

E. Greenfield, 'The Excavation of Three Round Barrows at Punchknowle', *Proceedings of the Dorset Natural History and Archaeological Society* 106, 1984, p. 63–76.

John W. Hedges, *Tomb of the Eagles*, London, 1984.

H. Kille, 'West Country Hobby-Horses and Cognate Customs', *Somerset Archaeological and Natural History Society Proceedings* 77, 1931.

J. G. Lalanne and Jean Bouyssonie, 'Le Gisement palaeolithique de Laussel', *L'Anthropologie* 50, 1941–6, pp. 1–163.

M. Lapidge, 'The Cult of St Indract at Glastonbury', in D. Whitelock, R. McKitterick and D. N. Dunville (eds), *Ireland in Medieval Europe*, Cambridge, 1981, pp. 179–212.

James Mellaart, *The Earliest Civilisations of the Near East*, London, 1965.

——*Çatal Hüyük*, London, 1967.

——*The Neolithic of the Near East*, London, 1975.

Steven J. Mithen, 'Looking and Learning: Upper Palaeolithic Art and Gathering', *World Archaeology* 19, 1988, pp. 197–327.

Ronald W. B. Morris, *The Prehistoric Rock Art of Argyll*, Poole, 1977.

Margaret Alice Murray, *The God of the Witches*, London, 1933.

——*The Divine King in England*, London, 1954.

Donnchadh O'Corráin (ed.), *Irish Antiquity*, Cork, 1981.

Michael J. O'Kelly, 'A Horned Cairn at Shanballyedmond', *Journal of the Cork Historical and Archaeological Society* 63, 1956, pp. 37–72.

R. I. Page, 'Anglo-Saxon Runes and Magic', *Journal of the Archaeological Association*, third series, 27, 1964, pp. 30–1.

Frederic F. Petersen, *The Excavation of a Bronze Age Cemetery on Knighton Heath, Dorset*, British Archaeological Reports, British Series, 98 (1981).

Lady Raglan, 'The Green Man in Church Architecture', *Folk-Lore* 1, 1939, pp. 45–57.

Philip Rahtz, 'The Roman Temple at Pagan's Hill', *Somersetshire Archaeological and Natural History Society Proceedings* 96, 1951, pp. 112–42.

Colin Renfrew and John F. Cherry (eds), *Peer Polity Interaction and Socio-Political Change*, Cambridge, 1986.

Alan Savile, 'A Cotswold–Severn Tomb at Hazleton', *Antiquaries Journal* 64, 1984.

J. G. Scott, *South-West Scotland*, London, 1966.

——*Temple Wood, Kilmartin, Stone Circle*, London, 1974.

W. Douglas Simpson, *Dunstaffnage Castle and the Stone of Destiny*, Edinburgh, 1958.

S. J. Tester, *A History of Western Astrology*, Woodbridge, 1987.

Julian Thomas, 'Neolithic Explanations Revisited', *Proceedings of the Prehistoric Society* 54, 1988, pp. 77–91.

Alasdair W. R. Whittle, *The Earlier Neolithic of Southern England and its Continental Background*, British Archaeological Reports, Supplementary Series, 35 (1977).

J. C. Wilson, 'The Standing Stones of Anglesey', *Bulletin of the Board of Celtic Studies* 30, 1983.

Index